"This book is absolutely the best resource available that clearly explains the learning challenges facing children, and I think that every educator and health professional who works with children and teens should read it and use it as a basic reference. It will also be on my recommended list for parents who are seeking help for their children."

— Margaret Gayle, executive director, The American Association for Gifted Children at Duke University, and co-author of *Education Renaissance*

"As informed physicians and informative writers, the Eides delineate children's mystifying behavior and ways to help them get in sync. I'm smitten by their content, wisdom, and compassion. For all of us who care about children with unlabeled or mislabeled needs, this book is a must!"

— Carol Kranowitz, M.A., author of *The Out-of-Sync Child*

"This comprehensive resource should be on the desk of every educator concerned about our youngsters and their path to success. *The Mislabeled Child* is filled with information that is practical and quick to find, in a very user-friendly format. I wish I'd had this book throughout my years as teacher and principal of both gifted and special education youngsters."

— Judith J. Roseberry, M.A., president, California Association for the Gifted

"This is the kind of book that parents will want to keep out and refer to again and again. The book provides a comprehensive, commonsense, and scientifically insightful overview of the causes and behaviors associated with a number of learning problems. This is done in a refreshingly 'nonpathologizing' manner. It also provides interventions designed to help each child overcome challenges by identifying and emphasizing le͟a͟r͟n͟i͟n͟g͟ ͟a͟b͟i͟l͟i͟t͟i͟e͟s͟ to achieve their maximum learning potential."

— Paul Beljan, Psy.D., presiden͟t͟, Pediatric Neuropsychology

"*The Mislabeled Child* is a practica͟l͟ ͟b͟o͟o͟k͟ ͟f͟o͟r͟ par-ents of children with learning and behavior disorders, as w͟e͟l͟l͟ ͟a͟s͟ ͟e͟ssential reading for educators, counselors, and healthcare professionals. Clearly written and solidly based, this book describes concrete strategies to help children with learning problems retrain and develop their brain. All too often children are given an incorrect label, and their parents are not given accurate and specific activities that they can use to help their children. This marvelous and clearly written book provides answers for many perplexing children. I wholeheartedly endorse this book and plan to recommend it widely."

— James T. Webb, Ph.D., clinical psychologist, founder of Supporting
Emotional Needs of Gifted Children, author of *Misdiagnosis and
Dual Diagnoses of Gifted Children and Adults*

"With their new book, the Eides have rendered a valuable public service in helping professionals, laypersons, and parents better understand complex, often subtle or self-contradictory mixes of talents and educational difficulties. They have helped us differentiate more clearly between various traits and labels, always looking deeply into the diverse nature of each individual. This is important work. Some of our brightest and most creative minds hang in the balance."

— Thomas G. West, author of *In the Mind's Eye* and
Thinking Like Einstein

"I think it will be a very helpful book for so many parents and families, struggling with a whole range of issues and complications at home and in school."

— Perri Klass, M.D., medical director and president, Reach Out
and Read National Center, associate professor of Pediatrics,
Boston University School of Medicine

"*The Mislabeled Child* represents a significant step toward a rethinking of our understanding of struggling children. It embodies an innovative, most helpful level of specificity, one that will enable us to customize education and parenting for children whose minds work differently from most!"

— Mel D. Levine, M.D., author of *Ready or Not, Here Life Comes*;
The Myth of Laziness; and *A Mind at a Time*

"In today's world of ADHD escapism, learning disability overdiagnosis, and medication–happy classroom environments, *The Mislabeled Child* is a much needed and called for resource for frazzled and frustrated parents."

— BellaOnline.com

"The best book we have read for a very long time. Highly recommended."

— Dyslexia teacher

The
Mislabeled
Child

The
Mislabeled
Child

**LOOKING BEYOND BEHAVIOR
TO FIND THE TRUE SOURCES—AND SOLUTIONS—
FOR CHILDREN'S LEARNING CHALLENGES**

BROCK EIDE, M.D., M.A., AND FERNETTE EIDE, M.D.

NEW YORK

A list of permissions, constituting a continuation of the copyright page, appears beginning on page 493.

Illustrations by Christine MacMillan

The Library of Congress has catalogued the hardcover edition of this book as follows:

Eide, Brock.
The mislabeled child : how understanding your child's unique learning style can open the door to success / by Brock Eide and Fernette Eide.
p.   cm.
Includes bibliographical references and index.
ISBN 1-4013-0225-4
1. Learning disabilities—Popular works.   2. Learning disabled children—Popular works.   I. Eide, Fernette, 1961–   II. Title.

RJ496.L4E44   2006
371.9—dc22   2005055053

Paperback ISBN: 978-1-4013-0899-5

Hyperion books are available for special promotions and premiums. For details contact the HarperCollins Special Markets Department in the New York office at 212-207-7528, fax 212-207-7222, or email spsales@harpercollins.com.

Design by Nicola Ferguson

FIRST PAPERBACK EDITION

10   9   8   7   6   5

For our children,

Krister and Karina:

You're simply the best,

and we love you with our whole hearts.

And for each other:

Like our love and our life,

this book neither is, nor could be,

the work of either,

but only, equally, of both.

Contents

Acknowledgments

One of the key themes of this book is the incredible effect that families, teachers, friends, and other caring persons can have on the lives of developing children. This is true also of developing books—and their authors.

Our greatest thanks and deepest love go to our children, Krister and Karina, who helped us see the need for a more holistic, brain-based approach to helping children with learning challenges. We thank them for their patience during busy times and for their unceasing love and laughter.

We also thank our parents, whose examples of love and care inspired every page of this book.

From Fernette: I'd like to thank the first "neurolearning couple" in my life, my father, Harry Chao-hung Fang, M.D., former chief of the neurology service at Rancho Los Amigos Hospital, and my mom, Marian Ching Fang, a teacher who received her M.Ed. from the University of Pennsylvania. From them, I first acquired a love of learning and the habit of looking beneath appearances for deeper answers.

From Brock: Thanks to my mother, Ruth Marie Eide, who surpasses anyone I know in her deep and abiding conviction of the goodness of God and her profound gratitude for His blessings. By word and example, she has taught me that hope is not wishful thinking, merely sanity. And to my father, Leonard Eide, whose courage and integrity as a husband, father, and man I increasingly understand and admire the longer I struggle to emulate them.

To the special teachers who have most greatly influenced us in our training as physicians, scientists, and scholars, our special thanks. As Hippocrates had us swear, "I will regard as father him who teaches me the art."

Fernette: My warmest thanks to Drs. Howard Fields, Louis Reichardt, Robert Fishman and all my wonderful teachers at UCSF, Ray Roos, and most of all to my dear father, friend, and first mentor in neurology, my dad. Thanks also to my dear friend, colleague, and enthusiastic supporter throughout college, medical school, residency, and beyond, Dr. Darel Butler. I would also like to acknowledge the giants of neurology's past, including Samuel Orton and Henry Head, who inspired me with their wonderful insights and careful observations.

Brock: My thanks to Kaj Johansen, Dan Bowen-Pope, Ed Krebs, Paul Ramsey (whose last-minute advice to change the order of my residency match list was responsible for this marriage and ultimately this book), Allan Spiegel, Donald B. Martin, Jaime Escobedo, Paul Friedrich, and Leon Kass. And to two special colleagues who have been constant friends, and at crucial times mentors, Eric Aguiar and Peter Juhn: my deepest thanks and my abiding respect.

To those who gave us guidance when we needed it most, our profound appreciation: Farrell Sheffield, Betty Meckstroth, Linda Silverman, Kimberly Alquist, Nancy Torgerson, Kristine Ganes, Susan Norton, and Meredith Warshaw. You are our models in the art of helping children. Special thanks also to a very wonderful teacher, Anda Adams.

Thanks as well to three special persons who generously gave us counsel when we decided to write this book: Carol Kranowitz, Lucy Miller, and Karen Gouze. Carol especially has been unstintingly lavish with her support, encouragement, and advice throughout this project. Her work and dedication have inspired us, and we're profoundly grateful for her help.

To our agent, Carol Mann, who provided essential guidance during the preparation of our proposal and who has been a watchful guide at every step: Thank you from the bottom of our hearts for all you've done, which from our perspective looks a lot like magic.

To all the folks at Hyperion who've made the book-birthing process so much smoother and more pleasant than we'd ever imagined: our deepest thanks. From the very beginning, we've been the grateful recipients of the uniquely attentive and individual treatment that are your hallmarks. Thanks to our initial contact and first editor at Hyperion, Mary Ellen O'Neill, whose enthusiasm and deep feeling for the project were essential as our book initially took shape, became chubby, and then—with her "personal training"—grew a little thinner! Thanks also to our second editor, Leslie Wells, who helped us, with legendary skill, through the crucial stages of editing and has been an ideal guide to the intricacies of the publishing process. Thanks also to Miriam Wenger, who, as assistant to both Leslie and Mary Ellen, has been an essential support from the beginning. Miriam is unfailingly cheerful and helpful, even when we e-mail her five times a day (and she usually seems to answer even before we hit the "send" button). Our heartfelt thanks also to the rest of the team at Hyperion, whose support we've felt at all stages: president Bob Miller, publisher Ellen Archer, editor in chief Will Schwalbe, marketing director Jane Comins, publicity director Katie Wainwright, sales director Sarah Schaffer, sub rights director Jill Sansone, and creative director Phil Rose.

We would also like to thank the folks at Hyperion for boosting our status at home. When you purchased our manuscript, we told our kids, "Hey, guys, we sold our book!" Their "Oh, really"s and "How about that"s were less than deafening. Then we added, "We sold our book . . . to *Disney!*" Since then we've been regarded with a kind of awe and have made no effort to deny rumors that we sometimes hang with Walt and Mickey in the Main Street fire station.

Thanks also to Christine MacMillan, who's been one of Fernette's closest friends since high school, when they first served together as candy stripers at Northridge Hospital. Christine is an amazingly talented artist who supplied much of the artwork in this book.

Thanks also to Bill Adams, Nancy Torgerson, and Dan Stachelski, who read and provided invaluable comments on various chapters in this manuscript. Thanks to Drs. Terri James Bellis and James T. Webb for helpful discussions. Thanks to Ruth Marie Eide for reading every word of this manuscript in several versions and providing essential quality control. And thanks also to whoever invented the spell-checker, without which Brock's life, as he now knows it, would be simply impossible (see "Dyslexia, Problems, Visual").

Finally, our profoundest gratitude to the families—and most of all the children—who have come to our clinic and have opened to us a special window into their lives. You have taught us, inspired us, and encouraged us. We are forever in your debt.

The
Mislabeled
Child

1

The
Mislabeled
Child

The beginning of wisdom is calling things by their
right name.

—ANCIENT CHINESE PROVERB

Michael was an eleven-year-old boy from a small midwestern town. When his parents brought him to see us, they shared the following painful but all-too-familiar story.

From his earliest years, it was clear that Michael was a bright and talented child. However, soon after he started school, it was also clear that he was experiencing a surprising degree of difficulty learning to read. Although Michael easily mastered all the names of the letters and many of their sounds, he couldn't seem to apply this knowledge to decoding whole words.

Michael's mother spent endless hours trying to teach him to read. Progress was slow at first—for a long time almost nonexistent. Finally, at the end of second grade, "something just clicked," and Michael's reading comprehension skyrocketed. During third grade, Michael earned a place in his class's advanced reading group, and he remained there for the next several years. He scored consistently above the ninetieth percentile on standardized tests of reading comprehension, just like the others in his group.

Yet Michael and his parents both knew that something was still wrong with his reading. While he could interpret the meaning of most long passages (at least as long as he read them silently), he often confused the meaning of short, succinct sentences—like instructions, test questions, or story problems in math—sometimes with disastrous consequences.

Michael also had difficulty reading aloud. He frequently skipped words or whole lines and constantly made mistakes when decoding even the simplest words. Before long, the thought of reading aloud before his classmates was his greatest fear.

Writing was not much better. Although Michael had an extremely strong knowledge base and a vivid imagination, he just couldn't get his thoughts down on paper. Instead of reflecting his interesting, intelligent, and often humorous thoughts, Michael's writing appeared childish, ungrammatical, and nearly indecipherable, as poor in content as it was in form. As time went by, Michael's parents noticed that he increasingly tried to "dumb down" his writing so that he'd only have to use the few words he knew he could spell. In addition, although his work always looked as if he'd dashed it off in a hurry, Michael never had enough time to finish his in-class assignments, and each night at home he spent hours struggling with work that should have taken just minutes.

Michael had problems beyond language as well. In math he frequently made "careless errors," despite the fact that he clearly had an excellent understanding of math concepts. In gym class and on the playground, Michael struggled with a severe lack of coordination. He particularly suffered when forced to participate in team sports requiring complex movements, quick reactions, or hand-eye coordination.

Although Michael had always been bothered by these difficulties, he managed (through heroic efforts) to get mostly A's during his early elementary years. However, by the time he reached fifth grade, Michael found that he could no longer keep pace with the growing demands for reading and writing. Midway through the year, he reached a crisis. Previously he'd had bouts of self-doubt and depression, but he'd always been able to bounce back. Now he seemed burdened beyond enduring. He grew increasingly self-critical, repeatedly calling himself stupid and dumb. He began complaining of headaches and stomachaches and of feeling too ill to go to school. He even began hitting himself on the head when he was frustrated, saying that he needed to be punished for being so stupid.

In the depth of his crisis, Michael confided in his mother, who recorded the following conversation. Michael's answers bear witness to the depth (and the causes) of his pain but also to his deep intelligence, insight, and verbal talents.

Mom: How would you describe yourself?

Michael: Not smart, maybe even below average. Maybe even stupid or at times worthless.

Mom: How do you feel about school?

Michael: I feel like school is hard because I can't get my answers down on paper. If I could answer questions out loud, I could snap the answers off. When I pick up a pencil, I feel like the task is actually getting my answer on the paper, not answering the question itself. I'm embarrassed at school about how I write, how no one can read my writing and how I can't spell, especially when we have a sub and have to pass our papers around for other kids to grade. Kids don't say anything just then, but afterward sometimes a few of my classmates will make me feel lousy about how bad I write and read. Sometimes I miss the whole worksheet because I can't read some part of the directions. I feel like an impostor when I'm sitting there in class and everybody else around me is reading. I'm trying to read the words in my own way, by memorizing what the word looks like, and I'm sitting there fearing that I'm going to be called on to read aloud. When I am called on to read aloud, feelings of fear, nervousness, and frustration all rush through my head, because I know I can't really read. I stumble over words and am embarrassed about what others think. My classmates think I'm a good reader because of the class I'm in, but I'm not. I'm an impostor because I'm a good guesser.

Mom: What are your educational goals?

Michael: I want to get the best grades I can. I'd like my work to get on the Principal's Pride Board. I'd like for things to be the way they are supposed to be. I'd like to be able to read and write and to be able to do the stuff normal kids do. I don't know how to read or write, and I want to be able to, like other kids do. I want to go to college and be successful. I'd like to become an engineer so I can build or design things, or go into politics so I can be famous. I want to do better at school academically.

Mom: What are you most proud of?

Michael: I don't know. I don't see anything to be proud of in myself.

Mom: What would you like to see happen?

Michael: I would like to learn how to help myself get better at schoolwork and would like to try to overcome my disabilities. I want others to understand how hard my disabilities make it for me to do my classwork.

Michael's parents were understandably heartbroken and more than a little frightened by this crisis they were witnessing in their son. They approached his school district for help, as they had on several prior occasions. They described Michael's emotional struggle and how his school problems seemed to be the cause. The school district disputed the connection. Michael's test scores and grades were all average or above. How could he have a learning problem? Maybe (they suggested) he just needed to try harder or pay more attention to his work. Most likely, they explained patiently, it was just a matter of unrealistic expectations. Maybe Michael really was doing the best he was capable of. Perhaps he expected too much of himself. Maybe his parents were pushing too hard. After all, not every child can be a genius. In any event, Michael certainly didn't fall two standard deviations below average, which is what the district required for children to qualify for services.

Michael's parents refused to accept the labels that the district offered to describe their son: lazy . . . careless . . . just not that smart. They were certain that Michael was far more intelligent than his schoolwork suggested. Their suspicions were confirmed when outside testing measured his verbal IQ at nearly 140. However, they wanted something more: They wanted a way to more accurately define the problems that were holding Michael back, and help in finding the interventions that would help him learn to his full potential.

Michael's parents brought him to our clinic. By the time we were finished meeting together, we were able to help them find a new and more accurate way to label his difficulties *and* to understand his tremendous strengths as a learner. Even more important, we were able to show them how Michael's difficulties could be diminished and his strengths developed to help him learn and achieve more, both in school and in life.

What's in a Name? Plenty!

Michael was like many children we see in our clinic. His struggles in school were caused not only by the brain-based learning challenges that made it hard for him to read, write, spell, and move in a coordinated fashion, but also by the fact that he was a *mislabeled child*.

Michael was neither lazy nor careless nor slow. Michael had dyslexia (see Chapter 10). Because he was mislabeled, his learning challenges were neither clearly understood nor properly addressed.

Michael's experience illustrates the wisdom of the saying we quoted at the start of this chapter: "The beginning of wisdom is calling things by their right name." This adage beautifully expresses our purpose in writing this book: to help you, as parents, teachers, or fellow child-care professionals, find the right names for the challenges that are keeping the children in your care from learning to their full potential.

This book is an outgrowth of our experience as physicians specializing in the treatment of children with learning challenges, but it's also the outgrowth of our experience as parents trying to find the right names for the challenges that confronted our own children. Ultimately, our experiences in both these roles have taught us the same truth: Labels really do matter, especially when they're applied to children.

Labels matter because they don't just express our thoughts, they can shape them as well, often without our realizing it. Labels can point us in the right direction or lead us astray. They can draw our eyes to truths we might otherwise have missed or hide important facts we might otherwise have seen. Labels can affect how closely we look at a child and what we see when we do. Labels can even mislead us into viewing the label as the reality and the child as the abstraction, rather than the other way around. This is a tragedy. We must never mistake the label for the child. Even accurate labels tell only part of the story. That's why a label should never be used as a shorthand for a child's whole existence. Statements like "He's ADHD" or "She's Asperger's" leave far too much unsaid to convey a complete or accurate picture of a child. Even among children who qualify for the same diagnostic label, differences in learning strengths and weaknesses, temperament, life experience, and personality can produce dramatic differences in the learning challenges these children face, the behaviors they display, and the treatments they need. As we'll argue throughout this book, a true understanding of a child's learning challenges—and what to do about them—always requires a complete assessment of a child's learning weaknesses *and strengths*. Simply determining which diagnostic labels fit is not enough.

Labels also matter because they can lead us to view children with learning challenges as diseased or disordered rather than as simply in need of further learning and development. In the age-old struggle between nature and nurture, nature currently dominates the battle for "expert opinion." As a result, the labels applied to children with learning challenges often sound as if they represent fixed and unchanging brain disorders, caused by irresistible forces that a child's development and experience have no power to change. Yet a growing body of research has demonstrated that brain development is an ongoing process that can be shaped and accelerated through the use of "targeted experience." As we'll show you, the nervous system has a remarkable capacity to "rewire" itself in response to stimulation. By carefully targeting the signals the brain receives (through teaching, therapy, or play), existing brain pathways can be trained to function more smoothly, old blocks can be bypassed by the development of new learning pathways, and children can learn to do things they previously found impossible. This is why we need to change the way we view labels—and the children to whom we apply them. We shouldn't see children with learning challenges as diseased, disordered, or deficient in various brain functions or chemicals, but rather as needing *new experiences* that can help them develop their capacities to learn and function better.

Labels matter because they can make us view the child as the sole source of learning challenges while overlooking the contribution of the environment. Children experience learning challenges when they have problems acquiring skills or displaying behaviors that are demanded by their school environment: in other words, when there's a mismatch between their developmental capacities and the school's demands. Unfortunately, we often forget that the environment as well as the child can contribute to this mismatch. For example, children who are easily distracted by sights and sounds may have difficulty learning in a conventional classroom yet learn well in a small class or homeschool setting. Children may even experience learning challenges in conventional classrooms because of learning styles and neurological "wiring" that actually predispose them to success in other settings. One well-known study showed that successful entrepreneurs in the United Kingdom were five times more likely than the general population to have had reading problems as children and that 70 percent "did not succeed" in school. Attributes like preferences for novelty, multitasking, intense high-frequency stimulation, visual rather than verbal reasoning, and interests that are detailed, deep, or narrowly focused, may also contribute to adult success but be poorly suited to many classrooms. When these attributes cause learning challenges for a child, it's important to see how the learning environment can be changed to better suit the child, rather than simply try to change the child to better fit the environment.

Labels matter because they can cause us to take an overly sterile, detached, and clinical view of a child's learning challenges and forget that these challenges occur in the context of a child's unique and complex life. They can make us overlook the important role that a child's unique temperament plays in dealing with learning challenges, and our need to help children develop character traits like optimism and resiliency. They can make us forget the importance of providing an information-rich and conversation-filled home, rather than one simply filled with electronic noise and bustle. They can also make us overlook the importance of clear, consistent, and patient adult guidance; the need to help children develop goals and visions for the future; and the need to help them develop the skills in self-monitoring and self-discipline that they'll require to reach them.

Finally, labels matter because of their peculiar tendency to expand over time to draw more and more behaviors (and children) into their orbit. Many of the labels applied to children with learning challenges tend to describe more than they explain and to say more about what those children do than about why they do it. Consequently, they tend over time to result in the labeling of more and more children with look-alike or "spectrum" diagnoses. This process of "diagnostic mission creep" has accelerated at such a pace in recent years that one might almost suspect that "abnormality" itself will soon become the new norm.

The last thing we want to do in writing this book is contribute to this trend. Our goal is not to prove that there are more "learning disabilities" than you ever dreamed possible but that there are more learning abilities than you ever dreamed possible, and that each and every child has abilities that can be better used to promote learning.

The human brain is remarkably *resourceful* in the fullest sense of the word: *full of resources*. As a result of this incredible versatility, it can learn and perform most tasks in a variety of ways. Yet too often we try to teach children using only a narrow range of options. This narrow approach actually aggravates—and in some cases even causes—many of the learning difficulties children encounter. Frequently we see children who, like Michael, could learn quite well in an appropriate setting but whose needs remain unmet in the standard classroom. To better teach these children, we must first recognize that they typically require educational experiences different from those that work for most children. What they need, in other words, is a form of education that is right for children who learn the way they do.

Most children currently identified as "learning-disabled" are literally "wired" to learn differently than most other children. These children use different routes of information intake, different techniques for storing and processing information, different formats for expressing information, and different patterns for interacting with the environment. Given the brain's incredible resourcefulness, in most cases these differences need never become disabling—unless we let them. We now have the ability not only to detect a wide range of differences in learning styles and approaches but also to meet many of the special needs that arise from these differences. The special learning approaches, strategies, and skill-building exercises you'll read about in this book can help you meet the needs of children who process information in ways different from most children, so they can learn and work to the best of their ability.

Our Use of Labels in This Book

After all we've said about the dangers of labels, it's a good idea for us to clarify how *we'll* use labels in this book. As we've said, the beginning of wisdom is calling things by their *right* name, not abandoning names altogether. Labels are like lenses. Used properly, they can sharpen our vision and help us see things we might otherwise have missed. Used poorly, they can render us all but blind. Appropriate labels can help us understand and anticipate the problems a child might face, increase our sense of empathy for her struggles, and enable us to find and deliver needed help. They can make it easier for parents, teachers, and the child himself to keep the "big picture" of a child's challenges in mind, without being overwhelmed by details. They can help us spot relationships between different learning challenges and the behaviors that accompany them, which can in turn teach us more about the underlying causes and true nature of learning challenges.

The labels we use in this book are not always the labels we would have chosen. Even within these labels, as you'll see, there are often enormous variations and tremendous room for confusion. In many cases, we'll point out explicitly what we think is wrong with these labels and how they are often misused. However, these are the labels that are currently in common use, and because our goal is to help you function in the real world (and not some ideal world of our imagining), we've chosen to look at these labels as they are commonly used.

Just one word of warning: Even the best and most accurate labels should always be used with caution. Labels only ever provide part of the picture: the part that describes a child's current level of functioning, not some fixed and immutable future. Labels are starting points, not destinations—and certainly not destinies.

In our next chapter, we'll show you how you can use this book to help children with learning challenges, many of whom, like Michael, have been mislabeled, misunderstood, and mistreated. We'll show you how to identify a child's strengths and weaknesses in the areas of *Information Input, Memory and Pattern Processing, Output for Action,* and *Attention.* We'll show you how these strengths and weaknesses can be used to design a program of education that can help your child learn and achieve to his or her greatest potential. Above all, we'll show you how you can correctly name and understand many of the things about your child that you've previously found confusing or mysterious. Which is, after all, the beginning of wisdom.

2

How to
Get the Most
from This Book

Of a good beginning cometh a good end.
—JOHN HEYWOOD, *PROVERBS*

Well begun is half done.
—MARY POPPINS, PROVERB

In this chapter, we'll discuss three things that you'll need to understand so you can use this book to help any child with learning challenges:

1. Our general approach to helping children with learning challenges.
2. How the nervous system thinks and learns.
3. How each of the chapters in this book should be approached.

Let's look at each in order.

Our general approach to evaluating and helping children with learning challenges involves three steps.

STEP 1: *Obtain a complete assessment* of a child's brain-based learning systems, including strengths and weaknesses in each of the following four areas of nervous-system function:

- Information Input
- Pattern Processing
- Output for Action
- Attention

(We'll discuss each of these areas in the next section.)

STEP 2: Use the information obtained from the assessment to *create a complete learning profile* of the child's strengths and weaknesses.

STEP 3: Use this profile of strengths and weaknesses to *design a program of education, therapy, and play* that will increase a child's capacities to think and learn more productively.

That's the big picture in a nutshell: assess, create a learning profile, and design a learning program. Obviously, performing each of these steps with an individual child will involve a lot of details, many of which will require at least a little understanding of how the brain thinks and learns. In the next section, we'll tell you everything you need to know in order to understand both these details and the information we present in the rest of this book.

HOW THE BRAIN THINKS AND LEARNS

When it comes to learning, thinking, and knowing, the bottom line is very simple: It's all about *connections*. Everything your brain can do and everything it can remember is a function of the connections that link its many nerve cells.

When you were born, your nerve cells made relatively few connections—just the ones you needed to cry, startle, breathe, suck, swallow, and perform a very few other automatic or reflex functions. Yet before your first birthday rolled around, your brain had formed countless new connections that enabled you to advance from smiling at your mother to reaching for a shiny toy to taking your first steps and probably even to saying your first words.

How were these connections formed? The answer is as simple as it is surprising: *Your brain itself formed them as you interacted with your environment.* During this process of brain-based "rewiring," which we call *neurolearning*, your brain absorbed information through your senses, processed it in your brain, responded to it using your various output functions, and monitored and coordinated the whole process using your attention system. By repeating this process over and over, your brain was able to assemble itself gradually into the capable and creative marvel it is today.

There are four basic steps or systems involved in this neurolearning process: (1) Information Input, (2) Pattern Processing, (3) Output for Action, and (4) Attention. As you'll see in the chapters that follow, each of these systems plays an important role in many of the learning challenges that are described in this book. Let's take a brief look at each.

Information Input

In order for your brain to begin to think, learn, and control your actions, it must first receive information about the world both outside *and* inside your body. This information is provided by your body's *Information Input* systems. These Information Input systems consist of the five basic senses you probably learned about as a child—sight, sound, touch, taste, smell—and several others that are essential for your daily function but may be less familiar: the *vestibular* system, which uses complicated inner-ear equipment to monitor your body's position in space; the *proprioceptive* system, which uses tiny nerve sensors in the joints and muscles to tell you about the position and movement of your muscles and limbs; and the *interoceptive* system, which gives you feedback from your internal organs.

Each of these Information Input systems plays a crucial role in learning and development. In fact, your abilities to think, reason, remember, and understand all began with—and were initially entirely dependent upon—your abilities to acquire information through these systems.

Because these Information Input systems play such a central role in the learning process, a child can have major difficulties when they malfunction.

When an input system malfunctions, every step in the neurolearning process that lies "downstream" of it will also be affected. Even a problem that lies outside of the brain—for example, in the eyes or ears—can have drastic effects on brain development, learning, and thinking if it prevents the flow of accurate information to the brain. For instance, visual problems can lead not only to poor visual perception of the environment but also to problems accurately remembering and understanding the environment. As you'll see, problems with the Information Input systems play an important role in children's learning problems.

Pattern Processing

Having functional input systems is absolutely necessary for learning about the world. However, by itself it isn't enough. You also have to be able to process the information that comes in through your inputs so you can form an accurate record of your experiences.

When information comes in through your input systems, it gets fed to various processing centers in your brain. These processing centers then analyze the incoming information to see if they can detect any patterns. When they do detect a pattern, they encode it into "brain language," then file it away as a memory in one of your brain's storage areas. Each time you observe this pattern in the future, like the sight of a cat or the sound of a skateboard, your memory of it will grow stronger and easier to recall. This is how you learn: by forming and reinforcing accurate memories of information patterns.

Once you've learned a particular information pattern, you should be able to recognize it whenever you encounter it, even when it's in a somewhat different form. Over time, as you repeat this *Pattern Processing* cycle on each new bit of input you receive, your memory stores become stocked with more and more remembered patterns. You also find that you can recall these patterns from your memory whenever you want to and reflect on them. The more you reflect on the patterns you've stored, the more you'll see the connections or associations between them, and as you discover these relationships, you'll begin to understand the nature of categories, rules, similarities, opposites, et cetera. As this process continues, you'll find that you've been building an increasingly clear, accurate, and complex model of the world.

(Note: Individual children often show big differences between their abilities to process or manipulate different kinds of patterns or images. Some children are better with visual images, some with auditory images, and some with images of bodily motion. As we'll see in Chapter 3, knowing which kinds of imagery a child handles best can play an important role in helping her identify her best learning style and strategies.)

Output for Action

Of course, learning isn't just about observing and understanding. It's also about acting. However, before you can act in a productive and successful fashion, you need to have some idea what you're doing. That requires having a detailed and accurate plan. How do you make such a plan? By following a pattern. Fortunately, you have a whole memory system chock-full of patterns to help you make your plan.

To develop a plan of *Output for Action*, you simply use the model of the world you've created from your past experiences to make predictions about what you think will work this time. In other words, your memory doesn't deal only with your past. It's important in the past, present, and future. It helps you understand your past and present, plan for your future (based on the predictions you make from your experience of the past), and act in the unfolding present, using your remembered model of the world. Your memory processing system is actually so important for every aspect of your thinking and learning that many learning experts consider it the fundamental basis of intelligence.

Attention

But all the memory capacity in the world won't help you if you can't pay attention to what you're doing. The *Attention* system is a collection of functions that helps you maintain mental focus, keep multiple things in mind while you're working on them, and balance creative and dynamic impulses with your need for order, restraint, and detailed planning. We'll discuss these functions in greater depth in Chapter 7.

HOW TO APPROACH OUR OTHER CHAPTERS

Before we leave this chapter, we'd like to take a few moments to familiarize you with the format we'll use in each of the following chapters. Each of these next eleven chapters will focus either on a single type of learning system and the challenges that affect it (like memory, vision, hearing, language, attention) or on a single broad type of learning challenge (like autism, SPD, or disorders of reading, handwriting, and math). Each chapter will follow the same basic format. After a brief case vignette (or vignettes) and a few introductory comments, they'll have four major sections, whose contents will be as follows:

Behaviors

The Behaviors section describes the common signs and symptoms displayed by the children with the learning challenges discussed in that chapter. The Behaviors section is the first place you'll want to stop if you're uncertain whether a particular chapter is relevant for your child. By quickly scanning the Behaviors sections, you can quickly identify which chapters are most relevant. However, irrespective of the child's problem, we would also recommend that you read Chapter 3, since many key concepts and learning strategies are presented in this chapter that will be helpful for any child with learning challenges.

Causes

The Causes section describes the brain-based processes that underlie the normal functions and the learning challenges discussed in that chapter. Our goal in this section will be to provide you with enough information to understand the learning challenges discussed and to help you understand why certain interventions work. In many of our chapters, these causes will be organized according to where in the neurolearning pathway they cause difficulty (i.e., Information Input, Pattern Processing, Output for Action, or Attention). In some chapters, we'll also include sections on social problems or other issues that can arise from the learning challenges covered in that chapter.

Evaluating

The Evaluating section in each chapter will discuss any specific information needed to determine whether a child is suffering from the learning challenges described in that chapter.

Because the basic evaluation we recommend for most children with learning problems will be very similar no matter what the child's challenges, we will not describe it in each chapter. Instead we will present it here. In general, the initial evaluation for all children with learning challenges should include:

- Descriptions by parent(s), teacher(s), and child of the particular challenges and issues in question.
- An evaluation of the child's schoolwork.
- A detailed developmental history that looks for evidence of pregnancy or birth problems, subsequent injury or significant illness, evidence of special developmental issues, and a detailed behavioral inventory.
- A personal and family history of particular psychological, psychiatric, or specific learning problems.
- A detailed physical and neurological exam that looks especially at sensory and motor functions the child will need to support academic skills.
- A detailed neuropsychological examination that looks at the lower- and higher-level cognitive functions the child will need to support academic skills.

The goal of this evaluation is not just to identify where a child is encountering problems but also to identify particular areas of strength that the child may possess, upon which interventions can be based. Some of the key questions we seek answers to are:

- What is the child's preferred route or routes of Information Input? Which of these routes, if any, present particular problems? Does the child prefer to take in information by reading? By looking at pictures or diagrams? By having others read to him or give him verbal explanations? By watching documentaries that combine words and visual images? Through active, hands-on approaches or personal experience in an informal setting?

- What is the child's preferred route or routes of Pattern Processing? Which of these routes, if any, present particular problems? How does she generally try to encode, store, retrieve, and manipulate memory patterns? As words? As visual images? As physical movements or gestures?

- What is the child's preferred route or routes of Output for Action? Which, if any, present particular problems? Is he fluent in both spoken and written expression? Does he have skills or difficulties with gross or fine motor function? Are fine motor difficulties limited to letter and word writing, or do they span many fine motor tasks? Are motor difficulties especially intense in activities that involve visual guidance, or are they apparent even in tasks that can usually be done without watching?

- In which Attention functions is the child particularly strong? Which are particularly weak? Does the child experience difficulties with particular aspects of paying attention in all environments, with all tasks, or with all forms of Information Input or only with some?

Although the child is being evaluated because of learning problems, the goal of the evaluation is not simply to identify weaknesses but also to identify strengths, because these can often be used to help the child overcome or circumvent the challenges posed by learning problems.

Helping

In the Helping section, we outline steps that can be taken to help children who are struggling with the learning challenges described in that chapter. Most of these "helps" will fall into one of three categories: remediations, compensations, or accommodations.

- Remediations are interventions that help a child develop new functions and areas of strength by "rewiring" the brain. Because of the way it works, parts of the brain that are usually used to process one kind of information (like hearing or touch or vision) can be "recruited" to process other kinds of information. This flexibility—which scientists call *plasticity*—is crucial for helping children with learning problems. Throughout this book, we'll discuss ways of taking advantage of this plasticity by using carefully tailored therapies (or "directed experience") to produce targeted changes in brain structure and function. Examples of remediations would include the use of targeted therapies to relieve brain-based deficits in hearing, vision, or motor function.

- Compensations are interventions that help children use their mental and physical strengths to work around problems caused by areas of weakness. An example would be helping a child who has impaired memory for rote math facts (e.g., memorizing the times table) to learn his multiplication facts by using narrative memory strategies (see Chapter 3).

- Accommodations are interventions that seek to minimize the negative consequences of learning challenges that cannot be (or have not yet been) entirely eliminated by remediations or compensations. An example would be the decision to let a child with a severe neurologically based impairment in handwriting (dysgraphia) use a keyboard to write his assignments. We have found that many persons (educators especially, but also parents and children) misunderstand the purpose of accommodations, so we would like to say a little about them here. Some people worry that accommodations can create "special advantages" or "tilt the playing field" in favor of children with learning challenges. Others respond that accommodations are needed to "level a playing field" that is already tilted against the learning-challenged child. We find these metaphors subtly misleading. Education is neither a game nor a form of competition; it is the process of helping each child learn and achieve as well as she possibly can. People who are worried about giving special learning advantages to children need to rethink their whole perspective. We should be trying to provide as many learning advantages as we can to all children. This does not mean relieving any child of the responsibility of making the kind of diligent effort that is needed to learn, but it does mean lessening the burden imposed by learning challenges that make certain kinds of work essentially impossible and channeling a child's energy into more beneficial forms of work. Accommodations, in other words, should not be thought of as ways of getting a child *out* of work but as ways of getting a child *into* the kinds of work that are best suited to promoting her education.

Of course, the most important kind of help that can be provided to any children who struggle with learning challenges is *an adult who believes in them totally and unfailingly*. Even children who face serious learning challenges can grow up to lead successful and satisfying lives if they are encouraged to develop their strengths, overcome their weaknesses, and maintain a clear and confident vision of their own eventual success. A child's ego is seldom strong enough to withstand constant negative feedback at school, unless she receives even stronger messages of optimism and hope from someone she loves and respects. Keeping alive a child's positive vision of herself and her future should be the number-one goal of parents, teachers, and adult mentors.

In the next chapter, we'll begin our discussion of particular learning challenges, learning strengths, and learning styles by considering the crucial topic of memory.

3

Gone in
Sixty Seconds

Memory Strengths and Weaknesses

Memory is the scribe of the soul.

—ARISTOTLE, PHILOSOPHER

Memory is what tells a man that his wife's birthday
was yesterday.

—MARIO ROCCO, COMEDIAN

Kendra was a sunny and delightful seven-year-old. Her parents believed she was bright in many ways, but they were often surprised by how little she remembered from school. Kendra could assimilate visual material, but her ability to retain auditory information was almost nonexistent. According to her parents, as soon as her teacher began to talk, Kendra's brain went out to recess.

During our evaluation, Kendra struggled to keep auditory information in mind for even a short period of time. She had difficulty following simple instructions or remembering even a short chain of numbers. Most six-year-olds can repeat a string of four numbers. Kendra, a year older, couldn't remember even three. Her auditory memory capacity became overloaded with even little burdens.

Fortunately, our evaluation showed that Kendra had a strong visual memory. She also had a strong ability to imagine and manipulate visual images. Kendra told us she actually preferred thinking in visual terms. We decided to see whether she might be able to remember more auditory input if she imagined it as pictures rather than sounds.

We asked Kendra to close her eyes and picture the numbers in her imagination as she heard them. With her first try, Kendra remembered three numbers, but four was still too many. We asked her how she was trying to remember the numbers. She said she was imagining them glittering and dancing on a stage in her brain. Unfortunately, when a new number was called, the old number danced off. Then she couldn't remember it. We asked her to keep all the numbers onstage together, so she could "read them off" at once. She closed her eyes, listened, and remembered five numbers in sequence—average for her age!

In retrospect, we saw that Kendra's school problems were caused not by one memory problem but by two. In addition to having difficulty remembering sound-based information, she also didn't understand how to use the memory strengths she possessed to learn and remember better.

Most children are like Kendra in being strong in some parts of memory, weak in others, and not really sure how to make the most of what they've got. In this chapter, we'll take a closer look at how the memory system really works and at how children can learn to use strengths in memory areas to become more effective learners and rememberers.

Memory: An Introduction

In Chapter 2, we described memory's central role in the neurolearning process. We showed you how memory is crucial for remembering the past, understanding the present, and planning for and acting in the future. We discussed how memory lies at the core of the way we think and know, and how it is in a very real sense *the essence of learning*.

During that discussion, we spoke of memory in rather a general sense. We focused on the common mechanisms underlying memory of all kinds and only briefly mentioned that children often show differences in their abilities to remember and manipulate different kinds of information patterns. Of course, most of us, children included, show big differences in our abilities to take in, remember, and manipulate different kinds of information.

We may not think about it too often, but we each have our preferred memory storage and retrieval systems, preferred routes of information input, and preferred forms of pattern reflection and manipulation. Each of us finds certain kinds of information easier to remember and manipulate than others. To minimize the impact of our weaknesses, we work around or avoid trouble spots and channel tasks toward areas of strength. Fortunately, all of us—even children who struggle greatly in school—have areas of strength that can be used to compensate for areas of weakness. Even better, the brain's plasticity or capacity for change can often allow us to strengthen our weaknesses.

Our goal is to show you how children can use their memory strengths to overcome their brain-based memory and learning weaknesses. We'll discuss how memory is intimately involved in each of the Pattern Processing steps we mentioned in Chapter 2 (i.e., encoding, filing, storage, retrieval, and reflection). We'll also discuss how problems with Attention and Information Input can affect memory. But before we get to the specifics, let's look at behaviors that often signal when a child is struggling with memory.

BEHAVIORS ASSOCIATED WITH MEMORY PROBLEMS

Some behaviors are relatively easy to identify as signs of memory difficulties, like:

- Trouble getting information into long-term memory.
- Forgetting quickly. ("Things go in one ear and out the other.")
- Tending to "leach out" information over time. (Getting it today, but it's gone by tomorrow or next week. Forgetting last year's work over summer break.)

- Frequently needing to relearn previously mastered material.
- Absentmindedness. (Seeming to forget what he is or should be doing.)

As we'll see throughout this book, these signs of memory problems may be signs of problems with memory per se or of problems with Information Input, Attention, or Output functions. A careful evaluation is needed to identify the true source of these behaviors.

Other behaviors may be less obvious as signs of poor memory, such as:

- Inattentiveness.
- "Spaciness."
- A tendency to experience "information overload" during rapid or complicated inputs.
- Difficulty with complex tasks, like writing or math, despite good conceptual understanding.
- Difficulty retrieving information from long-term storage, despite clear indications that it is there (e.g., a child who is better able to recognize something than spontaneously recall it).
- Slow, halting, or nonfluent speech.
- Difficulty learning and executing complex motor sequences.
- Difficulty learning and remembering complex cognitive procedures (e.g., the order of steps in a math problem or a recipe).
- Difficulties learning to read, write, or spell.
- A tendency to make "careless," "surprising," "bizarre," or "glaring" mistakes.
- A tendency to perform poorly on tests of information, despite good problem-solving and reasoning skills.
- An appearance of disorganization: always losing or unable to find things.
- A tendency to get lost or forget one's way around.

HOW MEMORY WORKS AND HOW MEMORY PROBLEMS ARE CAUSED

The memory system is distributed widely throughout the brain. In fact, every lobe of the brain plays some role in memory. Different memory tasks employ different parts of the brain, and some memory tasks involve multiple brain parts simultaneously, acting in coordination.

This broad distribution has both drawbacks and benefits. The chief drawback is this: The more parts of the brain that are involved in an activity, the greater the likelihood that some part will have problems. Brain development is a complex and risky process and rarely goes off without a hitch. Add to that the risk of injury or disease and you can see why most of us have problems with at least some part of our memory system. The chief benefit of memory's broad distribution becomes apparent when you look at these risks from another angle: It's almost impossible, short of a real catastrophe, to have *all* your memory functions impaired. This is the brain's version of "don't put all your eggs in one basket."

Another benefit of this broad distribution is that it gives the brain tremendous flexibility in making up for areas of dysfunction. As we mentioned in Chapter 2, the brain has two primary means of doing this. First, it can "recruit" or "rewire" new brain areas to take over missing functions. Such remediation is possible because of the brain's incredible plasticity (i.e., the ability of different brain areas to change and take on different functions). Second, the brain can use other memory functions to make up for functions that are impaired. This, as we mentioned, is called compensation, and it is the crucial response by which our brains increase our strengths to help compensate for our weaknesses.

At this point, you may wonder, *If the brain possesses these wonderful corrective mechanisms, why doesn't it just fix itself?* The answer is simple. Although these mechanisms *can* work on their own, they work much better when they're guided. In the Helping section of this chapter, we'll show you how to provide such guidance. However, before you can understand these treatments, you'll first have to understand a little bit about the memory system they're treating.

Let's begin our discussion of the memory system by looking briefly at the role the Information Input and Attention systems play in memory. Afterward, we'll look at memory's crucial Pattern Processing steps. By spending a few minutes now learning to understand how and why the memory system works as it does, you'll be able to understand much more clearly the reasons the interventions we describe later do their job.

How Information Input and Attention
Can Affect Memory Performance

Our Information Input systems consist of our various sense-receptor organs (like eyes, middle and inner ears, skin, etc.) and the nerves that carry signals from them to the brain. Our input systems are responsible for our ability to register events both in and around us. Problems with sensory registration usually weaken memory performance. In computer terms, it's a case of "garbage in, garbage out." If visual images, sounds, or other sensory inputs get garbled before they reach the brain's Pattern Processing system, then the memories formed from this input will be garbled as well.

Not only will these memories fail to accurately represent the environment, they'll also be hard to retrieve. Children with input problems tend to "misfile" information patterns in long-term storage. As a result, they have a hard time knowing where to look for them when they want to retrieve them later. This misfiling occurs because of problems in a step called *encoding*. Encoding is the process through which patterns are translated into the appropriate "brain language" for long-term storage. Because children with input problems don't register incoming patterns correctly, they tend to encode them improperly as well. Improving their initial registration of visual or sound input will help them encode, file, store, and retrieve memory patterns with greater accuracy and efficiency. We'll have much more to say later about optimizing this encoding process.

Memory problems due to impaired Information Input are often easy to recognize, because they cause highly specific problems. When a child has difficulty with a particular input route, she'll have difficulty remembering patterns that come in through that input. Any child with a cluster of memory difficulties that could have resulted from a single "upstream" problem with sensory input should be carefully checked for a problem in Information Input. For example, children who have problems remembering words should be checked for impairments in sound processing, and children who have trouble remembering spatial relationships (like what was nearer and what behind) should be assessed for visual problems. Not all memory problems are caused by impaired input, but many are, as we'll see repeatedly.

The attention system is also essential for learning and memory. Children can encode, file, and store patterns only after they've paid them careful attention. Contrary to popular mythology, children can't, for instance, memorize Lincoln's Gettysburg Address by having it played over headphones during sleep. Learning requires conscious attention.

Sometimes it can be difficult to sort out whether a child's troubles remembering things are due to a primary deficit in attention or memory. Children with both kinds of problems can have difficulty remembering what they've seen or heard. As we'll discuss later, most learning experts actually include one part of memory—called working memory—in the attention system as well. The similarities and distinctions between these functions should grow clearer as you read our discussion here and in Chapter 7.

Memory is also like attention in requiring firm foundations to function well. Any of the problems that weaken attention's foundations—like sleep problems, chronic illnesses, dietary or metabolic issues, sensorimotor issues, poor home or school environment, anxiety, or depression (see Chapter 7, Table 5)—can also cause significant problems with memory.

Memory Pattern Processing: Introduction

Memory experts sometimes disagree on the fine details of memory function, and some details aren't well understood, but despite this uncertainty, the overall framework we'll present in this section fits well with the known facts. This framework will help us understand both normal memory function and the kinds of memory problems that commonly affect children's abilities to learn.

Memory's Two Big Subsystems: Working Memory and Long-Term Memory

The memory system as a whole can be divided into two big subsystems: working memory and long-term memory. These two divisions of the memory system correspond with the steps of our Pattern Processing system, as we show in Figure 1: Working memory is essentially equivalent to encoding and reflection, and long-term memory is equivalent to filing, storage, and retrieval. Let's look at these in more detail, starting with working memory.

THE TWO BIG DIVISIONS IN MEMORY
1. Working Memory = encoding + reflection
2. Long-Term Memory = filing + storage + retrieval

FIGURE 1. Memory's Two Subsystems

Memory Pattern Processing: Working Memory

Working memory is the part of your memory that lets you "keep things in mind." It holds information patterns in your "mind's eye" so you can encode them for long-term storage; manipulate and modify them; use them to imagine, create, and solve problems; and plan what you're going to do next. Working memory helps you remember the words you've just read while you're reading the rest of this paragraph. It lets you keep in mind all the steps in a long-division problem while you're doing them and remember which step you're on. It keeps the words you've just heard in mind until you can write them in your notes. And it lets you remember the unfamiliar word you've just heard long enough so you can encode it and file it in long-term memory. We like to call working memory the Juggler because its main task is to keep as many memory "balls" in the air as possible!

Working memory operates in a relatively short time frame—typically less than a minute. It also has a far more limited capacity than long-term memory. You experience this limit all the time. Think how few things you can "keep in mind" all at once, compared with how much you can store in long-term memory.

Working memory—like the memory system as a whole—can be divided into several parts. At its highest level, it's made up of a central component that oversees and coordinates all of the working memory functions we'll discuss below. This central component is often called the central executive, because it coordinates the key processes in working memory. It provides the main workspace for encoding and reflection, and it coordinates the filing, storage, and retrieval processes with long-term memory.

Working memory can juggle patterns that come in from the sensory inputs or that are recalled from long-term memory. To keep incoming patterns in mind for more than a few seconds, it must divert them to one of several special short-term working memory "buffers," which we'll now describe.

The Auditory (Phonological) Short-Term Buffer: "Tape Loop"

The first short-term buffer is the *auditory (sound or phonological) buffer*, which is also sometimes known as the *auditory tape loop*. This buffer lets you replay sound patterns in your head. These may be actual sounds that you've heard or sound images that you've generated by reading, imagining sounds, or saying words to yourself.

The Visual-Spatial Short-Term Buffer: "Sketch Pad"

The second short-term buffer handles visual-spatial information and is often known as the *visual-spatial sketch pad*. This buffer lets you replay visual-spatial images or pictures in your mind's eye. As with the auditory tape loop, these visual or spatial images may contain either sensory patterns coming in from the environment or recalled patterns. Some children are extremely strong visual-spatial image generators and form visual-spatial images automatically in response to all sorts of stimuli (like heard or read words) or in response to particular thoughts or feelings. As we'll discuss below, they may even use these images as their preferred or primary form of memory and thinking.

The Motor/Kinesthetic Short-Term Buffer: "The Mime"

The third short-term buffer is called the *motor (movement-based or kinesthetic) memory buffer*, or *motor mime*. This buffer uses the mental or physical rehearsal of motor movements to help keep things in mind. These rehearsed movements can include everything from forming words with your mouth to retracing the eye or finger movements needed to outline a visual figure to using a finger to trace out the movements needed to spell a word to simply imagining the movements it would take to do so. The "mime" takes advantage of the fact that the body's motor or muscle-movement system has its own memory area, where it stores the memory patterns (or *motor maps*) needed to guide the body's movements. We'll discuss kinesthetic memory strategies that take advantage of this motor memory throughout this book.

Working Memory in Action

These short-term working memory buffers help with several key memory tasks. As we've mentioned, they aid in encoding (the process of preparing memory patterns for storage in long-term memory) and in reflection (the process of mentally manipulating memory patterns to understand and combine them in new ways).

One way these buffers help with these steps is by using the strategy of *rehearsal*. Rehearsal is the process of mentally repeating a pattern so it can be transferred from the short-term memory buffers to a longer-lasting form of memory. Rehearsal is a crucial strategy, because it allows you to keep much more information in working memory. As stated earlier, working memory has a limited capacity or span. In the early grades especially, a narrow span places real constraints on how much and how rapidly a child can process information. For example, a recent study from Australia showed that approximately one-third of kindergarten-age children have an auditory memory span of nine words or less, which means that they can't process any sentence longer than nine words. Although working memory span increases rapidly up to age twelve, it is still the case that by third grade one-third of children cannot process sentences longer than thirteen words. Yet many of the sentences teachers (and parents) use are longer than this. The simple sentence in Figure 2 is similar to instructions often given in class, *yet it would be beyond the reach of these children.*

Good teachers have always known this. Think of the slow, clear "teacher's voice" used by most skilled and experienced early-elementary teachers (and day-care workers, children's therapists, pediatricians, etc.). These professionals did not grow up speaking this way, nor did they gravitate toward their professions because they had a certain kind of voice. Instead they've learned over time what style of speech children best respond to, and they have adopted this style as their own.

Sit down, open your book to page twenty-five, and look at problem three. (This sentence is fourteen words long.)

FIGURE 2. Auditory Working Memory Span Is Narrow in Children

Children with very limited working memory spans tend to overload with even small amounts of information. As a result, they often show the classic "in one ear and out the other" pattern of forgetfulness and are frequently diagnosed with attention problems. These working memory difficulties may be limited to one short-term buffer (and as a result are seen only with certain kinds of input) or may be seen with all.

Working memory problems can be very serious. Studies have shown that children who have difficulty with their sound-based (phonological) tape loop often have problems with language acquisition. Likewise, children who have problems with their visual-spatial sketch pad typically show serious deficits in visual-spatial learning. Problems with working memory make it hard to learn and store new patterns in long-term memory. When severe, working memory problems can even cause delays in general cognitive development (i.e., mental retardation or low IQ).

Many children will show strong preferences for either their sound-based, visual-spatial, or motor working memories. These differences can play a big role in determining learning styles and preferences (as we'll discuss in our Helping section).

Memory Pattern Processing:
Long-Term Memory

When it comes to long-term memory, the name pretty much says it all: Long-term memory lets you store (and retrieve) patterns over long periods of time (from minutes to years). There are many different subtypes of long-term memory, each of which stores a different kind of information pattern in a particular part of the brain. Generally speaking, these long-term memory subtypes can be classified in two big groups: *personal memories* and *impersonal memories*. We'll describe each of these large categories briefly, then see how they're important for learning. We'll then go on to look at other important long-term memory subtypes.

This discussion is important because it will give you a practical basis for thinking strategically about how to help children learn and remember. Since memory is the essence of learning, we need to understand how the memory system works before we can understand how best to teach and learn. We'll refer to this information constantly in coming chapters when we discuss interventions and strategies that help children overcome learning weaknesses by relying on their strengths.

Personal (Episodic) Memory

Personal (also called *autobiographical* or *episodic*) *memory* gets its name because it stores patterns that deal with personal experiences (i.e., episodes or events in a person's life). Your personal memory patterns are highly contextual in the sense that they contain information about things that happened to you at particular times and in particular places. Often your personal memories are also connected with specific feelings, emotions, or sensory experiences that you had at the time.

Certain types of events are especially likely to generate powerful personal memories. In everyday language, these are the events that "leave a lasting impression." They include events that are highly novel (new or unique), surprising, humorous, fun, pleasant, or those that elicit a strong sense of emotional empathy. Less enjoyably, they include events that are notably shocking, irritating, unpleasant, painful, frightening, or embarrassing. Personal memories are especially valuable as aids to learning, as we'll see in a moment.

Impersonal (Semantic) Memory

Impersonal (or *semantic*) *memory* deals with facts that are impersonal in nature. They don't relate to you personally, or to events in your life. As a result, they are decontextualized with respect to time, space (particular place), and emotion, and they tell you nothing about when, where, or under what circumstances you formed your memories. Impersonal memory is like Joe Friday: "Just the facts, ma'am." Traditionally, most academic instruction focuses on generating fact-based impersonal memories.

Uses of Personal and Impersonal Memory in Education

Children vary tremendously in their skills at forming personal and impersonal memories. Those who favor the use of personal memory learn best through experience. These children thrive on novelty, humor, surprise, the flash of insight, and the "aha!" moment. Their interest must be provoked rather than solicited, and they often appear distractible, since their attention is easily hijacked by anything alluring. They tend to notice a lot and frequently have strong memories for things they pick up through personal experience. Often the parents of these children tell us, "I know he's got a good memory, because he can tell you all the names of his uncle's sheep from when he went to the farm three years ago. Yet he can't remember what he's supposed to be learning in history." Children like this require teaching in history, math, and science that embodies as much excitement, novelty, and personal engagement as does a trip to a farm. They need, in other words, to use their powerful personal memories to store the facts that most children store in impersonal memory.

Children who favor the use of impersonal memory are the classic "book learners." They have a strong capacity for storing decontextualized facts and may neglect observation and experiments because they find it easier to learn from books. Excessive reliance on impersonal memory is often compatible with success in school, but it's a poor preparation for adult life. Children like this need help developing strategies for learning through observation and experience.

Most children learn best by combining personal and impersonal memory. That's why in general we should try harder to add the power of personal memory to a child's learning experiences. Making sure that teaching is engaging and personally meaningful isn't just a concession to children who've been "spoiled" by attention-eroding electronic media (though such media aren't blameless, as we'll discuss in later chapters). It's simply the most powerful way to involve the whole brain in learning—and, as we'll show continually throughout, the more brain the better! In our Helping section, we'll discuss ways to get these two memory systems working more synergistically. First, though, we need to mention other important long-term memory subtypes.

Long-Term Sensory Memory Patterns

As we described in Chapter 2, we take in sensory patterns through our input systems, then store them in long-term memory to form a record of our environment. These patterns can subsequently be used to recognize similar incoming sensory patterns. They can also be recalled from memory, then modified or recombined to create new patterns through the process of reflection or mental imagery. As a result, our sensory memories are filled with images (remembered patterns) of real objects and imagined ones. Tolkien's Middle Earth, Lewis's Narnia, and Rowlings's Hogwarts were each cobbled together in their creator's imagination from sensory patterns their creator had previously stored. When we read these books, our mental images of these places are formed in the same way.

As you'll see, this ability to generate new sensory memory patterns through the process of reflection or mental imagery is crucial for many of the learning strategies we describe. One reason sensory memory patterns are so valuable as learning tools is that they can be easily linked to personal memory features like humor, surprise, novelty, or silliness to form particularly strong memories. Multisensory approaches are especially powerful because they allow us to simultaneously link one fact or idea with patterns from different senses — as well as with personal memory — and, as we've said before, the more links or associations a given memory has, the better it will be stored and retrieved. Many different types of sensory patterns — both real and imagined — can be used to create especially "memorable" memories, as shown in Table 1.

TABLE 1 *Types of Sensory Memory Patterns*

- Visual: real or imagined objects, creatures, faces, colors, shapes, symbols, printed words, charts, maps, graphs, etc.
- Sound (auditory): voices, word sounds, music, animal noises, machines or other inanimate noise sources.
- Touch (tactile): touching or being touched by certain things; feelings on the skin due to fright, cold or heat, vibration, etc.

- Muscle movement (kinesthetic/proprioceptive): voluntary motions, activities, signs, or signals.
- Taste: foods, spices, substances, chemicals, feelings or states (e.g., lactic acid taste after exercise, dry mouth from fear, iron taste of blood).
- Smell: things (e.g., animals, chemicals), places (e.g., seashore, forest), or processes (e.g., burning, machine exhaust, rainfall).
- Balance (vestibular): motions like rocking, jolting, bumping, or falling.
- Interoception (visceral, internal bodily sensations): nausea, deep pain, hunger or satiety, bodily contentment or pleasure.

Long-Term Word and Language Memory Patterns

Word and language patterns play a crucial role in the learning process. While multisensory learning should be the cornerstone of education, language-based instruction could be used more effectively than it often is.

First, children should be taught to use language-based memories to compensate for their difficulties with sensory-based memory. This compensatory use of language is known as *verbal mediation*. In verbal mediation, children who have difficulties memorizing sensory or motor patterns can compensate for their difficulties by memorizing verbal descriptions of these sensory or motor patterns, then "talking their way through" difficult situations or practices. For example, children with impairments in visual-spatial memory can use verbal descriptions to help them understand and remember things that most people remember visually, like the way from class to the restroom: "Turn right outside the door, then take the second hall to the left, then it's the fourth door on the right."

Second, all children should be taught to use language to enhance memory formation. Language can be used to elaborate (or form more memorable patterns for) essentially every kind of memory. Types of language patterns that can enhance memories are:

- Specific definitions of words, facts, or events.
- Verbal descriptions, including sensory or multimodal references (i.e., verbal mediation).
- Synonyms or similar facts or events.
- Antonyms or opposites.
- Words with similar structures (based on word families or word roots).
- Verbal *mnemonic* (memory) strategies, like acronyms (i.e., words that are formed from the first letters of a group of words, like *MADD* for "Mothers Against Drunk Driving"), rhymes, alliterations, and language usages that engage personal memory with personally interesting word associations, humor, absurdity, et cetera. We'll discuss these strategies in our Helping section. An example of strategies that can be used to elaborate memory formation for the word *great* are shown in Figure 3.

Story or Context Associations

creatures great and small
great leader
great ball player
great woods
great white shark

+ Synonyms
big
strong character
large quantity
powerful
super

– Antonyms
poor
small
insignificant

Homonyms
grate

Similar Sounds
grand ate
ground debate
gravel late

Visual Appearance
great

FIGURE 3. Language Elaboration Strategies

Long-Term Story or Narrative Memory Patterns

Story or narrative patterns are often especially valuable as memory aids, because they are closely related to personal memory. Like personal experiences, stories embed facts in the contexts of time, place, emotions, and personal relationships and are often novel, surprising, or humorous. Stories typically provoke the formation of many kinds of images and memory patterns (e.g., sights, sounds, smells, touch sensations, emotional feelings, linguistic narrative, etc.) that can be stored in linked sites or networks in both impersonal and personal memory. Stories are also more redundant than most abstract, nonnarrative approaches, which gives children more "second chances" to glean information. This can be crucial for children with language, reading, or auditory processing problems.

Long-Term Musical Memory Patterns

Musical memory is another powerful tool for elaborating and storing new memory patterns. Most of you have used a song at some point to learn collections or series of facts like the alphabet, names of the states, books of the Bible, or multiplication tables. Music forms especially strong and lasting memories, because music has a unique processing and storage system in the brain. When you learn a song, both its words and its tune are stored in different locations from where nonmusical sounds and words are stored. In addition, research studies have shown that when you learn a song with both words and music, you actually improve your ability to remember *both* the words and the music. Musical memory is especially valuable for children who have problems with nonmusical language. Such children can benefit enormously from specially designed music therapy.

Long-Term Procedural Memory Patterns

Procedures form a major part of the things children learn in school. Many procedures involve motor skills—like the motions needed to form written letters or the movements required to sharpen a pencil. Other procedures involve nonmotor elements, like remembering the steps to solve a long-division problem or to correctly label your math assignment and turn it in.

Some children have trouble learning some or all kinds of procedures. These children need special help to learn and follow these stepwise tasks.

Long-Term Rule-Based Memory Patterns

Children also need to learn many rules. There are important rules in every subject, like "*i* before *e* except after *c* . . . ," how to make singular nouns plural, how to punctuate a sentence, how to determine a city's population by the size of its name on a map, and how to change signs when you're multiplying with negative numbers. Many children are naturally good at inferring and remembering such rules, but other children have difficulty unless these rules are explicitly taught. In recent years, rule-based learning has fallen out of favor, because it's thought to be boring or restricting. This has created problems for children who have difficulty mastering rules in general or who struggle with particular kinds of rules—like those for which sounds go with which letters. Such children need special help learning rules, and they often make real progress when they are finally able to comprehend the rule-based nature of reading, spelling, and other subjects.

Long-Term Memory Patterns Embodying Relationships

Finally, many patterns embody relationships between ideas or objects. These relationships may be of several kinds:

- *Hierarchies*: Examples include the "phylogenetic tree" (i.e., kingdom, phylum, class, order, family, genus, species), military ranks, wholes and parts (body, leg, foot, toe), or hierarchies of size or value ("bigger or smaller," "more or less," "better or worse").
- *Categories*: Categories may be precise and well defined (like car models and makes, shoe brands, or dog breeds) or more subjective and fluid (like "foods I enjoy," "my friends"), including fluid categories like analogies or metaphors (e.g., "visual images that portray courage" or "analogies to birth and death").
- *Paired memories*: Examples include words and their definitions or simple math equations (like $2 + 2$ or 4×3) and their answers.
- *Relationships in time, order, or sequence*: Examples include the

letters of the alphabet, months of the year, days of the week, the number sequence, the steps in various procedures, or concepts like "before," "after," or "simultaneously."

- *Relationships of objects in space or in spatial characteristics*: Examples include relationships of position or relative sizes and shapes like *nearer, farther, left, right, north, south, higher, lower, inside, outside, bigger, smaller, rounder, longer, taller*, etc.

The brain's ability to group patterns into appropriate relationships is extremely important. A child who has difficulty linking memory patterns into appropriate networks of categories, relationships, and associations will have a hard time recalling those patterns, even if they are still stored in long-term memory. Children who have difficulties in this area are often much better at recognizing patterns than at recalling them. This type of difficulty is important to spot, because children with this problem can improve their recall greatly through focused training in understanding groups and relationships.

Key Points About Long-Term Memory Types

As you can see, your long-term memory can store many different types of patterns. This diversity has crucial implications for many of the learning approaches we describe in this book. Remember: Many children's learning difficulties are caused by highly specific problems affecting only one or a very few aspects of memory and information processing; yet these narrowly focused problems often coexist with intact memory skills that can be used for compensation. The tremendous diversity of memory routes means there is often more than one way that a child can remember a given piece of information—like alternate roads she can use to get to her destination when her favorite route is blocked. Pictures can be translated into words or words into pictures. Objects, shapes, or forms can be touched or described as well as seen. Stories can be heard, read, seen in a play or movie, or personally enacted. Developing such multimodal learning strategies is one of the keys to our neurolearning approach. We'll discuss such strategies in more detail in the Helping section and again throughout this book.

Problems at the Level of Long-Term Memory Storage and Retrieval

Before we move on to Evaluating, we should mention that some children face problems at a more fundamental level of long-term memory—in particular, at the level of long-term memory storage or retrieval. Severe problems with long-term memory storage are rare, but we sometimes see children with milder long-term storage difficulties. These children have relatively little difficulty getting information into long-term memory—that is, their encoding and filing systems work okay—but they have a harder-than-usual time keeping it there, especially when it's not being used. These children can typically master new information when it's presented in class, but as soon as it's not being put to use, it begins "leaching out." Soon it's gone. These children lose the most ground over the long summer break, and each fall it can seem as if they're right back where they started the year before.

Problems with long-term memory retrieval can occur with varying levels of severity. Milder and more narrowly focused difficulties (like word-finding or spelling problems) are usually caused by problems in the encoding and filing stages, as we described above. Such difficulties often cause more problems spontaneously recalling patterns than recognizing them when encountered. More severe retrieval problems may affect most or all forms of long-term memory, irrespective of the type of pattern.

EVALUATING CHILDREN FOR MEMORY IMPAIRMENTS

Medical History. Risk factors for memory problems include prematurity; difficult birth; known birth injury; the need for neonatal intensive care; early severe respiratory difficulties or hypoxia; later severe illness or ICU stay; traumatic head injury; seizures; auditory, visual, or behavioral disorders; or academic difficulties. A family history of learning problems, sensory input disorders, or seizures may be important.

Always think about seizures in a child with significant memory problems. Nonconvulsive (i.e., nonshaking) seizures are much more common in children under ten than most people realize—especially in children with memory or other learning disorders. In our own clinic, we find previously undiagnosed nonconvulsive seizures in about 5 to 10 percent of all children we see. Children whose performance fluctuates markedly or who lose a previously gained function are especially likely to have seizures (though other disorders may cause these problems as well). All children who show such patterns require a consultation with a neurologist. Children suspected of having seizures should receive an EEG (electroencephalogram, or brain-wave recording). If the suspicion of seizures is high, a child may need as many as three EEGs to reach a 90 percent certainty that he is not having seizures.

Memory and Learning Preferences. Ask about a child's preferred routes of Information Input and Pattern Processing. Does she prefer to take in information by reading text? By looking at pictures and diagrams? By listening to others read to her or give her verbal explanations? By watching documentaries that combine words and visual images? By active, hands-on approaches or personal experience in an informal setting? Does she generally try to encode, store, and retrieve memory patterns as words? As visual images? As physical movements or gestures? Does she prefer to imagine, reason, problem-solve, and create using verbal images? Visual images? Symbolic images? Through hands-on building strategies? Sometimes a child may have more than one preferred route of learning, remembering, and reflecting. Sometimes (though not usually) a child may prefer a route that is not her strongest and may need to be redirected. Careful questioning about memory and learning preferences will make the examination phase of the evaluation even more valuable (see Figure 4).

Physical and Neuropsychological Testing. Physical and neuropsychological exams should look for signs of problems with Information Input (e.g., vision or hearing problems) or attention that might impair Pattern Processing. Neuropsychological testing should then look for particular memory weaknesses and strengths.

HELPING CHILDREN WITH
MEMORY DISORDERS

Optimizing a child's memory performance is crucial for learning. In this section, we'll describe steps that you can take to help any child—but especially

Working Memory

Tape Loop   **Visual-Spatial**   **Sensory-Motor**
              Sketch Pad   **Mime**

Long-Term Memory

  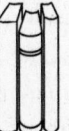

Personal Experience   **Feeling**   **Facts and Rules**

FIGURE 4. Inquire About a Child's Memory and Learning Strategies

a child with special memory challenges—become a more effective remember and learner.

There are *three basic steps* in improving a child's memory and learning:

1. Optimize Working Memory Performance
2. Optimize Long-Term Memory Performance
3. Develop an Optimal Learning Style Using Memory Strengths and Strategies

Helping Step 1: Optimize Working Memory Performance

Children differ markedly in their working memory capacities. Any given child may also show big differences between the capacities of his auditory, visual-spatial, and motor-kinesthetic working memories. Yet working memory capacity is not entirely fixed. Exciting new research has shown that children can significantly improve the capacity of their working memory. They can also learn strategies for retaining information in working memory for longer periods of time and for using their available working memory capacity more effectively. The following interventions can help them accomplish these ends.

Optimizing Working Memory Span

Working memory span can be increased through practice; like a muscle, it grows stronger with exercise. Recently Dr. Torkel Klingberg and colleagues in Sweden have shown that computer-based training in a variety of working memory tasks can not only increase working memory capacity but can also decrease the inattentive ADHD-type behaviors often exhibited by children with working memory problems. A commercial program based on their work (Robomed, from Cogmed Corp., www.cogmed.com) is now clinically available in Sweden, where it has shown promising results. Plans are under way to make this program more broadly available in Europe and through select clinics in the United States, beginning in 2006.

In addition to computer-based approaches, the following exercises can also be used to help build working memory strength:

- Expanding auditory working memory span. To build auditory working memory span, children should practice keeping longer and longer sentences "in mind" (i.e., in their short-term auditory memory buffer).

  - Start by finding a child's auditory (or phonological) short-term memory span. Have her repeat sentences of various fixed lengths (e.g., seven words, eight words, etc.), and determine where she drops from consistent retention (her current span length) to inconsistency. This is where she should start practicing. Remember: Repeating back sentences doesn't mean *memorizing* sentences—that's long-term memory. Just have her repeat sentences back right away, verbatim. Choose fun and interesting sentences with puns, jokes, alliterations, tongue twisters, or other sound plays to make things livelier.
  - When a child masters sentences at the initial level, she should practice sentences one word longer. Gradually increase sentence length as the child's span increases.

- Even five minutes of practice a day over a period of several months can produce significant gains in auditory memory span, and even small gains can result in big improvements in function.

- Expanding visual-spatial working memory span: Similar exercises can help children expand their visual-spatial working memory span. Here are two helpful procedures:

  - See how many of a line of simple geometric figures, patterns, or shapes a child can remember after looking at them for ten seconds. For this practice, use shapes or symbols that the child can't easily "turn into words" so he doesn't just use verbal mediation (auditory memory) to remember the figures. Verbal mediation is an excellent strategy and should be encouraged in most circumstances, but not when a child is practicing visual span length.
  - As an alternative, have children memorize the shapes of increasingly complex single figures or pictures. The symbols in Figure 5 are from a set of "dwarf runes" developed by Middle Earth fan Dan Smith and provide a good example of the kinds of figures that can be used. Using figures that cannot easily be verbally described (and therefore verbally mediated) will help ensure that the memory practice is really *visual*. As with auditory practice, children should move to gradually more complicated tasks as visual working memory span improves.

- Expanding motor memory span: Children with limited motor-kinesthetic working memory should practice motor imitation activities, like imitating hand and finger or whole-body (e.g., hopping) movements.

FIGURE 5. Practice to Optimize Visual Working Memory Span

- Because these children often have motor implementation problems (that is, difficulties getting each muscle to do what they want it to), involve only a few muscle groups at first. Have the child imitate a series of simple hand motions or a sequence of alternating hops from one leg to the other. Gradually increase difficulty as the child makes progress.
- A game like Simon Says can be a fun way to practice as the child improves.
- The video game Dance Dance Revolution, which is available for a variety of game console formats, can also be used to increase motor memory span.

Optimizing Working Memory Retention Using Rehearsal Strategies

While increasing working memory span is a top priority, children should also be taught to use the working memory space they have more efficiently. A great way to do this is by using repetition and rehearsal strategies. These strategies can help children retain more information in working memory so it can be better manipulated and processed.

- The most common rehearsal strategy is called *subvocalization*, which is essentially just talking to yourself.

  - Repeating things out loud is the most effective way to keep them in mind, because it combines auditory, verbal, and motor memory. However, it won't make you popular with teachers or classmates.
  - Whispering under your breath is more socially acceptable and still quite effective but also won't be possible in all circumstances, like during tests.
  - Silently forming words with your mouth while "pronouncing them" in your head is the next-best option.

- For children with better visual than auditory memory, forming and focusing on a visual image (mental "snapshot") can help as well.

- Motor strategies, like tracing over letters with a finger or tapping out the steps in a procedure, can also be used.
- Children begin discovering these strategies on their own around age seven. By age ten, most have. However, children as young as five or six can use these strategies if they are taught, and older children can often be taught to use them more effectively.
- Children will use these strategies most consistently if they are regularly prompted during the learning phase.

Optimizing Working Memory Efficiency by Making Skills Automatic

Working memory performance can also be improved by decreasing the effort required to perform different tasks. One way to decrease working memory burden is to teach a child to perform important tasks more *automatically*. The more automatic a process is, the less working memory is required to perform it, so more is available for other tasks.

- Automatic skills are especially important for frequently performed tasks like reading, writing, and math. If a child can't automatically decode when reading, form letters when writing, or recall basic math facts, then these functions will require conscious effort that steals working memory from other important uses.

  - Reading provides a good example of the benefits of automatic skills. When we first learn to read, we have to consciously "sound out" each letter, then hold each sound in working memory until we can decipher the whole word. With practice, this letter-to-sound matching process becomes more automatic. Eventually we no longer have to sound out words at all, and our conscious working memory resources are freed up for other tasks, like comprehension and analysis.
  - Writing shows a similar pattern. Greater automaticity in letter formation, grammar, and conventions like punctuation and capitalization leaves more working memory for formulating and expressing ideas.

- There's only one way to develop automatic skills, and that's through practice. Memory patterns—like those used to decode words or write letters—become more automatic the more they're used. That's why practice really does build speed and efficiency. Consistent, long-term practice should be part of the prescription for every child who's having difficulty developing automatic skills. But there's an important caveat: Many children have learning challenges that make them relatively resistant to the benefits of practice in certain areas. It's important that such children receive a course of practice and strategy development that's designed specifically for their needs.

Optimizing Working Memory at School: Teaching Styles and Strategies

Teachers can play an enormous role in helping children improve their working memory performance. Whether a child's working memory functions adequately in school depends both on its capacity *and* on the load it is asked to bear. By taking a few simple steps, teachers can significantly reduce the likelihood that their students will experience working memory overload.

- Step 1: Speak slowly and clearly! A child's working memory is highly sensitive to the rate of Information Input. Think Mister Rogers.
- Step 2: Use short, direct sentences! A child's working memory is highly sensitive to the amount of Information Input. Think Ernest Hemingway.
  (Note: If you're struggling to combine the images of Mister Rogers and Ernest Hemingway, just say slowly and clearly three times, "Hi, neighbors. It's a beautiful day on Mount Kilimanjaro!")
- Avoid presenting too much information at once. New information should be conveyed in small, manageable bits. This process is known as *chunking*.

  - Key words and key concepts should be clearly identified and nonessentials minimized. Informational "diamonds" should

initially be presented fully cleaned and polished, rather than in the rough. Over time, variations can be presented with gradual withdrawal of extra supports and explanations.
- We'll describe many specific chunking strategies throughout this book.

- Teachers can also help children learn new information by allowing them to preview or prelearn new terms, important concepts, or major themes before they're encountered in class. When children understand the terms and concepts being discussed, they can devote more working memory to processing and analyzing ideas, making inferences, and formulating responses and less to simply decoding terms.

Optimizing Working Memory at School: Accommodations

Although the strategies outlined above can greatly improve working memory function, some children need *accommodations* to lessen the burden on working memory. Many children experience working memory overload when tasks require extensive pattern processing, retrieval, and output. Sometimes the burdens of such tasks must be cut down so a child can learn to his full capacity.

- For example, for some children, handwriting imposes so great a burden on working memory that they can't express their thoughts clearly by hand. Such children should be allowed to keyboard or even orally dictate assignments whose focus is expressing ideas rather than handwriting per se.
- Likewise, if a child's difficulty remembering multiplication tables prevents her from practicing long division, she should be allowed to use a multiplication table or even a calculator for certain steps, so she can focus on learning the procedure.
- Printed tables and calculators are examples of external memory aids. So are desktop number or alphabet strips, printed lists of important groups or categories, printed descriptions or diagrams of steps in a procedure, sample problems, figures, charts, graphs, maps, printed time

schedules, or simple cues from a teacher or adult. External memory aids can also be more complex, like alarms and timers that remind children what they should be doing (and for how long), and data-storage devices like personal digital assistants (PDAs) that can store and display needed information. Used appropriately, external memory devices can be a big help for children with working memory limitations.

Helping Step 2: Optimize Long-Term Memory Performance

The steps in this section can improve long-term memory encoding, filing, storage, and retrieval. They are especially useful for children with diminished working memory but can help any child increase working memory performance.

Optimizing Long-Term Memory by Improving Encoding

Encoding is the step where patterns are prepared for filing in long-term memory. The encoding process takes place in working memory, but it has a tremendous effect upon long-term memory. In this section, we'll discuss three ways to improve encoding efficiency. These steps will play important roles in the development of the memory and learning strategies we discuss in Helping Step 3.

Optimizing Encoding Efficiency by Simplifying Patterns

The first way to optimize encoding efficiency is to simplify incoming information. Simplifying incoming sensory patterns ensures that they will consume the least possible space in working memory. The less space they consume, the more will be left to manipulate them in the encoding and filing processes.

- Simplification usually involves some form of summarizing or paraphrasing. Through these processes, incoming patterns are pared down and compressed so that only the most essential bits are kept in working memory. First, the most essential aspects of the incoming pattern are identified. These are generally its key words, images, or concepts. Second, these key patterns are "recoded" into a more manageable form. This form will vary for individual children, depending on their preferred memory and imagery styles, as we'll discuss below. For some it may be verbal, for others a mental picture or image. Whatever the form, this condensed version will then be ready for the final encoding steps of elaboration and association, which we'll discuss in the next section.

- Younger children should practice simplifying inputs from the outset of their education. After listening to a story, they should be asked to summarize the plot and to identify key concepts and characters. They will vary dramatically in their abilities to do this. Some may offer a sophisticated analysis of a complex Grimm's fairy tale as early as kindergarten. Others may struggle with even a one- or two-line proverb. But all should be asked to summarize, paraphrase, and simplify by putting things into their own words. Begin at their level of competence and progress to more challenging material.
- As children increase their simplifying skills, have them treat materials to successive rounds of simplification. Each round should be more succinct and concise. They should practice working at various levels of detail, from fairly complete and detailed summaries to big-picture views where only the "main themes" or "moral of the story" is expressed. Although successive summarizations involve a lot of work, they are worth the effort. More than most academic skills, summarizing and paraphrasing will be useful in essentially all adult careers.
- Children should also practice highlighting or circling key words, phrases, or concepts, when reading complex information. Have them write summaries using only the bits they've highlighted, restating these passages in their own words. Learning to recognize the patterns that mark key words and key ideas can be accomplished only through repeated practice.

- As children get older, they should practice taking notes on passages they read or movies they watch and should be given feedback on the content of their notes, level of detail, and accuracy in identifying key words and concepts. (Children who have problems with handwriting or the hearing skills needed to take notes should be allowed to dictate notes into a recorder or to a scribe.) Note taking should be taught as a specific academic skill, rather than leave students to pick it up on their own as they go along.

Optimizing Encoding by Elaboration and Association

Encoding and filing work best when they link new patterns to things that a person already knows in a network of associations. Associations are connections between memory patterns that make one pattern more likely to be retrieved when another is. Some associations give you the familiar feeling of "That reminds me . . . ," though most are so automatic you are unaware when you make them—like Pavlov's dogs, who salivated whenever they heard a bell because they had been trained to associate the bell with food.

Both conscious and unconscious associations can be used to help children overcome memory problems, as we'll describe in Helping Step 3 and throughout this book. For the moment, let's look at one example of a conscious association that may help make this process clearer. One of the authors of this book is an impressively awful speller and can spell many words correctly only by creating an auditory or visual association. For example, remembering that the word *persistent* ended with *-tent* rather than *-tant* required mentally associating the word with a visual image of a tent on the author's front lawn that persisted and would not go away. Likewise, mastering the irritating and illogical fact that *calculator* is spelled with an *-or* and *computer* with an *-er* required creating the images of a blue computer in front of a red calculator, and remembering the association that *-er* comes alphabetically before *-or*, just as blue comes before red.

This process of modifying patterns to associate them with other patterns is called *elaboration*. Elaboration takes the "crude materials" of one pattern and combines them with other patterns to create a new and more memorable image. Elaboration makes new memories easier to retrieve by organizing them within a network of previously stored patterns. The associations created by elaboration are like key words in a library search system. The more and better "key words" a memory pattern is linked to, the easier it will be to find it when it is needed. Elaboration techniques (like the use of spelling imagery described above) are often called *mnemonic* (or *memory*) *strategies*. We'll describe many of the most effective strategies in Step 3.

Improving Encoding Efficiency by Increasing General Knowledge

Creating new links and associations works best when a child has lots of memories or knowledge to connect to. The greater a child's supply of stored patterns, the greater her chances for finding relevant or analogous patterns that she can use to create associations with new patterns. Increasing a child's general fund of knowledge can create extra opportunities for forming new links.

Increasing the general fund of knowledge in children with working memory limitations can be challenging, because they often fail to learn well with traditional instruction. The following ideas can help:

- Children with working memory limitations often learn better incidentally (i.e., by doing or experiencing) than through formal instruction. The key is to provide them with interesting experiences.

  - Field trips to interesting places can be very instructive. They can be supplemented by quality documentary films or movies. Stories that illustrate through actions and events are often more involving and more easily memorable for these children.
  - Children with this learning style sometimes find that homeschooling offers the most flexible and effective learning environment.

Optimizing Long-Term Memory by Review and Rehearsal

Long-term memory performance can also be improved through review and rehearsal. A key principle of brain function is embodied in the saying "The neurons that fire together wire together." This means that for long-term memory, patterns that are frequently retrieved will be stored longer and accessed more easily than patterns that are neglected. "Use it or lose it" is the rule of thumb for storage. To ensure that patterns remain in long-term memory, it's important to have regular routines for reviewing or rehearsing important information.

- Patterns are stored best in long-term memory when they're initially subject to frequent (at least daily) review, followed by gradually lengthening gaps. Some children need frequent reviews for extensive periods. Others require only infrequent reviews and, if forced to spend too much time on review, may actually begin to perform worse. Finding an optimum frequency for an entire class can be a challenge.
- Review sessions shouldn't be boring, rote memory jam sessions. In fact, review sessions are good chances to employ elaboration strategies, so memories are left even better organized than before.

  - When retrieving and reviewing information, have children try to explain where each piece fits into a "larger picture" or framework of knowledge.
  - Have them make at least one new association in their previous memory network. Remember: *The more associations any memory pattern has, the more often it will be recalled, thereby increasing its durability in storage.*

- Review can also be unplanned, taking place whenever the opportunity arises. When encountering some new fact or phenomenon, refer back to previously learned material to show how these patterns are related: "You remember last week when you studied lizards? Well, snakes are similar to lizards in the following ways. . . ."
- Children who have problems with long-term memory decay need more "firing" than most children to solidify their "wiring." These children should become world-class note takers and list keepers. As we've discussed, notes and lists are forms of external memory aids,

and they can prevent important information from getting lost. Notes and lists are especially valuable for children with storage problems, because they can also be used for review.

- Children with storage problems should review their notes at home, especially over long breaks like summer vacation. Such children may also need to practice their handwriting, spelling, reading, and math skills over summer break so they don't slide back to square one. The same is true of any fact-based subject whose content will be built on year after year.

Helping Step 3: Develop an Optimal Learning Style Using Memory Strengths and Strategies

In this section, we'll discuss ways to help children use memory strengths to develop a learning style that is right for them. By memory strengths we mean memory in its broadest context: not just working and long-term memory functions per se but also the input systems that control the quality of information a child's memory systems have to work with. This combination of strengths will together determine a child's preferred learning style.

Identifying a child's preferred learning style is not simply a matter of finding out which route of input she prefers, or which types of patterns she can remember best. It also requires determining which types of patterns she can best manipulate and modify in working memory. Figure 6 lists these three key components of a child's preferred learning style. We'll briefly discuss each in turn.

1. Best Route of Information Input
2. Best Form of Working Memory
3. Best Form of Long-Term Memory

FIGURE 6. Three Key Components of a Child's Preferred Learning Style

Using the Best Route of Information Input

The first step in identifying a child's preferred learning style is to determine her best route of Information Input. As often as possible, information should be sent through the child's best input route, whether auditory, visual, or kinesthetic (hands-on). Multimodal formats are usually valuable, but one of the inputs should always be the child's best. Taking advantage of a child's strengths in Information Input will ensure she'll be provided with information in the best possible shape for her working memory to handle.

Using the Best Form of Working Memory: Manipulation and Modification

The second step in identifying a child's preferred learning style is to determine his best form of working memory. When we speak of a child's "best" form of working memory, we mean "best" in regard to two specific functions: span, or the amount of information (e.g., verbal, visual, motor-kinesthetic) that can be manipulated in working memory, and imagery, or the vividness and manipulability of information in working memory.

- We've discussed span extensively above. The bottom line: A child's preferred learning style should take advantage of her highest-capacity working memory system.
- Images are mental representations of feelings, sensations, experiences, or ideas. They may be sensory—visual or spatial, auditory (verbal or musical), tactile, kinesthetic, et cetera—or nonsensory symbols or emotions. These images can be used for daydreaming, reasoning, paraphrasing or summarizing, organizing, creating, finding analogies, making predictions, or problem solving. Strong imagery skills are very useful for manipulating, associating, elaborating, and recombining patterns in creative ways and will serve as the basis for many of the memory strategies we discuss later in this chapter.

  - Typically, children whose imagery skills are strong in a particular area will also have a large working memory span in that area.

These strong imagery and working memory abilities can be used to compensate for weaknesses in other areas of working memory. For example, some children have strong visual image-making abilities but weak auditory working memory. Often these children can better remember auditory-verbal inputs by quickly translating them into visual images, so they can be better held in working memory. (We'll discuss this in more detail later.)

• Particularly strong image makers can sometimes get distracted by their personal imagery ("daydreaming"). On occasion, younger children may even confuse imagined events with real ones (i.e., "false memories"). Strong image-driven thinkers sometimes get bogged down by the vividness of their images and may require extra time to formulate ideas and answer questions. They often do best in educational environments where they have plenty of time for personal experimentation and reflection.

Using the Best Form of Long-Term Memory

The third step in identifying a child's preferred learning style is to determine her best form of long-term memory—the one in which she most effectively files new memories and retrieves old ones. For example, some children are better able to learn new words than visual patterns and better able to retrieve those words later. Others are better at filing and recalling motor tasks. Often, but not always, a child's long-term memory preference will be similar to his working memory preference, because working memory plays such a large role in long-term memory effectiveness.

Two Important Caveats About Preferred Learning Styles

Now that we've discussed the three key elements of a child's preferred learning style, we want to add two important caveats:

• First, it's important to remember that a child's best input, working memory, and long-term memory functions may not always line up in the ways you'd expect. For example:

- We often see children who have poor auditory registration (or hearing) but who have excellent verbal working memories and prefer to think using words (i.e., auditory-verbal imagery). These children may have excellent long-term memories for verbal information that they've read but poor long-term memories for verbal information that they've heard. Melissa, whom we saw in our clinic, was a good example. Melissa was very bright but her grades began sliding from A's to D's when she moved from elementary to middle school. On testing, she showed an outstanding ability to take in information by reading but a substandard ability to take in information by listening. Melissa simply couldn't remember what came through her ears. When we arranged with her school to have her placed in classes taught by well-organized and sympathetic teachers who gave her handouts, teachers' notes, and stuck closely to their textbooks, Melissa did well. She also did fine on independent study with books or computer-based learning. However, in the few cases where her teachers refused to accommodate her needs in lecture-heavy courses, she continued to struggle.

- Similarly, we see many children who have difficulties with visual registration yet have strong visual-spatial working memories and prefer to think and reason using visual-spatial images. These children often do best taking in information through auditory-verbal routes, then translating it into visual-spatial images for reflection or long-term storage.

- Second, although we've recommended using a child's best input, best working memory, and best long-term memory routes in teaching and learning, you should remember that most children learn even better when they combine these "best" learning functions with additional forms of input, working memory, and long-term memory. Learning strategies that combine multiple routes of input and processing are often referred to as *multimodal* (or *multisensory*) *strategies*. Multimodal learning strategies can help every child learn better, but such strategies are especially important for children with specific memory problems.

- Combining verbal, visual, and motor/kinesthetic inputs with different forms of elaboration will embed knowledge much more firmly in an associational network, making it easier to understand and remember.
- Even within a particular sensory modality, children should be taught to employ different types of patterns. For example, when using visual strategies, children can use vivid colors and memorable graphic patterns as well as humorous, surprising, or interesting images.

Using Particular Strengths in Working and Long-Term Memory

In the rest of this chapter, let's look at ways to use focal areas of working and long-term memory strength to optimize a child's preferred learning style. (We'll discuss ways to optimize Information Input in Chapters 4 and 5.)

Building on a Child's Strong Personal Memory

Children with strong personal memories are especially good at remembering details of day-to-day events and sequences of personal experiences. These memories often associate information with specific places, events, and points in time.

- Because personal memory is located in a different part of the brain from memories for words, rules, or text, it can often compensate for blocks in verbal memory, rule-based memory, or text-based memory. Putting information into a form that children can experience rather than just hear about or read about can greatly increase their chances of remembering it.

- Teaching that builds on personal memory can emphasize personal experience through enactments, humor, surprise, and personal associations. For example, when we see children who have difficulty memorizing a list of unrelated words, we often find that they can memorize a similar list of words when they personally enact or weave the words into a silly or personally meaningful story. Once this information "touches them personally," it becomes part of their experience and then gets filed in (and is retrievable from) long-term personal memory.

- Interestingly, almost all memory experts and memory-contest winners ("mnemonists") use personal memory strategies to boost their memory skills. These strategies were first suggested over two thousand years ago by the Greek poet Simonides, and they've been in use ever since. These memory experts link (or associate) bits of new information (like lists of words, numbers, or other facts) with some sequence of objects with which they're already personally familiar. Often they'll use the sequence of features from a familiar walking route (like the houses or buildings on their block) or a familiar physical landscape (like the peaks in a mountain range or the objects in their bedroom) as "pegs" on which to "hang" new information. For example, a child who has trouble remembering the first five U.S. presidents could link their names to a sequence of familiar objects in her bedroom. Washington could be "linked" to her bed, Adams to her pillow, Jefferson to her stuffed dog, Madison to her nightstand, and Monroe to her dresser. Then, by mentally "traveling" around her room, she can use its familiar contents as prompts to help recall the linked presidents' names.

- Most commonly this "hanging" (or linking) is done using visual imagery, but it can also be done with auditory or even motor imagery (e.g., "hanging" memories on different fingers or different arm or hand movements). An individual child should use her best form of imagery and working memory, whatever it is. By linking new memories to previous personal experiences (visual or auditory), the new information is *"elaborated" to become part of personal memory*. In the sections that follow, we'll share additional examples of memory strategies that use similar "peg systems" to hang new information on previously stored patterns.

- *Narrative* or *story memory* is a related aspect of memory that can be extremely valuable as a teaching tool. Although stories don't deal with a child's personal experiences per se, they do deal with universal human experiences (such as facts embedded in specific times and places, emotions, and human relationships) that can evoke an empathetic response in the child. As a result, stories can form strongly contextual memories that are very similar to autobiographical memories.

- Stories can be made even more personal when children build their own fanciful stories around a group of facts. In our math chapter, we'll show you examples of story systems that have been created to help children who have difficulty learning their math facts simply by rote memory. Similar strategies can be used to remember any kind of information.
- Many children also find that physically acting out stories—both their own and others'—makes the stories even easier to remember, because they have a strong personal memory for physical movement.

Building on a Child's Strong Verbal (Word and Language) Memory

Strategies that help children build on strong memories for verbal patterns are useful either for children who are predominantly auditory-verbal learners (that is, those who learn best through auditory inputs) and those who learn best by reading.

- *One of the best strategies for strong auditory-verbal learners is verbal mediation, which, as we've mentioned, is the process of translating inputs or imagery (whether verbal, visual, or motor) into your own words.*

- Some strongly verbal learners seem to be talking all the time. We often find that many of the most talkative children have significant visual or motor memory problems and have learned through experience that they must engage in verbal mediation almost constantly if they are to remember things.

- When a child is using verbal mediation for deficits in visual memory, be sure to have him notice the spatial orientation of the material, if this is important. If not explicitly noted, it will be forgotten.

- *Peg systems* (like those described above) can also be an important mnemonic strategy for children with strong verbal memories. These systems are especially useful for memorizing lists of information, sequences of steps in procedures, or series of events in a story or a historical account. One good verbal peg system is the Number Rhyme System. In this system, each of the numbers one to ten (or more) is matched with a rhyming word to create a "peg pair" that the child memorizes: for example, "one: gun, two: shoe, three: tree, four: door, five: hive, six: chicks, seven: heaven, eight: gate, nine: mine (e.g., coal mine), ten: pen." These memorized rhymes can then be used to generate combined verbal images with a series of items that the child wants to memorize. Let's look again at our example of the first five presidents. A child with a strong verbal memory who wanted to remember this list could create little phrases with these peg pairs, like "Gun: General Washington carried a gun. Shoe: John Adams had very tight shoes. Tree: Thomas Jefferson liked to climb trees," et cetera. We'll see below how visual learners can use similar peg pairs to create visual associations.

- *Acronyms* are words formed from the first letter(s) of a string of words and can be useful memory devices for verbal learners. (For example, NATO is the North Atlantic Treaty Organization.) Acronyms can often be formed for lists of words or facts a child is trying to remember.

- *Initialization* is a similar strategy, but the initial letters are each pronounced separately and do not form a word. Examples include the NBA, FBI, CIA, and IRS. Initialization strategies are useful to help learn routine tasks—for example SLL for "stop, look, and listen" when approaching a street crossing, BJLH for "backpack, jacket, lunch, homework," to remember what to take to school.

- A related strategy is to use the *first letters* of a list of items you want to remember and create a short story or poem out of words with the same first letters. As medical students, we often used this trick to remember lists of anatomical names. One famous rhyme was designed for the thirteen "cranial nerves" that exit the skull. It begins, "**O**n **O**ld **O**lympus's **T**owering **T**op . . . ," with the first letter of each word standing for the first five cranial nerves: olfactory, optic, oculomotor, trochlear, and trigeminal. (You can ignore the other eight. We weren't so lucky!)

- Embedding facts in a rhyme scheme can also make them easier to remember. The previously quoted "*i* before *e* except after *c* . . ." is a good example of an academically useful rhyme. So is the common poem for recalling the number of days in the months, "Thirty days have September, April, June, and November. . . ." Verbally talented children should also be encouraged to make up their own rhymes for all sorts of uses.

Specific Tips for Strong Auditory-Verbal Learners

Children with strong auditory-verbal learning styles are nature's tape recorders. Often they can take in and repeat nearly verbatim all sorts of auditory information. These children are at a big advantage in the traditional learning environment, where listening and regurgitation are stressed. Because they have powerful word-based working memories, they can often hold and manipulate word-based patterns extremely well. As a result, they may become expert verbal reasoners, debaters, speakers, and actors.

- These children often prefer obtaining information through lectures or books on tape rather than reading. They may also find verbal dialogue (as with a tutor) a good way of learning.
- Auditory-verbal memory strengths can also be a useful source of compensations for children with spelling problems like those we'll describe in Chapter 10.
- Note: Not all children who can "repeat back like a tape recorder" are strong auditory-verbal learners. Some children with brain-based auditory processing disorders (see Chapter 5) may repeat back long passages of auditory information yet fail to comprehend it, or comprehend it only after a delay.

Building on a Child's Strong Visual-Spatial Memory

A strong memory for visual or visual-spatial patterns can also be a valuable learning tool. In this section, we'll describe a few of the ways that a strong visual or visual-spatial memory can support the development of learning and memory strategies. After discussing these strategies, we'll also discuss a few of the special challenges that children with strongly visual and visual-spatial learning styles can face in the standard educational environment.

- Children with strong visual-spatial imagery abilities often benefit from using visualization strategies. Visualization is the process of translating information (whether visual, verbal, auditory, tactile, or even abstract ideas) into "personalized" visual-spatial images that the child can more easily manipulate and file. These images don't have to be exact visual images of the things they represent, or even images of real things. They can be symbolic, schematic, dramatic, or even highly abstract representations that may have meaning for the child alone. The only important thing is that the child recognizes their association with the idea or set of ideas they are meant to represent.

- Different techniques can be used to make children better visualizers. One system we often recommend is *Visualizing and Verbalizing* by Lindamood-Bell. In this program, children are taught to convert information into visual imagery to aid with long-term storage. This information can be "replayed" like a "mental movie" for review.

- As we mentioned above, children with highly visual learning styles can also use visual peg systems to remember various kinds of information.

- For example, they could use the Number Rhyme System as described above to create visual rather than verbal images. To do this, they would create a visual image of George Washington holding his rifle, John Adams grimacing from his pinched shoes, Thomas Jefferson in the tree, et cetera.

- They could also use a strategy called the Number Shape System, where the "pegs" are created by visual images that physically resemble the numbers one to ten. For example, *1* could be a tall thin tree, *2* could be a swan with a curved neck, *3* could be a slithery snake that has shaped itself into a *3*, *4* could be the sail on a sailboat, *5* a seahorse, *6* a push-powered lawn mower, *7* a cliff, *8* a stylized bee with two body sections, *9* a balloon on a string, and *10* a thin woman standing before a large round mirror. Again, these pegs could be used to create striking and highly memorable visual associations with things the child needs to remember (for example, George Washington cutting down a tall *1*-shaped cherry tree, John Adams riding a swan, Thomas Jefferson holding the coils of the snake . . .). As with all memory strategies, bring personal memory into play by incorporating humor, surprise, absurdity, novelty, emotion, and important personal associations.

Special Challenges for Strongly Visual or Visual-Spatial Thinkers

Strongly visual or visual-spatial learners can be some of the most creative and talented learners of all. They can also be some of the most misunderstood, for several key reasons.

- Children with these predominantly nonverbal learning styles typically see information "all at once" (like a painting displayed on a canvas) rather than sequentially (like a story unfolding in a book). This tends to produce two problems:

  - First, they often perceive too much detail to process simultaneously. These details compete for attention and multiply relationships, which can be overwhelming.
  - Second, because these children see so much at once, they often find it hard to know where to begin and how to organize their thoughts when they want to express them. As a result, they may

speak or write in a rambling and nonsequential fashion, have trouble balancing fine details and larger themes, leave out important points or steps in a story, or suffer complete breakdown from a "mad rush of ideas" in which so many images compete for space in working memory that essentially nothing comes out.

- The output problems these children experience are often worsened by the fact that words are not their natural medium of thought. Verbal thinkers can directly express their thoughts in the form in which they think them. Nonverbal thinkers must first translate mental images into words before they can express them. This translation step can be slow, difficult, and a source of great frustration, yet it is essential for success in school and in life. Acquiring this skill requires lots of practice.

  - Have them describe visual scenes, either those encountered in real life or those displayed in photographs or other works of art. Have them practice identifying "big picture" themes, minor themes, and fine details, and help them learn to move easily between them. Having them create their own titles for pictures is also a useful form of practice.
  - Have them build sequential narrative skills. Practice recounting events of the day, stories that have been read or movies or videos seen, again trying to identify main themes, minor themes, and fine details. By practicing, they'll be building category and pattern recognition skills that will eventually make these steps automatic.

- While building verbal skills, children with nonverbal thinking styles may prefer organizing projects using pictures rather than words. Visual-presentation software like PowerPoint can be good for collecting and sorting ideas. Reports can also be written by collecting or drawing a series of pictures, then adding words later.
- If organization is a problem, use visual features and materials like color, visual symbols, or patterns to organize personal spaces, rather than alphabetical or verbal systems.

- Fortunately, as we have mentioned, there are also a great many positive aspects to this visual-spatial learning and processing style.

- Their strong attraction to visual images often makes these children strong incidental learners and highly visually observant. As a result, they will benefit from a learning environment that takes advantage of their particular learning style.
- Because these children see things in a different way than most children, they often make connections that others miss. As many observers have noticed (e.g., Thomas G. West, *In the Mind's Eye*), they often become quite good at seeing the big picture or imagining new possibilities. Although these children are naturally suited for work in highly visual fields, such as the visual and graphic arts, architecture, building and construction, engineering, radiology and surgery, history also shows that they also have great potential—perhaps surprisingly—as *writers*. While highly visual thinkers must learn to translate visual imagery into words, they are often extremely vivid verbal image makers once they do. Many of history's greatest writers and poets began life as tongue-tied visual thinkers and unsuccessful students before they learned to express their visions in words.
- Strongly visual learners may be especially well suited to learning through visually or graphically rich media. Computer-based programs or games, "distance" instruction over the Internet, videos or documentaries, graphs and tables, and hands-on or inductive learning strategies may all be useful.

Building on a Child's Strong Musical Memory

Music is a treasure trove of mnemonic potential. Every tune can become a peg system, full of useful hooks that students can hang information on.

- Musical memory is best known for preschool jingles like the "Alphabet Song" or "This is the way we brush our teeth . . .," but it can also be used for more advanced materials like multiplication tables (*Multiplication Rock/Schoolhouse Rock*), lists or sequences of information like history facts, state capitals, scientific classifications, and on and on.

- There are excellent online resources for musical memory, including www.audiomemory.com, www.musicalspanish.com, www.sing-smart .com, and www.lyricallearning.com.

- Most children are natural songwriters and should be encouraged to make up new songs about all sorts of information. One young child who constantly forgot his backpack both at home and at school fixed his problem by learning to sing on the way out both doors, "If I don't want to head back, I'd better take my pack."

- Songs can also help children who have difficulties with pacing, planning, organizing, or following procedures. Fun and bouncy songs can be used during cleanup or work time to keep kids on task (the theme from *Mission Impossible* is often a favorite). Specific instructions (like Barney's "cleanup" song) can also be set to music.

- Musical memory is particularly valuable for children who have primary language problems, because (as we have mentioned) music stores words at a different site in the brain than that normally used for language. Specially trained music therapists are available to help children with such problems.

Building on a Child's Strong Sensorimotor Memory

Children with strong sensorimotor (kinesthetic) memories often learn best by moving, touching, and interacting with objects or other people. It is no surprise that such children are likely to enjoy discovery-based learning and hands-on approaches. In addition, strengths in sensorimotor memory can also be used as an aide to information filing and retrieval.

- Children with strong sensorimotor memories can often improve their memory of objects or places by physically interacting with them (e.g., by moving in a three-dimensional space or feeling an object). This is especially true for children with visual weaknesses.

- Hands-on strategies are useful for both two- and three-dimensional materials. Tracing a finger or pencil over charts, graphs, geometrical figures, or other pictures (a procedure called *air-writing*)—can help children with strong motor-kinesthetic memories form better memory patterns. Air-writing the letters in words you're learning to spell is a useful mnemonic trick, especially for children with dyslexia (as we'll see in Chapter 10). For some children, large sweeps using the whole arm (i.e., movement at the elbow or shoulder) may be more effective than smaller motions with hands or fingers.

- Sensorimotor memory can help children with word retrieval problems as well. Recently researchers found that using body gestures when you speak can help you retrieve words more quickly and with less effort. This is true both in general and also for specific words and phrases.

  - Children with word retrieval difficulties can learn to associate specific gestures with certain words and phrases. Many of us already use such gestures for stock phrases like "I can't believe it" or "I'm cold!" or "I don't know" or "It doesn't matter to me." The possibilities for using such gestures are essentially unlimited.

  - Children with strong sensorimotor memories can also use motions (sometimes set to music) to represent the steps of a procedure or a sequence of facts. This is another type of motor-peg system.

Building on a Child's Strong Memory for Rules or Procedures

Children with strong rule-based or procedural memories can often use these strengths to learn to do things deliberately that they can't do automatically.

- Children who have difficulty mastering the phonetic rules that link sounds and letters can have difficulty learning to read and to spell. These children may benefit from intensive education in rule-based phonics.
- Children who meet criteria for autistic disorders are often better able to learn rules from others than to infer rules for themselves.

As such, they can be ideal candidates for rule-based instruction. This is especially true of the rules governing social interactions (see Chapter 8).

- In general, when a child is having difficulty mastering complex activities, those activities should be broken down to their most basic steps and taught to the child as rules or specific procedures.

A Final Key to Learning: Incremental Challenge

In addition to making use of a child's optimal learning style, parents and educators can maximize a child's learning potential by making sure that challenges are presented in a stepwise, incremental fashion. Research on motivation has demonstrated a critical relationship between success in learning and continued motivation: When children fail to achieve sufficient success or experience a sense of progress, their motivation plummets and they simply stop trying. Often children are diagnosed with attention and behavior problems when, after repeatedly facing challenges that demand unmakeable leaps rather than incremental steps in their exercise of skill, they simply lose heart and give up. But even thoroughly discouraged children can be reinvigorated by success. We often see children who have given up in school work hard on demanding remediative therapies once they've seen how small successes build in a stepwise fashion. Success *breeds* success by developing a taste for mastery. Research has shown that mental focus increases dramatically even in children who've been diagnosed with ADHD when they're given meetable challenges, and deteriorates both when challenges are unmeetable, or—crucially—*not challenging enough*. The desire to achieve mastery is natural; apathy is learned.

4

Overlooking the Obvious

Visual Problems in Children

All during my life I knew I had a problem; I just didn't
know what the problem was. At the age of twenty-
nine, I discovered it was connected with my eyes. . . .
How is it I never suspected, never complained, never
spoke of it before? The answer, I guess, is that we
tend to feel that all people see and feel things the
way we do. At least, having nothing to compare it
with, I assumed my vision was normal.

—JESS OPPENHEIMER, TV WRITER AND PRODUCER,
CREATOR OF *I LOVE LUCY*

Micah was six years old when his parents brought him to see us.
They were concerned about his worsening self-esteem, school
phobia, and behavioral problems. They had always thought he
was bright, and their observations seemed confirmed by tests during kindergarten that ranked his oral language skills at the ninety-ninth percentile.

That's why they were so concerned when he neared the end of first grade and was still having trouble learning to read, write, and do math.

As Micah fell further behind, his parents and teacher noticed that he was becoming more anxious, aggressive, and even hyperactive when expected to do work. When they asked him why he seemed unhappy, Micah said, "I'm dumb" or "I'm stupid." Soon it was a struggle just to get him to the bus in the morning.

When we first met Micah, it was clear that his prior testing was right on the mark: He was obviously very bright. He was also polite and well behaved. In many respects, we found it hard to imagine him as the aggressive, hyperactive, and withdrawn child we had read about in the school reports—at least until we began to test his visual and handwriting skills. As our demands increased, Micah's problems became apparent. He had difficulty reading even the simplest three-letter words, and when given two minutes to copy a printed sentence, he completed only three words, as shown in Figure 7.

As you can see from Figure 7, Micah had trouble keeping his letters between the lines, wrote repeatedly over letters he'd already written, and showed little regularity in his letter size or spacing. Yet he'd worked extremely hard to produce this meager output. After watching him struggle, we could easily understand why he was beginning to resist writing at all.

Writing wasn't the only thing Micah struggled with on our testing. On his tests of vision, he had difficulty telling the difference between similar letters. Figure 8 shows what happened when we asked him to circle the letters *dund*. To Micah, almost all these options looked the same—only when the tails of the two end letters pointed in opposite directions could he tell the difference. Yet despite his many wrong guesses, Micah was far from impulsive. He labored long and hard on this task and tried to check his work.

Micah also had difficulty copying a geometric figure, as shown in Figure 9.

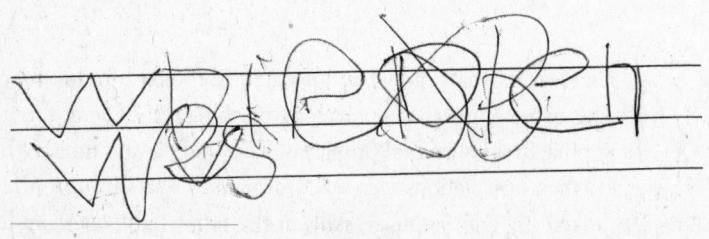

FIGURE 7

FIGURE 8

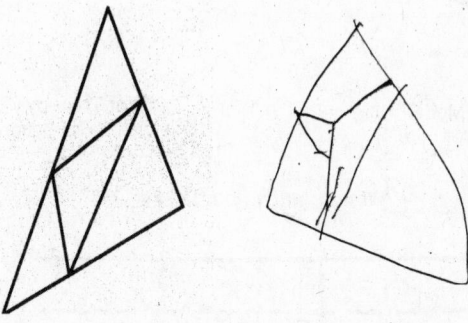

FIGURE 9

By the end of our testing, it was obvious where Micah's problems lay. Micah had severe visual difficulties. Fortunately, his story ended happily: With a combination of visual exercises and reading glasses, his visual function improved remarkably. So did his reading, writing, and copying. As his work improved, so did his attitude about school and his ability to pay attention in class. Figure 10 shows his excellent progress on word and figure copy after therapy.

Many children, like Micah, have unsuspected visual problems that stand in the way of their academic success. In this chapter, we'll discuss the most important visual problems affecting school-age children, the signs and symptoms they produce, and the best ways to help children who suffer from them.

BEHAVIORS ASSOCIATED WITH VISUAL PROBLEMS IN CHILDREN

Visual problems are often very hard to diagnose in children. One reason is that children with visual problems seldom complain of—or even recognize—their

Model   After Therapy
                              and Vision Correction

What will hatch from the eggs?

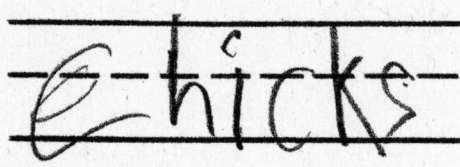

After Therapy and Vision Correction

FIGURE 10

difficulties. That's because (as Jess Oppenheimer described at the start of the chapter) *they don't know what it's like to see any other way.* Often the children we see recognize their problem only *after* it's been corrected. One young patient with a frequent squint protested all the way to the optometrist's office, "There's nothing wrong with my eyes!" Nothing, it turned out, but 20/50 farsightedness in one eye, 20/200 nearsightedness in the other, and an inability to coordinate eye movements. After glasses and visual therapy, this same child said, "Wow, I can't believe how sharp things look!"

The signs that a child has visual problems are frequently subtle and not clearly visually related. In addition, many common visual problems can't be detected on a routine eye chart exam. In this section, we'll list some of the most common signs and symptoms of visual problems in children, according to the settings in which they most commonly present.

Behaviors with Reading

Visual impairments are often suggested by difficulties while reading:

- Shows delayed mastery of reading skills.
- Moves head back and forth while reading instead of just the eyes.
- Frequently loses place while reading.
- Frequently skips lines or words.
- Uses finger to mark place while reading.
- Holds book unusually close to or far from eyes.
- Tends to tip books or papers sideways while reading, so lines are vertical rather than horizontal.
- Assumes "unnatural" or unusual body posture when reading or writing.
- Frequently misreads words or numbers or shows an excessive tendency to guess.
- Complains of blurred, doubled, moving, or wobbly letters or numbers, especially near the middle parts of words.
- Has unusual difficulty with letter confusions and rotations, (e.g., substituting not just b for d or p for q but b for q, p for d, m for w, or n for v or u).
- Problems worsen as text size shrinks and worksheets grow more crowded.

Behaviors with Writing

Visual impairments may also be suggested by the following types of difficulties while writing:

- Has trouble with consistent spacing between letters or words.
- Has trouble staying on lines or leaving margins at the edges of the page.
- Creates irregularly or inconsistently formed letters.
- Has a tendency to spell words in ways that "sound" right but are incorrect.

- Writes with head close to page.
- Has difficulty copying from the board.
- Has difficulty with tasks that require switching vision between near and far.
- Tends to "crowd" writing or drawing into specific areas or quadrants of the paper while leaving other parts blank.

Behaviors with Various Forms of Near Work

Difficulties with other forms of near work may also suggest visual impairments:

- Has difficulty staying within lines when coloring or scissoring along a line.
- Frequently rubs or pushes eyes.
- Closes or covers one eye.
- Turns or tilts head to use one eye.
- Squints or engages in unusual blinking.
- Complains of tired, burning, or itchy eyes.
- Complains of headaches, especially in the forehead or temple.
- Experiences recurrent unexplained nausea.
- Has an eye that turns in or out, wobbles, or wanders.
- Has an unusual tendency to look *away* from rather than at his hands when doing fine work.
- Has difficulty recognizing visual shapes or objects or copying shapes when drawing.
- Has difficulty identifying the big picture in visual images, while focusing instead on isolated parts or details.
- Has difficulty learning to tell time from a standard clock face.
- Has difficulty picking out visual objects from a cluttered background.

Behavioral Signs of Visual Problems While Moving or Playing

Problems engaging in gross motor skills may also suggest visual impairments:

- Has difficulty with coordination and balance.
- Frequently trips and stumbles.
- Has poor hand-eye coordination.
- Is awkward or clumsy with complex motor movements such as climbing, throwing, tying knots, riding a bike, et cetera.
- Has difficulty following rapidly moving balls in tennis, soccer, baseball, hockey, et cetera.
- Feels anxiety during rapidly moving games.
- Has difficulty following movements specifically on one side.
- Has difficulty performing integrated movements involving both hands or both feet.
- Has difficulty finding her way around or recognizing places where she's been before.
- Has a tendency to get lost.
- Has difficulty learning which desk in school is his or remembering where her classroom is located.

Behaviors That Mimic Attention Problems

Visual impairments can often produce behaviors that suggest difficulties with attention:

- Experiences visual distractibility—that is, the feeling that the eyes are drawn irresistibly toward moving, visually busy, or especially colorful objects.
- Makes careless errors (especially on visually challenging material like math problems, which worsen with crowded worksheets).
- Misses visual details.

- Has a tendency for work to take longer than expected or to remain incomplete.
- Complains of boredom.
- Has a tendency to tire quickly while reading or writing.
- Shows diminished written output.
- Copies inaccurately.
- Has a tendency to avoid tasks with heavy visual demands.

Behaviors During Social Interactions

Visual impairments may also present as difficulties with social interactions:

- Shows poor interpersonal skills.
- Has a tendency to miss social cues or subtle facial expressions (e.g., interest or disinterest, approval or disapproval, irony, etc.).
- Has difficulty following the flow of conversation.
- Tends to interrupt or fails to wait for others who wish to speak.
- Is drawn away from conversations by visual distractions.
- Has difficulty recognizing faces, even of close friends or family members.
- Makes poor eye contact. (Note: Poor eye contact is often an important cause of social challenges in children with visual problems. Eye contact is a fundamental sign of interest and engagement, and even well-meaning people can have difficulty "connecting" with children who don't look them in the eye. Too often poor eye contact is assumed to reflect a lack of feeling or empathy, when visual problems are commonly to blame.)

THE CAUSES OF VISUAL PROBLEMS IN CHILDREN

Most visual problems in children are caused by impairments in Information Input, Pattern Processing, or Output for Action. We'll consider each in turn.

Problems with Visual Information Input

Problems with visual Information Input usually fall into three main groups: acuity problems, eye-movement control problems, and visual-field deficits.

Problems with Information Input:
Impaired Visual Acuity

Impaired visual acuity is the basic "can't see the eye chart" problem most of us know from experience. Acuity problems usually result from difficulty focusing light on the retina at the back of the eye. Because the light image striking the retina (i.e., visual input) is out of focus, the brain can construct only a blurry or unclear image of the world. Light-focusing difficulties are usually caused by problems with the eye's internal lens, which produce near- or farsightedness, or by shape irregularities in the eye's visual surface (i.e., cornea), which cause astigmatism. Another focusing disorder, called *accommodative insufficiency,* is caused by a problem with the eye's lens that makes it hard to focus on objects close to the face—like words on a page—and is an important source of reading difficulties in children.

Acuity problems can show up at any age and in either eye or both. If the acuity difference between eyes is extreme, the brain may begin to ignore the weak eye. In severe cases, the child may actually lose sight in the weak eye. More commonly, the child will lack depth perception.

Problems with Information Input: Impaired Eye
Movement (Oculomotor) Control

Each eye has six tiny *ocular muscles* attached to its outside surface. These muscles help us look toward any angle, fix our eyes in one place, follow a moving object, scan across a line of text, or adjust our aim and focus from near to far away. There's even evidence that these muscles have special movement sensors that contribute to our perceptions of depth, distance, and motion.

Sometimes problems with these ocular muscles make it hard for the eyes to point in the same direction together (or work as a team), no matter where the child is looking. This condition is known as *strabismus*. Because children with strabismus are unable to look at the same spot with both eyes at the same time, they are said to lack efficient *eye teaming*. Strabismus may be present at birth, though it may also develop in infancy. Mild strabismus can often be treated with exercises or patching, though severe imbalances may require surgery.

More commonly, eye-muscle dysfunction will cause problems only during certain kinds of eye movements. One of the most important types of dysfunction for school-age children is *convergence insufficiency*, or difficulty coordinating eye movements when looking at near objects, as when reading. (Note: This is different from accommodative insufficiency, which is a problem of the lens.) Children with convergence insufficiency often experience visual doubling, difficulty viewing fine detail, and the feeling that objects they are looking at close up are wobbling or oscillating. Children with problems coordinating eye movements in general can have difficulty with the following functions:

- Focusing the eyes together when looking from place to place.
- Visually tracking a moving object.
- Systematically scanning a fixed object.
- Alternating focus between near and far (e.g., between the front of a room and the paper on the desk).
- Performing tasks requiring depth perception.
- Reading.

Children with eye-movement problems often have difficulty accurately registering (or "taking in") visual information. Because their visual Information Input systems fail to provide their brains with accurate and consistent information about their environment, their visual Pattern Processing systems will have difficulty working accurately as well. That's why children with eye-movement problems (like Micah, whom we described at the start of this chapter) often also have difficulties with "downstream" Pattern Processing functions like visual memory, visual-motor coordination, visual-spatial perception, and visual attention. As we mentioned in Chapter 3, it's the old problem of garbage in, garbage out. In our Helping section, we'll discuss ways to help these children improve their visual input.

Problems with Information Input:
Visual Field Cuts / "Blind Spots"

Visual field cuts are places in the normal field of vision where vision is absent. That's why they're often called blind spots. Field cuts may go undiscovered for years, because children who have them are usually unaware of them. In fact, the brain of a child with a field cut *actively tries to conceal it* from the child.

Field cuts may cause a child to look clumsy or anxious, to avoid physical play or large groups, or to have difficulty with social interactions. One kind of field cut, which is especially common in children born prematurely or with significant pregnancy or birth injury, blocks vision in the lower part of the visual field and makes it hard for children to see the ground in front of their feet. As a result, they may have trouble walking on uneven ground, stepping on or off curbs, or they may even accidentally walk off ledges. They are frequently terrified of escalators and small animals.

Fortunately, the visual fields from both eyes largely overlap, so each eye sends the brain similar information. As a result, to experience a field cut a child must lose the ability to process information about a particular area *from both eyes*. Defects that block the information coming in from only one eye usually don't cause problems at all. That's fortunate, because every eye has a naturally occurring blind spot, where the nerves pass through the retina to head to the brain. (We'll show you how to find yours in a moment.) These naturally occurring blind spots don't affect your vision when you look at something with both eyes, because they're "unmatched"—that is, they affect different areas of each eye's visual field, so the other eye compensates for them. Problems that affect only one eye rarely produce significant field cuts. That's why most visually significant field cuts are caused by problems in the brain itself—where vision is processed—because that's the only place in the visual system where the signals from both eyes are processed together.

Now let's "see" what it's like to have a field cut. Just to prepare you: It's different from what you probably expect. You won't see a dark spot in your vision. It's more like a trapdoor where things just vanish. To find your own blind spots, go to Figure 11.

Welcome back. Did you notice that when you'd found your blind spot, there was no hole or black space after the smiley vanished nor a gap in the lines of text immediately beneath it? That's because your brain filled in the

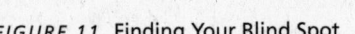

FIGURE 11. Finding Your Blind Spot

Close your right eye, then hold the book about eighteen inches from your face with the dot directly in front of your left eye. Now, keeping your eye focused on the dot, slowly move the book toward your face. Between six and twelve inches from your face, the smiley will "magically" vanish; however, if you move the book away again, the smiley will "magically" reappear. Congratulations. You've found your blind spot.

missing portions of the visual field using surrounding patterns to imagine what the missing part would look like. In the case of the smiley, that was blank page; for the lines of text, it was more text.

That's just what field cuts are like for the children who have them. It's a kind of trapdoor in their visual world where things just pop in or out as if by magic. Imagine how difficult this can be when the things that pop in and out aren't merely printed smileys but other children, flying baseballs, or moving cars! It's not just that they have a spot in their visual field where they can't see but that *there's actually an area of their visual field about which their brain is actively trying to mislead them.* Little wonder that field cuts can prove disorienting and even debilitating—especially when they involve crucial central visual regions.

Problems with Visual Pattern Processing

Like problems with visual Information Input, problems with visual Pattern Processing are an important and surprisingly common cause of visual challenges in school-age children. In fact, one study from Scandinavia showed that nearly half of all children referred to vision specialists for possible vision problems had central or brain-based visual impairments. Unfortunately, most children with brain-based visual impairments remain undiagnosed and untreated for far too long. Their problems are usually too subtle to show up on a routine eye exam and require detection by a specialist in visual processing, an expert in central visual impairments, or a neurologist. As a result, these children are often mislabeled as having attention deficits, autism, or other disorders.

In the sections that follow, we'll discuss the challenges children most often experience with visual Pattern Processing. While reading this section, it's important for you to remember what we've said above: that the Information Input functions lie "upstream" from Pattern Processing, so primary problems with Information Input can produce secondary problems with Pattern Processing. That's why it's crucial to make certain that a child who has problems with visual Pattern Processing doesn't also have an input problem with visual acuity, eye movement, or field cuts.

Problems with Pattern Processing: Impaired Visual-Spatial Perception

Probably the most common challenge school-age children face with visual Pattern Processing is difficulty perceiving the three-dimensional shapes of objects and/or their positions in space. Children who struggle in this area are said to have impaired visual-spatial perception, and they may show many problems, including:

- Difficulty learning to read, write, and do math.
- Difficulty processing the spaces between words (or "b et we e nw or ds") or math symbols (e.g., $14 + 12 = 38 - 12$ versus $14 + 1\ 2 = 3\ 8 - 12$).
- Difficulty distinguishing objects with similar visual features, which vary primarily in spatial dimensions (like pots versus pans, chairs versus benches, toothbrushes versus hairbrushes).
- Difficulty learning from graphs or charts that depend on the perception of proportions or size.
- Difficulty organizing three-dimensional spaces, backpacks, desks, closets, binders, or rooms.
- Difficulty remembering where objects and possessions are.
- Difficulty forming an accurate map of their own bodies, including (when younger) difficulty pointing to their various body parts, and (when older, and even as adults) telling right from left.
- Difficulty judging the positions of surrounding objects.
- Difficulty using visual information to plan motor movements.
- Difficulty with spatial directions, like mastering new routes or layouts.

Children with spatial impairments may have especial difficulty master-ing the "directional" nature of letters, numbers, and other printed symbols, including the distinctions between symbol pairs like *b/d, p/q, b/p, b/q, u/v, m/w, 6/9, 5/2, 5/3, </>,* or *+/x.* They may write these symbols in reverse, up-side down, or in a twisted form. Although some reversals are normal up to age seven, children with spatial-recognition problems are in an entirely dif-ferent league (see Figure 12).

Many children show some difficulties with letter and symbol reversals be-fore the age of eight or nine. As we'll describe in Chapter 10, some children with dyslexia may show difficulties with letter and symbol reversals beyond this age. However, dyslexic children do not usually show general deficits in spatial processing. In fact, dyslexic children may actually show heightened spatial abilities in certain contexts. One study by von Karolyi and colleagues found that dyslexic individuals were significantly better than nondyslexics at differentiating two-dimensional drawings that represented objects that could actually exist from drawings that represented "impossible figures." A number of writers, most notably Thomas G. West, have also written extensively about the special spatial-reasoning abilities found in many dyslexics.

Children with spatial challenges may also have problems with personal organization. They often appear messy and unsystematic in their behaviors, and, while very bad at finding things, they are very good at losing them. Spatial problems can be frustrating, for both the children who have them and the adults who care for them. That's why it's crucial to remember that these children are not disorganized because they lack character or will: They are *space-blind,* just as children who can't recognize colors are color-blind. They can't form a spatial memory that shows them where they've laid down their pencil or their backpack or their shoes, so these things may just

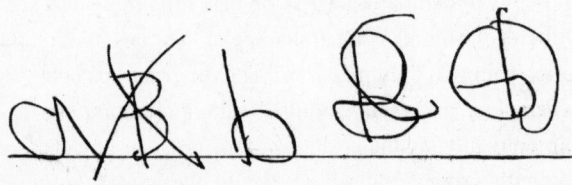

FIGURE 12. Spatial Impairments

seem to vanish into thin air. To improve their organization and make up for their flawed or missing visual-spatial maps, these children must be taught specific strategies that rely on other strengths, as discussed in Helping.

Problems with Pattern Processing: Trouble Recognizing Visual Objects

A second challenge with visual Pattern Processing that is much more common than most people realize is difficulty visually recognizing objects. Children with such problems are frequently mislabeled with a wide variety of other diagnoses, especially "nonverbal learning disorder," because their verbal skills are unaffected. Their difficulties with object recognition usually spring from impairments in one of three visual Pattern Processing functions: visual closure, visual figure-ground discrimination, and visual gestalt.

Visual closure is the ability to recognize a whole object (or symbol) when only part of it is visible. Children with visual closure problems typically have a hard time finding things that are only partly visible, like a milk carton in a refrigerator that's partially hidden by another object or a book partially covered by a piece of paper. They simply can't recognize the whole pattern based on the limited part that they see. Children with visual closure problems frequently have difficulty detecting errors in visual objects and performing complex visual planning, like that needed to draw a picture.

Figure-ground discrimination is the ability to recognize objects in the middle of a busy or crowded background. Children with impaired figure-ground discrimination often have difficulty finding objects in crowded backgrounds—even when those objects are "in plain sight." For example, they may have difficulty finding a pencil on a crowded desktop or a particular shirt in a dresser drawer, even if these objects are entirely exposed. Problems with figure-ground discrimination can be caused by problems with object recognition per se or by visual distractibility (see the section on visual attention below).

Visual gestalt perception is the ability to see relationships between the parts and wholes of objects. Children with impaired visual gestalt typically have difficulties with visual and spatial reasoning, like realizing how simple patterns can be combined to make complex ones, understanding how the parts of an object fit together, and perceiving how similar but different objects are related. They usually have a hard time guessing what an object does by its appearance and may show severe difficulties trying to assemble even simple multipieced objects. Children with poor visual gestalt perception also have difficulty using space in an organized fashion, like appropriately positioning a drawing on a page. These children often are skilled at noticing visual details but have trouble identifying the "big picture" that's formed by all the parts. Frequently parents of these children tell us, "We always thought he had such great vision because he notices things the rest of us miss." Figure 13 shows how an eight-year-old child with impaired visual gestalt perception interpreted a complex figure. Notice how he saw the small triangles as discrete figures (that is, he "missed" the larger shape) and had difficulty identifying even the triangular shapes of the smaller pieces.

Children with these types of object-recognition problems often have difficulty locating objects in visually crowded areas like their desks, bedrooms, or backpacks and are slow to complete visual tasks. They often "overlook the obvious" even when it's "right in front of their noses" and make "careless mistakes." They may also find it hard to distinguish similar objects and may get in trouble for confusing their own possessions with those of their classmates. Often their inability to see what everyone else finds obvious is interpreted as laziness, carelessness, or an attention problem, and

FIGURE 13

they may be criticized for shortcomings they cannot control or even understand.

Problems with Pattern Processing: Face-Blindness or Prosopagnosia

A third often overlooked challenge affecting visual Pattern Processing is difficulty recognizing a particular kind of object: human faces—a condition known as *face-blindness* or *prosopagnosia* (pro-soap-ag-NOSE-ee-ah). In some children, this condition is so severe that it prevents them from recognizing not only complete faces but even isolated facial features like mouths, eyes, or noses. More commonly, though, children with prosopagnosia have milder impairments that let them see faces "in parts," one feature at a time, but not as a single unified whole. Such children have difficulty discriminating between faces with similar features and may have difficulty reading facial expressions.

Children with face-blindness may struggle with social and emotional functioning. They usually show poor eye contact and are often diagnosed as autistic—in many cases inappropriately. They often have difficulty recognizing those around them, which may lead them to be suspected of rudeness, insensitivity, lack of warmth, or poor empathy. They may also behave awkwardly in social settings, because of problems picking up on facial expressions and other social cues.

Problems with Pattern Processing: Impaired Visual Attention

Many children have poor attention for visual tasks. Poor visual attention is often indiscriminately attributed to attention deficit/hyperactivity disorder (ADHD). Yet problems with visual attention are frequently caused by problems in the visual system itself, rather than primary impairments in attention. This is especially true when children have good sustained attention for less visually demanding tasks.

Most children whose attention problems occur primarily during visual tasks fall into one of two groups. First are the children who show difficulty with *visual task persistence*. These children have a hard time sticking with visual tasks, either because they experience unpleasant physical symptoms (like eyestrain or headaches) or simply because they find visual tasks too difficult and frustrating. Most often, their symptoms are caused by impaired visual Information Input, like uncorrected acuity or eye-movement disorders. Improving visual input usually improves visual persistence.

Second are the children who suffer from *visual distractibility*, or the feeling that their eyes are constantly being pulled away by irrelevant or competing stimuli. Visual distractibility usually results from problems processing patterns at an *automatic, preconscious level*. Take, for example, the way you're reading this page. Because your reading has become automatic, you don't need to "sound out" each letter, then "add them up" to make words; you recognize the entire word by sight, as a single unit. As a result, you're probably not even aware of the individual letters in these words.

This same kind of automatic processing allows you to dispense with other extraneous visual (and other sensory) data that are being sent to your brain, so you can focus on the text. The following exercise should show you how much visual information you process automatically, before it enters your conscious mind. In a moment, we'll ask you to focus your eyes on a single word, then allow your "visual attention" to drift. Without letting your eyes move, you'll let your attention wander first toward the objects on your right, then left, then up, then down. Go beyond the edge of the book to your hands, the table or your lap, the walls, the windows, or other objects. Ready? Begin when you reach the word . . .

NOW.

Okay, welcome back. Did you notice that when you focused your thoughts on objects beside the word NOW they "stole" your attention, even though your eyes continued to look at the word? If not, try it again. Although you'd previously ignored these objects, they became distractions when your attention began to wander.

Children who can't automatically dispense with distractions like these can face serious challenges in school. Sometimes these problems can be due to difficulties with the brain's *selective attention* mechanism, which decides what to focus on and what to ignore. (Impairments in selective attention are not visually specific, and we'll discuss them more in Chapter 7.) Problems with visual distractibility can also be caused by many primary visual and neurological difficulties. We'll discuss the best ways of improving visual attention in our Helping section.

Problems with Visual Output for Action

Children with impaired visual Output for Action have difficulty using visual information to guide their motor actions. Several types of visual disorders can result in such problems, including impaired visual-spatial processing (which we've discussed above), and poor hand-eye or visual-motor integration.

Problems with Output for Action: Impaired Visual-Motor Integration and Hand-Eye Coordination

Physical awkwardness (or motor clumsiness) is often a sign of visual problems. Studies have shown that well over half of all children with significant motor clumsiness have underlying visual impairments. When children have difficulty using visual information to coordinate their motor (muscle) actions, they are said to have *impaired visual-motor integration*. Problems affecting the visual-motor integration of fine hand movements are called *impaired hand-eye coordination*.

When a child wants to plan a movement, she must rely on her "mental map" of the environment to tell her where she is in relation to the things around her and how she should move to accomplish her goal. Although her eyes may be the "windows of her soul," her brain can't just look out those windows to see the environment. Instead her brain must use information from her input systems—primarily visual, but also balance and movement—to build an integrated three-dimensional map of the environment. If this map is wrong, any actions that she bases upon it will probably be poorly planned and uncoordinated.

Visual problems can prevent a child from forming an accurate 3-D map of the environment and can cause impaired visual-motor integration. The most common causes are problems with visual Information Input (like impaired visual acuity, depth perception, or eye-movement control) that cause secondary problems with visual-spatial perception. Children with impaired visual-motor integration often have difficulty with many fine-motor or hand tasks like drawing, cutting with scissors, tying shoelaces, and throwing or catching a ball. Children with impaired visual-motor integration also frequently have severe difficulties with handwriting, which we'll discuss in Chapter 11.

EVALUATING CHILDREN
FOR VISUAL IMPAIRMENTS

Accurately identifying a child's visual impairments is extremely important, because accurate diagnosis is the first step toward appropriate therapy. A thorough history is crucial. Begin by asking specific questions about the visual symptoms in our Behaviors section, and about the following factors, which greatly increase the risk of visual problems:

- Prematurity or low birth weight.
- Complicated pregnancy or delivery.
- Serious childhood illnesses.
- Head injury.
- Family history of eye problems.

Children with visual problems are often difficult to evaluate—especially when the underlying problems are complex. School-based screening tests miss many visual deficits, and so do visits to a licensed optometrist or ophthalmologist. If a child *acts* as though he might have a visual problem, he probably does. Finding the right specialist is the key to receiving the appropriate diagnosis and therapy. The right person may vary according to the child's age and type of problem. Acuity problems can be handled by most eye specialists. Children suspected of visual perceptual problems typically require evaluation by a vision specialist, neurologist, or neuropsychologist with expertise in visual perception. Specialized testing for eye movement, visual-motor, and some perceptual problems are best performed by a developmental optometrist, who should be a Fellow in the College of Optometrists in Vision Development (www.covd/fellow.html).

HELPING CHILDREN WITH VISUAL IMPAIRMENTS

In the following sections, we'll describe remediations, compensations, and accommodations that are useful for particular visual problems. First, though, let's look at some compensations that will be helpful for nearly all children with visual problems.

Steps That Help Most Children with Visual Impairments

Most children with visual problems will learn better when visual information is supplemented by other forms of input. As we mentioned in Chapter 3, this multiple-input strategy is often called *multisensory learning* and should be used with nearly all children with visual problems.

- *Auditory-verbal inputs* are especially valuable for supplementing visual inputs. Language is richly descriptive, and children with visual problems are often (though far from always) preferentially auditory learners who learn better by listening than by visual demonstrations or reading. Children with impaired visual memories can benefit greatly from storing information about visual images in the form of words through the process of *verbal mediation*.

- Parents and teachers should help children with visual problems learn verbal mediation skills by first describing all sorts of visual objects for them, then having the children provide descriptions of their own. Children should be asked to describe as many different features of objects as possible and to think about which features distinguish those objects from others.
- In addition to improving visual memory, verbal mediation can also improve visual reasoning and problem solving.

- *Tactile* (touch) cues can also be used to supplement visual information. Feeling an object can provide information about its spatial and physical characteristics. Adding tactile to visual inputs not only helps children learn about particular objects but helps to build their spatial skills as well.

- When a child studies pictures of objects, have her trace over these objects with her fingers or a pencil.
- Also, supplement her two-dimensional exploration with a three-dimensional model she can touch, like figurines or wood-block maps.

- *Kinesthetic* (or "body-position sense") cues can also be used to supplement visual input. Children can use physical enactment or role-play strategies to learn spatial orientations and relationships. Children who have difficulty remembering letter orientations or shapes (e.g., discriminating *b*, *d*, *p*, or *q* or remembering whether an *n* has one hump or two) can "enact" the appearance of the letter, as in the "Y.M.C.A." song. Additional kinesthetic (also called *proprioceptive*) strategies are detailed in Chapters 10 and 11 on dyslexia and dysgraphia.

Helping Children with Impaired Visual Information Input

Information Input: Help for Impaired Visual Acuity

Children with impaired visual acuity usually need corrective lenses like glasses or contacts. In addition to improving acuity, corrective lenses can improve the functional balance between eyes and help them work more smoothly together. Reading glasses may also reduce eyestrain.

Children with corrective lenses require regular checkups throughout childhood, since prescriptions often change during development. Any child whose vision does not fully correct with corrective lenses requires evaluation by a vision specialist.

Information Input: Help for Poor Eye-Movement Control

Eye-movement control problems can often be treated with special exercises, which are sometimes called *visual therapy*. Visual therapy works best when exercises are matched with particular problems. The best therapist to guide visual therapy will usually be an optometrist with special expertise in children's eye-movement issues (i.e., a Fellow of the College of Optometrists in Vision Development [FCOVD]), though for children with fine and gross motor coordination problems, occupational therapists who are members of the Neuro-Optometric Rehabilitation Association may also be helpful.

In addition to clinic-based therapies, there are also simple but effective home-based activities children can use to improve eye-movement control. At least thirty minutes a day of these activities is appropriate. Here is a list of activities, arranged roughly in order of increasing difficulty:

- Begin with scanning and tracking activities that involve slower eye movements; large, easier-to-follow targets; and a fixed position for the child.

  - Flashlight tag: Dim the room lights and have the child follow the path of a flashlight beam moving across the walls. Begin using large, slow movements. Advance difficulty as tolerated for a more challenging workout.
  - Visually follow the lines in shapes like those in Figure 14 to practice horizontal and vertical eye movements. Curves are more difficult than straight edges.
  - Practice pencil tasks like unidirectional tracing or simple maze exercises.
  - Play catch with a beanbag or a large, soft ball (like a Koosh), beginning with slow, easy tosses.
  - Reading is itself a helpful scanning exercise, but children with severe eye-control problems may need to build up skills beginning at very basic levels. Practice reading simple words in a large font while sweeping letter by letter under the words using a finger or other marker. Practice twice daily for at least fifteen minutes.

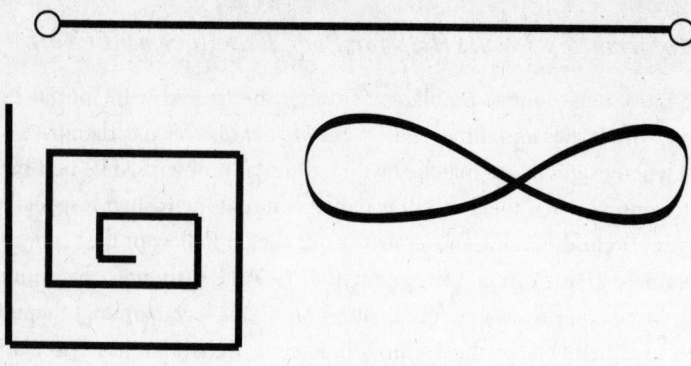

FIGURE 14

- After progress is initially made, add rhythmic or predictable movements onto eye-tracking practice. For example, have the child sit on a swing or rock on a balance board while fixing his eyes on a target.
- Play computer games with lots of horizontal movement. Some of the better such games are the older arcade sort like Pac-Man, Donkey Kong, and Pong. (Note: Sound cues can sometimes reduce the visual benefits from these games, so better results may be obtained with the sound off.)

- Advanced scanning and tracking exercises encourage complex and rapid eye movements by adding extra challenges such as time pressure, targets with less predictable movements, and activities where both the child and the visual target move.

- Practice following visual targets in three-dimensional space, like a swinging ball hung from the ceiling. To improve hand-eye coordination, have the child try to follow the swinging ball with a flashlight.
- Try to interact physically with a moving target, like touching or hitting a swinging ball with a tennis racket, bat, or broom handle.

- Practice speed-reading techniques that improve tracking speed and letter or word span (the number of letters or words that can be attended to at one time).
- Play games with faster and more complex two-dimensional movements, like air hockey.
- Try sports involving three-dimensional movement, such as handball, dodgeball, tennis, Ping-Pong, or air hockey.

- Children with convergence insufficiency benefit from *convergence exercises*, like "pencil push-ups." Have the child focus on the tip of a pencil, held initially at arm's length. Have him continue focusing on the tip as he brings the pencil slowly closer to his nose, until the image doubles or splits, then slowly go back to arm's length. With practice, a child should be able to get the pencil tip very close to his nose before losing focus. Pencil push-ups should be practiced fifteen to twenty times, two or three times per day. More severe convergence difficulties may require office-based optometric vision therapy.
- Other helpful visual therapy activities can be found in the book *Developing Your Child for Success* by developmental optometrist Dr. Kenneth Lane. In pursuing these exercises, frequency and consistency are even more important than duration. Practice sessions as short as five to ten minutes a day, if performed diligently, can reap huge benefits.

Information Input: Help for Visual Field Cuts (Blind Spots)

Helping children with visual field cuts is a complex process, and requires the help of skilled professionals. There are often two main components to therapy:

1. Visual therapy to help the child compensate better for her visual field deficit.
2. Prism glasses to "shift" a child's visual field so she can see parts of her environment that would otherwise lie hidden in her blind spot. (Prism glasses move incoming light waves away from the blind spot

onto parts of the retina that can better process them—the way car mirrors bounce light waves from the driver's "blind spot" to her field of vision.)

This combination of therapies can yield dramatic results. One of our young patients spent weeks giving her mother nonstop updates on her growing visual world. "Mama! The floor doesn't disappear when I look down anymore! . . . Mama, I can see the left side of the TV now!" and so on. She showed dramatic improvements socially and academically as well.

Children with field defects should also receive accommodations in school. These children should not be presented with papers or assignments where important information lies outside of their field of vision (i.e., in the area affected by the blind spot), nor should they be graded down for leaving blank portions of the paper that lie within their blind spots, as was one of our young patients with a left-sided field defect because he always began his writing in the middle of the page (Figure 15).

Care must also be taken in the classroom to seat children with field cuts where they can see everything they need to. For safety on the playground and in gym class, classmates should be given enough information about the child's difficulty seeing so they can avoid collisions or other problems. Special physical hazards for children with blind spots, like central doorjambs in the middle of double doors or low-hanging shelves or cabinets, should also be pointed out in advance. Often verbal or printed reminders (signs, colored dots at the beginning of the line) can be used to increase the frequency with which a child uses functional visual areas to look into the area affected by the blind spot.

Helping Children with Impaired Visual Pattern Processing

Pattern Processing: Help for Impaired Visual-Spatial Perception

Children with *impaired visual-spatial perception* typically have difficulty remembering where or how things are oriented in space, so they must learn

Left-Sided Neglect

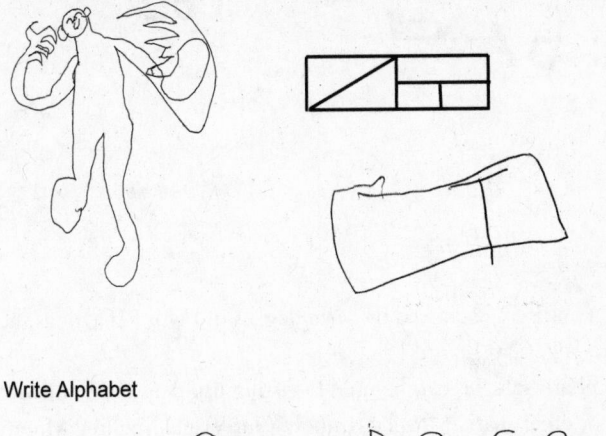

Write Alphabet

FIGURE 15. **Work from a Child with Left-Sided Field Neglect**

Notice on the drawing at upper left how the figure is shifted toward the right side of the page and that the figure gets progressively larger to the right. Notice on the figure copy at upper right that the entire left half of the figure has been omitted and the bottom-right portion constitutes essentially the entire figure. And notice on the written alphabet how the work begins more than a third of the way into the line.

to use other forms of memory to help fill in for "missing" visual-spatial information. Mnemonic strategies using personal or story memory, verbal descriptions or rules, kinesthetic memory, or memory for other visual features like colors can all be helpful.

Strategies to Help with Symbol Orientation

- Children who have difficulty remembering the spatial orientation of letters, numbers, and symbols often find it helpful to use visual or story mnemonics that provide memorable explanations for the three-dimensional orientation of symbols. For example, a child who has trouble remembering the shapes of *b* and *d* can imagine these letters

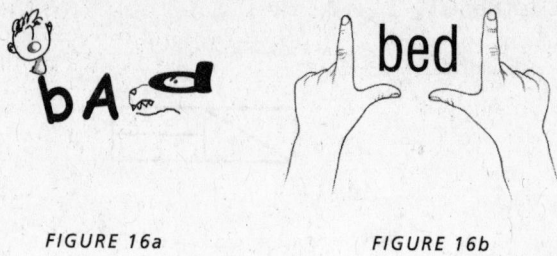

as a *b*oy being attacked by a *bad d*og, as in Figure 16a, or as the posts of a *bed*, as in Figure 16b.

- Similar strategies can be used to distinguish *p* and *q*, 6 and 9, < and >, or other spatially tricky symbols. Our Visual Spelling Mnemonics (as shown in Chapter 10, Figure 33) demonstrate how color memory, story memory, memory for rhyme, and other aspects of memory can be used to remember the letters in words. Similar strategies can be used to create pictures and stories to help children with spatial problems remember letter orientations.

- The company HTS (www.visiontherapysolutions.net) also makes a commercially available computer program to help children with rapid letter recognition and visual search.

- The kinesthetic strategy of tracing a finger over letters, numbers, or other symbols that a child is trying to copy or read can also help the brain form a proper spatial image of that symbol. Some children find that molding letters out of clay (or handling wooden or plastic ones) helps them better remember letter shapes, though it's important to distinguish clearly the orientation of the symbols in 3-D space.

- Verbal mediation can also be employed to create descriptions or lists that the child can use to verbally "walk through" predictable or repetitive spatial procedures, such as writing letters (see Chapter 11) or doing long division or geometry.

- Additional helpful suggestions can be found in the book *Unicorns Are Real* (see Resources, Chapter 3).

Strategies to Help with Personal Organization

- Verbal mediation can also be used to develop rule-based organizational systems. Developing verbal rules, descriptions, procedures, or lists can help children with spatial challenges become better at organizing, searching, and performing other spatially related functions. Using checklists of these rules and procedures can also help. Depending on the nature of a child's visual problems, auditory organizers like Dictaphones or MP3 players may be preferred to visual charts or graphics.

- Establish regular procedures for storage and organization and encourage the child to develop a special mnemonic system (like a peg system; see Chapter 3) to remember where she's put important things when these regular procedures can't be followed.

- Many children with visual-spatial difficulties have normal memory for color, so color coding may help them organize their things. Using color codes to organize binders, folders, cubbies, school schedules, dresser drawers, and cabinet space can provide these children with another way to conceptualize locations.

- For children who like animals, sports, or other subjects, stickers depicting animals, athletes, teams, and the like can also be used.

Strategies to Help Navigate Three-Dimensional Space

- Parents should help these children develop nonspatial strategies for "personal navigation." When going out, have your child help plan your route, whether it's cross-country or to the store. Emphasize the big picture first, then fine details. Practice reading maps. Have him trace the route with a finger or highlight it with a pen. Get him to think about landmarks or signs that can be used to guide him. When you're on your trip, encourage him to help you navigate (e.g., decide where to turn). Zooming in and out on the maps and satellite photos at www.earth.google.com can also be useful.

- Colored dots or lines on the floor can help the child who frequently gets lost. Routes to the library, bathroom, and other important destinations can be marked. One of our young patients showed how useful these markers can be. At the start of the school year, she surprised her teacher by asking to go to the bathroom every fifteen minutes. A bladder infection was suspected but ruled out. On careful questioning, she admitted that she thought she ought to "go" so often because she couldn't remember where the bathroom was, and she was afraid that if she waited until she really needed it, she might not find it in time. Colored floor markers remarkably tripled her "bladder capacity" overnight!

- At the start of a new school year, provide walk-throughs of rooms, buildings, and bathrooms and written descriptions of landmarks and routes. Verbal descriptions of landmarks will probably be more helpful than visual maps.

- When students need to walk between classes, pair the challenged student with a guide who is going to the same place.

Pattern Processing: Help for Impaired Object Recognition

Children with impaired visual object recognition usually require professional help for their difficulties. Still, there are lots of things parents can do at home to help a child with such problems improve his visual abilities.

- Because children with impaired visual closure have difficulty identifying objects of which they can see only part, they need to learn special strategies to help them identify objects. Most effective strategies involve verbal mediation.

- When children are looking for particular objects, they should look for distinctive features of those objects (like colors, printing or markings, or distinctive shape features such as height, width, curves, diagonals, long straight edges, etc.), rather than for the objects as a whole. Children should describe these features to themselves in words. For complex objects, they should make a checklist or voice recording of the features. Let's look at the example of the chocolate milk carton in Figure 17a. Because it's largely hidden behind other objects, the child with impaired visual closure will have difficulty finding it without special search strategies. Looking for the carton's combination of colors would be one strategy. Looking for the characteristic edge shape at the top of the carton would be another (Figure 17b) and can be combined with the kinesthetic and verbal strategies of tracing the edge of visual objects with a finger and describing their shapes in words.

- Strategies should also help narrow the area of the search. Teach children to start searching where the object is most likely to be, then divide the area into smaller regions to make the search more manageable. For example, the tall milk carton could fit only on the door or the top shelf.
- For children whose language deficits make verbal closure strategies difficult, tactile characteristics of objects (like texture, shape, size, etc.) can also aid in identification.
- Children with both visual closure and visual figure-ground problems can benefit from practice searching for partially concealed items and those in visually crowded fields. Simple *I Spy* or *Where's Waldo?*–type books or computer programs can be very helpful, as can real-world scavenger hunts in visually busy places, like grocery stores, shopping malls, or even in cluttered areas around the house. Sometimes it's helpful to build up to real-world environments by using a video recorder or digital camera to take pictures of visually

FIGURE 17a   FIGURE 17b

busy places like the school, church, or library, then identifying items in the pictures before visiting the real places.

- Because children with closure and figure-ground problems really do improve with practice, it's important not to help them too much when they have difficulty finding objects. Provide them enough hints and reminders so they don't become frustrated, but don't let them become "visually dependent" on others.

- Organizational strategies (like the color strategies described above for children with spatial difficulties) can decrease functional challenges by limiting misplaced items.

- Children with impaired visual gestalt can benefit from strategies that help them understand and remember the relationships between parts of objects and their wholes. These strategies fall into three main categories: visual, verbal, and kinesthetic.

  - Visual strategies create visual memories that clearly portray the relationship between parts and wholes. Color-coded models can be viewed assembled, then disassembled into parts, then reassembled to clarify relationships. LEGOs, Duplos, or model kits are ideal for this kind of practice. Be sure to start with sufficiently simple plans. Children can also create branching diagrams or visual flow charts to represent how parts go together to form wholes.

  - Verbal strategies use verbal mediation to describe whole-part relationships. Figure 18 shows the drawing of a nine-year-old boy with visual gestalt problems who was told to draw a floor plan for a pizza parlor that would have a kitchen, dining area, manager's office, storage area, entrance, and emergency and handicapped exits. While he carefully included all these details, he was confused over how the individual rooms should be combined to make a whole.

    When this same child was subsequently told that restaurants usually have square or rectangular floor plans (i.e., that he should start with a square "whole" rather than start with the individual parts), he was able to allocate space more effectively, as shown in Figure 19.

FIGURE 18

Getting children to talk themselves through whole-part relationships like this can make them much more proficient at understanding how parts and wholes fit together.

- Kinesthetic or hands-on strategies can help children feel the relationship between wholes and parts. To practice these strategies, the kinds of models, puzzles, and building kits we describe in our section on hand-eye coordination can all be useful. Give a child a few disassembled pieces and ask her to visualize a "whole" figure that could be made from them, and then have her build it. Or give her a constructed figure and ask her to draw or describe two or three pieces she could pull apart from it. You can also have her plan and build larger projects, like the pizza parlor shown in Figures 18 and 19. The next step would be to have the child actually lay out the "foundation" using LEGOs or some other building material. This sort of practice helps children with gestalt difficulties develop a better sense of space and spatial orientation.

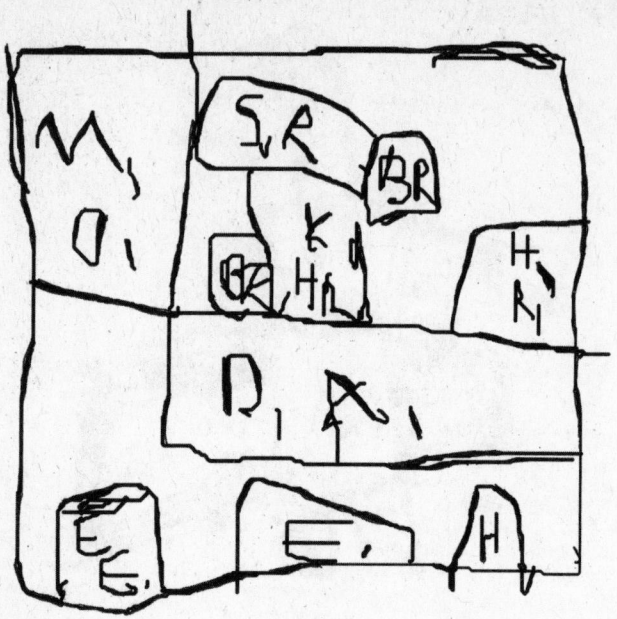

FIGURE 19

Pattern Processing: Help for Impaired Face Recognition
(Prosopagnosia or Face-Blindness)

Children who have difficulty recognizing faces or facial expressions can benefit from the following activities:

- For children who are not completely face-blind, practice can greatly improve their ability to read facial expressions. Some children prefer to begin practicing with simplified drawings of faces (like Figure 20a), then progressing to still photographs or paintings (as in 20b). When they are ready to advance to moving pictures, the exaggerated expressions seen in silent movies, professional wrestling programs, or soap operas are good places to start.
- Recently software programs have become available to help children practice recognizing faces and facial expressions (e.g., Mind Reading, www.jkp.com).

FIGURE 20a

FIGURE 20b

- Teaching children with face-blindness to anticipate whom they might see in various settings—such as the classroom, the playground, or the school office—can help them recognize people more quickly.
- Children who can recognize isolated facial features should also be taught strategies for identifying frequently seen individuals by going through a mental checklist of their most characteristic features (e.g., "Pug nose plus small ears plus blue eyes is Tanya").
- Children with prosopagnosia should also be given special assistance by their teachers, classmates, and parents, such as the following:

  - Clear voice cues, hand gestures, and animated "body language" should always be used when teaching or speaking with a child who has face-blindness.
  - Speech should be straightforward and without irony, satire, or sarcasm, unless accompanied by very clear voice cues.
  - Always introduce yourself by name when beginning to speak (e.g., "Hi, it's Coryn"), as this will greatly reduce confusion.
  - At the start of the year especially, classmates should wear name tags, and the student should be provided with a seating chart of classmates.

- Peers, teachers, and other adults must learn not to be offended by social slights or miscues that result from purely visual problems. A child with prosopagnosia may have difficulty recognizing even close friends in busy situations, so she may not always say "hi," seek them out, or return their smiles. Others should be taught to recognize and appreciate the special ways she shows her friendship.

Pattern Recognition and Recall:
Help for Impaired Visual Attention

When visual attention problems are caused by visual distractibility, a three-pronged approach is needed: (1) reduce environmental distractions, (2) improve resistance to visual distractions, and (3) improve visual search and error detection skills. Let's consider each separately.

Reducing Environmental Distractions

- Seat the child where visual distractions from windows, aisles, colorful or crowded wall displays, or other students are minimized. A study carrel, a desk against the wall, or a seat in the library may be ideal for quiet work or tests.
- Certain types of lights (especially fluorescent) may distract by flickering. Affected children will usually tell you if you ask. Indirect lighting, "pink" bulbs, or full-spectrum lighting from a specialty supplier like Verilux can markedly reduce distraction.
- Use large fonts. Limit printing on reading materials and worksheets and provide plenty of spaces at the margins or between lines. Sometimes these steps will be enough to eliminate a child's functional deficit.
- To make reader-friendly materials, scan printed documents into Word or another word-processing program (or download them from the Internet), then enlarge fonts, narrow margins, and increase spaces between lines.
- When pages are crowded, children should be taught to cover parts they don't currently need to see in order to reduce distractions.

- Some children may benefit from colored visual filters when reading (see Chapter 10 on dyslexia).
- Anti-glare filters can improve visibility of computer monitors, as can adjusting controls for color, contrast, and brightness.
- More information on viewing preferences (e.g., background color, font color, special fonts) can be found at *dyslexia.com* or at *schwablearning.com* under the topic of "Universal Design for Learning."

Improving Resistance to Visual Distractions

- Visual training can increase resistance to visual distraction. Recent studies have suggested that visual distractibility can be improved using computer programs that train children to ignore potentially distracting stimuli. To our knowledge, there are at present no commercially available programs that have been shown in large-scale studies to reduce visual distractibility, but it is likely such programs will become available in the near future. In the meantime, certain types of generally available computer or video games can be used to encourage similar skills.

- Useful games promote visual fixation and resistance to side distractions. In games of this sort, the central figure should remain the primary focus of vision. All the important action should take place near the primary figure or in the direction this figure is heading, rather than coming in constantly from all sides.
- One example of such a game would be Disney's Tarzan, which is available for use in many game systems. In this game, the character swings on vines and slides down branches but always remains the focus of action. Successfully getting Tarzan through the jungle requires persistent focus and careful resistance to visual distracters.
- Other useful games include race formats, where the important action takes place ahead of the car but not to the sides.
- It's important to realize that not all video games help reduce visual distractibility. In fact, many video games may significantly *worsen*

distractibility. In many attack, fight, or race-type programs, success depends on enhancing vigilance at the edge of vision. *This is precisely the kind of hypersensitivity that can worsen distractibility.* While such hypersensitivity is useful if you're a combat soldier or a race-car driver, it's considerably less useful when you're in the second grade. These programs may not be bad for all kids, but they should definitely be avoided in children who struggle with visual distractibility.

- Biofeedback training may also increase resistance to visual distractions. Studies evaluating clinically based biofeedback programs have shown that thirty- to sixty-minute sessions daily for about forty days can produce lasting gains in focused attention (see also Chapter 7). In practice, formal biofeedback training is expensive and time-consuming, and only those prepared to make substantial commitments in time and money are likely to benefit. However, several home-based computer programs are also available, and we have seen some children do well with these. The program Journey to the Wild Divine (www.wilddivine.com) is especially reasonably priced and provides several useful exercises that teach children to control their mental focus. Potential buyers should note that it does have strong New Age elements, though after an initial run-through these elements can mostly be avoided by focusing on specific practice exercises. Be aware that home biofeedback programs require a huge amount of computer memory, so make sure your system is adequate.

Improving Visual Search and Error-Detection Skills

- Teaching children cognitive strategies for monitoring their visual attention and engaging in systematic searching and error detection can help them avoid "careless mistakes," like overlooking problems on worksheets and tests, misreading symbols or words, or failing to discover errors of omission or commission in writing. Search strategies that involve highlighting key words or mathematical symbols, circling or checking completed problems, and simply

learning to systematically double-check work can all be very helpful.
See Chapter 7 for more information.
- Children can also improve their visual search and vigilance skills
  through practice with visually challenging materials. Books or
  computer games that contain hidden pictures, word searches, and
  "what's wrong with this picture?" type puzzles can all improve visual
  search and focus. Computer-based games like I Spy or Collapse
  (www.lovefreegames.com) can also improve visual search and
  scanning.

Helping Children with Visual Impairments in Output for Action

Output for Action: Help for Impaired Visual-Motor Integration

Children with impaired visual-motor integration usually need to improve
both their underlying visual system deficits and the integration of their
visual-spatial and motor systems. We've discussed the former above. To improve visual-motor integration, start with simple two-dimensional activities,
then advance to more demanding three-dimensional ones. The following
activities are presented in order of increasing difficulty:

- Hand-eye coordination can be built using many pencil tasks, like
  tracing figures, completing mazes, or connecting dots.
- Finger strength, dexterity, and coordination can also be built
  through many arts-and-crafts projects like drawing, painting with
  brush or finger (or using paint-by-numbers kits), making tissue or
  construction-paper mosaics (which require the excellent hand-
  strengthening activity of tearing paper by hand), stringing beads,
  making rubber-band patterns on a Geoboard, doing needlepoint, or
  using scissors to cut out increasingly complex patterns.
- Origami is also an excellent activity: The folding is useful for
  strengthening, and as a bonus it also helps foster visual-spatial
  reasoning.

- Hands-on building projects using LEGOs, K'nex, Quercetti Marble Runs, gear sets, or other model kits develop visual-motor integration and visual-spatial reasoning.
- Video-game play can strengthen impaired hand-eye coordination, though it is far from a complete treatment. Most video games don't involve all fingers, proximal hand and arm muscles, or near visual work, so other hand activities should be pursued as well. Fewer cautions are needed than for children with distractibility problems.
- Juggling and catching tasks encourage hand-eye and gross-motor coordination and provide practice in depth perception. The simplest tasks can involve Beanie Babies or Gertie or Koosh balls in a simple overhead midline toss.
- At the next level of difficulty, items can be tossed from hand to hand or back and forth with a partner.
- Difficulty can be increased by having the child and/or the partner move when tossing or by standing on a balance or tilt board.
- At the highest level of difficulty, sports can be fun and helpful ways of improving hand-eye coordination. Throwing or hitting a ball at a stationary target, hitting a ball on a string, hitting or catching a ball bouncing off a rebound net, or playing more challenging forms of catch or racket sports with a partner can all be helpful.

It's important to consider the role of physical education for all children with visual difficulties. Children with visual-motor coordination—or severe motor-coordination problems of any cause—need to be treated respectfully and thoughtfully when the class is engaged in complex coordinated motor activities that exceed their capacities. For some children, this can include activities as simple as running or performing tasks that require the coordinated use of both sides of the body. For many children with visual-motor impairments, it will involve care when playing ball sports. It's unreasonable and even dangerous to force a child who can't follow the trajectory of a moving ball or protect herself from it to play dodgeball, soccer, kickball, softball, basketball, or any other fast-moving ball sport. However, there's no reason at all why children who are excused from such activities need to remain idle. Fitness and strengthening activities are great alternatives for these children, as are safe ball activities using large, soft balls like the

Gertie balls sold by therapy-supply stores. Such activities are in fact therapeutic. Children with visual-motor impairments should be pushed to develop their physical skills just like any other child, only not in a manner that exposes them to significant risk of physical harm or the unnecessary ridicule of their peers.

Finally, as we have mentioned, children with impaired hand-eye coordination often have difficulties with handwriting. Interventions for these children will be discussed in Chapter 11 on dysgraphia.

5

What? Huh? Auditory Problems in Children

After the second or third grade at school, I started to get into trouble and seemed to spend a lot of time in detention or out in the hall. I was disruptive (because I did not hear what I was disrupting), and noisy (because I could not monitor the loudness of my voice). My behavior in some cases was inappropriate (because I could not pick up subtle conversational cues or follow fast-paced conversations). . . . Academically I was doing poorly. Socially, I was doing even worse.

—BEVERLY BIDERMAN, *WIRED FOR SOUND*

Kelly was a sweet and shy eight-year-old when her parents first brought her to our clinic. They were concerned about her hearing and attention. She was an only child from a quiet home where the TV and stereo were rarely on. She learned to speak on time and with good pronunciation and was reading independently at age four. Like her quiet, bookish parents, she could entertain herself for hours with her books, computer programs, or dolls. She had one close friend in the neighborhood with whom she played, spoke, and giggled normally.

Shortly after Kelly started kindergarten, her teacher surprised her parents by asking if Kelly was partially deaf. Kelly constantly responded to her teacher by asking "What?" and quickly lost interest when the teacher began to talk or read aloud.

Kelly was given a routine hearing tone test (audiogram), but it was normal. Her parents took her to their pediatrician for a follow-up, and he diagnosed attention deficit disorder, inattentive subtype. Kelly's parents questioned the accuracy of this diagnosis. They'd never seen signs of inattention in their daughter. When the doctor suggested Ritalin, they decided to hold off.

Over the next two years, Kelly continued to show the same problems at school. However, when we saw her in our clinic, she showed no signs of inattention. On our examination, she showed excellent higher-order language functions, though she occasionally "misheard" our instructions, thinking she'd heard one word instead of another. When we asked about school, Kelly told us she had a hard time paying attention when her teacher gave "talky" lessons, during circle or story time, or whenever the classroom got especially noisy. We also learned that she attended an aging school with bare tile floors and brick walls and sat near a heating vent that made constant knocking sounds.

Despite her normal audiograms, Kelly's history and exam suggested she was having difficulty hearing in certain circumstances, rather than with attention per se. We referred Kelly for specialized testing to check her central, or brain-based, auditory processing. Kelly's tests showed severe deficits in processing sound in the presence of background noise. At our suggestion, Kelly was given a desktop speaker, moved closer to her teacher, and separated from the noisy heater. Her "inattentiveness" improved dramatically.

AUDITORY IMPAIRMENTS: THEY'RE COMMON . . . AND DEVASTATING

Most of us drastically underestimate the importance of the auditory system in learning. Almost every school activity—from listening to teachers to interacting with classmates to singing along in music class to following instructions during gym—depends upon the ability to process sound.

Unfortunately, *auditory processing* (i.e., hearing) *problems* are surprisingly common among schoolchildren. In America, nearly one in five schoolchildren has a measurable problem with hearing, and studies have shown that 37 percent of children with mild to moderate hearing loss fail at least one grade. In this chapter, we'll discuss common auditory processing deficits, their effects on the children who have them, and the best ways to help.

BEHAVIORS ASSOCIATED WITH AUDITORY PROBLEMS IN CHILDREN

Auditory processing deficits can present with many different symptoms and behaviors. Often these behaviors resemble those seen with other learning challenges, like language difficulties, attention problems, or even autism, and mislabeling is common.

Most children with auditory impairments show only a few of the following behaviors. No child will show all. However, any child who displays several of these symptoms should be carefully evaluated for auditory difficulties.

Behaviors Suggesting Decreased Hearing

Behaviors that suggest a child is having difficulty hearing are the most easily recognized signs of an auditory processing disorder:

- Diminished response to voices or loud noises.
- Difficulty hearing in the presence of background noise.
- Worse hearing indoors than out, especially in echo-prone rooms with bare walls and floors.
- Difficulty understanding what's said.
- A tendency to ask for restatement or clarification, or repeatedly saying "What?" or "Huh?"
- Marked difficulty understanding speakers with particularly high- or low-pitched voices or with prominent accents.

- Significant day-to-day or situational variability in hearing, which may lead parents or teachers to suspect volitional or attention-related problems.

Behaviors That Suggest Unusually Sensitive Hearing

Surprisingly, behaviors suggesting unusually sensitive or acute hearing can also be signs of an auditory processing disorder:

- Sensitivity to sounds that don't bother others.
- Preference for quiet and solitary activities over group situations like birthday parties; preschool, school, or religious instruction classes; indoor malls; or swimming pools.
- A tendency in noisy environments to become withdrawn or anxious, to cover ears, to appear highly distractible, or to become "explosive."

Behaviors That Suggest Speech and Language Difficulties

Certain difficulties with language intake or output may be signs of auditory processing disorders:

- Delayed speech onset.
- Persistent articulation errors.
- Abnormally soft, loud, flat, formal, or "pedantic" speaking voice.
- Difficulty conducting casual conversations.
- Trouble reading or spelling due to difficulty discriminating word sounds.
- Difficulty following oral directions.
- Difficulty organizing behaviors.
- A tendency to appear quiet, distracted, or off topic during group discussions or to interrupt or blurt out answers.
- Long delays before responding to questions or instructions.

- Preferences for nonverbal tasks or a markedly higher performance IQ than verbal IQ.
- Difficulty taking notes.
- Worsening performance (or diminished attention) in higher grades as oral instruction load and receptive language demands increase.
- Difficulties with inference, abstraction, and figurative language that are greater with "listened" than "read" material.

Behaviors That Suggest Impaired Attention or "Low Intelligence"

Some behaviors suggesting poor attention or low cognitive potential may be signs of an auditory processing disorder:

- Difficulties paying attention, especially with auditory-intensive materials.
- Unusual difficulty following directions.
- Avoids talking to others.
- Does not enjoy being read to.
- May appear slow or spacey.
- Becomes confused or frustrated when spoken to.
- Seems to exist largely in a self-contained world.
- Tunes out or daydreams a lot.

THE CAUSES OF AUDITORY PROBLEMS IN CHILDREN

Hearing isn't simply a matter of detecting the presence or absence of sound. After sound waves strike your eardrums, they're converted in your middle and inner ears into nerve impulses. These impulses then travel to your brain along the auditory nerves. In your brain, these impulses are analyzed for patterns that tell it where the sound originated, what kind of sound it is, whether it carries linguistic information, whether it's worth paying attention to, and what meaning is contained in any parts that have become garbled in transmission. Your brain's ability to perform all these tasks requires the interaction of both your *auditory Information Input* and *auditory Pattern Processing* systems. In this section, we'll describe these two systems and how they work together to perform the complete range of auditory processing functions.

Problems with Auditory Information Input: Peripheral Auditory Processing Deficits

The structures of the auditory information Input system are most often collectively referred to as the *peripheral auditory system*. The structures of this system are shown in Figure 21.

Nearly one in six school-age children has a peripheral auditory problem severe enough to produce learning challenges. Some of these children have congenital or familial impairments. However, by far the most common cause of peripheral hearing impairments is collections of fluid, or *effusions*, in the middle ears (i.e., behind the eardrums).

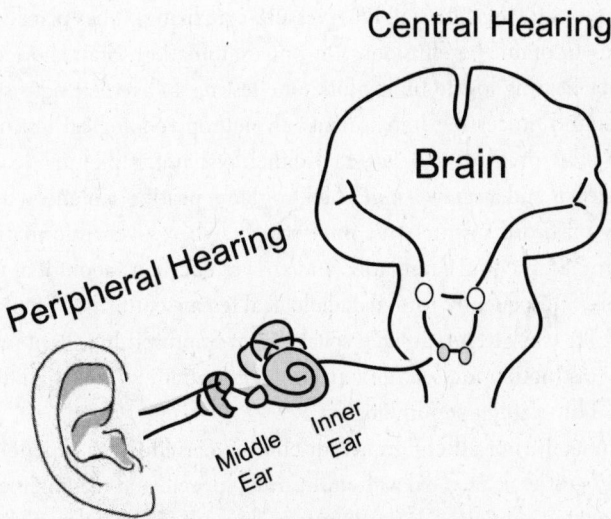

FIGURE 21. The Auditory Processing System

Middle ear effusions have three primary causes: infections, allergies, or blockages in the eustachian tubes that drain the middle ear, often due to enlarged tonsils or adenoids. These effusions dampen sound transmission through the middle ear, causing an average hearing loss of 25 decibels. This can have enormous implications for learning, because *at this level of hearing loss a child can miss 30 to 50 percent of what a teacher is saying.*

Many middle ear effusions are caused by viral upper respiratory infections (URIs). The average child in day care, preschool, or early elementary school contracts a URI seven times per year, and while most infections will not form significant effusions, some children seem especially prone. Once formed, an effusion takes (on average) forty days to drain, so an effusion-prone child can have fluid in her ears almost constantly. Academic impairment from an ear effusion can last weeks to months. Small wonder many children with learning challenges (some studies suggest as many as one-third) have a history of chronic ear infections.

One of our patients, Stan, had many of the problems we commonly see in children with chronic middle ear effusions. Stan's parents brought him to us when he was seven because he was distractible, had a tendency to daydream, and was having difficulty learning to read. Stan had a history of chronic ear infections, for which he'd recently had his tonsils and adenoids removed. He'd also had PE (pressure-equalizing) tubes placed in his eardrums to drain the effusions. On our examination, Stan showed low-frequency hearing loss to tuning-fork tone testing and several signs suggestive of sound processing impairments on neuropsychological testing. He thought *moss* rhymed with *hot*, had difficulty naming pictures (called a ruler a *stencil* and a screw a *nail*), had trouble repeating sentences, and repeatedly misheard instructions. Interestingly, when given information in story form, Stan could summarize and answer questions about it at above-age levels. Subsequently, formal audiological testing confirmed Stan's hearing loss. He was given a desktop speaker that improved his attention, and phonics instruction and computerized auditory training that significantly improved his reading performance.

Fortunately, not all children with chronic ear effusions experience as many difficulties as Stan did with mishearing, speech, and reading. Because the brain plays a crucial role in interpreting sounds (as we'll discuss below), children with strong brain-based processing may suffer fewer effects from effusions. Chronic effusions seem to magnify brain-based processing difficulties in children who are at risk but who would experience fewer problems if their peripheral hearing were intact. Since it's impossible to tell beforehand which children will experience serious problems as a result of chronic effusions, it's a good idea to treat children with effusions carefully, as we'll describe below.

Other causes of peripheral hearing impairments, such as head or surgical trauma, neonatal meningitis, and inborn or inherited defects of the auditory structures, are significantly less common but are often more severe. Table 2 shows a list of conditions that put children at risk for auditory processing impairments.

One increasingly important source of auditory impairments in school-age children is peripheral hearing damage due to environmental noise, from sources like loud concerts, stereos, and TVs, and portable electronic devices like MP3 players. In one recent study, 12.5 percent of children aged 6 to 19 years were found to have evidence of noise-induced hearing loss. Avoiding prolonged exposure to loud noises is essential to preventing unnecessary hearing loss.

TABLE 2 *Risk Factors for Impaired Auditory Processing*

- Neonatal ICU stay of greater than forty-eight hours.
- Problems serious enough to require mechanical ventilation.
- Family history of hearing loss.
- In utero infection with herpes, cytomegalovirus (CMV), rubella, syphilis, toxoplasmosis.
- Abnormal ear or head shape or other congenital malformations.
- Bacterial meningitis or other severe infections.
- Hyperbilirubinemia.
- Head trauma.
- Recurrent or persistent middle ear infections or effusions for at least three months.

Peripheral hearing problems are relatively easy to diagnose—if you remember to look for them. If you think your child has an ear effusion (or a simple canal obstruction caused by wax buildup), have her evaluated. *Tympanograms* can be performed in most doctors' offices and can quickly detect the pressure imbalances across the eardrums that result from effusions and eustachian tube blockages. If you think your child has hearing loss, an *audiogram* (tone-detection test—see Evaluating) is necessary and should be done by an audiologist. Any child with significant hearing loss—or an effusion or pressure imbalance that fails to clear within ninety days—should also be seen by an ear, nose, and throat specialist (ENT).

Problems with Auditory Pattern Processing: Central Auditory Processing Deficits

The other part of the auditory system consists of the nervous system structures that perform the brain's auditory Pattern Processing functions. These structures are collectively referred to as the *central auditory processing (CAP) system*. This CAP system is responsible for extracting useful information from the nerve impulses sent in from the peripheral auditory system.

Unlike peripheral hearing impairments, *central auditory processing deficits* (CAPDs) cannot be detected by routine audiometry. In fact, most children with CAPDs have entirely normal audiograms, and in many situations their hearing may seem completely normal or even hypersensitive. Yet these children show problems processing sound in certain situations— problems that clearly correlate with sophisticated tests of central auditory functions.

Unfortunately, most children with CAPDs go undiagnosed and untreated. Many doctors, teachers, and therapists have never even heard of CAPDs, and many who have heard have only a vague knowledge of this rapidly evolving and often confusing field.

Although there are various ways of categorizing CAPDs, in this chapter we'll group them according to the functional problems they cause. These problems include:

- Impaired hearing in the presence of background noise.
- Impaired sound discrimination and mishearing.

- Impaired hearing of the music or "prosody" of speech.
- Impaired sound localization.
- Delayed sound processing.
- Impaired auditory memory.
- Auditory hypersensitivity (hyperacusis).

We'll discuss each separately.

Pattern Processing: Impaired Hearing in the Presence of Background Noise

Many children with CAPDs have difficulty hearing in the presence of background noise. Although they often hear well enough at home or in quiet environments, they may appear hard of hearing or even functionally deaf in noisy environments—like school. Frequently they're suspected of attention problems, because they have difficulty attending to speakers or taking in information when there's background noise. Kelly, whom we described at the beginning of this chapter, was a typical example of a child with this problem.

One reason these children are frequently misunderstood and mislabeled is that their functional hearing impairment depends as much on their listening environment as it does on their underlying brain wiring. The greater the level of background noise and the more surrounding surfaces create echoes, the greater their hearing problem will be. That's why modifying the environment plays a huge role in their treatment, as we'll see in Helping.

The other fact about children with background noise difficulties that's crucial to recognize is what an enormous role their other hearing and language functions play in determining how well they can piece together sounds to interpret underlying messages. Let us show you what we mean.

Suppose a boy with background noise difficulties is trying to hear his teacher while several classmates are talking. Their noise will muffle the teacher's words, so that when she says, "Jessie rode to school on the bus this morning," all our child will hear is, "Jessie rode . . . school on the . . . sss this morning." Based on sounds alone, both the sentence as a whole and the word *bus* would be uninterpretable. Fortunately, our student's brain can use other information to fill in the gaps. Having heard that Jessie "rode . . . on" something this morning and that it had something to do with "school," our student can use his knowledge of transportation, schools, Jessie, and grammar (by knowing what things people ride "on" versus "in") to fill in the gaps and determine that Jessie rode *to* school on the *bus*.

This process by which the brain fills in missing information is known as *closure*. In auditory closure, the brain determines which patterns would best complete or "close" the information it does receive, so it can predict what the initial sound patterns actually were. As we'll see in our Helping section, closure has important implications for improving hearing performance in many children with auditory processing deficits.

Pattern Processing: Impaired Sound Discrimination

Impaired sound discrimination (or the inability to distinguish different sounds) is another common CAPD profile. The most important sound discrimination problem affecting school-age children is called *impaired phonological discrimination*. Impaired phonological discrimination causes difficulty distinguishing the sounds (or *phonemes*) in spoken words, especially those in complex words and sentences. To a child with impaired phonological discrimination, words may sound indistinct or garbled, and many may simply sound alike.

Children with severe phonological discrimination problems may be slow to develop language skills. They may have trouble speaking and listening, because of problems learning basic grammar and word meanings. Children with milder discrimination problems learn to speak fairly normally but often struggle with finer sound distinctions. Many vowel and consonant sounds may sound the same to them, especially when spoken quickly. As a result, not only will they have difficulty hearing the differences between words like *thin, fin, thing, think*, and *fink*, they'll have even more difficulty understanding the connections between those words and the letters used to represent them. That's why they often have trouble with reading and spelling. Since they can't clearly hear the sound distinctions between words, the rules linking sounds to letters and letter groups can be hard for them to master. As we'll see in Chapter 10, problems with phonological discrimination are a contributing factor for the majority of children with dyslexia.

Not surprisingly, children with poor sound discrimination have a tendency to *mishear*, or to think they hear words other than those that have been spoken. We've had several children with this problem respond to our requests to draw several *lines* on their paper by drawing *lions*. Children who have trouble hearing in background noise or perceiving the music of speech (i.e., prosody, see next section) can also have problems with mishearing.

Pattern Processing: Impaired Perception of Speech Prosody

Impaired perception of the *prosodic* or "musical aspects" of speech— including rhythm, pitch, and tone—is another CAPD profile. Children with impaired perception of prosody simply don't hear these aspects of speech and often have problems both listening and speaking. When listening, they may miss a speaker's intent, since this is often conveyed by inflection and emphasis as much as by the words themselves. They may interpret ironic or sarcastic comments as rude, paradoxical, or silly and may miss a speaker's earnest, pleading, or even threatening tones. Misunderstandings, suspicions, hurt feelings, confusion, and even personal injuries can sometimes result. When speaking, their voice may sound droning, monotone, or robotic and may hide both the depth and intent of their feelings. Their odd or idiosyncratic speech style often draws ridicule from other children and may cause them to be shunned. Frequently these children are diagnosed with autism spectrum disorders, despite normal empathy, affection, and attachment (see Chapter 8).

Severe deficits in the perception of speech prosody can actually impair a child's ability to learn language. Remember: The first step in language processing is breaking words down into their component sounds (phonemes). Yet a child begins the process of learning language without actually knowing all of the basic word sounds that are used in her language. Instead she must discover these sounds by breaking down the bits of sound she hears (in phrases like "pretty baby" and "I love you") while looking for repeated patterns. One of the keys to being able to recognize these basic sounds is hearing over and over again where the breaks occur between clustered sounds. These breaks are often signaled through prosodic clues, like tone shifts. That's why a child who has difficulty hearing these prosodic elements of speech will have difficulty both identifying basic word sounds and recognizing the combinations of these sounds that form the various word patterns.

Pattern Processing: Impaired Sound Localization

CAPDs can also cause impairments in *sound localization*. The inability to tell where sounds are coming from makes it extremely hard to tell who or how many people are speaking and whom they are speaking to. As a result, children with poor sound localization often have difficulty telling when someone is speaking to them. They may be easily distracted by competing noises, have difficulty maintaining eye contact, look in the wrong direction during conversations, direct their statements and attention to someone other than the person speaking to them, or appear "spacey" and oblivious when conversing with others. These symptoms worsen dramatically with background noise, because the brain needs to determine where various sounds are coming from before it can filter out competing noises.

Pattern Processing: Delayed Auditory Processing

Children with CAPDs often show *delayed auditory processing*, or time lags between hearing a message and understanding it. Typically, they can repeat back a message like a tape recorder yet not comprehend it until several seconds or more have elapsed. Children with language impairments can also show processing delays, but delays due to CAPD are specific to the auditory system in the sense that they delay processing only when listening, not reading.

Children with this problem typically use the strategy of *subvocalization*, or repeating to themselves what they've heard, to keep information in working memory until it can be processed. Like children with impaired auditory working memory (see Chapter 3), these children may experience "auditory overload" when incoming information is too fast, lengthy, or complex. However, unlike children with auditory working memory deficits—who lose information so quickly that they have trouble repeating it back—these children can often retain and repeat very long messages; it simply takes them a while to understand them. Children with significant delays are most likely to have problems during discussion formats, oral questions, or other situations in which they must process auditory information quickly.

For example, one eleven-year-old girl we saw with this problem answered most of our questions quickly—but initially incorrectly. After a second or two, she'd correct herself without prompting, getting most answers correct. When we asked her why she tried to answer so quickly when she could be more accurate by waiting, she said she'd been criticized for slowness. She also frequently subvocalized and often said "What?" or "Huh?" when we talked too long or quickly, so she could gain time to process.

Pattern Processing: Impaired Auditory Memory

Problems with *auditory memory* can be caused either by peripheral hearing deficits or by CAPDs. Problems with the auditory working memory buffer (or phonological "tape loop," as described in Chapter 3) are particularly important causes of auditory memory impairments, because every pattern that gets stored within auditory memory must first pass through this buffer. Impairments in the auditory working memory buffer can severely impair not only long-term auditory memory but also language development and comprehension (as we'll see in Chapter 6).

Pattern Processing: Auditory Hypersensitivity (Hyperacusis)

Other children with auditory processing disorders are *hypersensitive* to certain sounds. This can be one of the most confusing features about auditory disorders: They may make children more sensitive to certain sounds, even as they make them less sensitive to others (see Figure 22). Sound hypersensitivities often keep children from being correctly diagnosed with hearing impairments, because they can make hearing seem so acute in certain situations. In addition to causing discomfort, auditory hypersensitivities can cause distractibility and overstimulation in noisy environments, and, when overstimulated, children with auditory hypersensitivities may react by becoming anxious, hyperactive, or aggressive. These behaviors are especially likely to lead to a diagnosis of ADHD.

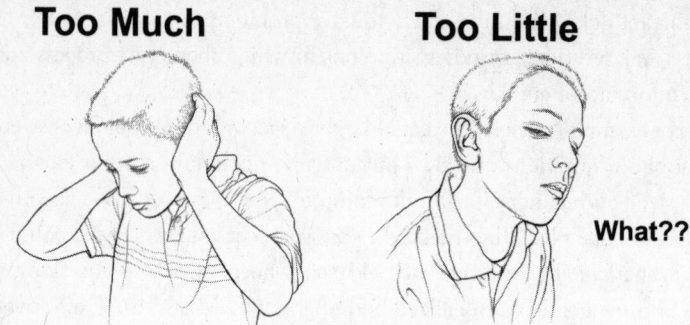

Too Much   **Too Little**

What??

FIGURE 22. The Paradox of Auditory Disorders

Sometimes the same child can hear too much of some sounds and too little of others—and both problems can be equally crippling.

Another irritating (and potentially disabling) problem is called *tinnitus*. Tinnitus is commonly called "ringing in the ears," though some children may describe it as sounding like buzzing, scraping, scratching, ocean waves, or waterfalls. The key is that they hear this noise in the absence of an external sound source. Most often, tinnitus is a benign problem, and is only perceived by children when they are in a quiet place, like lying in bed before sleep. However, in approximately 1 percent of cases, tinnitus is severe enough to block out other sounds and cause functional hearing impairment. Tinnitus is especially common in children with a history of chronic ear infections.

Distinguishing Auditory Problems from Other Disorders

Children with auditory problems often show many of the same signs and symptoms as children with language, memory, or attention challenges or even autism. But undoubtedly the diagnosis with which children who have auditory impairments are most frequently mislabeled is ADHD, or attention deficit/hyperactivity disorder. Because of the frequency of this confusion, let's look at some of the features that can help to distinguish between auditory problems—especially CAPDs—and ADHD.

Auditory Impairments and ADHD

Like children with ADHD, children with auditory disorders often appear distractible or inattentive. In fact, they may even meet the criteria in the American Psychiatric Association's *Diagnostic and Statistical Manual of Mental Disorders*, Fourth Edition (*DSM-IV*) for diagnosing inattentive ADHD *entirely on the basis of auditory impairments* (see Chapter 7). This was the case for Kevin, a sweet-tempered eight-year-old who was brought to us for inattention and behavioral problems at school. Kevin was bright and cooperative—usually—but became inattentive whenever his teacher read a story or talked at length. He was also easily distracted by noises or movements. Worse still, during school assemblies and music class he became anxious and disruptive, and on more than one occasion he broke down in tears. Recently he'd begun refusing to go to school.

Kevin's parents told us that he'd always had "sensitive ears" and that he often covered them at birthday parties or in noisy restaurants. Although he loved movies, he hated to go to theaters because they were so loud. At home, he would focus so intently on the computer or TV that he wouldn't hear his parents when they called his name—even when they were standing right next to him. His pediatrician interpreted this as "hyperfocusing," consistent with ADHD. However, Kevin showed no other signs of disordered attentional focus (like difficulty shifting his attention from one thing to another or trouble transitioning between tasks), and he quickly responded when his parents tapped him on the shoulder. We thought hearing rather than attention might be to blame.

We sent Kevin for a hearing evaluation. His peripheral audiometry was normal, but his CAPD testing was not. He scored in the second percentile when trying to hear words in the presence of competing voices and had great difficulty combining auditory information presented sequentially to different ears. His auditory attention, though, seemed just fine. On a demanding selective auditory attention test, he scored 100 percent—as long as there was no background noise—but when he took the same test in the presence of background speech, his score dropped to 45 percent—far below age norms. Kevin, in other words, could focus his attention just fine, but he couldn't piece together word sounds in the presence of background noise. Small wonder he found it hard to pay attention in a noisy second-grade class.

With just a few simple changes, Kevin was able to focus much better in class. He was given a desktop speaker to help him hear above background noise, and a seat closer to the teacher cut down on auditory distractions. He was also allowed to use earplugs for assemblies and music class, which helped him do just fine.

Kevin's story highlights several important features that can be used to distinguish attention difficulties due to auditory disorders from those caused by impairments in the attention system proper. First, auditory disorders are likely when attention problems seem to worsen in the presence of background noise. Second, auditory disorders are likely when a child has greater difficulties following auditory directions than written or visual directions. Third, auditory problems are likely when a child consistently has more behavioral problems (including distractibility and inattentiveness) during auditory-intensive tasks than tasks of other kinds. Finally, children with impaired auditory processing usually show abnormalities on auditory processing tests that correlate with their symptoms. We'll discuss these tests in the Evaluating section.

Auditory Problems and Social Functioning

Many children with auditory processing deficits experience significant challenges in social and emotional functioning. Terry was a classic example.

Terry was a very bright eleven-year-old boy who easily handled school's academic demands. Unfortunately, school's social demands were another story. He was quiet in the classroom, had no close friends, and tended to spend recess by himself. He was affectionate with his family but was sad about his lack of friends and blamed himself for his isolation. Increasingly, he tried to avoid school by claiming vague symptoms of nonexistent illnesses. A behavioral pediatrician diagnosed him as having PDD-NOS (an autism spectrum disorder, which we'll describe in Chapter 8). He was tried on various medications, including antidepressants, an antianxiety drug, and several stimulants, all without significant benefit. When the doctor suggested trying an antipsychotic medication, Terry's parents felt it was time for a different approach.

When we met Terry, one of the first things we noticed was his unusual speech pattern. His voice was flat and monotone, and his speech was rather slow and unusually deliberate. During our testing, Terry had difficulty hearing when we were trying to be emphatic, ironic, humorous, or questioning. However, he was able to understand the humorous and ironic aspects of various jokes and stories when they were not dependent upon inflection.

When we sent Terry for an auditory evaluation, his peripheral hearing tested normal. In contrast, his CAPD testing showed substantial deficits in the ability to process speech prosody. In conjunction with the audiologist, we prescribed several exercises to help Terry improve both his receptive (listened) and expressive (spoken) prosody. Special accommodations were also made at his school. Gradually, Terry began to make progress in his social interactions.

As Terry's case illustrates, auditory processing disorders can impair social skills in a number of ways. Children with prosodic deficits, processing delays, mishearing, or background noise problems often have difficulty with social communication. They can have difficulty following conversations and may fall off topic or stay one step behind. They often have difficulty adopting the speech patterns and inflections used by their peer group. They may speak too loudly, employ an odd tone, or use styles of diction, cadence, or emphasis that they've picked up from books or documentary films and that make them sound different than their peers. They may have difficulty with reciprocal conversations because of missed auditory cues or because they're slow in answering questions or following up on others' interests. They may have difficulty catching the point of a joke or may laugh only after a long delay. They may seem rude, unresponsive, slow, "uncool," or just no fun to be around. Children with defective sound localization or auditory hypersensitivity may have poor eye contact, due to confusion about the sound source or increased distractibility. They may also ignore (or appear to) people who are speaking to them. The obstacles these behaviors pose to making and keeping friends are obvious.

Children with auditory difficulties often receive discouraging feedback from both peers and adults. They may be berated for their slowness, failure to listen or follow directions, apparent selfishness and self-absorption, or lack of interest in others. They will frequently be mislabeled with Asperger's syndrome or other autism spectrum disorders, even though they have strong social and emotional attachments, are very capable of empathy and emotional understanding, and desire to be with and to be like other children. This is especially likely with intellectually gifted children, whose vocabularies and interests often appear unusual for their age and who pursue their interests with intensity.

Children with social challenges caused by auditory processing deficits often suffer feelings of guilt and low self-esteem. They feel unloved, unlovable, a burden to others, and somehow deserving of the hostile treatment they receive. All too often, they become anxious, depressed, and socially withdrawn. When help is offered, it is usually in the form of counseling or medications aimed at treating the emotional and behavioral consequences of their mislabeling and the resulting mismanagement, while the underlying auditory disorder goes undiagnosed and untreated.

Beverly Biderman, whom we quoted at the start of this chapter, has poignantly recounted the childhood experience of social isolation caused by her own auditory processing disorder. The following passage from her book *Wired for Sound: A Journey into Hearing* shows the variety of social and behavioral impairments that resulted entirely from her difficulties with auditory processing:

> Recess time in the school playground was an ordeal. All the games the little girls my age played seemed to require hearing. There was the chanting for skipping games, especially double Dutch, that made me hold back for fear that I would not jump in (or out) at the right point. There were the elastic rope games, where the others dipped their toes over and under and between the elastics, all the while reciting some nonsense verse that I could only mutter indistinctly, praying that nobody would realize I had heard it hopelessly wrong. ("Yogi in the Kaiser?") Then there were the folding-paper games, where the other girl chattered as she opened the folded paper onto little printed messages while I was supposed to look at the folds. I didn't understand these games either, for I could look at the paper the girl was wiggling in her hand, or I could watch her face and understand what she was saying, but not both.

EVALUATING CHILDREN FOR AUDITORY IMPAIRMENTS

Auditory processing problems in children seldom affect hearing at all sound frequencies. They also seldom produce complete hearing loss at any frequency. Most often, they produce partial hearing loss at only certain sound frequencies. They may also cause impairments only in certain environments or with certain kinds of sounds. That's why a thorough auditory exam is important whenever you suspect a hearing problem. If you wait until you're sure, you've waited too long.

Auditory processing disorders are best evaluated using a multidisciplinary approach, including medical evaluations, neuropsychological testing, and audiological evaluation. History should look for the behaviors or predisposing conditions mentioned above and for a history of an abnormal screening audiogram. Physical exam should include otoscopic (i.e., ear speculum) inspection to look for evidence of prior surgery or damage, auditory canal obstruction with wax or another foreign object, or middle ear effusion. Simple office-based hearing tests can be performed using a set of tuning forks to evaluate high- and low-frequency hearing and lateralization and localization of sound with air and bone conduction. Discrimination of whispers can also be tested by whispering in one ear while providing background noise (rubbing fingers) in the other. Neuropsychological testing should check formally for language, memory, or attention disorders; frequent mishearing; errors of articulation or pronunciation; auditory overload or impaired auditory short-term memory; auditory (versus read) language comprehension; the tendency to subvocalize.

Audiological evaluation usually begins with *peripheral audiometry*, which is also known as an audiometric tone test. Peripheral audiometry assesses the function of the peripheral auditory system (ears and auditory nerves), and its results are displayed on a graph called an *audiogram*. Several key points should be kept in mind when evaluating the information provided by initial auditory testing.

First, the accuracy of these hearing tests depends greatly upon the age and cooperation of the child being tested. For children younger than age five, the examination can often detect only fairly severe hearing impairments, because it often depends on the use of techniques that don't require the child's cooperation. For older and more cooperative subjects, peripheral audiometry usually yields more detailed and accurate information. If you suspect hearing problems in a younger child, an evaluation is important and may yield helpful results, but if testing fails to show problems at age three, repeat testing annually is still warranted if the child continues to show problems.

Second, when an audiogram is obtained, it will report a child's hearing "thresholds" (or sound-detection levels) at various frequencies. These thresholds determine whether a child will have difficulty hearing certain speech sounds. Figure 23 shows the hearing sensitivities needed at various frequencies to hear different speech sounds. As you look at this figure, remember that hearing thresholds are like golf scores: The lower the threshold in decibels (dB), the better or more sensitive the hearing.

Now, note from Figure 23 that a hearing impairment that lowered a child's sound threshold at a frequency of 500 Hz (Hertz) to 30 dB will affect that child's ability to distinguish *d* from *b*, *m* from *n*, and *u* (*uh*) from various sounds including *ah*, *eh*, and *ih*. It can also be seen that even a relatively mild hearing loss of 15 to 25 dB at the high-sound-frequencies range

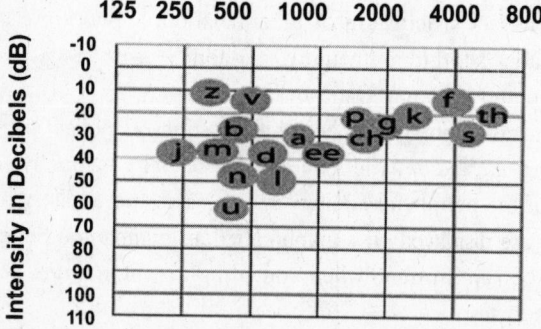

Different Sounds Are Heard at Different Frequencies

FIGURE 23. Sound Discrimination at Different Intensities and Frequencies

of 4 to 8000 Hz can impair the perception of high-frequency sounds such as *th*, *f*, and *s*.

The important message in this figure is that difficulties discriminating speech sounds can start at hearing thresholds as low as 15 dB (e.g., discriminating *z/v*). This is crucial to understand, because school screening tests use cutoffs as high as 35 dB for diagnosing hearing disorders! In other words, a child can have a hearing threshold of 30 dB across the board and still be sent home with a report stating she has "normal" hearing. However, if you look at Figure 23, you'll see that such a child would have difficulty processing most of the sounds in speech! That's why it's crucial not to accept the reassurance of a "normal" school screening exam if you think your child may have hearing problems.

Third, once peripheral audiometry has been completed, you must decide whether these results fully account for a child's problems or whether a specialized assessment for CAPD is indicated. If CAPD testing appears warranted, there are several important facts you should consider.

- CAPD testing is very operator-dependent, so its accuracy hinges greatly on the skill and experience of the audiologist. Even with a skilled operator, these tests are not perfect. In our experience, the sensitivity of these tests for identifying deficits in children with very strong clinical evidence of CAPD is in the range of 85 to 90 percent.
- It's important that the audiologist use a battery of tests sufficient to evaluate the full range of CAP functions. Many centers that claim to offer CAPD testing in reality perform only a limited battery of tests known as the SCAN-C. This test can detect only about half of children with CAPD, so by itself it's far from adequate for evaluating CAPD.
- CAPD testing is rarely helpful in children younger than age seven or eight. Younger children find it hard to cooperate with these demanding tests, and broad variations in normal development at younger ages have made it difficult to establish valid norms.
- Children with significant difficulties in receptive language, attention, and oppositional behavior also have difficulties cooperating with these tests.

HELPING CHILDREN WITH AUDITORY IMPAIRMENTS

The auditory system has a tremendous capacity for change in response to targeted interventions. In the sections below, we'll share many strategies to remediate or compensate for the auditory processing difficulties we've described. First, though, let's look at accommodations that can help essentially any child with auditory problems.

Accommodations for Children with Auditory Problems

Accommodations for children with auditory processing disorders can be divided into three categories: those that optimize the classroom environment, those that optimize Information Input, and those that are necessary in test settings.

Optimizing the Classroom Environment

To make the classroom a more acoustically friendly environment:

- Seat children with auditory processing disorders close to the teacher (or other speakers), in a place where they can hear well and have a clear vision of the teacher's face.
- Minimize background noise and auditory distractions by seating children away from sound sources like buzzing lights or heaters, blowing air ducts, noise-permeable partitions (like walls or doors), and particularly noisy classmates.
- Minimize visual distractions by seating children where they can't see windows or busy wall displays.
- Improve classroom acoustics by using carpets and wall hangings to cover echo-prone surfaces.
- Teach children and teachers how environmental factors affect sound perception. Helpful hints are provided in the book *Speechreading* (see Resources).

Optimizing Information Input

Provide students information in forms that children with auditory processing disorders can easily process.

- Because they must often devote all their mental energy just to listening, children with auditory impairments typically have tremendous difficulty taking notes. When instruction is given in auditory form, they should be given access to the teacher's notes or to notes taken by another student. If textbooks are available on the topic, they should be allowed to take them home. They should also receive all important instructions, assignments, and due dates in written form.

- Students with auditory impairments will be able to follow auditory instruction more easily if they are familiar with the topics and terms under discussion (see our discussion of auditory closure). Let them prelearn new key terms and topics through textbooks or the teacher's notes before these new materials are presented in class.

- Because children with auditory impairments often have difficulty following class discussions, they will have difficulty answering oral questions (especially those requiring inference) on the spot. Let them know the night before or at the start of a session what question they'll be asked to discuss, then let them lead off the discussion, to make sure they can have a chance to speak before the topic changes.

- Use multisensory forms of instruction whenever possible.

  - Use visual or tactile cues to reinforce important auditory information (e.g., printed copies of the teacher's notes, lists of key words, pictures, charts, maps, graphs, models, or hands-on learning projects).

  - Use closed-captioning with all audiovisual materials. Since nearly a quarter of students have some degree of hearing difficulties and many more need practice reading, closed-captioning is *always* a good idea.

Special Accommodations for Testing

Testing accommodations are essential for all children with auditory impairments.

- Provide all test instructions in writing.
- Oral testing is usually not appropriate. Children with auditory processing disorders typically show a large discrepancy between their ability to analyze and infer meanings from written texts versus auditory inputs. Usually they'll be better able to "show what they know" when analyzing written as opposed to auditory information.

Helping Children with Auditory Information Input Problems

Peripheral hearing loss (i.e., impaired auditory Information Input) is an important problem in children and one with potentially devastating consequences. Children who suffer peripheral hearing loss should be aggressively treated and frequently evaluated. Any child suspected of peripheral hearing loss should receive a careful evaluation from an audiologist and an ENT specialist. She should also receive follow-up examinations at least yearly until the problem has clearly stabilized or resolved. Interventions for confirmed hearing loss should be tailored to address the precise problem.

- Children with persistent ear effusions (longer than three months) should be referred to an ENT (ear, nose, and throat) specialist for evaluation. These children may benefit from PE tubes, antibiotics, treatment of allergies, or the removal of tonsils or adenoids to relieve eustachian tube dysfunction. Children with persistent allergies or chronic nonallergic rhinitis may also benefit from treatment by an allergy specialist.
- Children with significant peripheral hearing loss will often benefit from the use of an assistive listening device in school. The right device for a particular child will depend upon age, developmental stage, and the type and severity of problems. Three general types of

assistive devices are available (not including cochlear implant devices, which are used for children with essentially complete hearing loss).

- Desktop amplification is a simple solution with broad benefits and should be used far more commonly than it is. The teacher speaks into a desktop or lapel microphone, and the sound is projected to the student's speaker by a local FM transmitter (or, less commonly, through wires). Studies have shown that these devices can actually improve academic performance for all children, not simply those with measurable hearing loss. However, for children with hearing thresholds above 15 dB, especially in the early-elementary grades, when language and reading skills are being developed, these devices should be mandatory. Most schools already have some of these devices, but their guidelines for use are often more restrictive than they should be.
- Students can also be equipped with headphone (or earpiece) amplifiers that receive direct transmission from the teacher's microphone. These devices may work better than desktop amplification for children with severe background noise problems, auditory distractibility, or sound localization difficulties. However, they are much more expensive (around two thousand dollars), more intrusive and difficult to use, and more likely to make children self-conscious (especially above the early-elementary grades). Still, they will be useful for select children.
- Standard in-ear hearing aids can be useful for children whose hearing problems are impairing both classroom and social performance. Children should be considered for such devices (especially during the crucial early years, when they're learning to read) at thresholds lower than those used for adults — in some cases as low as 25 dB.
- The choice of an assistive device should be made only after consultation with an audiologist or ENT, skilled in the care of children with hearing impairments.

Helping Children with Auditory Pattern Processing Problems (CAPDs)

In this section, we'll discuss interventions for children with each of the seven categories of CAPDs described in our Causes section. Table 3 summarizes the main interventions for each category.

TABLE 3 Helping Children with CAPDs

Background Noise	Auditory Closure Practice with Noise Song Lyrics Closed-Captioning	FM Amplification Teacher's Notes Computer Learning Preview & Prelearn
Discrimination	Train Discrimination Guided Oral Reading Auditory Closure Closed-Captioning	Visual Supports Teacher's Notes Rule-Based Phonics
Prosody	Train Music, Pitch Train Timing, Rhythm Guided Oral Reading Poems, Jokes	Animated Teacher
Localization	Train Localization Emphasize Visual Cues Auditory Closure Learn Sound Acoustics	Environmental Changes Carpeted Floors Preferential Seating
Delayed Processing	Visual Learning Visualization Chunk Information Key Words	More Time to Answer Online Learning Prepared Questions
Memory	Train Auditory Memory Chunk Information Subvocalization Context, Personalize Visual Learning Visualization	Visual Supports Teacher's Notes Book at Home Written Instructions
Hypersensitivity	Sound Desensitization	Environmental Changes Sparing Use of Musicians' Ear Filters

Pattern Processing: Help for Impaired Hearing with Background Noise

Children who have difficulty hearing with background noise can benefit from the following interventions:

- Auditory training exercises. Targeted exercises can be specially designed to improve the ability to interpret speech in the presence of background noise. This training can range from "low-tech" to highly sophisticated.

  - The simplest form of auditory training is to have a child practice listening to a speech source (like a book on tape or a parent reading aloud) in the presence of background noise from a TV or music player. Start with the volume of the background noise source very low, then gradually increase it as the child's listening skills improve. Fifteen to thirty minutes of practice a day can be very productive.
  - Auditory training can also be performed using Internet sites like Randall's Cyberlistening Lab (www.esl-lab.com). These download-able recordings (which are intended primarily to teach English as a second language) are ideal for auditory training, because they feature short recordings followed by a series of comprehension questions. Listening to these tapes (then trying to answer the questions) in the presence of increasing levels of background noise is a great form of auditory training.
  - Some children have more difficulty with background noise when competing messages are presented in the same ear at the same time. Others may have more difficulty when competing messages are presented into opposite ears at the same time. They may also experience more difficulties in one ear (i.e., right or left) than the other. If the precise nature of a child's problem has been determined by CAPD testing, specific computer-based practice programs can easily be constructed using music or video mixing software, like Adobe Premiere or the free downloadable program Audacity (www.sourceforge.net). These programs can be designed to present competing speech messages,

whose volumes can be separately adjusted in the same or opposite ears. Commercial programs that perform this task will likely soon become available.

- Another good form of focused listening practice is to have a child listen for the lyrics in favorite songs. Most song lyrics are now available on the Internet.

- Closed-caption TV and video programs. In addition to improving auditory comprehension, closed-captioning can show children how much they are missing through hearing alone. If programs are watched in the presence of a competing sound source, they can also be used for auditory training.
- As we've mentioned, a child with background noise problems will experience fewer practical difficulties if she's good at "filling in" the information she misses through auditory closure. Auditory training exercises (like those described above) can be very helpful in improving auditory closure skills. These skills can also be improved by increasing general knowledge, expanding language and vocabulary skills, and improving phonologic processing. A course of speech therapy with a speech-language pathologist who's experienced in working with hearing-impaired children will often benefit a child with poor auditory closure skills—especially if the child has underlying language weakness.
- Helpful classroom accommodations include textbooks, teachers' notes, and opportunities for computer-based and multimodal learning.
- Sound-amplification or other assistive devices can also be helpful for children with severe background noise deficits.

Pattern Processing: Help for Impaired Sound Discrimination

Most problems with phonological discrimination are caused by the brain's inability to hear the fast changes in sound that distinguish different words. Fortunately, brains that lack this ability can develop it through appropriate training.

- The most extensively tested and best-documented treatment for children with impaired phonological processing is intensive training in phonics, which we'll discuss in detail in Chapter 10. Properly conducted phonics training helps children more accurately hear the differences between word sounds and better link these sounds to the letters that can be used to represent them.
- Speaking slowly and clearly to these children can also improve their sound processing. Stress the distinctions between words like *dime* and *time*, *pig* and *peg*. Remember, most deficits in phonological processing are caused by brain-based difficulties processing *rapid* sound changes. By drawing out and exaggerating sounds, you can gradually improve a child's ability to hear these changes.
- Several computer programs that can train the brain to better hear these sounds are now commercially available.

  - The most sophisticated and best studied of these programs is called Fast ForWord (www.scilearn.com). This program begins by assessing the user's current skills in phonological discrimination, then adjusts the speed and frequency of the signals it delivers to a level that the user will find challenging but not overwhelming. Over time, the program gradually increases the level of challenge until it presents word sounds at fairly rapid rates. Gains made with this program have been shown to translate into real-world progress in phonology, speech comprehension, and auditory memory. Unfortunately, not all children with phonological deficits benefit from this program, though available studies (and our personal experience) suggest that up to two-thirds of appropriately selected children do. This program is also quite expensive, costing in excess of a thousand dollars, and is seldom covered by insurance, though in some cases it may be available through school. It is quite rigorous, demanding forty-five to ninety minutes per session for a period of up to six weeks, and individual training sessions cannot be stopped once started. Consequently, this program is useful primarily for highly motivated children with strong attention skills and good physical endurance.

- A simpler computer program called Earobics (www.earobics.com) has been shown capable of producing comparable gains in phonological processing. Earobics is similar in many ways to Fast ForWord but is not as interactive. Instead the user selects among several fixed levels of difficulty which exercises he wishes to perform. In general, the auditory tasks are simpler than with Fast ForWord. Because the lessons can be paused and resumed at the user's convenience, this program is probably better suited than Fast ForWord for younger users or those with less endurance. Earobics is also considerably cheaper (around three hundred dollars).

- Like children with background noise impairments, children with impaired phonological discrimination typically benefit from strategies designed to improve auditory closure. The strategies discussed in the previous section will be useful.
- Children with severe impairments in phonological discrimination often experience significant delays in language development and require intensive language therapy (see Chapter 6).
- Closed-captioning video displays allow children to simultaneously listen to and read words. This can improve sight-sound correlations.
- Other useful treatments and accommodations will be discussed in Chapter 10.

Pattern Processing: Help for Impaired Perception of Speech Prosody

Children who have difficulties processing the musical (prosodic) aspects of speech typically benefit from exercises designed to improve their perception of speech rhythms, inflections, and intonations. Improving a child's perception of speech prosody can also improve her expressive speech prosody (i.e., the musicality of the child's own speech).

- Children with prosodic speech impairments often benefit from practice listening to and speaking with markedly exaggerated speech patterns.

- Speakers should speak to them slowly and with exaggerated inflection. The children should then be asked to imitate the speech pattern. Practice exchanging speeches. Make them elaborate and fun. Use plays, poetry, jokes, short skits, or famous speeches.

- Practice using facial gestures and expressions of emotion while delivering these lines. Have an adult go first, then have the child focus on the adult model's use of expressions, postures, and gestures. If the child initially has difficulty perceiving these gestures, begin by making them very broad. As the child becomes more perceptive, make the gestures more natural. Have both the child and the adult model critique each other's performances in regard to inflection, emphasis, breath control, expressions, postures, and movements.

- Children with prosodic speech deficits often use poor breath-control techniques, because they are not aware of the effect that breathing in different places has on speech communication. Paying attention to and practicing breath control on longer sentences can be extremely helpful.

- Charades is a great way to practice gestures and expressions. So is speaking in front of a mirror. Use a video recorder (or a voice recorder) to copy these sessions so the child can play them back. Focus not only on sounds but also on mouth movements, facial expressions, body postures, and hand gestures.

- Practice imitating the motions of an actor on TV or video. Have the child critique both the actor's performance and her own.

- Children with prosodic speech deficits often benefit from musical training in pitch and timing. Start by playing a single note on a musical instrument or sing a note out loud, then have the child imitate it. Repeat the process with different notes. When this is mastered, move on to a more complex series of notes.

- A similar process can be used for practicing rhythms and timing. Have a child practice clapping or repeating rhythmic sequences. Begin with short, slow sequences, and then get faster and longer.

- One additional piece of equipment that can be used during this practice to help children with pronunciation difficulties is called a *pacing board*. As we've mentioned, children with impaired prosody often have difficulty pacing or segmenting their speech production, so that some words or word parts get jammed together while others have unusually long pauses. The purpose of the pacing board is to help a child become more aware of, and better able to regulate, the rhythm of her speech. A pacing board is basically just a series of colored boxes that the child can tap on when she utters a word or a word sound, to make her more conscious of her vocal patterns.

  - If a child is having problems pronouncing individual words (usually the long ones), model the word's pronunciation by saying it with appropriate pacing and spacing (though slowed and exaggerated at first), while accompanying the sounds with taps on the board. Have the child repeat. Similar practice should be performed for whole sentences, focusing both on appropriate spacing and pacing and also on inflection or word emphasis.
  - Adults should encourage children by informing them that most famous actors and actresses work with "vocal coaches" to change their voices.

- The pitch and temporal perception exercises in auditory training programs like Fast ForWord can also be helpful for children with prosodic deficits. However, parents be warned: One of our patients with prosodic difficulties was so inspired by her new ability to perceive the joys of music that she became an incorrigible shower singer!
- When prosodic deficits cause problems in social interactions, a course of *pragmatic language training* may be useful. Pragmatic language is the language of everyday social interactions, and pragmatic language training can help children understand the roles of tone, emphasis, inflection, and diction in ordinary speech. Pragmatic language training should initially be conducted one-on-one. Too often, children with prosodic speech deficits are placed in "social skills groups" where noise and commotions may prevent necessary attention from being paid to the subtle sound qualities. Such classes

are more helpful in improving social behaviors than prosodic language deficits. Adults should also model the speech patterns they are trying to teach. Take the child places where she can hear adults engaging in social conversations, then ask her to critique and imitate the adult performances. For more information on pragmatic language, see Chapter 6.

- In the classroom, speak to these children with straightforward language but with animated voices and expressions.

Pattern Processing: Help for Impaired Sound Localization

Since children with impaired sound localization also have trouble hearing in the presence of background noise, they'll benefit from the suggestions described above. They'll also benefit from:

- Practicing localizing sound sources, like a beeping telephone or key locator, egg timer, or other hidable sound source.
- Playing the classic children's game Marco Polo. This game will be easier or harder in different acoustic environments. Play first in an echoless, distraction-free environment. Gradually progress to environments with more echoes and background noises.
- Instruction in searching for visual cues that allow them to tell who is speaking in various settings.
- Optimizing the acoustic environment in the classroom (as above).

Pattern Processing: Help for Delayed Auditory Processing

Children with delayed auditory processing typically experience functional difficulties when their delays in processing cause backups in encoding and working memory. The best way to help these children is to make them better encoders. A complete discussion of this topic is provided in Chapter 3; however, the main principles are:

- Use multimodal or multisensory learning strategies to spread out the information load across several input systems. Adding visual and kinesthetic inputs (as we described in Chapter 3) can greatly improve a child's ability to process incoming information.

- Use visualization strategies (like those described in Chapter 3) to quickly translate auditory into visual information, freeing up more space in auditory working memory.
- Provide classroom accommodations like computer-based learning strategies (where the rate of input can be better controlled and can be supplemented by printed text).
- Allow more time for answering oral questions in class, and inform them in advance what questions they'll be asked to discuss in class.

Pattern Processing: Help for Auditory Memory Problems

Many approaches to helping children with auditory memory problems were discussed in Chapter 3. The primary strategies include:

- Auditory memory training (to increase auditory memory capacity or span).
- Visual and hands-on supports, to supplement auditory processing.
- Visualization strategies, to improve encoding.
- Chunking and key word strategies, to use auditory working memory resources more efficiently.
- Personal memory strategies, to make incoming information more memorable.
- Written backup for auditory information, such as teachers' notes, books, and written copies of instructions and assignments.

Pattern Processing: Help for Auditory Hypersensitivity

Hyperacusis and auditory hypersensitivity typically diminish as children age. Still, they can cause substantial problems for younger children. Helpful interventions are as follows:

- For the most severely affected children, sound-desensitization treatment may be required. Currently the best established desensitization treatments involve the use of *pink noise*. Pink noise is a form of broad-spectrum noise (like white noise) that places extra sound on lower frequencies and less on higher. Since auditory hypersensitivity usually results from too many high-frequency processors in the brain, pink noise can actually "convert" some of these extra high-frequency processors into low-frequency processors, eliminating hypersensitivity. Pink noise therapy usually involves listening to pink noise for approximately two hours a day for a span of several months. Treatment is provided through centers that specialize in the treatment of auditory hypersensitivity and tinnitus (see below).

- Children with auditory hypersensitivity may benefit from the occasional use of earplugs. Caution is needed, though, because excessive use of earplugs can actually worsen sound sensitivity. Children with the most severe problems (i.e., those who require earplugs on an essentially daily basis) should use musicians' earplugs, which block out only selected (usually high) frequencies. Even then earplugs should be worn for no more than two or three hours a day—and only when an activity would be impossible without them. Children who need earplugs only during recess or assemblies can usually use nonfitted earplugs, which can be obtained online at sites like www.etymotic.com.

- Watch for signs of sensory overload in children with auditory hypersensitivity. Limit exposures to situations that cause problems, but don't entirely avoid challenging situations. Use earplugs if needed, and don't exceed the child's tolerance levels. Promote socialization in smaller, quieter groups. Encourage kids to improve their noise tolerance, but just a bit at a time. Don't overwhelm them by asking too much at once. This can fill them with a sense of failure or insecurity.

- Tinnitus (ringing in the ears) is usually most bothersome when children are trying to fall asleep in a quiet bedroom. Soothing background music, or a pink or white noise generator, is often all that's needed. For children with tinnitus severe enough to cause functional hearing problems, evaluation by a specialist is crucial. Treatment generally involves the use of sound generators (like the pink noise generators we described above) that help "retrain" parts of the brain that produce the abnormal sound. Centers that provide this service (and treat children with auditory hypersensitivity) are listed by the American Tinnitus Association (www.ata.org).

Auditory Impairments and Alternative Educational Settings

Sometimes, despite everyone's best efforts, a student with significant auditory processing challenges may find it impossible to get the education he needs at a typical school. Two alternatives should be considered:

- Many school districts will have designated low-hearing schools. In these schools, amplification systems are more readily available, teachers are more aware of special issues for hearing-challenged children, and multisensory approaches are stressed. Although these schools are typically intended for children with peripheral hearing impairments, their teaching methods are usually effective for children with CAPDs as well, and determined parents may be successful in getting their child enrolled in such a school.
- Homeschooling is also a good alternative for some children with auditory processing impairments. The environment is usually fairly customizable, so distractions and background noise can be kept to a minimum. In addition, computer-based or online instruction can be used. These resources offer controllable acoustics, single-direction sound sources (i.e., the speakers), the potential to emphasize visual learning, and an essential absence of background noise. If homeschooling is chosen, it's still important to provide children frequent exposures to unfavorable auditory environments, so they can learn to function in a broad range of settings.

6

The Communication Gap

Language Problems in Children

> Apt words have the power to swage
> The tumors of a troubled mind.
>
> —JOHN MILTON, *SAMSON AGONISTES*

Marshall was a cheerful but very quiet young six-year-old whose parents sought our opinion on his across-the-board school difficulties. At home, Marshall was a contented and creative child who loved doing puzzles, building elaborate structures with LEGOs and K'nex, looking at picture books, and drawing beautifully detailed animals and insects. At school, he usually just looked lost. Marshall couldn't follow even simple directions unless they were acted out for him, wouldn't respond to the teacher's questions, and could never explain anything he was learning in class.

Marshall had seen the school psychologist. She gave him an IQ test and concluded that he was borderline mentally retarded; he wasn't learning because he was "slow." Marshall's parents rejected the "slow" label. They could see from his other interests and talents that he had some strong intellectual abilities. They could also see that, in Marshall, history was repeating itself.

Thirty years earlier, Marshall's father, now a successful businessman, had also been labeled "slow" when he was eight years old and still largely

nonverbal. In fact, his school district had been so certain he was mentally retarded that they recommended full-time placement in an institutional care
setting. It was "obvious" he'd never be able to care for himself. Fortunately,
his parents insisted he remain at home and in school. Although no special
services were provided, they spent endless hours barraging him with oral language (talking and reading). Because they always suspected there might
be something wrong with his hearing—although the tests were all normal—
they spoke slowly and loudly and with exaggerated inflections. Over time,
Marshall's father began to respond. By fourth grade, he was reading. By eighth
grade, he was at grade level in all subjects. In high school, he made the honor
roll. At the university, he made the Dean's list. And from what we could tell
when we met him in our clinic, as an adult his self-care skills were pretty
much intact—not to mention his ability to care for his many employees.

As we examined Marshall, we, too, began to feel that history might be repeating itself. During our testing, Marshall often had difficulty understanding what we wanted him to do, unless we *showed* him rather than simply
asked. It was easy to understand how he might have performed poorly on an
IQ test in which all the task instructions were given orally. (This is a perfect
example of why it's so important to consider not just the *results* of a test but
also its *nature* and how its structure can influence its results.) Our testing re-
vealed strengths as well as weaknesses: Marshall actually showed above-
average performance in a variety of mechanical and spatial reasoning tasks.
In short, he had a fairly focal deficit in language development—based, it
turned out, on a severe difficulty processing the sound structure of words.

Marshall was referred for an intensive course of therapy with a speech-
language pathologist and a reading tutor, and his teacher began to use a
more multimodal teaching approach. Together, these steps started to yield
dramatic results.

LANGUAGE: THE PRIMARY
MEDIUM OF LEARNING

Language skills are crucial to a child's well-being, both in school and
in life. In a very real sense, language is the primary medium of learning
and knowledge. In the classroom's "information economy," it is the coin
of the realm and the fundamental means of exchange. While there are

nonlinguistic ways to learn and communicate information, these are neither as versatile nor as valuable as language-based communication.

Language is equally important outside the classroom. It provides the clearest and most versatile means of sharing and critiquing ideas, explaining feelings and opinions, persuading others to adopt your point of view, communicating goals and visions, showing interest, concern, and empathy, establishing and explaining rules, and peacefully resolving conflicts. Children who struggle to comprehend or communicate through language will face challenges in all these areas. That's why language problems can be devastating not only academically but also socially and emotionally.

In this chapter, we'll discuss many common—and commonly neglected—language challenges and what can be done to help children who struggle with them achieve all the success and satisfaction that language skills can bring.

BEHAVIORS ASSOCIATED WITH LANGUAGE PROBLEMS IN CHILDREN

Two general categories of behaviors point to language problems in children: behaviors suggesting problems taking language in and behaviors suggesting problems putting language out. Let's look at each category.

Problems Taking Language In: Understanding Language

The following signs suggest that a child may have difficulty taking in or understanding language:

- Shows little or no interest in being read to by age two.
- Unable to understand simple terms or phrases like *yes, no, Kiss Mommy,* or *Take the ball* by age two.
- Has difficulty understanding contrasts like *good/bad, nice/naughty, in/out, hot/cold,* after age three.
- Has difficulty understanding simple questions involving *who, what, where, when, why, how,* after age four.

- Has difficulty with simple conditional or relational words like *before, after, very, by, next to, unless, until,* et cetera, after age five.
- Has persistent difficulty understanding routine conversations at home or in preschool by age five.
- Displays lack of interest in learning to read. May or may not have difficulty with decoding (see Chapter 10), but typically significant problems with comprehension.
- Has difficulty understanding the increasingly complex, layered, clause-filled sentences that come into use around grades three and four.
- There is a general sense that the child appeared "brighter" or more intelligent when younger but seemed to grow progressively less perceptive (especially relative to peers) as she grew older.
- Makes surprising errors in understanding comments, requests, or instructions.
- Misunderstands test or assignment instructions or questions.
- Has poor comprehension when listening or reading.
- Doesn't "get" jokes.
- Poor problem solving.
- May do far worse with math story problems than other math formats.
- Has a tendency to "subvocalize" (repeat everything to himself) in order to understand.
- Has problems with word meanings, including:

  - Limited vocabulary.
  - Difficulty learning new words or phrases.
  - Frequent confusion or "forgetfulness" about word meanings.
  - Difficulty comprehending multiple word meanings.
  - Difficulty with ambiguous or figurative language.
  - "Selective" problems understanding language, so that some language skills exist along with impairments.
  - Difficulty understanding how different grammatical forms affect word meanings, including tenses, singulars and plurals, verb forms, adverbial forms, adjective forms, et cetera.

- Has difficulty paying attention in class.
- Has difficulty following instructions.

- May become physically active when teacher talks for prolonged periods.
- May frequently commit social mistakes or "say the wrong thing."
- May be socially isolated or a "hanger-on" with a group.
- May try to dominate social speech and play to avoid having to listen to others.

Problems Putting Language Out: Speaking and Writing

The following signs suggest that a child may have a disorder of language output:

- Fails to speak single words by eighteen months or to combine words by two years.
- Is unable to speak in complete sentences by age four.
- Has unusual difficulty pronouncing words or making the proper speech muscle movements needed to speak words.
- Speaks "baby language" after it's no longer appropriate.
- Has difficulty recalling the right words or names when needed.
- Has difficulty telling stories or relating experiences.
- Has difficulty summarizing, paraphrasing, elaborating, or identifying and stating the main point.
- Has difficulty describing relationships or similarities.
- Has a tendency to echo or copy the statements of other speakers.
- Frequently relies on stock words and phrases or fillers like *thing, stuff, junk, those guys, like, um, no way,* and so on.
- Has a tendency to confuse pronouns, tenses, or other grammatical features.
- Has a tendency to avoid being drawn into conversations.
- Has a tendency to remain silent in groups and avoid participation in class.
- Has a tendency to give brief answers to questions, like, "Okay," "Yeah," and "No."
- Has a tendency to speak in incomplete sentences or to rely on others to complete statements.
- Appears to know more than she can express.
- May be quite glib in informal or social speech (especially when

there's lots of known or shared context) but has more difficulty speaking about decontextualized or abstract material (like what's going on at school, what he's thinking about, etc.).

- Has difficulty solving problems using words, both in school and in social, family, and other interpersonal relationships.
- May speak little or on a fairly limited range of topics or using a fairly limited vocabulary.
- May become frustrated at his inability to explain needs or wants or to resolve conflicts verbally, sometimes resulting in explosive or aggressive behaviors.
- May demonstrate comprehension by answering direct questions with short answers but be unable to answer in full sentences.
- May show extreme resistance to writing or write only very short, very simple, direct declarative sentences, sentences with poor grammar, or sentences with impoverished idea content.

THE CAUSES OF LANGUAGE PROBLEMS IN CHILDREN

In this section, we'll describe how the language system works, how it develops, how it's organized in the brain, and how it sometimes encounters problems. In discussing the many *neurolearning* systems that underlie language, we'll use the illustration of a Filing Cabinet:

- Information Input functions will be likened to an inbox in which language-based information is placed before being processed and filed in the storage areas of the brain.
- Pattern Processing will be likened to the files that are stored in the cabinet.
- Output for Action will be likened to pulling those files from the cabinet and expressing their contents.

By studying the language processing pathway, we'll be able to see how language is processed in the brain, how language skills develop, how language problems occur, and, most important, how they can be treated.

Information Input: The Language System's Inbox

Two Information Input routes bring most of the information into the language system's inbox: auditory inputs that receive spoken or sung words and visual inputs that receive printed words or sign language. (Tactile inputs can also take in language, as when blind children read Braille.)

For most young children, auditory inputs play by far the greatest role in language intake and development. In fact, until a child can read or is taught sign language, all of her language development will depend upon auditory inputs. That's why even subtle (or temporary) problems with the auditory processing systems (either peripheral or central) can result in major problems with language development (as discussed in Chapter 5).

Auditory processing deficits are responsible for many language-related problems, especially in younger children (though they may be diagnosed at any age). Since we've discussed both visual and auditory impairments in detail in Chapters 4 and 5, we won't repeat those discussions here. Instead we'll focus on the language problems that result when these input systems fail to adequately stock the language inbox, and on primary deficits in the language Pattern Processing system.

Pattern Processing: The Language Files

After language-based information is placed in the "inbox," the language Pattern Processing system must properly process and file this information if language is to be learned. To do this, the brain must create a series of files for each kind of pattern that makes up language: word *sounds,* word *definitions,* word *relationships* (like synonyms, antonyms, homonyms), and *higher-order language features* (like grammar, paragraph and story organization, and writing style).

The files that store each of these kinds of information are located in different areas throughout the brain. However, they can be connected through a complicated network of connections, or "cross-references," that mirror their associations and relationships. Let us show you what we mean: Figure 24

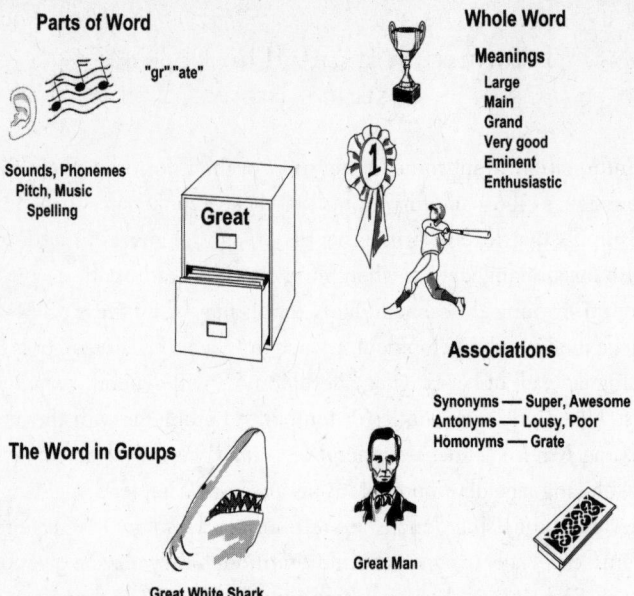

Parts of Word

"gr" "ate"

Sounds, Phonemes
Pitch, Music
Spelling

Great

Whole Word

Meanings
Large
Main
Grand
Very good
Eminent
Enthusiastic

Associations

Synonyms — Super, Awesome
Antonyms — Lousy, Poor
Homonyms — Grate

The Word in Groups

Great White Shark

Great Man

FIGURE 24. Language File and Network for the Word *Great*

shows a network of associations for a single word, *great*. Reading or hearing this word places it in your language inbox. Your language pattern processing system locates and opens the primary word file for *great*, which contains both the word's primary definition and various links to associated files. By opening this single file, you suddenly have access to a huge variety of relevant information, like word sounds, alternate spellings, various word meanings, illustrations or examples, synonyms, antonyms, homonyms, visual images, phrases, quotations, names, songs, and on and on (see Figure 24). The broader and richer a child's exposure to language (and the better her ability to process language patterns), the richer her network of associations will be.

Language files aren't just organized around individual words, like *Great*. In fact, each of the definitions, phrases, word parts, and other items listed in Figure 24 has a file of its own. By accessing any of those files directly, we could work our way back through our brain's network of associations to *Great*.

Let's consider the different types of files that exist in the language system and also the difficulties in forming, storing, or accessing those files that can cause language problems. These language files fall into three main categories: those that contain information about *word parts,* those that contain information about *individual words,* and those that contain information about *words in groups.* Let's look at each.

Pattern Processing: Word Parts

As we discussed in Chapter 5, before the brain can recognize individual words, it must break those words into their component sounds (or phonemes), then analyze those sounds for the patterns that represent whole words. This ability to correctly process the basic sound component of words is one of the key foundations upon which higher language skills are built. Children who have severe difficulty recognizing and discriminating between the basic sounds in spoken words may have difficulty at every level of the language process, from word recognition (spoken or read) to grammar to sentence and discourse comprehension.

It's easy to understand why difficulties with this basic process should have such dramatic effects on language at all levels when you remember how a child learns language: by observation and imitation. To acquire new language skills, a child must be able to accurately observe how words are used by others, and to do this she must be able to clearly and consistently perceive the sounds that make up those words. When a child has difficulty processing and perceiving the sounds in the words spoken by her parents, teachers, and others, she'll miss the consistent patterns that make learning words and the rules that govern their use possible. As a result, she'll fail to form accurate and useful files for word meanings (or vocabulary), rules of grammar, and elements of style or language usage.

Children with milder sound discrimination (or phoneme recognition) problems typically have less difficulty understanding spoken language. In fact, they may have an easier time understanding whole sentences or even longer discourse than short fragments like individual words. That's because longer fragments usually provide more contextual cues to help them "fill in" poorly heard sounds through the process of closure that we discussed in Chapter 5. However, these children can often have major difficulties learning to read, as we'll describe in Chapter 10.

Difficulties understanding and learning whole words can also be caused by trouble hearing the cues (like pauses and tone shifts) that signal breaks between words or word parts. A child who can't perceive that the simple phrase "I don't know" is made up of three distinct words may use this phrase appropriately in certain situations yet have no idea what each of the individual words means. In his mind, *iduhno* will be stored in a single file that has no links or relationship to *I, don't,* or *know*. (He may not even have files for these other words at all.) This inability to distinguish words in simple phrases means that each phrase will be stored as a kind of "compound word" in a separate unconnected file and will be useful only for a narrow range of settings. As a result, the child will develop a highly inflexible and poorly integrated language system where there are few cross-references or interconnections and little understanding of how individual words can be combined to create different meanings. Children with this problem often have extensive language difficulties and require intensive therapy.

Fortunately, intensive therapy can usually improve a child's ability to hear the fine distinctions in sound. Even children with relatively severe sound processing difficulties can achieve significant—and in some cases fairly rapid—gains in language function.

Pattern Processing: Individual Words (Semantics)

The next level of language Pattern Processing involves files that store information about whole words. This "whole word" level is often referred to as *semantics*. The formation of files for whole words is dependent not only on word part processing, as we've just discussed, but also on auditory working memory. Children usually learn new words by repeatedly "saying" them to themselves using their auditory working memory's "tape loop" (see Chapter 3). Studies have shown that the better a child is at retaining and repeating words with this auditory tape loop, the better she will be at learning new words. Children who have deficits in auditory working memory typically have fewer primary word files in their memory stores.

As we mentioned previously, when the brain's language Pattern Processing system recognizes that an incoming sound pattern forms a particular word, it retrieves the primary word file for that word. This primary word file contains the first definition a child thinks of when she hears or reads that word. It also contains links to any word association files that the child has cross-referenced to that word (as we showed in Figure 24). Many of these association files contain secondary or alternate word meanings. These files are very important, especially in English, where an estimated 60 percent of words have multiple meanings (like *bat*, which can mean a small flying mammal, a club used in baseball or cricket, a provocative motion of the eyelids, a waving motion of the hands, a sheet of cotton wadding used for filling quilts, and several other things as well). Understanding which meaning is intended depends upon contextual cues (see below).

Primary word files can also be linked to association files that contain information about words in different grammatical forms or parts of speech—for example, as a noun, as various verb forms, an adjective, an adverb, et cetera (e.g., *runner, run, runs, ran, running, runny*). These association files can also contain various types of memories, like personal memories (of events or sensory or emotional experiences), or previously learned ideas, concepts, objects, actions—essentially anything that can be known or imagined. Working memory also plays a crucial role in the process of creating associations. Having an extensive network of word association files is useful in many ways, as we'll discuss below.

Some of the most confusing language problems occur with children who have difficulties forming associations for specific types or classes of words. Let's briefly consider several specific classes of words that children sometimes struggle with.

Pattern Processing (Semantics): Concrete and Abstract Words

Some of the hardest words to understand are those that denote nonsensory ideas or concepts: things a child can't touch, see, hear, smell, or taste. Words like these are called *abstract words*. Abstract words include concepts like *noun* and *verb*, *love* and *hate*, *virtue* and *vice*, *democracy* and *tyranny*. Abstract words are usually defined using other words and concepts rather than physical examples. As a result, they can be especially hard to understand for children with underlying language impairments, who have difficulty understanding concepts expressed through language.

In contrast, *concrete words* are usually much easier to understand and remember. Concrete words denote things you can experience with your senses: nouns like *car, girl*, or *cat*; verbs like *run* or *eat*; adjectives like *hot* or *big;* or even adverbs like *quickly*. Even children with fairly severe language challenges can usually learn these words.

Understandably, children grow in their ability to understand abstract words as their language skills grow. For most children, this begins around age seven. Those with the most highly developed networks of word associations will have the easiest time understanding abstract words and concepts.

Pattern Processing (Semantics): Problems with Other Specific Classes of Words

Some children have difficulties understanding other types of words. In some cases, these difficulties may be caused by input or memory problems rather than language processing problems per se. For example, children who have trouble understanding sequences (whom we described in Chapter 3) will have trouble understanding *words* that describe sequence-based concepts, like *before, after, until,* or *since*. Similarly, children who have spatial processing deficits (whom we described in Chapter 4) may struggle with spatial terms like *beside, behind, next (to),* or *under*.

Other children may have difficulty remembering specific types of words because of structural problems in various brain regions. Because particular types of words are usually stored together in specific brain areas, injuries or structural problems in those brain areas may result in difficulties processing very characteristic types of words. For example, proper nouns are stored together in one region, object names in another, and action names for various kinds of processes in another. Particular parts of speech (like prepositions, relational words, or conditional words such as *before, behind, with, and*), various types of categories (like people, animals, tools, etc.), and many other specific kinds of words are also stored in local brain regions. This is one more reason a detailed evaluation by a trained language specialist is necessary for any child with language problems (see our Evaluating section below).

Pattern Processing (Semantics): A Final Comment on Semantic Skills

Having good semantic skills isn't just a matter of having lots of word files stored in your language cabinet; those files must also be extensively cross-linked with related words and concepts. Children whose word files store only single or simple word definitions and have few associations with other ideas or concepts will be overly simplistic or literal in their understandings of words. They'll have difficulty understanding multiple word meanings, inferences, allusions, metaphors, images, ambiguities, many forms of humor or irony, and literary style. For example, such a child might have difficulty understanding why another child was called "bright," since that child did not appear more "shiny" than any of her peers. We'll discuss such children in more detail below in our section on pragmatic language.

Pattern Processing: Words in Groups

The next level of language Pattern Processing contains files that store information about words in groups. Many statements or questions can be understood only if you first understand how words work on and with one another when they're used together in groups—like sentences or paragraphs. There are two basic types of interactions: those that depend on specific linguistic rules, called *grammar* or *syntax*, and those that depend on elements of vocal emphasis or tone, or literary style, and are called *pragmatics*. Let's briefly look at each.

Pattern Processing (Words in Groups): Grammar/Syntax

The specific linguistic rules that govern the interactions of words in groups are called grammar (or syntax). Figure 25 shows some examples of just a few of the many ways that grammar can affect sentence meaning and why a proper understanding of these rules is essential for comprehending sentences and paragraphs.

Children who have difficulty recognizing the grammatical patterns that affect the meanings of words in groups are at a big disadvantage when they try to understand sentences or longer language passages (discourse). Many children learn these patterns "automatically," through observation and imitation alone. Others require intensive and detailed instruction and will suffer from errors in comprehension and underachievement until they get it.

Sometimes children with milder problems understanding grammar go undiagnosed, because they function adequately in casual settings where

Word Order
- "Every morning, I have trouble waking up."
- "I have trouble waking up every morning."

Subjects and Objects
- "I gave the teacher a letter."
- "The teacher gave me a letter."

Active and Passive Voices
- "The teacher gave me a letter."
- "A letter was given to me by the teacher."

Tenses
- "I went to the store."
- "I have gone to the store."
- "I had gone to the store."
- "I go to the store."
- "I am going to the store."
- "I will go to the store."
- "I will be going to the store."
- "I will have gone to the store."

Conditionals
- "He *might* have won the game if he hadn't missed that shot."

FIGURE 25. Words in Groups, or Word Patterns That a Child Must Understand to Understand Sentences

the language used is more simple, direct, and informal and they have plenty of background cues. However, these same children may "inexplicably" struggle with tests or assignments that pose questions using complex grammar with few contextual cues (which is often the case on high-stakes, standardized tests) or that require detailed responses. Too often, these children are thought to be deficient in knowledge rather than simply unable to understand language. Over time, though, this may become a self-fulfilling prophecy, as language problems prevent them from acquiring new information. That's why early remediation is essential for these children.

Pattern Processing (Words in Groups): Pragmatic Language

The meanings of words in groups can also be affected by nongrammatical factors like word emphasis, tone of voice, rhythm of speech, language style, and word choice. These factors constitute the pragmatic aspects of language. Let's take a closer look at some of these factors.

One important aspect of speech pragmatics is word emphasis. Consider, for example, the sentence "Markus gave the car to Carol." This sentence can take on many shades of meaning, depending on how the words are emphasized:

- "*Markus* gave the car to Carol." (*Markus* was the one who gave it.)
- "Markus *gave* the car to Carol." (He didn't make her *pay* for it.)
- "Markus gave the *car* to Carol." (Not some *other* thing.)
- "Markus gave the car *to* Carol." (As opposed to getting it *from* her.)
- "Markus gave the car to *Carol*." (To *Carol*, and no one else.)

Emphasis and inflection could also be employed in various ways to form this sentence into various questions (e.g., "Markus gave the car to Carol?"). Another pragmatic factor—the tone with which these words are spoken—could further alter the meaning of the sentence, by giving the words humorous, ironic, or sarcastic meanings or conveying warmth, anger, impatience, or friendliness. Failure to recognize factors like speech tone and emphasis greatly hinders a child's ability to understand hidden meanings conveyed in sentences.

The meanings of words in groups can also depend upon the context in which the words are spoken. For example, depending upon who speaks the words and in what context, the phrase "I'm sick" could mean:

- "I have a stomachache" (from a person who's eaten too much ice cream).

- "I have a cold" (from a person with a runny nose and sore throat).
- "I have stage fright" (from a person who's about to give a speech).
- "I'm worried about my test today" (from a child who's just been told it's time to catch the bus).
- "I'm mentally ill" (from a compulsive shopper who just purchased her thirty-second pair of shoes in one week).

Pragmatic language elements are even more important in interpreting longer fragments of language (or discourse), since the meaning of each new sentence must be interpreted in light of what's come before. These factors play a growing role as a child advances through school. So do elements of literary style, such as word choice, order, and format (e.g., humorous sketch, persuasive essay, legal notice, scientific text, informal note, etc.).

Another aspect of pragmatic speech is recognizing word groups that have important nonliteral meanings, like idioms, figures of speech, poetic language, similes, and metaphors. A child who has difficulty understanding the nonliteral use of common phrases might respond to his father's request to "throw me that wrench," with disastrous results! Even when they don't result in mayhem, figures of speech like "She's a real piece of work" or "A rolling stone gathers no moss" may seem baffling or irrelevant to a child who struggles with nonliteral word meanings.

Aspects of nonverbal communication, such as facial expressions, gestures, and body language, and even the social rules that govern conversations, are often considered part of pragmatic (or social) language as well. Problems in these areas of communication are produced more by sensory input and processing difficulties than by language deficits per se, so we have discussed them extensively in other places (see Chapters 4, 5, 8, and 9). We will, however, discuss a few of the practical problems that can result from difficulties in these areas later in this chapter.

Output for Action: Retrieving Files from the Cabinet

Problems with language output (also commonly called expressive language) can be divided into three categories. These categories are analogous to the language Pattern Processing problems we've just discussed: problems with the *output of word parts*, problems with the *output of individual words*, and problems with the *output of words in groups*.

Output at the Level of Word Parts: The Clarity and Accuracy of Spoken Words

Children who have difficulties with language output at the level of word parts have difficulty pronouncing words clearly and accurately. Two kinds of problems can cause such difficulties: problems *processing* the *sound-based* (or phonological) structure of language and problems *producing* the *motor* actions with the lips, tongue, and other speech muscles that are needed to clearly *articulate* the various speech sounds. Let's look at each.

Sound-Based (Phonological) Problems with Word-Part Output

As we've already mentioned, a substantial minority of children (as many as 15 to 20 percent) have a hard time hearing the different sounds (phonemes) in words. Because they have difficulty hearing these sounds, they may also have difficulty saying them. Children with sound-based language output problems often show a wide variety of errors in pronunciation, which may reflect difficulty hearing the sound structures in words. These pronunciation errors may either be subtle (*libary* for *library*) or dramatic (*ca* for *cat*), but if they're caused by errors in sound perception, they'll usually be consistent. Figure 26 shows some of the common types of pronunciation errors made by children with difficulties in sound processing.

When evaluating children who make sound-based errors in word pronunciation, it's important to remember that the ability to hear and speak the different sounds in English is acquired over time and that there is some natural variation among children in the ages at which they acquire these abilities. Several Web sites list the normal age ranges for acquiring these different sounds, such as www.chatterboxkids.com/speech_chart.doc.

Sensorimotor-Based Articulation Problems with Word-Part Output

Pronunciation errors may also occur because of difficulties coordinating the muscles needed to produce the appropriate speech sounds. Children with such

Cluster Reductions:	*top* for *stop*
Weak Syllable Deletion:	*nana* for *banana*
Final Consonant Deletion:	*ca* for *cat*
Initial Consonant Deletion:	*at* for *cat*
Vocalization:	*caa* for *cat*
Stridency Deletion:	*at* for *sat*
Affrication:	*jo* for *doe*
Deaffrication:	*dud* for *judge*
Epenthesis:	*horsie* for *horse*
Metathesis:	*aks* for *ask*
Consonant Devoicing/Voicing:	*fan* for *van*
Stopping:	*toup* for *soup*
Fronting:	*tar* for *car*
Backing:	*go* for *doe*
Assimilation:	*peep* for *deep*

FIGURE 26. Common Patterns in Sound-Based Pronunciation Errors

difficulties may *know* what sounds they're trying to produce and *hear* them perfectly well when others say them yet be unable to coordinate their speech muscles in the ways needed to produce the sounds. These children are said to have *sensorimotor speech articulation deficits* (also called *oromotor apraxia*).

Often these children will have other oral motor problems as well. They may be generally poor eaters, dislike especially sticky or hard-to-chew foods, have poor saliva control, a flat smile, hesitating speech, poor volume control, flat or monotone voice, and impaired mouth movements. Early in life, they may have had difficulty learning to nurse. They may also have had difficulty learning to eat (e.g., a tendency to overstuff their mouths, incompletely chew their food, or have difficulty swallowing).

Distinguishing Sound-Based from Motor-Based Output Problems

Distinguishing sound-based from motor-based speech output problems is important, because these problems require different treatments. However, both problems are common and not mutually exclusive, so some children may have both. In general, there are four important features that distinguish children with sound-based pronunciation problems from those with motor-articulation difficulties.

1. Children with sound-based pronunciation problems pronounce words the way they sound to *them*. As a result, they are often blissfully unaware of their mistakes. If they ask you for a Hot Wheel by saying, "Give me the *tar*," and you reply, "You mean *car*?" they'll respond, "That's what I said: *tar*." In contrast, most children with articulation difficulties will be aware of their error and might even get angry with you for "making fun" of them.

2. Children with sound-based pronunciation errors usually don't try to correct their mistakes. They are usually content with the way they speak and see no need to change it. By contrast, children with motor-articulation difficulties pronounce words in ways that they don't intend and often try to correct their mistakes.

3. The pronunciation mistakes made by children with sound-based deficits are more consistent: Because they don't realize they are making mistakes, their words will sound the same every time. By contrast, children who realize their mistakes will often try to correct their articulation errors and will show more variability.

4. Children with sound-based deficits are usually physically capable of producing the sounds they mispronounce and often will produce those sounds in other words. Children with motor deficits show more signs of an actual physical struggle to produce certain sounds.

Output of Individual Words

Children who struggle with sound-based (phonological) word processing can also have language output problems caused by difficulties with *whole-word retrieval*. Because they have difficulty hearing word sounds, their brains can have trouble accurately filing and retrieving words, since word files are organized in the brain by sound.

Children may also have more specific whole-word retrieval problems, involving particular types of words. Brain injuries or malformations involving memory areas for particular types of words (like proper or common nouns, connecting and relational words, or other parts of speech), can cause specific word-finding difficulties.

Often children with word retrieval difficulties become "children of few words." If they have relatively good language comprehension (i.e., solid vocabulary and grammar), they may show a rather halting style of speech with frequent pauses to find the right word and an overreliance on "filler words" (like *things*, *stuff*, *junk*, or little phrases like *you know*). However, their use of grammar will be correct, and the informational content of their speech will be good.

When children struggle with both language comprehension and word retrieval, they'll typically show more extensive problems with language output. Since they have fewer word files to choose from—and the files they have contain fewer cross-references—their language output will not only be halting but vague, informationally poor, and grammatically inaccurate. The following sentences were taken from children with combined language intake and output problems:

- "I read how different dogs eat different things."
- "I liked when I went over to John's."
- "The robbers melted gold because they covered their trace."

Output of Words in Groups

Problems with the output of words in groups can cause progressively greater difficulty as children advance through school. These deficits often go unnoticed in younger children, especially those with adequate language comprehension. Younger children spend most of their time in casual family, social, or day-care settings, where incomplete sentences, imitated phrases, or sentence fragments are the norm and where everyone shares a great deal of experience and context. In situations like these, they may appear quite talkative and outgoing (though a careful analysis of their output would reveal their language restrictions). These children are often first discovered to have language problems when they have difficulty speaking with new acquaintances, with whom they may appear unexpectedly shy despite a temperament that's basically outgoing.

These children also frequently come to attention during third or fourth grade, when expressive demands increase. Their writing and speaking will show problems, including grammatical errors, like subject-object disagreements or inconsistent use of tenses; difficulty using complex constructions to convey complex ideas; poverty of detail and description; a narrow range of word choice and usage; a limited range of sentence constructions; difficulty describing relationships between ideas or facts, like relationships in meaning or time; and difficulty understanding what background information the listener or reader needs to understand their message.

As children advance through school, they should also show an increasing awareness of stylistic elements like word sounds, rhythms, and images. Look, for example, at this brief but acoustically and visually vivid sketch from Dickens:

> Oh! but he was a tight-fisted hand at the grindstone, Scrooge! a squeezing, wrenching, grasping, scraping, clutching, covetous old sinner! Hard and sharp as flint, from which no steel had ever struck out generous fire; secret, self-contained, and solitary as an oyster.

A child with output difficulties will usually try to avoid confusions in grammar and style by describing the same character using just the unvarnished kernel of thought: "Scrooge was . . . bad."

Language output skills are valuable not only for expression but also for thinking, learning, and memory. We've described the value of verbal elaboration (or the practice of putting information in your own words) as an aid to memory, learning, and understanding. Because children with poor language output skills can't effectively elaborate information, they'll have far greater difficulty with many kinds of language-based learning.

Output of Pragmatic Language

Children who have difficulties with the output of pragmatic language can have problems with any of the "nongrammatical" elements of speech we mentioned previously, like tone of voice, word emphasis, rhythm of speech, language style, and word choice. They may have difficulty conveying meanings through the tone and rhythm of their own voice; speak with an oddly flat, whining, singsong, professorial, or pedantic tone; struggle in adapting the tone and rhythm of their expression to the message being conveyed; show an overly formal, literal, inflexible, and restrictive choice of words;

have difficulty correctly using words with multiple word meanings; avoid idioms and common forms of speech; and have difficulty explaining thoughts or feelings that require imagery, analogy, or metaphor. These children require a variety of interventions, which we'll discuss in Helping.

Social and Emotional Consequences of Language Output Problems

Children with language output challenges have difficulty putting their thoughts and feelings into words, using words to resolve conflicts with others, or using words to solve personal problems. As a result, they are at special risk for social, emotional, and behavioral problems. Children with significant output difficulties may become socially isolated or become social "hangers-on" who latch on to a group and adopt its manners and mores. They may experience a heightened risk of peer-provoked behavioral problems like delinquency, drug abuse, promiscuity, and even criminal behavior. Often they have difficulties dealing with anger and frustration and may display a tendency toward "explosive" behaviors or rage attacks.

Children with output challenges specifically in the area of pragmatic language may have difficulty understanding the unspoken social rules that govern conversations, like taking turns, speaking at appropriate length (which will vary depending on listeners, topics, and settings), knowing how much to focus on themselves and their own interests, and knowing when and what types of humor are appropriate. Children with these problems are often shunned or have difficulty "fitting in" or may be ridiculed by their peers. As they move into upper elementary and middle school, they may have difficulty maintaining friendships if they lack the language skills needed to share interests, express friendship, confide secrets, tell jokes, soothe hurt feelings, pay routine compliments, or solve special problems.

Problems with Language Output Due to Nonverbal Thinking Style

Children who have nonverbal thinking and learning styles often have difficulty with spoken or written output. Most children, when they hear or read words, create both a language-based model, which organizes the information in a logical or sequential format, and a visual-spatial model, which organizes information into webs or networks of symbolic representations. They then develop their thoughts by jumping back and forth between these two models.

About one-third of children, though, seem far more skilled with visual-spatial than with verbal reasoning. These children often perceive their ideas as pictures, shapes, symbols, energies, or forces rather than words, and they may have difficulty translating their ideas into language. This type of thinking is very common among those who work in visually or spatially related fields, like scientists, mathematicians, engineers, architects, and artists (see Resources).

Albert Einstein was such a thinker. In fact, his strongly visual-spatial thinking style often made it hard for him to communicate—especially as a child. Fortunately, as he matured, he learned to "translate" his thoughts into words so others could understand. In a famous letter, he described his thinking style as follows:

> The words of the language, as they are written or spoken, do not seem to play any role in my mechanisms of thought. The physical entities which seem to serve as elements in thought are certain signs and more or less clear images which can be voluntarily combined.

Children with primarily visual-spatial or nonverbal thinking styles may find it hard to put their ideas into words. Not only do they not think primarily in words, but their thoughts are often organized spatially rather than sequentially, which can make them hard to organize into speech. They frequently describe their ideas as being present before their mind all at once—like a great stained-glass window in a cathedral, where all the scenes of the Bible are shown simultaneously—rather than in sequential order. Because they "see" so many ideas at once (and so many connections between ideas), they often have difficulty knowing where to start when putting their thoughts into words.

Despite their difficulties with verbal output, these children often develop into powerful thinkers. In addition, because they see so many connections between ideas and can think in such vivid detail, they have the potential to develop into outstanding writers, too—but only with extensive practice, patience, and guidance.

EVALUATING CHILDREN FOR
LANGUAGE CHALLENGES

Children with language challenges often go undiagnosed or are mislabeled as having attention deficits, reading disorders, autism or autism spectrum disorders, mental retardation, or as being "not very bright." Such misdiagnoses are entirely unnecessary, and they can have devastating consequences. Language problems often improve greatly with intensive therapy—especially in younger children. That's why it's crucial to carefully assess the language skills of every child who appears to have difficulty either understanding or expressing language.

All children who are strongly suspected of language problems require a thorough language evaluation by a speech-language pathologist (SLP), neuropsychologist, or other competent professional. An experienced professional not only should be able to perform standardized tests but can watch how the child behaves during the evaluation. Some children may score well on tests by using strategic approaches yet show clear signs of difficulty. This may be an indication that additional testing is needed and that the child may be in danger of falling behind as language demands continue to increase during progress through school.

Finally, all children with language processing difficulties require careful examinations of their memory, auditory, and attention systems as well, as described in Chapters 3, 5, and 7.

HELPING CHILDREN WITH
LANGUAGE CHALLENGES

It's impossible to overstate the need for intensive help in children with language problems. Language is the portal through which most of a child's education must pass, and when this portal is blocked, all parts of a child's education will suffer. We often see children with language difficulties treated as if their challenges were confined to a narrow part of their education called "language arts." This is a serious mistake. Language problems pose a threat to *all* aspects of a child's education—and to a child's entire future as well. Children with language problems struggle in every area of learning, because they have trouble understanding instructions, principles, and questions on tests. Too often, the widespread problems they experience are attributed to low intellectual potential. Unfortunately, when language problems are not addressed, this can become a self-fulfilling prophecy. Language skills are needed for many aspects of intellectual development, and when they are neglected, a child's mental growth will be greatly impeded.

When language problems are discovered, they must be treated from the roots up—not beginning at ground level. We often see children with serious language problems getting speech therapy to help them pronounce words correctly, when their problem is at the level of understanding. This is also true for reading disorders: When a child has difficulty reading because of a language disorder, it's important to aggressively treat the language problem, not just the reading problem. The ability to decode words will be of little value to a child who cannot understand them. Language as well as reading training is required.

Fortunately, many resources are available to help children with language problems, and with intensive therapy, even children who have serious language problems can make substantial progress. In the following sections, we'll discuss many steps you can take to help children with various language problems.

Improving the Language Environment for All Children

Before we discuss specific language problems, let's look at an intervention that will help all children—even those without language problems— become better language users and learners: creating a good *language environment*.

You may have noticed that our society isn't currently doing a very good job of promoting healthy language growth in children. In fact, over the last forty years children's language skills have declined significantly. Ironically, at a time when children are exposed to more talking, singing, and other word sounds than ever before, their functional language stores are being depleted. While this may seem like a paradox, the cause is not hard to understand.

Children acquire language skills by trying to understand, imitate, and interact with others. Research has shown that the encounters that best promote language growth are *interactive:* back-and-forth, face-to-face exchanges conducted in a relatively quiet background. Unfortunately, the trend in recent years has been away from this kind of language experience rather than toward it. Children who spend the bulk of their formative years receiving auditory stimulation primarily from TVs and music players, or through early group exposures in day care, may be receiving more noise stimulation than language stimulation. In fact, too much noise can actually serve as a barrier to language development and create a condition of communication deprivation.

In our practice, we often see children with language problems who have no clear evidence of specific brain injury, auditory input impairments, working memory deficits, or sound processing problems yet have nevertheless failed to develop the language skills they need to succeed in school or to communicate effectively with their parents, teachers, and peers. Often these children respond so well to focused language therapy that they seem unlikely to have been suffering from a significant brain-based deficit. Instead they appear to have been suffering from a kind of *language malnutrition.* They simply haven't received enough language "face time," especially in the home. Research suggests that the amount of interactive language a child is exposed to in the home correlates highly with the development of verbal expression and reading skills. (This does not, of course, mean that most reading disorders are caused by less-than-ideal language exposures, but rather that children will usually learn to read more easily if they've had a broad language exposure.)

To put your child on the right track for language development, make sure your home is a rich and nurturing language environment:

- Speak in complete sentences and use words with precise meanings. In our harried home lives, our speech often degenerates until it becomes telegraphic or impressionistic: *"Mom, where's that thingy— you know . . . the metal thing with the pencil sticking out of the side that I use to draw, like, circles and stuff for math?" "Oh, your* compass: *It's by the whatchamacallit—behind the junk where your brother dumps his stuff.*" Such speech may get the job done, but it will not develop a child's vocabulary or grammar. You don't need to speak as formally as if you were delivering the eulogy at a funeral, but you should try to speak with precision.

- If your child has difficulty getting her words out, don't interrupt or fill in the blanks. Patience is crucial for encouraging language development in children. Give your child time to put her thoughts into words and opportunities to practice.

- Model the richness of language for your child by adding color and variety to your own speech. Use multiple word meanings in wordplay and use different words to express the same thought.

- Spend time each day having your child describe the events of the day or particular topics or ideas. The dinner table is a natural conversation venue if you can fit it into your schedule. If not, make a special time before bed where you can exchange words and ideas in a relaxed but challenging format. Practice commenting on common "kids' topics" like movies, video games, sports, or other interests, and then move to more challenging, abstract topics. Kid Talk cards (from www.speechtx.com) or conversation-starter books like *Come to the Table* provide plenty of great ready-made ideas for discussion as well.

- Make home a place where your child feels free to take risks with language, to make mistakes, to ask questions, and to discuss complex topics she might otherwise be afraid to struggle with. But don't always wait for your child to take the lead: Make sure her skills are constantly challenged and forced to grow.

- Reading together is a great spur to language development. Often parents stop reading to their children once the children learn to read for themselves. This is a mistake. Parental reading skills are usually more advanced, so they can expose children to more advanced grammar, vocabulary, images, and ideas and demonstrate the prosodic aspects of speech. Be aware when reading to a child that he often may not ask what an unfamiliar word means. If you encounter a word you suspect is unfamiliar to your child, ask him to define it. If he can't, provide him with definitions, synonyms, antonyms, physical enactments, stories, or as many other associations as you can.

Helping with Language Pattern Processing

Now let's look at interventions for the language problems discussed above. Since helps for Information Input were discussed in Chapters 4 and 5 and helps for processing word sounds are discussed in Chapters 5 and 10, let's begin our discussion by looking at interventions that can help children who have difficulty processing individual words.

Helping Children Who Have Difficulty Processing at the Individual Word Level

Children who have difficulty processing individual word patterns can benefit from two kinds of help. First, those with too few words stored in their filing cabinets need to learn more words. Second, those whose problem is less a lack of words than a narrow, inflexible, or incomplete understanding of words need to increase the associations or "cross-references" between word files. Let's discuss strategies for each.

Filling the Filing Cabinet with More Words

Children who have too few words stored in their filing cabinets need to add word files on a word-by-word basis. Children who enter school knowing too few words may be so overwhelmed by the flood of strange sounds that they have difficulty picking out and learning new words—the "noise-to-signal" ratio is just too high. Unless they are given specific language instruction, their language development will continue to languish, with disastrous consequences for all subjects. What these children really need is a period of intensive language "boot camp" that focuses on improving their word-recognition skills to a level where they can profit from a normal classroom environment.

In our own practice, we have seen children with such difficulties progress far more rapidly when given intensive, one-on-one, multihour therapy sessions over a period of a few months than when given similar amounts of therapy stretched out over years in thirty-minute weekly sessions. Children do best when their problems are identified and treatment begins as

early as possible. In addition to formal language therapy, the following steps
will be useful:

- Expand auditory working memory to improve word learning. As we
  mentioned above, the better a child is at retaining and repeating
  words with her auditory tape loop, the better she will be at learning
  new words. In our Helping section in Chapter 3, we discuss a variety
  of ways to improve auditory memory span.
- Focus on individual words or word classes the child is having difficulty
  learning. For example, if a child has trouble remembering names for
  common objects, conduct "naming safaris" to practice naming items
  around the house, in the park, or in a store. If he has difficulty learning the names of objects, hold a scavenger hunt in which you give
  him a list of objects (or even a single object), then have him search for
  them. When he finds them, have him say the name of each object several times, then make up sentences about them. If he's old enough to
  read and write, have him write the name of the object on a card, then
  decorate the card with a picture of the object he's drawn, cut out of a
  magazine, or taken with a digital camera.

  - Children who have difficulty understanding verbs, adjectives,
    adverbs, or relational words should act out the words by playing
    Simon Says: *"Simon says run in place 'quickly'"* or *"Simon says
    show me what 'sliding' means"* or *"Simon says show me what a
    strong person is like."* Then have them describe their pantomimes
    in words. Drawing picture definitions or demonstrating meanings
    with blocks, figurines, or other models is also helpful.

- Expand your child's vocabulary by reading together. Choose books
  with short and simple sentences, on subjects the child finds
  interesting. To maintain a child's interest, it may be necessary to let
  her select the book. For the purposes of word learning, an old
  favorite that's been read before is entirely acceptable and in some
  ways preferable: Going over the same book multiple times can help
  reinforce new words and is fine as long as there are still new words
  to master. Series books are often good, because they deal with

familiar characters and settings and because they tend to employ consistent vocabularies. Don't worry if your child doesn't select Shakespeare. If *Calvin and Hobbes* is both challenging and interesting, it's a good enough place to start. Words learned reading comic strips are as valuable as any in *Hamlet*.

- *Most importantly, teach your child the habit of inquiring about any word she doesn't understand.* Teach the child to be assertive in asking for clarification on words that are new, strange, or unclear to her. Have her keep a file or list of these new words for practice. Check on her progress by asking her to define words as they come up in sentences, and define them for her if she can't. Habitual use of these practices can yield significant progress, even for children with serious language problems.

Filling the Filing Cabinet with More Word Associations

For children who need to increase the number of cross-references between existing word files, the following steps can be useful:

- Teach the child about word classes and word relationships, and help him develop the habit of looking for these. Important classes and categories include:

  - Synonyms and Antonyms: Many words have synonyms and antonyms that help explain what they're like and what they're not. The more comparative terms like these the child knows for each word, the more precise, varied, and colorful his speaking and writing will be.
  - Word Roots: Many words have recognizable roots that can be used to clarify meanings and relationships to other words. Prefixes and suffixes (like *co-*, *-able* or *-ible*, *a-* or *an-*, or *un-*) can be especially useful.
  - Categories: Examining which categories a word belongs in is a powerful way of expanding word definitions and relationships. For example, the word *mustang* belongs to many categories including: animals, cars, horses, quadrupeds, herbivores, mammals,

warm-blooded animals, forms of transportation, *m*- words, words with two syllables, et cetera. Have the child think about all the categories that a particular word might go into, whether by thinking about its physical features (e.g., size, shape, color), its functions, its word class (e.g., noun, verb, adjective), and so on. To make categorizing activities multimodal, have the child sort toys, other possessions, or household items into various categories.

- Semantic Webs: Have the child create semantic webs that use verbal and visual information to represent each kind of association. Figure 27 is an example of a semantic web for the word *great*. Note how the word *great* in the center of the web is surrounded by associations of many different kinds. Children who have difficulty remembering word associations verbally can often improve their recollection with these visual depictions of the relationships. These associations may be made even more memorable for children with word association problems if they add pictures like those in Figure 24 or create their own pictures.

- Multiple Word Meanings: One of the most useful strategies for helping children become more aware of multiple word meanings is to familiarize them with the use of idioms, like "I'm feeling mighty low," "She's shooting the lights out tonight," or "I feel like a ham sandwich." *The Scholastic Dictionary of Idioms* is a fun and interesting way for children to explore these broad and flexible word usages. Looking for puns or multiple word meanings in their own or others' speech can also be useful and a lot of fun, too. Other helpful materials to help children build word associations and analogies are available at www.criticalthinking.com.

- Figurative and Symbolic Language: Expose your child to lots of figurative and symbolic word usages. Poetry is a great source for metaphors, similes, and analogies that can broaden a child's understanding of language.

Helping Children Process Words in Groups

Children who have difficulty comprehending sentences or longer passages need intensive, carefully directed instruction. This is especially important

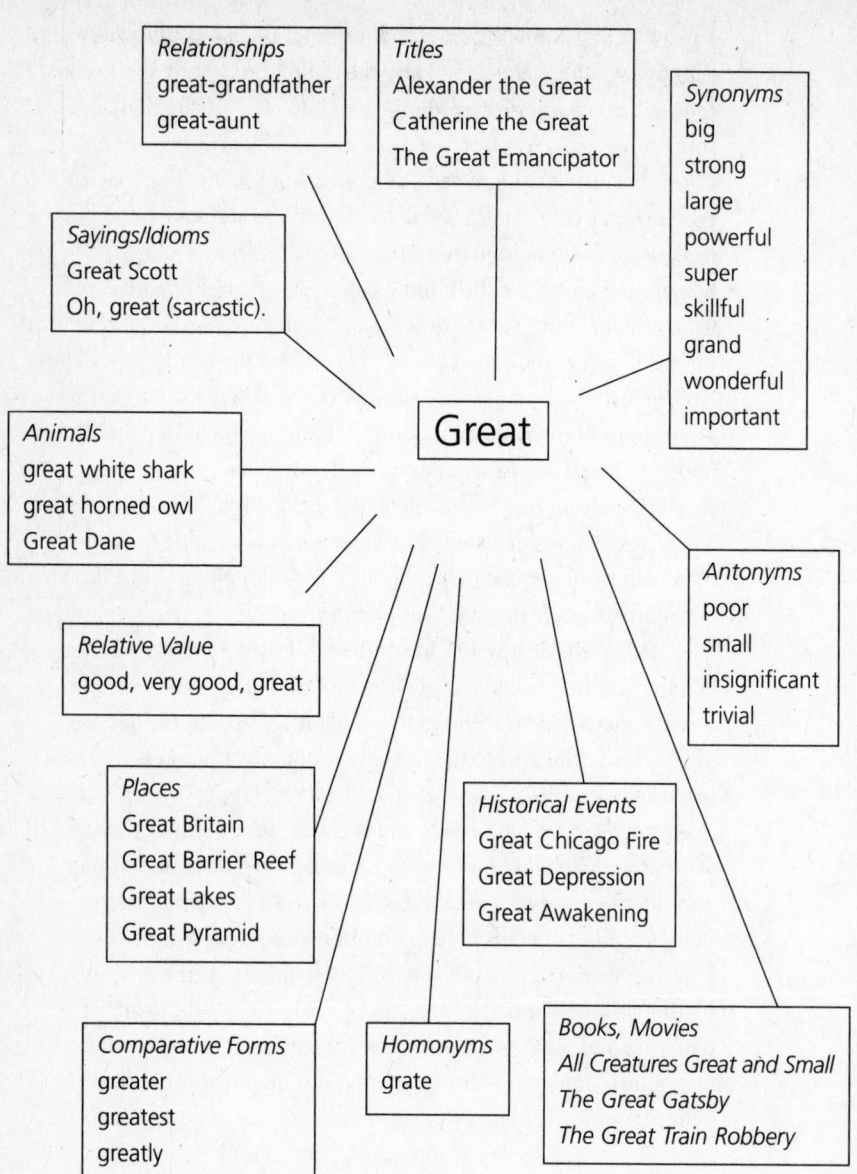

FIGURE 27. Semantic Web for the Word *Great*

by the middle elementary grades, when increasingly complex sentences begin finding their way into the curriculum.

Helping Children Who Have Difficulty
Comprehending Individual Sentences

Let's begin with strategies that can help children better understand the meanings of complex sentences. The following four sentences illustrate the kinds of complex grammar that children begin to face as they make the transition from the early to the middle grades.

1. The boy that sees the girl chases the cat.
2. The boy chases the girl that sees the cat.
3. The boy chases the girl that the cat sees.
4. The boy that the girl sees chases the cat.

The first sentence is the easiest of the four, and most children have little trouble keeping track of the fact that the first subject they encounter (the boy) is the one who does both the chasing and the seeing. The second and third sentences are harder, because they involve a "change in perspective." In the second sentence, the boy is still doing the chasing, but the girl is now seeing, so the reader has to shift her perspective of who the subject is in the middle of the sentence. The third sentence is even trickier, because the second subject (who does the seeing) is now the cat, who is the third character encountered. Still, this third sentence involves only one change in perspective, because the girl remains the object of both the chasing and the seeing. The fourth sentence, by contrast, is the trickiest of all, because it requires two changes in perspective. When we first read "The boy," we naturally begin by thinking of him as a subject but then have to switch to thinking of him as an object (of the girl's seeing); then we have to switch back to thinking of him as the subject who does the chasing. This kind of heavy grammatical lifting is just about impossible for children with significant difficulties understanding grammar.

- Children who have difficulty understanding the effects of word order and grammatical word forms on sentence meaning need intensive practice with sentence diagramming. Remember: Don't rely excessively on verbal explanations—that's the problem in the first place. Visually based approaches (like the use of color coding, arrows, or branching diagrams to connect related words) are usually far more effective. There are many resources available to help with sentence diagramming and other basic grammar skills. One that we've found especially useful for children with a strong visual-spatial orientation is the handbook *Better Sentence Structure Through Diagramming*, which is available at www.frankschaffer.com.

- Different resources will be appropriate for children with different problems, different skill levels, and different ages. A speech-language pathologist or a school resource specialist may provide a recommendation, or you can investigate materials online or at an educational supply store. You may need to try several resources or strategies to find one that "clicks" for a particular child.

Helping Children Who Have Difficulty
Comprehending Longer Passages

Children who do well at the sentence level but have difficulty comprehending language in larger doses can benefit from the following:

- Study the kinds of words that mediate the transitions between sentences, passages, or arguments. These transitional words may signal reasons, arguments, causes, or conclusions (e.g., *because, since, then,* or *therefore*); hypotheticals or conditionals (e.g., *if* or *unless*); additions (e.g., *and, plus,* or *also*); contrasts (e.g., *however* or *on the other hand*); changes in point of view or counterarguments (e.g., *but* or *however*); or various other meanings.

- Have them highlight words that tie together the clauses and sentences in longer passages, or words that indicate that an idea or argument is continuing. Do the same with words that indicate breaks or changes.
- Have them highlight the entire portion of the discourse that is affected by each transitional term. For example, if the child finds a

then or a *therefore*, ask him to highlight the clause or section that the term refers to.

- Finally, have the child draw lines connecting each transitional term that is connected within the same argument. For example, connect *if* with any relevant *then*, *since* with *therefore*, et cetera.

- Learn the following elements of basic literary analysis to help determine a passage's meaning:

  - Practice looking for the author's overall purpose or goal in any piece of writing. To tell a story? To describe a person, place, or thing? To convince or persuade? To entertain or amuse? Recognizing an author's overall intent or purpose will provide useful clues for children if they stumble at the individual sentence or word level.
  - Focus on the author's choice of words. Is it formal? Informal? Academic? Legal? Slangy? What does the word choice say about the author and what he or she considers important?
  - Look for the use of figurative language, like similes, metaphors, and idioms. Use pictures or dramatizations to help children see the point of these figures of speech. Have the child come up with her own explanations of phrases like "A stitch in time saves nine." Practice changing similes into metaphors and vice versa (e.g., change the simile "She's as good as gold" into the metaphor "She's a real treasure," or the metaphor "He's a wall" into the simile "He's as solid as a rock").
  - Look for clues that the author is trying to be humorous or ironic (like intentional over- or understatement, sentences that seem to reverse their point without warning or that seem to be arguing for something ridiculous).
  - At first, the child will need plenty of hints when engaging in such practice. Ask specifically whether this or that word sounds formal, whether this phrase is a simile or that one a metaphor, whether the author is trying to tell a story, to persuade, and so on. Gradually withdraw the prompts as the child progresses. (Use this procedure for the following items as well.)

- Children who have difficulty understanding longer passages should also practice identifying key concepts or themes in passages.

  - Children who have difficulty recognizing major ideas, concepts, and themes usually feel overwhelmed when asked to identify the big picture in a longer passage. Have the child begin by practicing on a more limited basis, using very simple stories or passages.

    - Start looking for key words and key ideas on a sentence-by-sentence basis. Have him identify and highlight the most important word or short phrase in each sentence; then look at each key word and phrase on a paragraph-by-paragraph basis, to identify the most important word or phrase in that paragraph.
    - Next use these key words and phrases to make a summary or to paraphrase the passage. It's important that the child express this summary in his own words, using complete sentences. Then go through several rounds of condensation until the child feels he has identified the key ideas and concepts in the passage.
    - Children who use primarily visual-spatial or symbolic thinking styles may prefer to use visualization approaches (like *Visualizing and Verbalizing* from Lindamood-Bell) in this process of key-idea identification, paraphrasing, and summary (see Chapter 3).
    - Many other materials can also help in this process. *The Reading Detective* (www.criticalthinking.com) is a good place to start (also see Resources).

  - Children who have difficulties with inference (i.e., finding implied meanings in texts or statements, which is a very common problem in children with language challenges) can benefit from a game called Here, Hidden, or In My Head. The child begins this game by reading a short passage (chosen by a guide) containing at least one implied meaning (from which she can draw an inference) and one direct statement. The guide then makes a statement to the child that is either a direct claim from the text, an implied message from the text, or something that is neither claimed nor implied in the text and asks the child to decide whether the statement is *here* (i.e., explicitly stated in the text), *hidden* (i.e., implied but not explicitly stated), or *in my head* (i.e., neither implied nor explicitly stated in the text but is only "in your head"). This fun form of practice can make children much better at finding implied meanings in the text.

Helping Children with Language Output for Action

As we discussed in Causes, children can have language output difficulties at the level of word parts, whole words, or words in groups. In this section, we'll discuss interventions for children with problems at each level.

Helping Children with Impaired Articulation and Pronunciation

Language output difficulties at the word-part level can be caused by deficits in the auditory word processing system or the oral sensorimotor system.

Helping Children with Sound-Based Pronunciation Problems

The most important intervention for children with sound-based pronunciation problems is providing help for their underlying sound processing difficulty. Such help is described in detail in Chapters 5 and 10.

- In addition, these children can benefit greatly from practice reading aloud with careful feedback on word pronunciation, stresses, pauses, and the music of speech. Practice with a tape recorder can also be useful.

Helping Sensorimotor-Based Articulation Problems

Children who struggle to make the movements necessary to produce speech can benefit from the following strategies:

- Practice making difficult word sounds in front of a mirror. Just as visual guidance can help a child perform difficult finger movements, it can also help coordinate the proper movements of the lips and tongue. This articulation practice can be made more fun by using tongue twisters and humorous poetry.
- Activities that build oral sensorimotor strength and coordination should also be introduced into the diet or daily routine. Helpful activities include chewing double sticks of bubble gum, sucking thick liquids (like milk shakes) through a straw, or playing blowing games with straws or whistles.
- Children with more severe articulation difficulties usually require therapy with a speech-language pathologist or appropriately trained occupational therapist. Formal speech-therapy programs often merge visual and tactile cues to help children create memories for certain sounds.

Helping Children with Impaired Output of Individual Words

Children who have difficulty with the output of individual words often display the "tip of the tongue" phenomenon: They know what they want to say, but they just can't seem to spit it out. As we mentioned above, this problem is often caused by impairments in sound processing, which hinder sound-based word filing and retrieval. The most important way to help children with sound-based word output problems is to improve their phonological processing system, as described in Chapters 5 and 10. There are other important helps as well.

- Words can be retrieved not only on the basis of sound but also through memory files that are associated with those words in other ways, like word definitions, synonyms, antonyms, categories, images, muscle movements, personal memories, or any of the other types of associations shown in Figures 24 and 27. This is what you do when you say to yourself, "Oh, what's that thing you use to hit a baseball . . . that long, thin stick you swing and it makes a *crack* when you hit the ball?" and then you put your hands together and swing. Taking advantage of all forms of memory can be a big help for children with individual word output problems.

- As you can see, the more associations a word has, the more ways there are to retrieve it. Encouraging children to expand their word associations by practicing word elaboration (as described in Chapter 3) can be a big aid in word retrieval.

- The chances of becoming stuck and not able to get a thought out also diminish when a child has many ways of saying the same thing. That's why children with individual word output problems should also be encouraged to practice using new and different words. Have them practice expressing their ideas in several different ways, and when they're redrafting their written work, have them use more vivid and descriptive words with each draft. Using a thesaurus can be helpful. In addition to print versions, a thesaurus is included on many word processing programs, or one can be found on the Internet at sites like www.visualthesaurus.com or www.thesaurus.com.

- Too often, children with word retrieval problems end up in a vicious circle where their difficulty speaking leads them to speak even less, leaving them less verbally fluent. At home, encourage children with word retrieval problems to speak more. Have them make short, impromptu speeches on topics that interest them, or, if necessary, prompt them by asking a specific question. Provoke them by taking a stance with which you know they'll disagree. For instance, if the child loves gargoyles, say, "Some people think having gargoyles on buildings is a bad idea, because they cost a lot and don't serve any purpose. What do you say?"

- Avoid the temptation of completing sentences for children with word retrieval problems. If simply waiting doesn't do the trick, prompt them with a ridiculous alternative. For example, if your child says, "I'm looking for the, uh . . . um . . . er . . . ," ask, "Hippopotamus? Space shuttle? *Mona Lisa?*" Often these prompts will trigger a giggle and "free up" the right word. Try it. It really works.

- If they remain stuck and you know what they're trying to say, give them a helpful prompt (like the beginning word sound, a rhyming word, an association [e.g., peanut butter and . . ."], a charadelike physical cue or gesture) without simply giving away the answer.

- Interestingly, recent research has also shown that the use of hand gestures can help with word retrieval. So if you have a child who's perpetually tongue-tied, have her use her hands more when she speaks (see Resources, Chapter 3).

Helping Children with Impaired Output of Words in Groups

Language output challenges due to problems with grammar can be helped using the same techniques described above for language comprehension. In addition, children with more severe difficulties desperately need intensive formal therapy provided by a specialist like a speech-language pathologist (SLP).

- Some of the best therapy options employ multimodal formats in which children form sentences using picture cards from different piles that visually represent words belonging to the different parts of speech (e.g., articles, nouns, pronouns, verbs, adjectives, adverbs, etc.). One program that employs this format is called the Fokes Sentence Builder and has been used effectively for many years. Newer computerized versions, like the Boardmaker program from Mayer-Johnson (www.mayer-johnson.com), can also be used. However, before investing in a system, it's best to have an evaluation from a qualified language therapist.
- Children whose language output problems hinder their ability to communicate effectively through writing should always use a drafting process when trying to write.

  - The first stage should be a very free-form brainstorming step where children free-associate and let their minds wander, jotting down anything that comes to mind without extensive elaboration on notecards, PowerPoint slides, or a word processing program where ideas can later be cut and pasted together. More visually or spatially oriented children may also prefer to use a visually based format like Mind-Mapping or Kidspiration (www.inspiration.com)—which are both similar to the semantic map format we discussed earlier—at this stage. Whatever format is chosen, there should be little attention paid at this point to lower-order writing features like grammar or spelling. As much working memory as possible should be devoted to getting ideas down on paper.

- Having a repertoire of "first steps" or "opening moves" available can often help unlock the floodgates of creativity. Start by making a silly, controversial, or obviously wrong statement, and then list all the reasons it might be wrong. Look at each idea that gets written down, and see what words need more explanation. Gradually build "rings" of expanding ideas without worrying about how those ideas will fit into the final disucssion.

- Next, children must ask certain stylistic questions. What are the major questions they wish to ask and answer? Will their purposes be best served by writing a narrative structured around a temporal sequence of events? Or an essay structured around a particular set of ideas? Or a persuasive argument used to support a particular point of view? Or a dialogue between two opposing points of view?

- Now that they have settled on an overall structure, they should go through all the ideas they've written down earlier and begin to organize them by asking certain questions. Are these all the major points or facts they wish to convey? Is more background needed? Are there major transitions or holes that need to be filled?

- Only when they have reached this stage and have developed a complete outline should they begin to put their thoughts into full sentences.

- Once a draft is complete, they should redraft . . . then redraft again. During the redrafting process, they should again look for "gaps," "bumps," or "holes" between ideas or words that need to be filled in until the text is "smooth." Have them read the paper out loud to look for rough spots in the wording or arguments. Is the word choice consistently formal or informal? Can more interesting sound features be added, like alliteration, assonance, rhyme, rhythm? Or interesting structural features like parallel constructions, visual or symbolic images, similes, metaphors, idioms, or humor? Encouraging experimentation, daring, and growth can yield big rewards over time.

- Sometimes parents may be overwhelmed by their child's need for writing help. If the writing challenges are truly language-based and not related to problems with the mechanical formation of letters and words (see Chapter 11 on Dysgraphia), a writing tutor can often help. Sometimes one can be arranged through school. Extra-curricular writing programs or online tutors are also available (see Resources).

Helping Children with Impaired Social/Pragmatic Language

Children with pragmatic language deficits can often benefit from instruction and modeling in social communication and interactions. We've discussed some of the steps that can help children with prosodic deficits in Chapter 5. In addition:

- The conversational skills of these children can often be greatly improved by helping them become good "questioners" who can draw others out to talk about themselves. By developing good questioning skills, these children can become valued friends and skilled conversationalists, even if they have difficulties with language output. By learning to ask the right questions, they can keep a conversation going without speaking a great deal themselves. We often recommend the book *Conversationally Speaking* by Alan Garner as a helpful conversational skills resource for persons with output difficulties. Garner shows how people can become skilled conversationalists simply by learning how to ask short how and why questions.
- Adults should teach and model nonverbal ways of showing interest in others. Have the child practice in front of a mirror, displaying appropriate signs of interest, affirmation, friendship, questioning, et cetera.
- Adults should also teach and model contextually appropriate speech. Provide explicit instruction regarding social language conventions and extensive practice in role-playing social situations.

- Various materials are available that provide specific scenarios and discussions of rules that parents (and teachers) can use to help children learn and practice social interactions (see Resources).
- Filming a child's performance in role-play scenarios, then reviewing the film together with both child and guide critiquing the performance, can be a good way to reinforce the lessons.
- Parents can also help children develop explicit rules for conversation and social interaction. For example, a child who tends to "monologue" rather than converse can be given a rule like, "First you tell me something, then ask me a question, and then I'll tell you something back." Discuss the reasons for these rules while developing them, then practice and consistently enforce them.
- A speech-language pathologist with special expertise in the specifically *social* aspects of language can also provide important help.

Helping Children with Output Problems Due to Nonverbal Thinking Styles

- Children who think primarily in nonverbal images often have difficulty expressing their thoughts in writing. They may struggle with word order, punctuation, background, continuity, and large-scale structure.

  - These children often benefit from using visual approaches to grammar and sentence organization, such as those described in books like *Image Grammar* or *Writeful* (see Resources). In the latter, for example, author Gary Hoffman suggests visual techniques like imagining a comma as a "telescopic lens" that helps readers zoom in on images. So instead of a plain sentence like "The palm sat in a container," commas provide the opportunity to zoom in for a closer look: "The palm sat in a large, white container, the branches stretching into the air." Children can use this approach to study the works of famous, image-rich writers (or speakers), then apply the language lessons learned to their own writing.

- These children can also benefit from practice using the Visualizing and Verbalizing method from Lindamood-Bell (see Resources, Chapter 3).
- For composing reports, these children often enjoy using visually based software programs like PowerPoint, because such programs allow them to set down their thoughts in largely visual format without having to worry about either words or sequence. Words can then be added and the slides arranged in appropriate order.

7

Getting It
All Together

Attention Problems in Children

Every young thing . . . is incapable of remaining calm
in body or in voice, but always seeks to move and cry:
young things leap and jump as if they were dancing
with pleasure and playing together, and emit all sorts
of cries.

—PLATO, *THE LAWS*

Nichole was a lively young eight-year-old who struck us when we
met her with her intelligence, self-confidence, and poise. She
also struck us with her occasional obstinacy, explosiveness, and
unwillingness to finish our testing! She'd previously been diagnosed with
oppositional defiant disorder (ODD) and attention deficit/hyperactivity disorder (ADHD) and was on medicines for attention and anger management.
Although she looked fairly alert when she entered our clinic, after five minutes of testing she looked completely exhausted: yawning, floppy, slumped
in her seat, and head on the desk.

. . .

Tyler was a carefree young gentleman of seven. Although he seemed eager to cooperate, he had difficulty understanding the point of many of our questions. Even when he understood what we were asking, he had a hard time organizing his responses, especially verbally. Still, he managed to remain relatively focused and compliant through two hours of testing. When it was time for him to play by himself while we talked with his parents, his activity level began to increase dramatically and soon spiraled out of control. He seemed to be energized by activity and was quite literally bouncing off the walls, furniture, floor—and us! Despite repeated requests that he "put on the brakes," Tyler seemed unable to control his physical activity.

Rachel was an adorable and lively second-grader whose parents were concerned about her attention. In school, whenever her class began reading or writing or doing math, Rachel started squirming as if someone had set her seat on fire, and began looking around the room, out the window, or anywhere but at her work.

Lucinda was an extremely bright and observant seven-year-old who began peppering us with questions and comments from the moment we met her. What style was the pottery in our office? How old was the fish in our tank? Was he a goldfish? Did we know goldfish came originally from China or that they were bred from green carp? Did our goldfish come from China? What was the name of that light thingy we were sticking in her ear? Could we see her brains? Could she look in *our* ears? And so on, for three solid hours. Yet despite her steady stream of commentary, Lucinda easily complied with the demands of our testing, which she seemed able to perform almost as an afterthought. She did remarkably well, except for a few "silly mistakes." At school, Lucinda always completed her work on time (early, in fact), and seemed to be learning well. However, Lucinda's eyes were always wandering around the classroom, and when she finished her work, she tended to wander as well, checking in on what her classmates were doing and frequently offering advice. Her teacher was concerned about Lucinda's attention.

Franklin was a friendly young man with an impish gleam in his eye. He was only in third grade but seemed well on his way to fulfilling his life's goal of becoming an astronaut—he certainly zoomed around our exam room like he was riding a rocket! Franklin had been placed on stimulants a year before for a diagnosis of ADHD. Although the doses and medicines had been changed several times, it wasn't clear to his adoptive mother that they were doing any good.

Melanie was a friendly but soft-spoken fourteen-year-old who was having increasing problems in middle school. Although she'd been an A student in elementary school, her middle-school teachers complained that she frequently drifted off to "her own world" during lectures. They often had to call on her two or three times to get her attention, and when they finally did, she typically responded with a bewildered, "Huh?" Her grades fell to C's and D's, mostly because she didn't turn in homework. When her parents investigated, they found most of her papers—completed—stuffed in wads in her backpack or locker. One thing they couldn't find was any evidence that she ever took notes during class. All her notebooks contained were a few scattered doodles of horses, dogs, and kittens.

INTRODUCTION: ATTENTION AND ADHD

Most parents who come to our Neurolearning Clinic believe their child has an attention problem. In fact, in a random sample of fifty consecutive children visiting our clinic, forty-nine had a parent or parents who thought their child had problems with attention! One thing about attention is clear: Parents are sure paying attention to it.

This interest in attention is in many respects desirable. Problems with attention can both cause learning challenges and be an important sign that other learning challenges are present. There's only one catch: Most people aren't quite sure what they mean by the term *attention*. This is true not only of parents and teachers but also of many physicians, psychologists, and educators who work with children. Like *happiness, attention* means different things to different people. Coming up with a definition that makes sense both practically and scientifically has proved surprisingly difficult.

Most parents and educators we work with use the term *attention* basically as a way of describing a child's ability to stick with schoolwork or other activities requiring sustained focus without being excessively physically active, distracted, or disruptive. In short, they see attention as a child's ability to do what he's told, when he's told, how he's told, and for as long as he's told.

Clinicians have avoided the problem of defining attention by instead defining what an absence (or deficit) of it looks like. Most use the American Psychiatric Association's (APA) diagnostic framework for attention deficit / hyperactivity disorder (ADHD), as outlined in the *Diagnostic and Statistical Manual of Mental Disorders, Fourth Edition, Text Revision (DSM-IV-TR)*. This ADHD framework is probably at least a little familiar to anyone who's had or worked with school-age children during the last two decades. In fact, it's become so familiar that many people now believe that "ADHD" is essentially synonymous with "attention problem."

In reality, there's far more to attention than ADHD—and far more to discovering how to help a child with attention problems than simply determining whether she shows a certain number of behaviors on an ADHD checklist. The practice of labeling all children who behave in certain ways as having ADHD—as if they all suffered from the same disorder and all required the same treatment—is mislabeling of the first order. Attention is not just a single function that children either have enough of or suffer from a "deficit" in. Attention is the end result of many more basic functions that work together to allow a child to "pay attention." The key to discovering how to help a child with attention problems is to look carefully at these more basic functions to see where malfunctions are occurring and how those malfunctions are contributing to the child's difficulty paying attention.

This is the same kind of "troubleshooting" approach people use to investigate the breakdowns that occur in any other complex system—like the laptop computer we're using to write this book. If our laptop malfunctioned (knock wood!), we could simply declare that it had developed "laptop deficit disorder" and apply some generic intervention for that disorder—or we could troubleshoot the problem to see which of the computer's basic systems is actually at fault, then apply a specific solution. Is the problem with the power cord? The battery? The motherboard? The screen? Did our kids stuff HoHos under the keys again? Obviously finding the right "treatment" for our laptop depends upon finding the breakdown that is causing it to fail.

Like a computer, attention is a complex system and requires troubleshooting and targeted intervention when it breaks down. That's why a diagnosis of ADHD should never be viewed as an endpoint, but only a beginning. It's not enough to know *that* a child shows ADHD-type behaviors; you need to know *why* the child shows those behaviors. Only when you know the source of a child's attention problems can you find a complete set of solutions.

Before we discuss the mechanisms underlying attention and attention problems, let's look at the behaviors commonly seen in children who have difficulty paying attention. The *DSM-IV-TR*'s list of ADHD-type behaviors provides a good (and for many people familiar) summary of behaviors often seen in children with attention problems.

BEHAVIORS ASSOCIATED WITH ATTENTION PROBLEMS

The *DSM-IV-TR* divides its list of ADHD-type behaviors into three general categories: *inattentive*, *hyperactive*, and *impulsive*. Table 4 displays the full *DSM-IV-TR* diagnostic criteria for ADHD. Let's review these categories one by one.

Inattentive-Type Behaviors

"Inattentive" basically means "doesn't pay attention." Consequently you'd expect that this category would pretty much cover the waterfront, and that's exactly what you find. "Inattentive" behaviors include problems with error checking, multitasking, forgetfulness, listening, processing auditory-verbal input, organization, sustaining attention, task persistence, and motivation. As we'll see later in this chapter, many of these behaviors are caused by problems with different aspects of the attention-control system and require specific interventions. We'll also see that each of these behaviors can be produced by various causes—not just primary attention problems (or ADHD).

TABLE 4 *Diagnostic Criteria for ADHD from the* DSM-IV-TR

(Reprinted with permission from the *Diagnostic and Statistical Manual of Mental Disorders*, Fourth Edition, Text Revision [Copyright 2000]. American Psychiatric Association.)

A. EITHER (1) OR (2):

1. Six (or more) of the following symptoms of *inattention* have persisted for at least 6 months to a degree that is maladaptive and inconsistent with developmental level:

INATTENTION
a. Often fails to give close attention to details or makes careless mistakes in schoolwork, work, or other activities.
b. Often has difficulty sustaining attention in tasks or play activities.
c. Often does not seem to listen when spoken to directly.
d. Often does not follow through on instructions and fails to finish schoolwork, chores, or duties in the workplace (not due to oppositional behavior or failure to understand instructions).
e. Often has difficulty organizing tasks and activities.
f. Often avoids, dislikes, or is reluctant to engage in tasks that require sustained mental effort (such as schoolwork or homework).
g. Often loses things necessary for tasks or activities (e.g., toys, school assignments, pencils, books, or tools).
h. Is often easily distracted by extraneous stimuli.
i. Is often forgetful in daily activities.

2. Six (or more) of the following symptoms of *hyperactivity-impulsivity* have persisted for at least 6 months to a degree that is maladaptive and inconsistent with developmental level:

TABLE 4 *(Continued)*

HYPERACTIVITY:

a. Often fidgets with hands or feet or squirms in seat.

b. Often leaves seat in classroom or in other situations in which remaining seated is expected.

c. Often runs about or climbs excessively in situations in which it is inappropriate (in adolescents or adults, may be limited to subjective feelings of restlessness).

d. Often has difficulty playing or engaging in leisure activities quietly.

e. Is often "on the go" or often acts as if "driven by a motor."

f. Often talks "excessively."

IMPULSIVITY:

g. Often blurts out answers before questions have been completed.

h. Often has difficulty awaiting turn.

i. Often interrupts or intrudes on others (e.g., butts into conversations or games).

B. Some hyperactive-impulsive or inattentive symptoms that caused impairment were present before age 7 years.

C. Some impairment from symptoms is present in two or more settings (e.g., at school [or work] and at home).

D. There must be clear evidence of clinically significant impairment in social, academic, or occupational functioning.

E. The symptoms do not occur exclusively during the course of a Pervasive Developmental Disorder, Schizophrenia, or other Psychotic Disorder and are not better accounted for by another mental disorder (e.g., Mood Disorder, Anxiety Disorder, Dissociative Disorder, or a Personality Disorder).

Hyperactive-Type Behaviors

The *DSM-IV-TR's* list of hyperactive-type behaviors is similarly varied. As you can see in Table 4, they range from relatively mild behaviors like fidgeting, squirming, a preference for standing over sitting, or "excessive" talking to more dramatic behaviors like inappropriate running and jumping and compulsive or "driven" motor activity. The breadth of these behaviors can create confusion about what constitutes abnormal motor activity in children and what to do about it. Several points require clarification:

- Hyperactivity is not a new phenomenon, as indicated by our quote from Plato at the beginning of the chapter. Children have been wiggly and squirmy for as long as there have been children. However, over the last several decades there does seem to have been a rise in more extreme types of hyperactive, impulsive, and oppositional-type behaviors in younger children. (We'll discuss some of the potential reasons for this shortly.) The best studies indicate that 1 to 2 percent of children (mostly boys) engage in behaviors so extreme and pervasive that they create a severe impediment to learning and behavior in essentially every environment. These children are hard to care for at home, have a difficult time interacting with other children, and are extremely difficult to manage in the classroom.
- For such children, excessive physical activity clearly does represent a severe impairment, because it prevents them from achieving their goals or interacting productively with their environment. However, many other children show "excess" motor activity that does not interfere significantly with their learning. In our practice, we often see children who wiggle like the proverbial can of worms or prefer standing while working to sitting but have no clear attention problem. "Excess" motor activity can have many causes besides attention problems. Sometimes these causes may require specific interventions—like problems with sensory processing (see below), sleep, energy, mental excitement or boredom connected with giftedness, anxiety (often as a result of problems arising from learning disorders), or inadequate training in impulse inhibition.

However, some children just seem to think and focus better when they're moving. (This relates to what we said in Chapter 6 about the relationship between hand motions and word recall.) Providing these children with some space to swing their legs, chew gum, stand as opposed to sit, rock in their seat, or even occasionally pace can help them feel comfortable and more focused in the classroom.

- One group of physically active children needs a little extra explanation. Children with a condition called *sensory processing disorder* (which we'll discuss in Chapter 9) often engage in sensory-seeking behaviors (such as fidgeting and squirming, standing from their seat, or even rough play like jumping from heights or rolling on the ground) because their body requires extra sensory stimulation to feel oriented, alert, and comfortable. Children with sensory processing disorder often perform motor activities to improve their attention and increase their level of alertness. Pursued appropriately, these behaviors actually improve focus. Often these children require special accommodations for motor activities.

- It's also important to realize that there are enormous natural variations in the rates and ways in which children develop, both physically and emotionally. Some children are ready for the highly structured, basically sedentary, auditory-intensive demands of the classroom quite early on, while others (especially boys) develop these abilities more slowly. It's important not to mislabel children who are simply developing in a way that is quite normal but is not ideally suited for the educational structures we have created as having fundamental deficits in attention.

- It's also important to determine whether a child's environment is contributing to the functional impairment caused by ADHD-type behaviors. Frequently it's the mismatch between the environment and the child's behaviors—not simply the behaviors themselves—that cause learning problems. Studies have shown that approximately half of all children who qualify for the ADHD diagnosis based on hyperactive and impulsive behaviors do not have any clinically significant impairment in function either at home or at school. If behaviors alone were responsible for learning problems, we'd expect to find that all children who showed ADHD-type behaviors were significantly impaired. That's why it's so important to determine whether the child's environment might be contributing to his problems and not simply assuming that the child is the source of all the problems.

Impulsive-Type Behaviors

Impulsivity is the tendency to "leap before you look." Impulsive children often act before establishing goals, identifying alternatives, assessing possible consequences and relevant rules of conduct, and planning out strategies.

While children naturally vary greatly in the ease with which they can be taught to exercise self-control, available research clearly shows that there's a strong learned component to impulse control. All of us begin life unable to control our impulses, and we acquire this ability only gradually, through consistent, clear, and patient training. Impulse control is not something most children "pick up" by hanging out with the other kids at the playground or in day care. Quite the opposite! Yet many popular parenting approaches downplay or even deny the need for this essential form of attention training. Too often, we see children who've been placed on medicines to control impulsivity but have never received the training they need to control their own behavior. Practice can greatly increase a child's resistance to impulsivity and his ability to delay gratification, just as it can increase resistance to sensory distractions. As an example, in studies with children the ability to delay gratification (which is a sign of impulse control) was increased when students practiced ignoring recordings that tempted them to quit working and go out and play.

CAUSES OF ATTENTION PROBLEMS IN CHILDREN

Attention is not the product of a single brain structure or function but rather of *a whole network of brain functions*, requiring the coordinated actions of structures throughout the brain. We have divided the *attention-control functions* that help children pay attention into three major categories and have given each category a symbol to represent its functions.

The first category contains functions that help us focus our attention.

These functions are represented by the symbol of the *Spotlight*. The second category contains working memory functions that help us keep information in mind. These functions are represented by the symbol of the *Juggler*, because they help us "keep lots of balls in the air" at once. The third category contains functions that help us plan and implement actions. These functions are represented by the symbol of the *Creative Corporation*, which is a partnership between a Chief Operations Officer and a Chief Creativity Officer.

Problems with the functions in any of these categories can cause difficulties paying attention. Attention problems can also result from difficulties with a number of basic factors that are needed to "lay the foundation" for attention. We call these factors *the Foundation Builders*.

In the following sections, we'll consider each of these categories of attention-control functions and attention supports. Let's start with the Foundation Builders.

Laying the Foundation: The Foundation Builders

While not attention functions per se, the factors in this category provide the physical and mental foundations that a child needs to pay attention. If these Foundation Builders fail to do their jobs, the whole attentional structure will come crashing to the ground. Table 5 shows each member of the foundation-building team, divided into two categories: those that provide physical and neurological preparation and those that provide psychological preparation. Let's consider each category in turn.

Physical and Neurological Preparation

It's essential to remember the crucial role that the body plays in allowing and preparing the brain to do its tasks. In this section, we'll review the many physical and neurological factors that can affect a child's attention.

Sleep/Alertness/Mental Energy

A well-rested and alert mind is the cornerstone of attention's foundation. Unfortunately, as many as one quarter of children diagnosed with ADHD

TABLE 5 *Attention's Foundation Builders*

PHYSICAL AND NEUROLOGICAL PREPARATION
- Sleep/alertness/mental energy.
- Auditory and visual processing functions/impairments.
- Learning disorders and learning styles.
- Sensorimotor issues.
- Diet and metabolism.
- Chronic medical illnesses.
- Other significant neurological impairments.

PSYCHOLOGICAL PREPARATION
- Home environment.
- School environment.
- Temperament.
- Anxiety.
- Depression.
- Substance abuse.
- Major psychiatric diagnoses.

---

may have sleep disorders such as *frequent periodic leg movements of sleep* (FPLMS) or *obstructive sleep apnea.* Sleep disorders often cause daytime drowsiness, marked irregularity in bedtime, difficulty falling asleep, disordered nighttime breathing, snoring, or leg kicking during sleep. Nichole, whom we mentioned at the start of this chapter, was exhausted during our testing because she had severe obstructive sleep apnea, due to a floppy upper airway. After being given a CPAP (continuous positive airway pressure) breathing machine for use at night, she no longer met criteria for attentional impairment, and her medications were stopped.

Unlike Nichole, some children with sleep disorders don't always look or even feel sleepy. Sometimes they may complain that they're just too tired to think. Thinking really does consume tremendous amounts of energy, and children who sleep poorly may not have enough for the job. This complaint can be confusing, though, because such children may actually increase their physical activity to keep from falling asleep.

Auditory and Visual Processing

Children with significant auditory or visual processing disorders may lose interest in material they have difficulty processing and become restless, inattentive, fidgety, or distractible. It's important to determine whether their attention problems occur primarily during activities that place heavy demands on their dysfunctional processing system or whether they occur across the board. Rachel was a typical example of a child whose attention problems showed up only during tasks that involved extensive visual processing. In young boys especially, auditory working memory limitations are a common problem (see Chapter 5).

Learning Challenges and Learning Styles

Learning challenges and learning styles have a complex relationship to attention problems. Some studies have found that over half of all children given the ADHD diagnosis have learning challenges such as dyslexia, dysgraphia, dyscalculia, or language disorders. Attention problems can aggravate any learning challenge, but some learning challenges can make children show ADHD-type behaviors even in the absence of attention problems. That's why it's important to determine whether a child's attention problems show up only during reading, writing, math, or language-heavy tasks or across the board. Task-specific attention problems are more likely due to learning or sensory processing problems than to primary attentional impairments, though language disorders can cause more broad-based impairments. Tyler, for example, had significant difficulties with both language input and output that made it hard for him to attend to essentially all classroom tasks. (Tyler also had a history of head trauma, as we'll mention below.)

Certain learning styles can also make children look as if they have attention problems, particularly if their learning style is not accommodated in the classroom. Highly gifted children often appear inattentive or restless if not adequately challenged (see Chapter 13). So do children with strongly visual-spatial or nonverbal learning styles. The latter children may also show problems with organization, task initiation, flexibility, diminished interest in class activities, delayed responses to questions, and strongly independent approaches to learning that can make them appear inattentive to the activities of the class.

Sensory Processing Disorder

Children with sensory processing disorder often show sensory-seeking or sensory-sensitivity problems that can either mimic attention problems or really cause attention problems. They may show sensory distractibility, intrusive sensory-seeking behaviors, or sensory overload. We'll discuss this disorder, and its relation to ADHD, in more detail in Chapter 9.

Diet and Metabolism

Despite many claims and anecdotal reports, there is no convincing evidence that particular supplements or diets (including allergy-testing and elimination diets) produce benefits for most children with attention problems *as a group*. However, individual children often show important behavioral differences in response to particular foods, like sugars or dairy products. Parental observation has been shown to be a fairly reliable means of determining food sensitivities, so parents should watch children carefully for signs of diet-related behavioral change. There is also some recent evidence that attention can be improved in children with motor-coordination problems by the use of fish oil supplements.

Medical problems like thyroid abnormalities, anemia, and lead poisoning (more common in children living in houses built before 1965) can also produce symptoms of inattention. While allergies and asthma are often cited in books and Web sites on ADHD as causes of attention problems, there is little solid evidence to show that these very common health issues actually cause problems with attention, except during severe allergy or asthma flares. High-dose allergy or asthma medicines can sometimes diminish attention, though newer medicines generally have fewer and milder effects.

Neurological Disorders

Subtle *seizures* are a surprisingly common cause of attention problems in younger children. In fact, up to 5 percent of children under age ten will have occasional seizures. In many, these events go undetected. Two types of seizures are especially important:

- *Absence seizures*, which cause a child to briefly lose awareness. Although they may cause fluttering of the eyelids, they usually cause no clear signs of seizure like shaking, loss of posture, or loss of balance.
- *Partial seizures*, which produce abnormal electrical activity in one particular part of the brain.

Children with both types of seizures may "zone out" for as little as a few seconds or for several minutes at a time. Typically they have no memory of their seizures but may appear "off topic" or repeat themselves when coming out of a seizure or have a period of postseizure confusion or forgetfulness that may last from minutes to hours. In our own clinic, we find unexpected seizures in about 5 percent of the children we see. In many of these children, the seizures occur throughout the day but in very short bursts (less than two or three seconds, and often less than one)—in other words, often enough to significantly impair a child's focus and learning.

Tourette's syndrome is another relatively common neurological disorder that can impair attention. The most obvious features of this disorder are the characteristic tics, which may be physical (grimacing, jerking, blinking) or vocal (throat clearings, grunts, animal noises, or even whole words or phrases).

Structural brain injuries or malformations can also undermine the foundations for attention. Brain injuries caused by ministrokes during gestation or delivery are much more common than often thought, especially in children born prematurely, at low birth weight, or after prolonged or complicated deliveries. When they involve the frontal lobes, cerebellum, or other important brain structures, they may cause impaired attention. The same holds true for traumatic brain injuries in young children. Tyler was a typical example: His problems with inattention and language began after he was hit in the head by a baseball bat while playing with some friends, suffering a depressed skull fracture. Prenatal brain injuries from maternal substance abuse with cocaine, methamphetamine, or alcohol can also impair attention. Franklin, for example, was born prematurely to a teenage mother who abused methamphetamine (the same medicine in the stimulant Ritalin that's often used to treat ADHD) and alcohol throughout pregnancy. Children with structural or drug-related brain impairments often respond less well to stimulant medications for behavioral control than children with other types of attention problems.

Psychological Preparation

To enjoy psychological and emotional health, a child must be free of major stressors, both without and within. Environment, experience, and genetics each help to build a solid psychological foundation for attention.

Environmental Factors

Several environmental factors play an especially important role in producing or worsening attentional impairments:

- Inappropriate or unrealistic expectations. When adults demand more of a child than the child is capable of delivering, the anxiety produced may result in inattentive or hyperactive behaviors. Often this is a sign of an underlying learning disorder.
- Stress at home. Children are barometers of their environment. Attention problems at school may indicate problems at home, like physical or mental illness, death of a loved one, family conflict, change of household, neglect or abuse, or even poor parenting practices.
- Stress at school. Student-teacher or student-student conflicts may cause ADHD-type behaviors, as can inadequate stimulation (for gifted or novelty-seeking children) or learning styles that are not properly addressed.

Anxiety, Depression, Conduct Disorders, Substance Abuse, and Other Psychiatric Disorders

The relationships between attention problems and psychological disorders like anxiety, depression, oppositional defiant disorder, conduct disorder, and substance abuse are complex. Each of these disorders is present at higher rates in children diagnosed with ADHD. However, these other disorders may also disrupt attention, even in children without a history of ADHD. Any child suspected of one of these serious disorders requires a comprehensive evaluation from a qualified mental-health professional, like a psychiatrist or clinical psychologist. Urgent psychiatric evaluation is essential for any child who appears to have problems with violent or frankly delusional behavior. While rare, psychotic disorders are possible in children and will sometimes present with extreme impulsivity and motor activity.

THE ATTENTION-CONTROL FUNCTIONS

Once the Builders have laid the foundation, the true *attention-control functions* can do their jobs. As we mentioned above, we divide these functions into three main categories: functions that help us *focus* attention (the *Spotlight*); *working memory* functions that help us *keep things in mind* (the *Juggler*); and functions that help us *plan and implement tasks* (the *Creative Corporation*). Let's consider each in order.

Category I: Focusing Attention (the Spotlight)

The attention-control functions in this group work together to "spotlight" or focus attention on particular objects and to control the quality and effectiveness of that focus. There are three main Spotlight functions (as shown in Table 6), each of which also begins with an S: *selective attention, sustained attention*, and *stimulated attention*.

TABLE 6 *The Spotlight's 3 S Functions*

- **Selective Attention:**   **What to focus on.**
- **Sustained Attention:**   **How long to focus on it.**
- **Stimulated Attention:**   **How brightly to illuminate it.**

Selective Attention: What to Focus On

Selective attention determines what a child's attentional Spotlight will focus on. At each moment, enormous numbers of stimuli in a child's environment, body, and mind all clamor for her attention. Before she can productively focus on any of these, her Spotlight must first choose what to illuminate and what to leave in the dark. This requires a delicate balancing act. On the one hand, the Spotlight must be sensitive enough to focusing on new and unexpected stimuli that it doesn't miss important items. On the other hand, it must exclude enough irrelevant and potentially distracting stimuli so that the child can focus effectively. To accomplish this difficult balancing act, a child's selective attention system must be able to quickly scan through everything that's presented to it and decide what deserves more careful illumination and what should be ignored. For most children, this selection process occurs largely below the level of consciousness, so that the child remains unaware of most stimuli clamoring for her attention.

In contrast, a child with a weak selective attention system will have difficulty automatically distinguishing between important and irrelevant stimuli. As a result, his Spotlight is as likely to focus on unimportant objects as important ones, and he will have difficulty preventing irrelevant stimuli from crowding his conscious attention. Because his attentional focus is constantly diverted by one intriguing distraction after another, such a child is said to be distractible.

Often—though not always—distractible children will suffer from their problems with selective attention. However, even a very distractible child may suffer no real consequences from distractibility if he shows good task persistence and returns to what he was doing before without needing to be reminded (see "Sustained Attention," next section). In fact, in children who are highly persistent, distractibility may actually be a strength. Distractible but persistent children are typically observant and sensitive and are frequently creative and intellectually "gifted" (see Chapter 13). Lucinda was just such a child. Although her Spotlight constantly jumped from one thing to another, it returned quickly to where it was shining before. As a result, she not only showed few ill consequences of her distractibility but she was also an excellent incidental learner, picking up every piece of new information that came her way. This is why it's important not to view distractibility itself as a problem, unless it produces a significant functional impairment.

One final point: Distractibility represents a balance between selective attention and sensitivity to sensation. Children with sensory impairments often have such strong sensitivities in certain areas that they literally overwhelm their selection mechanisms, even if their selective attention is normal for most tasks. For example, children with auditory processing problems often struggle with visual distractibility, because they "rewire" their visual fields to be more sensitive to movement at the edges of vision rather than in the center. From a protective standpoint, this rewiring is beneficial: If you can't hear what's approaching you, increasing your peripheral visual sensitivity may help you better see what's approaching. Unfortunately, it can also pull your eyes away from the teacher who's standing in front of you. Auditory distractibility in visually impaired children works in a similar fashion. (For more on visual and auditory distractibility, see Chapters 4 and 5.)

Sustained Attention: How Long to Focus on It

Sustained attention determines how long a child's attentional Spotlight will shine or focus on a particular object. Children with impaired sustained attention have difficulty knowing how long to shine their Spotlight on various objects. As a result, they may show either or both of two seemingly opposite problems: They may shine too briefly on objects to sufficiently illuminate them, or they may shine longer than they need to on objects that don't deserve such scrutiny. These problems can cause difficulty taking in new information, completing work, and persisting with tasks.

When evaluating a particular child's sustained attention, it's important to realize that there are large natural variations in the ways children prefer to use their Spotlights. Some children learn best when shifting their Spotlight rapidly from one object to another, preferring multiple quick views to a few deep and steady ones. Often these children are born multitaskers. They are more at home in a fast-moving, constantly changing environment with a dozen projects going at once than they are in the relatively slow-moving classroom, where they are expected to shine their Spotlight in one place for a long time.

We sometimes see this "frequent-burst" pattern of sustained attention in children with birth injuries or autism-like syndromes. Often these children seem better able to open up their learning and memory channels by "tricking" their brains into perceiving a piece of information as "new," by continually turning their Spotlight away from it, then turning back to it again. For example, such a child might try to learn to read a new word by walking away from his book and around the room but returning on several occasions to view the word again over the course of a few minutes. As challenging as it can be to accommodate this learning style, it can make a big difference for some children.

This raises an important question: whether such a sustained attention pattern truly represents a learning problem or is simply a different learning style. In general, if a child is able to make progress with work and learning—even in fits and starts—he should probably be considered to have a variation in sustained attention rather than an actual impairment; if, however, she's constantly falling behind with her work and is unable to bring her projects to completion, it's an impairment.

One final point about sustained attention: Recent research has shown that sustained attention depends heavily on a child's sense of reward and motivation. Children with the best task persistence, especially for tasks that aren't particularly interesting, are better able to activate the "reward centers" in their brains—that is, they're able to stimulate their own attention. Children who lack this ability are much more dependent upon the task itself to hold their interest. This brings us to our next subject: stimulated attention.

Stimulated Attention: How Brightly to Illuminate It

Stimulated attention determines how "brightly" a child's attentional Spotlight will shine on some object. Children with impaired stimulated attention can't seem to find the necessary interest, enthusiasm, or motivation to engage productively in many tasks. Their Spotlight only flickers faintly across objects, yielding vague and partial impressions, which keeps these children from paying full attention. Unless the object itself is unusually "bright" (i.e., interesting and stimulating), it will fail to hold their focus.

Not all children who appear uninterested or unenthusiastic about school have impairments in stimulated attention. Children with learning challenges may be unable to maintain attention on tasks they find excessively hard and confusing. Conversely, children who find the level of instruction in a class beneath their ability may be bored by the repetition and slow pace. Finally, some children may feel that certain subjects have no direct relevance to their personal goals and interests and are not worth the effort needed to master them.

Of course, all children occasionally find some school tasks difficult, repetitious, or lacking in direct relevance to their future. Yet they usually muddle through because they're motivated by the indirect relevance of school success to their future: "If I don't finish this report, my mom will kill me!" "If I don't study for that test, I'll get an F, and everyone will think I'm an idiot." "If I don't turn in that paper, Mrs. Harriman will be disappointed in me." "If I don't get straight A's, it's good-bye, scholarship." For children with impaired stimulated attention, factors like these are insufficiently motivating to get them to pay attention and do their work.

This brings us back to the point we raised at the end of the last section: The intensity with which a child shines her attentional Spotlight on an object is closely related to issues of motivation and reward. Children are much more likely to "shine brightly" on tasks they find rewarding than on ones they don't. Two types of rewards can stimulate a child's attention: *intrinsic rewards* and *extrinsic rewards*.

- Intrinsic (or internal) rewards are rewards a child gets from doing tasks she enjoys for their own sake. They are the feelings of satisfaction or pleasure she receives because she finds these tasks interesting, enjoyable, challenging, or otherwise worthwhile.
- Extrinsic (or external) rewards are rewards a child gets for doing tasks from some outside source, like other people. Extrinsic rewards include money, treats, privileges, or emotional strokes.

Both intrinsic and extrinsic rewards have a place in education. In an ideal world, every child would be motivated by the intrinsic joy of learning and the love of discovery. This, you will not be shocked to learn, is not the world we inhabit. Almost all children require extrinsic rewards (like grades, threats of punishment, fear of shame, desire for esteem, etc.) at least some of the time. Children who have difficulties with stimulated attention often require more enticing motivators—at least initially. Through the careful use of extrinsic rewards, children with too little stimulated attention can often be motivated to learn more effectively.

It's also important to think creatively about the ways *intrinsic* rewards can be used to motivate these children. Almost all children have some interest that they find motivating for its own sake. Finding ways to use this "favorite thing" or things to motivate them to tackle important learning tasks can be a key to promoting their education. For example, allowing children to do reports or assignments on a slightly off-topic personal interest may give them the extra motivation they need to get some work done.

There's one other pattern of stimulated attention we should consider. Some children have Spotlights that seem to shine most brightly on particularly new (or novel) stimuli. Their tendency to focus primarily on "novel" forms of stimulation can be a weakness or a strength, depending upon the rest of their neuropsychological framework and upon environmental factors as well. However, novelty seeking is not an abnormal brain condition; it is a naturally occurring learning pathway in the brain.

Children who are primarily oriented toward new or novel stimuli are especially skilled at noticing differences or changes in the environment. They are also often natural tinkerers or "tweakers" who are constantly looking for ways to make things better. In fact, many young novelty seekers are highly creative and self-directed learners—in other words, a kind of learner we should be trying to encourage. Often these children are highly motivated to pursue learning in their areas of interest—but in their own ways—and they may bristle when the things they're doing in the structured classroom environment don't seem so novel anymore.

Finding the best educational environment for such children can be a challenge, but it can be helpful to realize that the areas of the brain that are activated by novelty are closely related to areas geared toward insight or inductive learning, rather than deductive learning. Inductive approaches start with particular facts or embodiments of ideas, then work back from these to discover general principles. For children who favor inductive learning, hands-on or discovery-based approaches may be a more "natural" way of learning than conventional auditory-verbal instruction.

Unfortunately, some children seem to require so much novelty and stimulation to hold their interest that their focus is unable to be fixed by all but the most extreme forms of stimulation. These children really do have a problem with stimulated attention. Some experts call this problem *insatiability*. Insatiable children constantly seek out intense and thrilling (and often dangerous) activities for the rush of stimulation that only they seem able to provide. They're always looking for the next big thrill and are rarely able to finish or even fully attend to the task at hand. These children may be able to focus on sufficiently stimulating activities (like video-game playing) for hours on end but are often hard to engage in the classroom, regardless of the lesson plan.

Category II: Working Memory (The Juggler)

Our second major attention-control function is working memory. Because of working memory's great importance, we've chosen to give it its own section, though many experts consider it to be one of the brain's "executive functions" (which we'll discuss in the next section). We've chosen to represent working memory with the symbol of the Juggler, because working memory helps us "juggle" lots of information at once.

We've already discussed working memory in detail in Chapter 3, so we won't repeat all that information here. In this section, we'll focus instead on a few points that highlight the role of working memory in attention.

Working memory is a crucial but often underappreciated aspect of the brain's attention system. In addition to helping us rehearse and encode information coming in from the senses, working memory also aids in recall and reflection and provides other brain functions the time and space they need to perform complex operations. We can reason, reflect, imagine, infer, solve problems, create and critique plans, acquire new information, speak and write sentences and stories, and comprehend written or spoken language only if our working memory capacity is large enough to hold all the information we must simultaneously process.

Limitations in working memory capacity are very common in children with attention problems. Typically children with working memory deficits show inattentive-type behaviors like those listed in Table 4, including "careless mistakes," failure to listen (or "in one ear and out the other" forgetfulness), failure to follow instructions, difficulty with organization, a tendency to lose things, and forgetfulness. They also usually have problems with the "executive function" tasks overseen by the brain's "Chief Operations Officer," which we'll describe in the next section. Auditory, visual-spatial, and kinesthetic working memory may be particularly affected, while other aspects of working memory are spared. (Remember: Problems with sensory input [i.e., seeing or hearing] may also masquerade as working memory problems, so it's important to check for these, too.)

Children who experience attention problems due to limitations in working memory capacity need a regular program of intervention to help improve their working memory function. Fortunately, there are some exciting interventions on the horizon that can help them do precisely that. (For more information, see the sections that deal with how to optimize working memory performance in Helping, Chapter 3.)

Category III: Planning and Acting (The Creative Corporation)

Our third major set of attention-control functions helps us conceive new ideas, plan their implementation, and oversee their execution. Together, these functions create a powerful mixture of flexibility and discipline that lets us both imagine the possible and determine the practical. In short, they create an ideal partnership of creativity and structure that any organization must have to function successfully. That's why they're often called executive functions. It's also why we've chosen as their symbol the Creative Corporation. As you'll see in this section, the Creative Corporation is an ideal pairing of two very different executives, who bring together two very different sets of executive skills to create the perfect organizational partnership.

Executive #1: The Chief Creativity Officer (Creating and Conceiving)

Our first executive plays a crucial role in the life of our corporation, though his job description is rather limited. We call him the Chief Creativity Officer, and his job is basically to act as the corporation's "idea guy." He sits in his office (primarily in the brain's right frontal lobe) and essentially brainstorms all day—that is, when he's not just dreaming or playing wastepaper basketball! His role is to generate alternative goals or approaches, to expand the realm of possibilities, and to combine ideas, sensations, and images in new and creative ways. Although he can sometimes seem like a bit of a slacker, he's recognized around the corporation as the creative "talent," and he's generally considered to be worth every penny he's paid, because he's got "that vision thing" in spades. Whenever the corporation faces a new challenge or an unexpected complication in one of its plans, he's the guy they look to for potential solutions. His primary focus is on the "big picture" rather than the "bottom line" and on the possible rather than the practical or realistic. He's always got a million new things he'd like to try and a thousand ways of doing each one of them. Most of his sentences start with, "Wouldn't it be cool if . . ." Problem is, he's a little bit sketchy about exactly how he's going to carry out any of his ideas. Those are the details he leaves to his partner.

Some children have trouble getting the best from their Chief Creativity Officer. As a result, they have difficulty developing alternative concepts or creative ideas and find it hard to engage in the kind of flexible thinking that's necessary to develop alternatives. They're often rather rigid or concrete in their thinking. Some may even seem unwilling to consider more than one potential strategy for their actions.

For other children, it's just the opposite. We often see children who are identified as having attention problems who have an extremely dynamic Chief Creativity Officer but a relatively inactive Chief Operations Officer (see below). This was part of Lucinda's challenge. With children like this, the goal should be not to blunt or tone down the Creativity Officer but to strengthen the Operations Officer (see next section).

Executive #2: The Chief Operations Officer (Planning and Implementing)

Our second executive is the Chief Operations Officer. The Chief Operations Officer is the corporation's practical manager. She's the highly organized—and rather compulsive—"suit" who's responsible for making sure all the trains run on time and for overseeing and harnessing the somewhat scattered energy of the Chief Creativity Officer.

The Chief Operations Officer has a more complex job description than her creative colleague. She oversees a group of functions (located primarily in the brain's left frontal lobe) that are responsible for most of the brain's detailed planning and implementation. Let's consider these planning and implementation functions separately.

Functions of the Chief Operations Officer: Planning Phase

To plan an action, the Chief Operations Officer must perform five crucial functions.

- Step one is to analyze and prioritize the goals of the action. After the Creativity Officer has submitted a list of possible actions, the Operations Officer must decide which to implement and in what order. She must determine what the proposed actions would achieve if successful and whether such success would promote the company's long-term goals. As the old saying goes, "If you aim at nothing, you're sure to hit it." Actions begun without clear goals in mind are literally aimless and unlikely to be productive.
- Step two is to perform a cost (or risk)/ benefit analysis. Even strategies that achieve their intended goals can be losers if the costs of "success" are too high. The Operations Officer must consider not only the potential benefits of an action but also its potential consequences.
- Step three is to consult the lawyers. Before acting, the Operations Officer must run all plans by the corporate legal office to determine whether a considered action will violate any rules. Potential action: *Take candy from classmate's backpack*. Relevant rule: *Taking without asking is stealing*. (Obviously it is important to make sure that the company's "lawyers" have actually been taught the law! Such knowledge is largely learned, not innate.)
- Step four is to refrain from hasty, unplanned, or impulsive actions. There's a constant tension between the Chief Creativity Officer, who's always eager to give his ideas a try, and the Operations Officer, who wants to make sure "all the ducks are in a row" before beginning a project. Children who have difficulty waiting until they've fully formed and vetted their plans are impulsive. Improving a child's ability to restrain impulses can pay long-term dividends. Studies of preschoolers have shown that the ability to delay gratification (waiting for a marshmallow or some M&M's) correlates highly with parental assessments of self-control throughout childhood and with later SAT achievement. While there's a great deal of natural variation in impulsiveness, consistent, firm, and

patient guidance can help most impulsive children develop effective self-management. There is, however, a small group of children who seem essentially unable to restrain their impulses despite inducements and whose actions look less like poorly inhibited voluntary behavior than compulsory, driven, involuntary behavior. In many cases, their difficulty is related to significant neurological problems like stroke or trauma (especially to the frontal lobes) or to maternal substance abuse. Franklin was just such a child. Despite the firm, consistent, and loving care of his adoptive mother, he often "leapt before he looked" and had tremendous difficulty regulating his own actions. We'll have more to say about such children in our Helping section.

- Step five is to develop a careful and detailed plan of action. During this detailed planning step, the Operations Officer must devise a series of steps that lead to the desired goal. Not all planning difficulties are due to attention problems. Poor planning can be caused by trouble with procedural memory, gestalt organization, or specific sensory processing or learning problems. For example, children with visual memory deficits are often unable to perform spatial or visual planning tasks (see Chapter 4). Different problems require different solutions.

Functions of the Chief Operations Officer: Implementation Phase

When planning is complete, the Chief Operations Officer must oversee the implementation of her plan. There are three important steps in this phase.

- Step one is initiation. Some executives can have trouble getting started, even when they know their objective and how they intend to pursue it. These are the anti-impulsives who suffer from "analysis paralysis." Often children with this problem just need to be reassured (and shown) that the world won't end if they make a tentative, exploratory start, then have to back up a few steps or begin again.
- Step two is monitoring implementation. During implementation, the Operations Officer must keep track of several things at once, including:

- Materials management. The Operations Officer must keep track of whether she has everything she needs to implement the plan (like pencils, paper, space on the page, etc.) and how these things are located and organized.
- Rate and time. The Operations Officer must also keep track of how much time is available for a task (throughout implementation) and at what rate she needs to go to finish her tasks on time (e.g., to finish twenty addition questions in five minutes or to finish a ten-page research paper in two weeks).
- Synchronization. The Operations Officer often needs to coordinate the performance of several activities at once, like idea generation, sentence construction, and written output.
- Style. The Operations Officer must also monitor whether the "style" of implementation matches the demands of the job. A child needs to monitor not only what he's saying but how loudly he's speaking, whether he's bumping his classmates too hard while playing tag, or whether he's bothering anybody by clicking his pen in class.
- Error checking. When implementing a task, the Operations Officer must be on the lookout for errors: "Are the words all spelled correctly?" "Is the punctuation correct?" "Did I perform the right operation on that math problem?" "Did I form that 3 like a capital *E*?" Failure at this monitoring phase usually results in "silly mistakes."

- Step three is to modify the plans as necessary. While the Creativity Officer must assist in developing alternative strategies when needed, the Operations Officer must determine when the overall plan or strategy has gone off course and a new approach is needed.

The Creative Corporation: Summary

Many children have trouble with one or more of the executive functions performed by the Creativity and Operations Officers. In addition, children with working memory challenges also typically show difficulties with these executive functions, because working memory provides the "desk space" on which the corporate officers do their work.

Developing skill in these executive functions is a normal part of maturation and involves a great deal of learning and practice. While some children with underlying brain problems (like a stroke, head injury, or maternal substance abuse during pregnancy) show hard-to-treat problems with many of these functions, most children can improve their executive functions substantially with training, instruction, and maturation, as we'll describe in our Helping section.

EVALUATING CHILDREN WITH ATTENTION PROBLEMS

Every child with attention problems requires a thorough evaluation. Many different conditions can cause attention problems, and each may require a different solution. One-size-fits-all approaches and behavioral checklists are simply not enough.

The evaluation should begin with a detailed history, in which information is obtained from parents, child, and, if possible, teachers or other caregivers. Evidence of the environmental, temperamental, medical, or psychological factors we've described should be noted, as should evidence of task-specific inattention during reading, writing, math, or heavy auditory or visual work. Information should also be sought regarding the degree of social and academic impairment the child's attention-related behaviors are causing.

Every child with attention problems also needs a complete physical, neurological, and neuropsychological evaluation. Over half of children diagnosed with ADHD have learning disorders, and similar numbers have neurological and sensory problems. A single brief visit to a primary caregiver or even a specialist is inadequate to identify the sources of a child's attention problems or the full range of the child's needs.

In addition to this basic evaluation, a child may also need evaluations (or treatments) by a psychiatrist or psychologist, a vision or hearing specialist, an occupational therapist, a speech-language pathologist, or other professional. Because the attention system is so complex, its evaluation and treatment will also be complex. Both evaluation and treatment should be thought of as processes rather than single events. Those who are looking for quick fixes or magic bullets will usually be disappointed.

HELPING CHILDREN WITH ATTENTION PROBLEMS

There are five general points to remember when trying to help a child who has difficulty paying attention:

1. The primary goal of treatment should always be to improve the Foundational, Spotlight, Juggler, and Creative Corporate functions that are required for attention, not simply to suppress unwanted behaviors.
2. Most children with attention problems need help in several areas, and each should be addressed to provide maximum benefit. Even small improvements in several weak areas can combine to create large gains.
3. Most children require both specific measures that address their particular problems and general measures that can help anyone with attention problems.
4. While concern is appropriate, panic isn't. Although the issues facing a child with attention problems can sometimes feel like an emergency, there's rarely a need to rush into diagnosis or treatment. Seek early assessments, not early conclusions.
5. While medications are often recommended as the first line of treatment for children with attention problems, they are never the entire solution for any child with attention problems, nor are they a necessary part of the treatment for many children with attention problems. (We'll discuss medications in more detail at the end of this chapter.)

With these general points in mind, let's turn to some specific solutions.

Helping Fix the Foundation: The Foundation Builders

Interventions for many Foundation Builder problems are covered in other chapters, so we won't repeat them here. However, two require more comment.

Sleep Disorders

If you suspect that a child might have a sleep disorder, the first step is to follow these four basic principles of "sleep hygiene."

1. Respect your bed! Beds are for sleeping, not doing homework, calling friends, watching TV, instant messaging, or playing video games. When a bed is used for fun and stimulating activities, the brain becomes conditioned to think of it as a place for alertness, not sleep. If space is an issue, consider a foldaway or drop-down bed or a futon that can be made into a sofa during the day.
2. Get plenty of exercise, but not too close to bedtime. Children who lie around all day often have difficulty falling asleep. Physically active days promote restful sleep.
3. Establish regular sleep/wake times. Children with attention problems often have irregular sleep patterns. Establishing regular sleep/wake times can help them develop a more regular sleep cycle.
4. Use background noise. Some children's brains are just too active to fall asleep. A white noise generator or favorite musical recording can provide enough calm to help them fall asleep. Children with auditory distractibility who wake up at every little noise can also benefit.

If these "hygienic steps" fail to help the child become well rested (or if he shows obvious signs of snoring, frequent arousal, or thrashing or kicking movements in sleep), then it's time for an evaluation by a children's sleep expert.

Environmental Stressors

Environmental modification should be part of the treatment plan for every child with attention problems. Some modifications can help in any environment. Others will be especially useful at home, or in school.

General Environmental Factors

Three key steps can make any environment more attention-friendly for children with attention problems:

1. Identify and eliminate environmental triggers that worsen a child's attention. If a child is distracted by certain stimuli, eliminate them—or at least lessen the frequency of contact. Sounds, visual distractions, tactile stimuli, or even foods are the major culprits.

2. Make the environment more stable and predictable. Most children like occasional surprises, but when all of life is uncertain—or even threatening—they become anxious and less capable of focused and sustained attention. A constant lack of predictability encourages vigilance and distractibility rather than sustained focus. Orderly and predictable environments allow children to "let their guard down" so they can devote more of their mental resources to the work of the moment. Novelty is important, but for most children it should be controlled novelty, delivered against a background of stability and security.

3. Provide stable, supportive, consistent, and patient guidance. Confusion and inconsistency in the lessons taught and the behaviors shown by the adults in their lives can produce confusion, anxiety, and uncertainty about what constitutes acceptable behavior. Children need positive, consistent reinforcement when they behave well and clear feedback and consistent discipline when they break the rules.

Factors at Home

When stresses at home seem to be contributing to a child's behavior and attention problems, family counseling is crucial. A good family counselor can provide guidance on rule setting and rule following, behavior modeling, communication techniques, conflict resolution, reward and discipline strategies, and other interventions that can help relieve household stress.

Factors at School

In Chapters 4 and 5, we discussed helpful interventions to decrease visual and auditory distractions in the classroom. The following steps can also help make the classroom a more attention-friendly place:

- Provide information in small, easily digestible chunks. These will be easier to process for children with poor sustained attention or small working memory capacity.
- Use multimodal teaching strategies. Provide examples in multiple formats to reinforce lessons.
- Provide plenty of structure to classroom rules and activities. Post a schedule and stick to it. Do the same with rules of behavior.
- Be consistent, persistent, and insistent in providing and enforcing rules. It is important that parents support teachers in enforcing classroom rules, so long as those rules are clear, fair, and fairly enforced. They will be a great help—not a hindrance—in your child's development of self-command and self-respect.
- Watch for negative peer interactions and minimize their occurrence.
- Watch for specific tasks that seem to provoke ADHD-type behaviors. These will often provide clues to a child's underlying learning or sensory problems.

Helping with Focused Attention: The Spotlight

Before we discuss specific Spotlight problems, let's look at three steps that can help any child who's struggling with focused attention:

1. Teach children that their attention is like a Spotlight and that they can learn to control the direction, duration, and intensity of its beam. Tell them that their Spotlight can help them ignore distractions, remain focused, and even become more interested if they learn to control it well. Teach them, in other words, that they should play an active and not just a passive role in determining where their attention is focused. The Spotlight can be hard to control at first, but with practice most children can learn to control it far better than they realize.

2. Give them explicit and practical strategies for increasing their control over the Spotlight. Help them develop the habit of asking themselves frequently, *Where is my Spotlight focused? Where should it be?* and *How brightly is it shining?* When you see them drifting, ask them the same questions.

3. Help them to understand how, and in what circumstances, their Spotlights work best and in what circumstances they struggle most. By understanding their own cognitive strengths and weaknesses (i.e., in sensory processing, memory, verbal and nonverbal reasoning, reading, math, etc.), they can be especially alert for times when they're more likely to have problems.

Spotlight 1: Helping Improve Selective Attention

Children with impaired selective attention must learn how to focus their Spotlight on important (or relevant) things and to leave unimportant ones in the dark. Three steps can help them achieve this goal: increase their understanding of task requirements, improve their resistance to distractions, and eliminate distractions. We'll discuss each.

Improving Selective Attention by Increasing the Understanding of Task Requirements

Selective attention can be improved by teaching children what they should focus on and what they should ignore. Most of us make these decisions automatically, but children with selective attention problems must be taught to make them deliberately. Three basic steps can help the child with selective attention problems understand better where to direct his focus.

1. Teach him the rules for each task he performs. Every task, whether reading or writing or doing math (or picking up his room!), has a set of rules that help distinguish the important from the irrelevant. When a child knows the particular types of information he should focus his Spotlight on (e.g., certain types of sensory information, key words, essential principles, etc.), he can better make such distinctions and focus more effectively.

2. Have her subvocalize or visualize the rules. Have the child repeat the rules to herself while performing tasks: "Eyes on my paper, ignore any movements or noises to the sides" or "Listen to the teacher, ignore any whispers from my friends." Practice is essential. Soon these rules will become automatic and she will no longer need to consciously repeat them.

3. Act as their "surrogate Spotlight." When the child's attention wanders, don't simply tell him to "stay on task." Ask him (and if you must, tell him) what kind of task he's performing and what rules he should use to direct his Spotlight: "You're doing math now, so focus your Spotlight on your book, your paper, and my voice, and try to leave everything else in the dark."

Improving Selective Attention by Increasing Resistance to Distractions

Children with poor selective attention can be trained to resist distractions:

- Studies have shown that video games that encourage central visual focus can improve visual attention and efficiency. As we mentioned in Chapter 4, it's important to select games that build resistance to (rather than awareness of) peripheral distractions (see Resources, Chapter 4).
- Also, as we mentioned in Chapter 5, training that improves auditory focus in the presence of background noise can be used to improve auditory selective attention. Simply reminding a child to ignore distractions, as mentioned above, can help train her to ignore distractions. If a child has difficulty dealing with distractions during tests or class work-periods, give her practice tests at home during which she has to do her work while ignoring distractions you provide, like whispers, crinkling paper, coughing, et cetera.

Improving Selective Attention by Eliminating Potential Distractions

Selective attention can also be improved by eliminating potential distractions. These distractions will most commonly be environmental factors, like noises, visual distractions, irritating touch sensations, or even off-topic thoughts (daydreams). Chapters 3 through 5 contain extensive discussions of ways to deal with working memory overload, visual distractions, and auditory distractions. Chapter 9 contains an in-depth discussion of ways to help children who suffer from sensory-seeking and sensorimotor distractibility.

Spotlight 2: Helping Improve Sustained Attention

Children who have difficulties with sustained attention often benefit from interventions that help them maintain focus for longer periods of time or help them manage their learning better given their particular attention style.

- Children with impaired sustained attention can benefit from training in self- and task awareness as described above.
- Children with weak sustained attention often have a poor internal sense of time and pacing and may simply have an inadequate sense of how long they need to focus their Spotlight in a particular place. Children with poor time awareness should practice various tasks using a stopwatch or egg timer to improve their sense of pacing.
- As long as these children progress toward their goals and finish their work, allow them some flexibility in their work habits. Some children may have "birdlike" appetites for knowledge: They may return repeatedly to the feeder but consume only a small quantity of food each time. For children who require frequent breaks, see if there are activities they can perform during breaks (e.g., physical exercise, tactile fidgets, snacks, quiet time) that make their bursts of attention more efficient when they occur.
- Children with brief attention spans may learn better by being exposed to many different examples, each of which reinforces a single principle, than by being given a single example that must be studied in depth to learn the principle.
- The strategies described in the next section for increasing motivation should also be used.

Spotlight 3: Helping Improve Stimulated Attention

Children with inadequate stimulated attention often feel as if learning is simply more trouble than it's worth. Before teaching them, you must help them see learning as a rewarding and worthwhile endeavor.

As we mentioned in Causes, two types of rewards can help motivate these children: intrinsic rewards (or things they find rewarding for their own sake) and extrinsic rewards (or rewards they receive from others for doing things they don't find rewarding in themselves). Let's see how each can be used to motivate learning.

Using Intrinsic Rewards to Increase Stimulated Attention

In her book *Creativity in Context*, psychologist Teresa Amabile identifies two factors that can help make learning more intrinsically rewarding for most children:

1. Choice: Individuals who choose some aspect of their tasks show greater persistence and enjoyment than do persons assigned tasks at random.
2. Feelings of competence: Individuals persist more on tasks they can perform well than on tasks they can't.

Let's discuss these two aspects of choice and competence in greater detail.

Using Choice to Make Learning More Intrinsically Rewarding

When we discussed personal memory in Chapter 3, we mentioned that children (like adults) learn and attend better to things they find funny, odd, unusual, or relevant to their persons or interests. When children are given an element of choice so they can approach materials from avenues of special interest, they will often find learning more intrinsically enjoyable.

- Use areas of special interest to teach information of all kinds. For example, a child with an interest in trucks could learn history by studying ancient modes of transportation, the Roman system of roads, or the role of the steam engine in the industrial revolution; language arts by reading and writing about trucks; math by doing story problems about payloads, tire pressures, gas-tank readings, or distances traveled; social studies by researching the effect of cars and trucks on the development of contemporary life. Similar linking strategies can be used to teach information of all sorts and are especially important for children with very narrow and intense interests.

- Teach children personal memory strategies (see Chapter 3) to enhance interest and improve memory. Encourage these children to create interesting or amusing stories or associations with material they are trying to learn and to develop the habit of looking for personal associations and links to previously learned material whenever they encounter new information. Encourage children with visual thinking styles or an artistic bent to doodle their associations, and children with verbal or musical bents to turn information into poems, songs, or raps.

- Learn what the child finds interesting and important. Children come to learning with their own agendas, and these agendas sometimes conflict with ours. When doing math, some children may place a higher premium on being the first done than on getting all the answers right, while others may be so afraid of making mistakes they are paralyzed into inaction. It's always important to understand the motivational structure that may be influencing a child's work patterns.

Using Feelings of Competence to Make Learning More Intrinsically Rewarding

Children quickly lose interest in tasks where they seldom succeed. Recently a study of motivation found that children seldom persisted on tasks where they couldn't succeed at least two-thirds of the time.

- Make sure that your unmotivated child isn't suffering from a learning challenge that prevents him from achieving enough success to remain attentive.

- Conversely, make sure your unmotivated child is not being taught at such an unchallenging level that it gives her no sense of accomplishment.

- Demand success, but make sure it is achievable. Maintain "positive momentum" by pushing for continued small gains at a level the child can reach. Take a long-term view. A child who makes consistent incremental gains will achieve more than one who's pushed so hard that he simply gives up.

Using Extrinsic Rewards to Increase Stimulated Attention

Extrinsic rewards can also be used to help children persist in those aspects of learning they find intrinsically unrewarding. Before you turn up your nose at the idea of using "mercenary motivators," remember that grades, praise from parents or teachers, the esteem of friends, and the chance to get into a good college or get a desired job are all extrinsic rewards. Remember also that helping children develop the necessary self-discipline to put up with at least some work that they find immediately unrewarding is an important part of building the patience and character they will need throughout their lives.

For younger or more impulsive children, more immediate and tangible rewards (like stickers, music CDs, books, video-game rentals, etc.) may be needed. Rewards should initially be relatively easily attainable, but gradually the effort needed to obtain them should increase. Eventually the need for extrinsic rewards should fade substantially (or even altogether) as the child develops enough skill to experience success and the intrinsic rewards that come with competence.

Helping Working Memory: The Juggler

Steps to help children with difficulties in working memory are discussed extensively in the Helping section of Chapter 3.

Helping with Creativity, Planning, and Implementation: The Creative Corporation

For the Creative Corporation to function optimally, each partner should be as strong as possible, so that neither partner is overwhelmed by the other. The goal in helping most children with imbalances in executive function is to strengthen their weaker partner rather than to weaken or curb the stronger. We'll discuss each "executive" individually, starting with the Chief Creativity Officer.

Helping to Maximize the Performance of the Chief Creativity Officer

As you recall from Causes, the Chief Creativity Officer is responsible for generating alternative goals or approaches, expanding ideas and possibilities, combining images and ideas in new and creative ways, and spotting deficiencies in the status quo. Children who receive too little input from their Creativity Officer (or rely too much on their Operations Officer) can benefit from the following strategies:

- Clarify big-picture goals and objectives. The Creativity Officer works best when he knows what he's aiming at. Most of the time, creativity doesn't just "happen"; it's the result of sustained thinking about specific objectives. Identifying specific objectives makes it easier for children to generate creative alternatives, because objectives can provide them with a starting place from which various alternatives can be generated.
- Imagine alternatives. One of the Creativity Officer's biggest strengths is his ability to imagine alternative approaches, scenarios, or realities.

- Ask the right questions. Teach children to ask the questions the Creativity Officer normally does when presented with a problem: *How have other people approached this problem? How might I have done it instead? How could this be better? Is there a different way this could be solved? How could I frame the question differently?* Then get them to explore the implications of these answers.
- Train in tweaking. Get children in the habit of asking their own questions as well, so that they develop a "tweaker's" mentality, always looking for ways that they could change things and make things work a little bit better. Encourage them to develop a critical eye and to always ask themselves classic tweakers' questions, like,

How could that work better? What could make doing this easier?
What problems do I have doing things at school or around the
house? and *What kinds of solutions could I imagine that would*
eliminate those problems?

- Demonstrate creative and flexible approaches to thinking at
  home. Use humor, metaphor, analogy, alternative word choices,
  and wordplay in daily conversations with your child to teach
  her about the flexibility and opportunities for choice available
  in language.

- Study different problem-solving approaches. Having a variety of
  problem-solving approaches available can be a huge asset for a
  child. Often there will be more than one way to approach or solve a
  problem, and knowing several alternative approaches can make it
  easier to find a correct answer. Children who have difficulty generating alternatives on their own should be taught specifically to think of
  different problem-solving strategies, including verbal strategies, pictorial or diagrammatic strategies, metaphorical strategies, or, if appropriate, mathematical strategies. (See Resources for information
  on problem-solving skills.)

- Study examples of alternative solutions to various problems. Study
  different inventions or products that are intended to perform the
  same function. Compare and contrast features, and discuss what still
  needs work. Share your own opinions, and explain how you arrive at
  your conclusions. Study historical examples of improvements and
  innovations (e.g., ships moving by oar power, wind power, steam/coal
  power, diesel power, nuclear power), as well as "bad examples" of
  tweaking (New Coke, anyone?). Study also different movie versions
  of the same story, different literary accounts of the same legend, or
  compare and contrast successful and unsuccessful movies, music, or
  works of art.

- Practice generating alternatives. Give assignments that require a
  range of different possible approaches and solutions. Instead of assignments with lots of problems each requiring a single solution,
  give the child some assignments with fewer problems, and have him
  solve each using several different approaches.

- Encourage a willingness to make mistakes. Some children resist generating alternatives or trying new approaches because they fear making mistakes. Let them know that exploring possibilities and making mistakes is an important part of learning and that nothing great is ever created without a lot of mistakes or half successes along the way. Share with them some examples of your own mistakes and wrong approaches and what you learned from them. Teach them also that most innovations and improvements are incremental, not earth-shattering, and that they should look for step-by-step improvements as well as more dramatic improvements.

Helping to Maximize the Performance of the Chief Operations Officer

Children with weak Operations Officers need to become more thoughtful and deliberate in planning their actions, better able to restrain their impulses to act, and more controlled and perceptive in overseeing their actions. The following interventions can help them reach these goals.

Helping the Chief Operations Officer Plan

The Operations Officer's first responsibility in the action-generating process is to supervise planning. The tasks in this stage include narrowing and focusing on immediate objectives; analyzing potential risks, costs, benefits, and relevant rules; and creating a detailed plan of action.

- While children with weak Creativity Officers need to focus more on "big picture" goals and objectives, children with weak Operations Officers must become more mindful of immediate goals and objectives. As such, they can benefit from the same training in understanding the nature of tasks that we described above in "Improving Selective Attention. . . ." In particular, they should practice identifying, stating, and describing the goals for various types of projects.
- These children also require more explicit teaching about the potential risks, benefits, and relevant rules that are involved in different types of tasks.

- In addition to going over such information before children initiate an action, it is also important to review this information after they have completed the action. Through repeated practice, they will learn to internalize these questions and ask them of themselves.

- Having children apply the same analysis to carefully selected stories or vignettes about the actions of other persons will also help them develop the habit of automatically analyzing costs, benefits, and rules. Many children find it easier to learn these general principles while looking at stories and examples rather than by trying to analyze their own actions. You can even give them a little checklist they can use to remember the questions they should ask. This is not a new concept; this has been the central focus of children's literature throughout the ages. One of our favorite resources on this topic is *Books That Build Character* (see Resources).

- Practice generating plans. When it comes to developing detailed plans, most children with weak Operations Officers will initially need some "scaffolding" or structured help in learning what's involved in plan generation. Planning difficulties may involve a variety of problems organizing work, organizing space, and organizing time. An important place to start is by providing a framework of routine and structure in daily activities. Establishing general rules for routine activities, like "No video games until the homework is done" or "No snacks after five and before dinner," can encourage children to develop the habit of planning and thinking ahead. Also, in the daily events of life, encourage children to become involved in planning: School assignments, family outings, school activities, meal preparation, or even cleaning up around the house can all provide opportunities for practice. Sit down beforehand and plan the necessary steps. Write them out if necessary. Provide explicit instructions about the kinds of planning that need to take place for different types of activities.

- Set aside regular times for planning. For longer-term scheduling, sit down at the beginning of each week for weekly planning. Note due dates, tests, and requirements, and develop plans for getting work done on time—then enforce them. For shorter-term scheduling, sit down each evening and go over any new assignments. Make concrete plans for completing them, even if the due date is a long way off. (Note: Older children, especially teens, may prefer to plan with an outside "ADD coach" [see below] by phone or e-mail, especially if tension has built up between parents and children as a result of missed assignments, failure to communicate, or intentional deception.)

- Organize materials and assignments. Various visual and mnemonic strategies for organizing materials have been discussed in Chapters 3 and 4. It can also be helpful to have a checklist or assignment folder that the child can carry between the parent and the teacher each day to improve communication and planning. Teachers can play an important role in providing scheduling information in advance to children with planning difficulties and their families.
- Organize time. Time organization is important for both planning and implementing actions. Many children with planning difficulties lack a clear internal sense of the passage of time. As a result, they have difficulty judging how long certain tasks will take and allocating their time during tasks. These children require intensive practice in time management so they can internalize the sense of time and develop a better awareness of how much time different tasks take. Time management goes all the way from years (e.g., life goals and major planning decisions), down to months and weeks (managing projects), down to days and hours (managing assignments and homework), down to minutes and seconds (allocating time on a test). Helping children develop strategies to deal with planning on all these levels will be essential.

  - To manage the longer framework of days and weeks, calendars or day timers should be displayed in prominent places at home and in school and should be frequently referred to. Color-code important dates and assignments and things that a child has to do and wants to do.
  - To manage the hours in a day, clocks or desktop computer information-management programs that chime at regular intervals

or preset times to remind of specific responsibilities can also be used to help reinforce the sense of time passing. Helpful programs are available at timetimer.com. Wrist alarms, like the Watch-Minder (www.watchminder.com) or PDAs can also be programmed with reminders to perform certain actions at certain times of the day (see Resources).
- To manage the minutes, practice *pacing activities* using a clock (described under Helping the Chief Operations Officer to Implement Actions).

- One important caveat should be made regarding the child who chronically fails to turn in his homework. In our experience, most such children, especially after third or fourth grade, don't simply "forget" to turn in their work or merely misplace it. Either they are ashamed of their work, or they don't want to be criticized for their mistakes, or they haven't done it because they don't find it worth the effort, or they are angry for some reason at parents or teachers. Chronically missed assignments are usually a call for help rather than a product of poor planning or forgetfulness.

Helping the Chief Operations Officer Restrain Impulses

As we've mentioned, simple, clear expectations and firm, consistent discipline should always be a part of efforts to help a child develop impulse control. Beyond that, the following steps can greatly help children delay gratification and restrain impulses so they can effectively plan and implement actions:

- Make a partner of the child. Increase a child's awareness of his own tendency toward impulsivity, and teach him to monitor his behavior. Use a notebook or chart to follow progress and to keep track of rewards (if used). Help the child become more aware of how emotions and physical states (like hunger and fatigue) can increase impulsivity. Teach him to monitor his bodily signals and "emotional thermometer" for signs that he's becoming overly excited, distractible, or irritated—all of which can contribute to impulsivity. Being aware of these factors can help him rein in his behavior before he acts.

- Children can also benefit from the use of simple rule-based strategies, like counting to three before acting and using that time to think about goals, rules, and consequences; reading questions three times before answering them; circling math-operation signs (+, −, /, %, etc.) before solving problems; and so on. Though simple, such strategies can work if consistently applied.

- Parents and teachers should provide frequent reminders of the need to slow down, take time, and plan, either with a touch, a hand signal, or some other gesture.

- Simon Says is another great way to practice impulse control (especially with younger children), since it requires a combination of following directions and refraining from actions.

- More elaborate computer or clinic-based programs (e.g., Interactive Notebook, Physioneurotherapy, Doree, etc.) have also been developed to help children improve their impulse control. Most of these programs are based on principles similar to those described in this chapter for developing mental focus and resisting distractions, improving working memory span, and inhibiting the initiation of action. There are many anecdotal reports of the effectiveness of these programs, but at the present time (as with many of the techniques currently used by educators and therapists) there is little carefully controlled research documenting their effectiveness. Families who require the discipline of a formalized program and an outside therapist to diligently practice effective exercises, and are not frightened away by the cost of these programs (often from two to five thousand dollars and up), may want to look more closely at them.

- Biofeedback training is another technique that can be used to help children monitor and control their tendencies toward impulsivity. Published studies have actually shown that biofeedback can significantly decrease behaviors associated with poor attention, and in a lasting fashion.

  - The most elaborate form of biofeedback is called EEG biofeedback, during which a child's brain waves are monitored by an electroencephalograph (EEG). This EEG can show when children are generating brain waves that are associated with functional attention and those associated with inattention, and it can provide feedback on these states to the children. By receiving feedback during various tasks, the child can learn to modify her own brain activity to increase the kind associated with good attention.

- EEG training can be received in a formal clinic with elaborate equipment and professional monitoring. The primary drawbacks with this therapy are that it requires daily or several-times-weekly visits over a two-to-three-month period and that it is expensive and may not be covered by insurance. For those willing to bear the inconvenience and expense, however, the benefits may be significant and lasting.

- Biofeedback can also be pursued at home using simple systems that can be run off a PC. One relatively affordable (less than two hundred dollars) program that some of our patients have found helpful and easy to use is called Journey to the Wild Divine. (See Resources and "Improving Resistance to Visual Distractions" in Chapter 4 for more information.)

- For children with emotional impulsivity who show frequent tantrums or outbursts, we have found the approach described by the psychologist Ross Greene in his book *The Explosive Child* to be extremely helpful.

- Children who are so physically impulsive that they pose a danger to themselves or others require immediate professional attention by a trained psychiatrist.

Helping the Chief Operations Officer to Implement Actions

The following steps can help children with weak Operations Officers better initiate, monitor, control, and modify their actions.

- Help children get started. Clarifying the goals and procedures required for particular tasks can help some children with difficulty initiating actions.

- Often children with initiation problems have undiagnosed learning challenges that keep them from engaging in their work, or they may not understand the point of the work. Clarify goals and provide access to examples of successfully completed work, so they can check their own against it.

- Children who seem to understand what's called for but simply don't know where to begin often benefit from learning a repertoire of "opening moves" that can unlock their flow of creativity. (For math problems, this may mean highlighting operation signs or breaking down problems into individual steps. For essays, this may involve restating the question in the opening paragraph, then clarifying the definitions of the words in the question that can be understood in more than one way.) Early on, it may be necessary to provide the student help with the first step or provide examples of a problem similar to the one they're being asked to solve so they can get some idea of what they should be doing.

- Improve self-monitoring of pace. Children who have difficulty monitoring their pace can benefit from the interventions described above for planning the use of time. These children should also practice time monitoring as a game. Encourage them to find an appropriate pace (say, for doing a page of math problems), then do "speed checks" at various points in their assignment. Reward work that is done carefully, thoroughly, and at an appropriate pace.

- Improve error detection. Children with weak Operations Officers often need to develop reliable systems for checking errors.

  - Teach children to do work in stages or drafts. Trying to do too much at once often results in working memory overload and more mistakes. For example, a child who makes many errors of grammar, spelling, and punctuation when writing should be allowed to produce shorter writing samples that he redrafts multiple times, focusing on one specific aspect of performance with each draft.

  - After each stage and before the work gets turned in, the child should review and critique it with an adult. The child should be asked to provide her own critique and to make it very specific (need to write more, use clearer word choice, etc.). Do the same after graded work comes home. Discuss how mistakes that went unnoticed might have been picked up, whether mistakes are small—like spelling errors or simple math mistakes—or large—like a paper or deadline forgotten. Encourage the child to problem-solve and think how a better "system" might help reduce such mistakes in the future. Teach her that checking and rechecking her work is not "something extra" or a punishment but an essential part of any work.

- Make practicing error detection fun and rewarding. Instead of "detecting errors," have him "look for spies" that have "infiltrated his homework" or "weeds that are growing in his garden." Provide rewards for errors detected.

- Formal training programs, like Kumon (www.kumon.com), are also available to promote error detection by having children repeatedly take the same tests until they've mastered them. The idea is to get children accustomed to producing work that contains no errors by increasing their vigilance in error checking. These programs work well for children whose errors really do result from insufficient oversight by their Operations Officer, but they are less valuable for children who make "silly mistakes" because of underlying sensory input or learning challenges.

The Benefits of an "Attention Coach"

While building their operations skills, most children require the help of an "attention coach": some adult who helps them monitor their focus, plan and implement actions, and critique their performances, while providing support, advice, and encouragement. Any adult can be a coach, including parents and teachers, though some children prefer to have an "outside" adult who can encourage, advise, and motivate without being responsible for grading or discipline. There are also programs that specifically train coaches in techniques that are especially useful for children with attention problems.

Coaching works best when a regular schedule is set up for meetings, phone calls, or e-mails. During exchanges, the coach and the student review how things have gone, discuss strategies for making things go better, and make a list of skills the student should be practicing. Coaching works well for students who want to improve their attention and organization, but not so well for those who don't. No matter how good the coach, the student must be motivated if the relationship is to be effective. Fortunately, most children really do want to do well and succeed, and they respond well to caring and competent oversight.

THE ROLE OF MEDICATIONS IN CHILDREN WITH ATTENTION PROBLEMS

The role of medications in children diagnosed with ADHD is a complex and controversial subject. Doing it full justice would require an entire chapter—if not an entire book. Unfortunately, we don't have the liberty of that much space, so in this brief section we'll narrow our discussion to the basic facts and principles that have shaped our own approach in this area.

Important Facts on the Use of Medications in Children with Attention Problems

Let's begin by looking at the different classes of medications used to treat children diagnosed with ADHD. The most common include:

- *Stimulants*: amphetamine-related drugs including Ritalin, Adderall, Concerta, Metadate, and Dexedrine. These are the most widely used medications for ADHD and those with the longest history of clinical use.
- *Nonstimulant*: Strattera, which has come into use only recently and is primarily used as a backup for children who've experienced unacceptable side effects or haven't responded well to the stimulants, or who have problems for which the stimulants are relatively contraindicated, like Tourette's syndrome.
- *Antidepressants*: less commonly used for ADHD than for other disorders, but sometimes used for children diagnosed with ADHD

who have responded poorly to stimulants or have unacceptable side effects. Two classes of medicines are most commonly used, including selective serotonin reuptake inhibitors (SSRIs, like Prozac, Zoloft, and Lexapro), and older *tricyclic antidepressants* (like imiprimine).

The stimulants are by far the most commonly used, so the rest of our discussion will focus on those.

The Benefits, and Risks, of Stimulants

On the *benefits* side, research has shown that stimulants work best in controlling the inattentive, hyperactive, and impulsive behaviors associated with ADHD (like those listed in the *DSM-IV-TR*). Some of their beneficial effects may result from improvements in working memory. There is, however, no solid evidence that these medications significantly improve academic performance in most children who take them. In the largest controlled trial of stimulant use (i.e., the National Institute of Mental Health's Multimodal Treatment Study of Children with ADHD [or MTA Cooperative] Trial), children receiving stimulants showed decreases in hyperactive and impulsive behaviors but no improvement at all in math and spelling and only a slight improvement in reading. (Reading achievement improved from an average score of 96.1 to 97.9, but this is of negligible practical significance.) Other studies have shown a similar absence of significant academic benefit. Parents should realize that stimulants are primarily a form of behavioral regulation, not a learning aid. While they can help children *conform* to the behavioral demands of the classroom, they will probably not help them *perform* better academically.

On the *risk* side, stimulants are known in the short term to cause appetite suppression, headache, stomachache, insomnia, angry episodes, sadness and depression, and occasionally psychosis. In general, these problems are reversible when the stimulants are stopped.

In the long term, stimulants are known to cause growth and height suppression. Recently, Ritalin has also been linked with an increased incidence of sudden cardiac death. Many questions also remain unanswered about the effects of long-term stimulant usage on the developing brain.

Strong promoters of stimulants often point to the lack of evidence that long-term usage causes harm as proof that they are entirely safe. Yet, in point of fact, there has never been an adequate study of the effects on the brain of long-term stimulant usage in childhood to show whether these drugs are harmful, beneficial, or neutral.

Almost certainly such a study would show effects of one kind or another. As we have discussed throughout this book, there is overwhelming evidence that any form of long-term brain stimulation—whether via negative factors like environmental stress or emotional deprivation, or positive factors like early musical or language exposure—produces lasting structural and functional changes in the brain. Brain development isn't just the product of our genes; it results from the long-term interaction of our genes and our environment—including the "chemical environment" created in our brains by the medicines we take. Bathing a young child's developing brain for long periods of time in medicines that are known to alter levels of important brain chemicals will unquestionably affect long-term brain development, just as it unquestionably affects short-term brain function (as displayed by behavioral alteration). The question is simply how. At present, there is no way of answering this question with any degree of certainty, as has been clearly stated by the National Institutes of Health Consensus Development Conference Statement of 2001.

What we do have are a variety of troubling but inconclusive studies that suggest there may be reason for concern. A number of studies have shown that amphetamine-type drugs (like those used to treat ADHD) can damage nerve cells in the same parts of the brain where they are believed to exert their effects in ADHD. The subjects in these studies include young animals exposed to stimulant-type medications, children like Franklin who were born to mothers who abused methamphetamine (i.e., the medicine in Ritalin) during pregnancy, and adolescents who have abused amphetamines or drugs contaminated with amphetamines.

In addition to these studies on brain structure, studies on animal brain function have shown that amphetamine use in young animals decreases their responsiveness to naturally rewarding stimuli. While these studies used higher doses of stimulants than are used to treat children with ADHD, they are concerning, because the studies on brain structure mentioned above showed diminished brain size in areas of the brain that control reward and motivation.

Most concerning to us was a recent study conducted by researchers at Harvard Medical School and elsewhere (Kessler, et al.), that looked at risk factors for persistence of ADHD into adulthood. They found two. The first, as might be suspected, was the severity of symptoms in childhood. Children who showed problems with both attention and hyperactivity had a risk of ADHD persisting into adulthood that was 2.4 times greater than for those who had only one or the other. This risk climbed to 3.4-fold for the most severely affected children, who showed "pervasiveness of childhood role impairment." The second risk factor was even more predictive of persistence of ADHD symptoms into adulthood, and that was *whether the adults had been treated for ADHD as children.* After controlling for the severity of disease symptoms, adults who had been treated for their ADHD as children were 4.5 times more likely to have persistence of ADHD as adults. This means if you took two groups of children who showed equivalent ADHD symptoms and levels of impairment, treated one group, and didn't treat the other, the children in the treatment group would be almost 5 times more likely to have ADHD symptoms as adults. To us, this is a profoundly worrisome finding. It's important to stress that the authors of this study asked the respondents only "whether they had ever received professional treatment for ADHD" but did not obtain information "about type or persistence of treatment." Yet the treatments prescribed for attention and hyperactivity disorders at the time the adults surveyed in this study were children were overwhelmingly treatments with stimulants, and unless and until some other explanation for these results can be found, we believe it should be assumed that stimulants may have played a significant role in this increase in symptom persistence.

While these studies do not yet prove that the long-term use of stimulants is harmful to the developing brain, we believe they are concerning enough to play a role in deciding whether to use stimulants in children. In our next section, we'll describe how we help the parents who come to us approach the difficult question of whether to use stimulant medications in children diagnosed with ADHD.

Our Approach to the Use of Medications

We'll divide our discussion of the use of medications in children diagnosed with ADHD into two categories: things to do prior to starting medications and rules to follow after starting medications.

Things to Do Prior to Starting Medications

Before deciding to use medications in a child who shows signs of attention problems, keep in mind the following three points:

1. **Don't rush your decision.** Unless a child's extreme hyperactivity or impulsivity puts him at serious risk of harming himself or others, there's no need to start medications until a complete evaluation has been performed and the effectiveness of the different environmental and behavioral modifications we've discussed has been assessed. Typically this process takes three to six months.

2. **Remember the big picture.** Attention is not just a chemical process in the brain but a skill or achievement that emerges from the proper blending of many different brain functions. Because it's a skill, it can often be learned, trained, and developed. Children are people who can develop and learn, not hardwired machines that can be changed only through chemical and physical manipulation of their brains. While medications can suppress troubling behaviors, they don't teach self-awareness, self-restraint, the ability to delay gratification, persistence, resiliency, or any of the other aspects of character that children must develop to better control their own behavior. Always remember that you're trying to help a child grow and develop into a responsible adult, not simply to behave in certain ways in the short run.

3. **Avoid the temptation of "one-stop shopping."** Too often, attention challenges are approached as if they all come from a single uniform disorder (ADHD) and all require a single "magic bullet" (medications). Yet many different factors can lead to difficulties paying attention, and many different developmental, environmental, and

therapeutic approaches can help to improve attention. Medications, if used at all, should always be just one part of a broader therapeutic approach.

4. Be certain that you're treating a true impairment in function that cannot be adequately addressed in other ways and not simply a set of behaviors that are causing no harm or can easily be addressed in other ways.

Rules to Follow After Starting Medications

If, after a child has been carefully evaluated and the above information carefully considered, the decision is still made to try stimulants, we would recommend the following three basic rules:

1. Continue medications only if the child shows evidence of clear and substantial benefits. As we mentioned above, in our judgment the potential risks of continued medication usage outweigh the benefits in children who show minimal or even modest benefits with stimulants. You should know within just a few weeks of starting what the medication's effects will be. If you're not convinced that the medication is making a substantial difference, don't continue having the child take it. This is also true when trying different doses and different varieties of medications. The principle for each change remains the same: If you haven't noticed a big difference the first month at the outside, it's time to try something else.

2. Continue the medications for only as long as they're clearly needed. Many children eventually outgrow their ADHD symptoms, even without specific therapy, and even more do with appropriate interventions, yet there's no way besides periodic reassessments to know when a child can function adequately without medications. Often children can also be given "medication holidays" over longer school vacations, especially over summer break. This will allow reassessment at the beginning of each new school year to determine whether medications are still necessary.

3. Except in extreme cases, children should receive stimulants only if they can tolerate them as single agents or, rarely, double agents. Far

too often we see children who were initially begun on a stimulant for ADHD, then had other medicines added on to help them control the angry spells they developed (like Clonidine or Depakote), then had antidepressants added on when they became depressed, then antipsychotics for mood swings. . . . In the end, the child is on four or five highly potent psychoactive medications—most of which are being used to treat the side effects of the others—with little solid proof that such multidrug regimens are either safe or effective. The notion that a child's cognitive or psychological functioning can be "fine-tuned" by mixing multiple medications is simply not justified.

8

Making the Right Connections

Autism and Autism-Like Disorders

> Principles for the Development of a Complete Mind:
> Study the science of art. Study the art of science. De-
> velop your senses—especially learn how to see. Real-
> ize that everything connects to everything else.
>
> —LEONARDO DA VINCI

Noah was fourteen years old when he was brought to see us for various behavioral issues. Unlike most children we see, Noah hadn't
really struggled with the academic aspects of school. In fact, he'd
always been in the top third of his class, whatever the subject. Noah was
having problems interacting with his classmates and responding appropriately to the demands of different situations.

Noah had trouble understanding what other people were thinking. According to his family, he couldn't tell when others were being friendly or unfriendly
to him. Noah himself told us he often didn't "get" what other people were talking about. Noah also had difficulty understanding how his actions appeared to

other people, and he sometimes upset people with his "unusual" facial expressions. He had alienated most of his classmates and had no real friends, either close or casual. He also had trouble knowing how to show affection for family members, though he did seem to take comfort when they were around.

Noah's thinking wasn't delusional, but he had some very fixed ideas and a few unusual rituals and routines. He absolutely insisted on being the last one in his house to go to bed, so he could make sure that all the doors were locked. Whenever he got upset, he insisted on using a tape measure to measure everything he could see around the house. For the last several years, he'd been trying to make a complete collection of paint samples (color squares) from all the paint and hardware stores in town, and he grew frantic whenever his parents refused to stop at one of these stores when they drove by. Sometimes he had "meltdowns" at school, especially when the schedule was unexpectedly changed or when things got really noisy.

Most recently, Noah had gotten into trouble at a family funeral because he'd begun giggling and making faces during the eulogy. He'd been surprised to discover that his behavior was considered rude, since laughing was such a good thing. As he confessed to us, he just couldn't seem to figure out what people expected of him.

Noah's unusual pattern of difficulties met criteria for the autistic disorder known as Asperger's syndrome.

Sean was a ten-year-old boy who'd also been diagnosed with Asperger's syndrome — in his case by a psychologist who'd used a behavioral rating scale (checklist). Sean was very large for his age and employed an advanced vocabulary. This was consistent with his verbal IQ, which had been measured in the 150 range. He had few friends his own age, though he did have several significantly older friends in the neighborhood with whom he enjoyed interacting, typically on advanced computer projects, which he pursued with an intensity unusual for a ten-year-old.

During his visit with us, Sean spoke freely on a wide range of topics and made many sophisticated jokes involving wordplay, absurdities, and complex analogies. He was easily able to follow our conversational leads and to switch topics at our suggestion. He showed a creative approach to problem solving and was easily able to come up with many good and realistic alternatives to problems we gave him. We had to remind ourselves repeatedly that he was just ten years old.

Sean's speech was also a bit unusual: His very loud voice was somewhat lacking in musicality, though he did vary his tone, pitch, and volume to emphasize statements appropriately. According to his mother, hearing problems ran in her family, and many of her relatives spoke the same way. Sean had a history of difficulty hearing in noisy places and sometimes wouldn't respond when the teacher spoke to him. Frequently he had difficulty following social cues during group discussions, though he generally did very well one-on-one in a quiet place. He also displayed good social judgment with his younger siblings and a strong ability to empathize with their needs.

Sean did show difficulties making eye contact, a point his psychologist had made much of. He'd also shown difficulties on the "performance" portion of the IQ exam the psychologist had administered (which tests primarily visual-spatial and motor functions), where he scored a 115—significantly lower than his verbal score. The psychologist had attributed these visual-spatial difficulties to the kinds of higher-order processing problems characteristic of children with autistic disorders. However, on our examination, Sean also showed a prominent visual field defect and problems with visual motion control.

On the basis of our exam, we did not believe that Asperger's syndrome was an appropriate label for Sean.

Noah and Sean. Two children so vastly different that no one seeing them together would ever think they were suffering from the same disorder. Yet both received the same diagnosis from qualified professionals.

In this chapter, we'll look at the many reasons why Asperger's syndrome and other autistic (i.e., autism-related) diagnoses are so difficult for professionals to diagnose and for parents and teachers to understand. We'll describe the behaviors associated with these complex disorders, the brain-based problems underlying these behaviors, and the many nonautistic disorders that can lead to similar behaviors—*and to mislabeling*. Most important, we'll describe interventions that can help children suffering from autism and autism-like disorders to lead richer, fuller lives. To understand these issues, we should first consider what autism is and what it isn't.

AUTISM: WHAT IT IS . . . AND ISN'T

"Autism" was first proposed as a specific diagnosis in the 1940s by psychiatrist Leo Kanner, who used the term to describe a group of children who showed severe deficits in social interaction and communication, and who also manifested unusually focused and repetitive interests. Kanner initially applied this term exclusively to seriously disabled (and usually mentally retarded) children who showed grave difficulties in their abilities to interact with others.

For the next half century, the term *autism* continued to be used primarily to describe this same group of seriously disabled children. Then, in 1994, the *DSM-IV* (*Diagnostic and Statistical Manual of Mental Disorders, Fourth Edition*) introduced a new set of diagnostic criteria for autism (available at www.autism-biomed.org/dsm-iv.htm). These new criteria both broadened the various core symptoms that are used to diagnose autism and introduced two additional autism-related diagnoses: *Asperger's syndrome* and *PDD-NOS*. (The criteria for these diagnoses are also available at the above Web address.) These new diagnoses were intended to describe children who showed behaviors which were similar to those seen in children with autism but less severe or pervasive: Asperger's syndrome was intended to describe children who show greater strengths in certain areas of language than children with autism, and PDD-NOS was intended to describe children who show a variety of autism-like behaviors but too few to qualify for a diagnosis of autism (or Asperger's syndrome).

These diagnostic changes have produced several important results. First, the numbers of children being diagnosed with autistic disorders has skyrocketed. Currently, three-quarters of the children being diagnosed with autistic disorders are labeled with Asperger's or PDD-NOS. (Prior to 1994, most of these children would not have received an autism-related diagnosis.) Second, many of the children now being diagnosed with autism spectrum disorders are less seriously disabled than those previously diagnosed with autism. Prior to the *DSM-IV* changes, at least two-thirds of children diagnosed with autism showed IQs in the mentally retarded range. This proportion is now closer to one-quarter. Third, since the broadening of diagnostic criteria, there's been a growing tendency to *mislabel* children with autistic diagnoses who show superficially similar behaviors yet fail to show the core deficits in emotional empathy and social affiliation (described below) that characterize autistic disorders. Before we begin a detailed discussion of the ways autistic and nonautistic disorders can be distinguished, let's look carefully at the behaviors associated with autistic disorders.

BEHAVIORS ASSOCIATED WITH AUTISM AND AUTISM-LIKE DISORDERS

The behaviors listed in this section are often seen in children diagnosed with autistic disorders. We'll divide these behaviors into three categories, which will be similar to the categories used in the *DSM*: *social impairments, communication impairments,* and *other impairments.*

Behaviors Associated with Social Impairments

Impairments in social functioning are the most characteristic of all autistic problems. In fact, *children who lack serious deficits in their ability to understand (or empathize with) the emotional life of others, their desire to "affiliate" with (or be with) others, and their desire to imitate (or be like) others should not be considered autistic.* The following behaviors are characteristic of autistic social deficits:

- Children with autism often *seem strangely unaware of or uninterested in others* around them.

  - They often show little interest in the actions, words, or experiences of others.
  - They may focus almost exclusively on personal interests and concerns.
  - They typically show less interest in making friends or being with others.
  - They often show less interest in sharing personal interests, enjoyments, or achievements with others or entering into others' interests.

- Often they appear unmotivated to imitate the actions of others, which is the main route of most learning in childhood.
- Children with autism often show little pleasure in the praise of others and little interest in doing things simply to please others.

  - Often autistic children learn primarily as a way to increase personal pleasure, rather than to imitate or earn the praise of others.
  - They may show diminished response to signs of physical affection or a diminished ability to understand the significance of physical affection.

- Children with autism often appear indifferent to the displeasure of others and show a diminished capacity to be negatively influenced by others' disapproval.
- Children with autism often fail to understand that others have interior lives (thoughts and feelings) similar to their own. As a result, they often have difficulty understanding what others think or feel (empathy).
- They may also appear unconcerned about effects of their behavior on others.
- Children with autism also have difficulty engaging in reciprocal (back-and-forth, mutually enjoyable or beneficial) social interactions.

Behaviors Associated with Communication Impairments

- Children with autistic disorders often have a variety of problems with language comprehension.

  - They often show delayed development of language skills (though this is not true of children diagnosed with Asperger's syndrome or many children with PDD-NOS).
  - They often show a highly "concrete" understanding of words, which may include a very narrow, restricted, or idiosyncratic understanding of the meanings of individual words (especially abstract words), concepts, humor, irony, or implied meanings.

- Children with autistic disorders typically have difficulty understanding nonverbal aspects of communication as well, such as tone-of-voice cues, physical gestures, body postures, or facial expressions.
- Autistic children also often show problems with language expression.

  - They typically have difficulty initiating or sustaining conversation.
  - They may show stereotyped, repetitive, or idiosyncratic use of language.
  - They may speak with unusual intonations, pitch, rate, rhythm, or stress, and they may have difficulty integrating tone with words and gestures.
  - They occasionally show *echo speech* or *echolalia*.
  - They often have difficulty expressing needs, feelings, and abstract ideas through language.

- Autistic children also typically have difficulty communicating non-verbally.

  - They may show diminished or unusual use of facial expressions, physical gestures, or other bodily movements.
  - They often have a poor sense of "personal space" in social interactions.

Behaviors Associated with Other Impairments

- Autistic children typically have difficulties with certain aspects of attention.

  - They may show difficulty selecting appropriate objects to focus on, sustaining focus for the right duration, and shifting focus between objects.
  - They tend to value the familiar and repetitive over the novel and show a lack of curiosity about new things, even to the point that activities become perseverative (i.e., unusually repetitive), stereotypical, or ritualistic.

- They often adhere inflexibly to schedules or rituals.
- They may stick with previously learned procedures even in situations where they're clearly not called for and are not effective.
- They may engage in self-stimulating or repetitive play with spinning objects or may show stereotyped motor mannerisms, like hand or finger flapping or twisting, or complex, repetitive whole-body movements.
- They may show a persistent preoccupation with parts of objects while ignoring the whole.
- They often show great difficulty imagining, pretending, or assuming hypotheticals.
- Typically their interests and activities are very restricted and are unusual both in their content and in their duration and intensity.
- Because they may care little about provoking the pleasure or displeasure of others, typical reward/punishment strategies often do not work well with them.
- Often they have difficulty understanding how they should act to achieve their goals.

- Children with autistic disorders typically show difficulties with motor, sensory, and emotional self-regulation.

  - Often they show difficulties with motor coordination.
  - They may show unusual sensory over- or underresponsiveness (and any of the signs of sensory processing disorder described in the next chapter).
  - Sometimes they show unusual patterns of fears, with excessive fear of harmless objects or little fear of harmful ones.
  - Frequently they will show unusual emotional responses (or lack of responses) to a variety of circumstances.
  - Often they experience emotional overload or breakdowns with excessive emotional or sensory stimulation, which frequently results in tantrums.

THE CAUSES OF AUTISM AND AUTISM-LIKE DISORDERS

Recently researchers have discovered that the brains of autistic children often possess several unusual but characteristic features. In this section, we'll discuss these unique brain features and how they may help to explain the autistic behaviors just described. We'll also discuss what these features might be telling us about the true nature of autism. Finally we'll discuss how truly autistic children can be distinguished from nonautistic children who may show similar behaviors.

Characteristic Brain Abnormalities in Autistic Children

There are currently no brain tests or imaging studies that can diagnose autistic disorders in individual children. However, researchers using various pathological and imaging techniques have discovered several characteristic features that distinguish the brains of autistic children (in general) from those of nonautistic children. These distinguishing features can be grouped into two main functional and structural categories: first, those involving primarily the frontal lobes of the brain and, second, those involving the structures that support the interaction of the widely separated brain areas that together produce "higher-order" brain functions. Let's look at each category.

Frontal Lobe Abnormalities in Children with Autistic Disorders

As we saw in Chapter 7, the frontal lobes of the brain play a crucial role in many aspects of attention. They're involved in the Spotlight functions of selective, sustained, and stimulated attention, the Juggler functions of working memory, and the Creative Corporation's functions of creativity, flexibility, imagination, planning, impulse inhibition, and implementation. As a result, the frontal lobes can be rightly thought of as the "headquarters" of attention and executive function.

The frontal lobes also serve two other key roles. First, they play host to a fascinating set of structures that are involved in a child's ability to imitate, understand, and empathize with others; these are the brain's so-called *mirror systems*. Research into these mirror systems is currently one of the most fascinating areas in neurobiology, but it all began by accident. While setting up for an experiment, a researcher happened to notice that his monkeys activated the same parts of their brains (including the parts of the frontal lobes involved in planning and acting) when they observed him moving his fingers as they did when they moved their own! The brain activity of these animals was essentially "mirroring" his own, because they were "mentally re-creating" the brain activity needed to generate the same movements.

Humans display this same basic mirroring process. When we observe others performing actions, the areas of our brains that we would need to perform identical actions become activated. This appears to be how we learn by imitation: We essentially replicate the brain waves we would need to produce the actions we witness, then use these brain waves both to understand and to perform the action.

This mirroring process is also activated when we watch other people move their facial muscles to form expressions. This "facial mirroring" is especially important, because the motor systems controlling facial expressions are closely linked with the emotion centers of the brain. That's why if you form your face into a smile (try it, and don't forget the muscles around your eyes!) you'll probably feel the stirring of some happy feelings; that's your "smile" muscles triggering a direct link to your emotional centers. These same centers are activated both when you smile yourself and when you watch someone else smile. That's why advertisers put so many smiling people in their commercials: Their smiles not only help us understand that they are happy (presumably because they use Brand X), but they make us feel happy, too—we can't help it, even when we know the trick! This is believed to be one of the key sources of emotional empathy: We know what others are feeling by watching their reactions, because we experience those feelings as we watch. We're literally replaying—and experiencing—their emotional drama in our own brains. In just a moment, we'll discuss the relevance of these mirroring systems for autistic children and their special difficulties understanding, imitating, and empathizing with others, but first let's look at another key role of the frontal lobes.

The second key role played by the frontal lobes is that of a giant switchboard, which helps to *integrate the interactions of widely separated brain structures*, making higher-order thinking and acting possible. The frontal lobes are helped in this integration process by the *cerebellum* at the back of the brain and the *white matter tracts* that connect the different parts of the brain. We'll discuss this integration function in greater detail in the next section. For now, let's consider how problems with the frontal lobe functions supporting attention and mirroring may produce some of the characteristic behaviors seen in children with autistic disorders.

Impaired Frontal Lobe Function and Autistic Behaviors: Attention and Mirroring

Children with autistic disorders tend to show two particular kinds of changes to the brain cells in their frontal lobes. First, they show an increased number of frontal lobe brain cells—so many, in fact, that the cells become "crowded" and disrupted in their normal function. Second, the brain cells in their frontal lobes are far more connected with each other and far less connected to cells in other parts of the brain than are comparable cells in nonautistic children.

Both kinds of changes impair frontal lobe function, leading to impaired performance of the brain's attention and mirroring functions. Attention system dysfunction can result in many characteristic autistic behaviors, including repetitive, perseverative, or ritualistic behaviors; difficulty shifting attention between objects; an abnormal reward structure; lack of interest in (or avoidance of) novelty; lack of imagination; cognitive and emotional

---

TABLE 7 *Three Key Frontal Lobe Functions Affected in Autistic Disorders*

1. Controlling attention
2. "Mirroring," to understand and imitate the actions of others
3. Integrating higher-order brain functions

inflexibility; and difficulty generating and implementing plans to reach goals.

Dysfunction of the brain's mirror systems may result in many of the characteristic motor, sensory, and social and emotional difficulties seen in autistic children. These include difficulty imitating others' physical movements, difficulty understanding others' facial or bodily expressions (or making their own), and difficulty understanding another's feelings (like the pain she experiences when she cuts her finger or the fear and revulsion—as well as the physical sensation—he feels when he discovers a snake crawling over his foot). This difficulty understanding and empathizing with the interior lives of other people—or even recognizing that they have such lives—is sometimes called a problem with "theory of mind" and is one of the most fundamental and characteristic deficits seen in autistic children.

Abnormalities in Long-Distance Interactions in Children with Autistic Disorders

The second characteristic set of autistic brain abnormalities involves structures that mediate the interactions of different parts of the brain and help support complex, higher-order functions. These structures include the white matter tracts that provide the "wiring" connecting different brain structures; the frontal lobes (which we've already mentioned), which act as a switchboard to direct traffic between these areas; and the cerebellum, which sits at the lower back part of the brain and helps to integrate and regulate the interactions between different brain areas.

Children with autistic disorders have been found to have abnormalities in each of these structures. As a result, they typically have difficulty performing complex higher-order tasks that require the coordinated interactions of multiple brain areas. Such higher-order tasks include using or understanding abstract or social language; coordinating visual and verbal functions (e.g., forming a visual image from a verbal description or looking at and listening to multimodal information at the same time); processing sound or visual cues in complex environments (like a busy classroom or a birthday party); interpreting nonverbal social cues like facial expressions, tone-of-voice cues, and "body language"; and performing complex motor functions like riding a bike or jumping rope. While lots of children struggle to master these complex functions, the difficulties encountered by autistic children are of an entirely different magnitude. It's not just that they have a problem performing these functions, but that they often have difficulties even comprehending the nature or purposes of those functions. The common response from others when they see autistic children struggling with these functions is often one of bewilderment: *How are they missing it? Why can't they understand? Why can't they make that connection?*

Of course, as we've discussed in previous chapters (and will discuss in more detail shortly), children with all sorts of brain-based learning challenges can have difficulties performing complex higher-order functions. However, unlike many of the Information Input and Pattern Processing difficulties we've discussed previously, in children with autism these higher-order problems don't simply occur as the "downstream" results of low-level processing problems (as, for example, visual memory problems often occur as the result of deficits in visual input). These higher-order problems in autistic children seem to be caused mainly by problems in the connections that allow different higher-level processing centers to cooperate with each other to perform complex, multisystem functions.

In fact, most autistic children show normal (or even better) functions in certain low-level tasks that don't require complex combinations of sensory, memory, or motor functions, or in high-level reasoning or language tasks. This combination of low-level skill and high-level impairment explains why, for example, children with Asperger's syndrome often show strong (or even outstanding) abilities to define individual words but have difficulty understanding the same words when they're used in complex structures, like idioms, proverbs, or abstractions, that require higher-order processing (like generalizations or visual imagery) to understand. As a result, their ability to process language depends too heavily on individual word meanings and can be highly "rigid" or "concrete" at the sentence level.

Autistic children often show this preference for simple low-level processing, not only in the area of language but also in memory, sensory processing, motor output, abstract reasoning, and social interactions. This contributes to several of their common behavioral characteristics, like a preference for the familiar over the new; a tendency to rely on old and familiar strategies (even in situations where they don't work well), rather than trying to generate new strategies for new situations; and a tendency to focus on isolated details while ignoring more important (and complex) aspects of whole objects or events.

Conditions That Can Mimic Autism

Often it can be difficult to distinguish truly autistic children (that is, children whose "autistic-type behaviors" result from the kinds of autistic brain changes we've just described) from children who show similar behaviors but for other reasons. *There are, however, many other conditions that can cause children to behave in ways that resemble the autistic behaviors listed in our Behaviors section.* These conditions often cause autistic-type behaviors, because they produce difficulties with some of the same kinds of higher-level brain connections we've just discussed.

In general, children whose behaviors result from these other conditions can be distinguished from autistic children in two primary ways:

- First, children with these other conditions typically show abnormal behaviors in more restricted areas of function than do truly autistic children. (For example, their abnormal behaviors may be restricted to predominantly visual, predominantly auditory, or predominantly language-related areas.)
- Second, children with these other conditions don't show the severe deficits in emotional empathy, "mirroring," and social affiliation (or the sense of bonding with others) characteristic of autistic disorders.

Still, these distinctions can be challenging. In our experience, there are two key reasons children with these other conditions are commonly mislabeled as autistic. First, like children with autism, children with these other conditions have areas where they "just don't make the connections" that appear obvious to everyone else. As a result, they often act in ways that seem baffling and unaccountable to others. Second, these children typically have problems with social interactions. However, unlike the problems faced by children with autistic disorders, these difficulties are not due to a lack of emotional empathy or affiliative drive but to practical issues caused by the conditions we'll describe in more detail below.

As a result of their difficulties, these children may behave in ways that seem strange to others, and this perceived "strangeness" can make it hard for observers to empathize with their experiences. Remember, "mirroring" works both ways: *When an observer can't understand or relate to what a child is thinking or feeling, the observer will have difficulty feeling empathy for that child, too.* Thus the observer may "project" the sense of emotional distance or lack of empathy *he feels* back upon the child, and attribute this perceived "emotional flatness" to the child's supposed autism.

Of course, children with these other conditions may still have significant (and in some cases quite severe) impairments in social functioning. Typically, however, they have relatively normal desires to affiliate with others, strong attachments to those to whom they feel close (such as parents or siblings), and an ability to engage in reciprocal social interactions under the appropriate conditions.

In the following sections, let's take a look at conditions that commonly "mimic" autistic disorders.

How Auditory Impairments Can Mimic Autism

The relationship between auditory impairments and autistic disorders is quite complex. Many autistic children have disorders of auditory processing, but many other children with auditory impairments may show certain autistic-type behaviors yet not have the characteristic autistic deficits in social affiliation. Children with sound processing or background noise impairments will have difficulty following social interactions and may miss social cues. They may fail to acknowledge, respond, or make eye contact with someone who is speaking to them. Children who mishear may change the thread of conversations or respond to questions in odd ways. Children with auditory hypersensitivities may avoid or become anxious in noisy social environments and act in odd ways when overloaded. (See Chapter 5 for more detail on social functioning in children with auditory problems.)

Some of the behaviors seen in children with auditory impairments can look very "autistic" and are far less likely to be attributed to auditory causes. For example, children with hearing impairments often engage in repetitive activities with objects that produce certain noises, like tapping or clicking pens or spinning coins or bottle caps on a tabletop. They may also repeat things in ways that mimic autistic echolalia (or echo speech). However, far from being purposeless (like autistic echolalia), these repetitions may help them process sound. Author Beverly Biderman describes her own tendency to echo things as her hearing failed:

> I found myself unable to trust what I heard with my ears. People would say, "Thanks, Bev." I would respond, "Thanks, Bev." They'd say, "How is Tuesday for lunch?" I would say, "How is Tuesday for lunch?" Talking on the telephone seemed like a drill to me, and I needed to repeat what I heard to confirm that I had understood correctly.

How Visual Impairments Can Mimic Autism

Visual impairments also commonly result in autistic-type behaviors. Children with visual problems may show poor eye contact, have difficulty interpreting facial expressions, miss social cues, avoid visually busy or challenging environments, have problems with visual distractibility, and have difficulties with higher-order visual processing (like understanding visual whole/ part relationships or recognizing faces).

Poor eye contact probably leads to a suspicion of autistic disorders (particularly Asperger's syndrome) more than any other visual behavior. However, this behavior is often misunderstood. Many conditions other than autism can cause poor eye contact, including temperamental shyness, primary eye-motion-control problems, visual field cuts, and working memory overload. Working memory overload is a particularly common and frequently unrecognized cause of poor eye contact. Studies on adults have shown that the ability to remember a verbally communicated string of numbers is inhibited by looking at faces. Additional research on developmentally normal children (ages six to ten) shows that children can remember visual information better if they look away or down while talking to a person. These studies suggest that poor eye contact may be a compensation for limitations in memory resources: that many children (and adults!) need to avert their gaze to remember what they were planning to say or to keep information in mind. While children should be encouraged to make at least intermittent eye contact to help maintain social contact, it is also important not to overemphasize its importance, from either a diagnostic or a functional standpoint.

Children with brain-based visual processing issues (*cerebral visual impair-*

ments, or CVIs) may also engage in various odd or self-stimulating visual behaviors that lead to suspicions of autism. Nonautistic children with visual difficulties may engage in repetitive activities involving light or visual movement (like flapping their hands or moving an object before their eyes), or they may stare for unusually long periods of time at visually interesting materials. They may also bring objects very close to their eyes, despite an apparently normal visual acuity (presumably in order to block out visual distractions).

How Language Impairments Can Mimic Autism

Children with language impairments are commonly suspected of having autistic disorders. Children with impaired language input may have difficulty interpreting, following, or understanding language. They may answer questions in odd or idiosyncratic ways. They may interpret words or statements in concrete ways. They may also appear easily frustrated and inflexible with change, because they don't understand why things are being done or have missed the warnings that changes were approaching.

Children with impaired language output may also display behaviors that mimic autism. They may show signs of frustration, emotional lability, or cognitive inflexibility, because they cannot express their ideas, preferences, or opinions clearly.

Children who have impairments in social or pragmatic language are particularly likely to be diagnosed with autistic disorders. The social use of language is in many ways the most demanding of all language functions. The need for rapid back-and-forth exchanges, simultaneous detection of social cues, and the need to interpret context, idioms, slang, and figurative language all add to the extent of the challenge. Children who experience long conversational delays in language output or processing, who use advanced vocabularies, who prefer to converse about advanced interests, who speak with an abnormal voice quality, or who show signs of variable language comprehension may all be suspected of autistic disorders.

While autistic disorders can unquestionably cause problems with social language, many children with pragmatic language difficulties are not autistic. Problems with language at any level (including word

retrieval, categorization, semantics, and grammar) can cause difficulties
with high-level social language functions. Social language problems
should not be attributed to autism unless a child also has clear difficulties with social affiliation or emotional empathy. Mistakes at this level
will lead to improperly focusing treatment on higher-level social language while ignoring the child's underlying deficits with the building
blocks of language. The best way to improve social language function is
to start at the roots of language and build up, not simply to memorize
higher-level language "scripts."

How Attention Problems Can Mimic Autism

Children with severe impairments in attention can show many features
characteristic of autism. Those with impaired working memory may appear to "tune out" when they are spoken to and may even show delays in
language learning similar to autistic children. Those who have impaired
selective, sustained, or stimulated focus may appear inflexible and rigid
and may at times even appear to show deficits in social affiliation, because
they may not shift the focus of their attention easily in response to the leading of others. Some children with attention problems may show diminished
imagination, cognitive inflexibility, and difficulties generalizing their ideas
from one area to another, similar to children with autism. Children with
significant attention problems may also miss social cues, have trouble applying social and behavioral rules, and have difficulties with reward and
motivation similar to children with autism.

How Sensory Processing Disorder Can Mimic Autism

The condition called sensory processing disorder (also sometimes called
sensory integration disorder, which we'll discuss in detail in Chapter 9) can
also cause children to exhibit many of the same behaviors that are seen in
autistic children. In fact, there is some relationship between sensory processing disorder and autism. Many children with autistic disorders also
have sensory processing disorder, and some experts actually consider sensory processing disorder to be a part of the autistic spectrum. Both children
with autistic disorders and those with sensory processing disorder show

difficulties with high-level tasks involving the integration of different brain areas. These include complex sensory (e.g., vision, hearing, position, balance, motion, and touch) and motor functions and also emotional regulation. Typically, though, the deficits seen in children with sensory processing disorder are "patchier" than those seen in children with autism, with greater sparing of higher-order functions in areas like language, social affiliation, and empathy. In the next chapter, we'll discuss our suspicion that the behavioral similarities between autism and sensory processing disorder result from certain structural similarities in the problems affecting the brains of those affected. Like children with autism, children with sensory processing disorder typically show signs of problems with the long-distance connections that integrate different areas of their brains, with the cerebellum (which helps to regulate and "smooth out" the brain's different perceptions and responses), and with the frontal lobes (which help coordinate brain activities).

Because of these structural similarities, children with sensory processing disorder will often show behaviors similar to those seen in autistic children. Because of their problems accurately perceiving their environment, they may resist transitions and appear rather rigid and inflexible. They may insist on unvarying environmental layouts and routines. They may adjust furniture precisely and be upset by minor changes in a room, because these changes may dramatically upset their ability to orient themselves or to know where things are. They may have difficulties with smooth emotional and motor control and struggle with behaviors caused by sensory seeking, sensory avoidance, and sensory overload.

Children with sensory processing disorder may also engage in repetitive self-stimulating activities like body rocking or hand flapping. These types of motions are present in many autism checklists and often set off "bells" in people's minds about autism, but they are not particularly specific for autistic disorders. These same kinds of movements are also commonly seen in children with sensory processing disorder, mild developmental injuries, or sensory deprivations due to severe hearing or visual deficits (like Ray Charles). From a physiological standpoint, these rhythmic movements provide motor and sensory inputs that help to improve body imagery, balance, and localization, so they are not as purposeless as they appear.

How Giftedness Can Mimic Autism

As we will discuss in Chapter 13, intellectually gifted children are often mislabeled as autistic. This is particularly likely when they also have learning challenges. Gifted children often have intense and specialized interests, are socially awkward (because of introversion and emotional sensitivity), and often have little affiliative bond with their same-age peer group, with whom they share little in common. In addition, their speech patterns are quite different from those of others their age, containing more advanced vocabulary and focusing on more advanced topics. While it is possible that gifted children can be autistic, they should never be diagnosed with autistic disorders unless they show the severe impairments in social attachment and emotional empathy characteristic of autism.

EVALUATING CHILDREN FOR AUTISTIC DISORDERS

Children suspected of autistic disorders require the same thorough workup as do children with other learning problems. Although various behavioral rating scales (checklists) have been developed to help diagnose autistic spectrum disorders, in actual practice the ability to fill out these checklists accurately takes a great deal of clinical judgment. Simply counting behaviors on checklists filled out by observers inexperienced with autistic children is not enough either to make a diagnosis or to determine the treatments needed.

The primary goal of evaluation should be to determine the specific areas of function with which a child needs help. Finding a single overarching label is less important—especially as children age and can be more thoroughly and accurately tested. In fact, given the extreme variability with which autistic labels are currently applied, the greater danger is that a child's individual needs will be obscured through mislabeling. At its worst, the misdiagnosis of autism can result in inappropriate conclusions about a child's abilities to become emotionally attached or to develop creativity and problem-solving skills. It can also result in failure to address treatable sensory input and processing problems, if they are incorrectly attributed to higher-order integration deficits. In the future, as the ability to diagnose and treat the underlying causes of autism develops, this balance will change and the need to precisely identify autistic disorders will increase. At present, it is most important to identify the specific learning problems that need to be addressed.

HELPING CHILDREN WITH AUTISTIC DISORDERS

As we've mentioned, our focus in this chapter is primarily on school-age children with milder autistic-type symptoms: that is, on children who are typically diagnosed with Asperger's syndrome, PDD-NOS, or high-functioning autism. We'll organize our discussion around three major categories of autism-related behaviors:

1. Autistic social issues
2. Autistic communication issues
3. Attention and self-regulation

Before we address these specific issues, let's begin by discussing a number of approaches and interventions that can help all children with autistic diagnoses.

General Principles for Helping Children with Autistic Disorders

Teaching children with autistic diagnoses can be highly rewarding. Seeing these children begin to make difficult connections for the first time or to develop new and sometimes creative strategies for circumventing areas of weakness is as exciting and rewarding as any experience in education or parenting. Of course, teaching these children is also very challenging for several reasons. Often they are not motivated by the kinds of factors that normally engage children. They may show narrow, intense, and highly specialized patterns of interests. They may vary greatly in their abilities to process information of different kinds, with some being particularly strong visual but poor verbal learners, while others display an opposite pattern. They may also show a surprising discrepancy between their ability to process low-level and complex higher-level information, even in the same area. In this section, we'll discuss ways to deal with these issues while educating children with autistic disorders.

Reward and Motivation

Before you can teach any child, you must first engage her sense of reward and motivation. As we've mentioned, autistic children typically have a diminished desire to imitate others or to please and earn praise from others. In this way, they differ from most children, who quite naturally want to imitate and please parents and other adult authority figures—like teachers. Usually we take these desires to imitate and please others for granted in designing our educational and therapeutic systems. However, when a child has little intrinsic motivation to imitate or please, we must find a way to motivate her using things she finds extrinsically rewarding.

- Step one is to determine what a particular child enjoys, whether favorite foods or snacks, toys, activities or trips, or sensory sensations like spinning, swinging, bouncing, squeezing, or even tickling. If possible, ask the child to help you identify these items and set up a system of rewards for desired actions.
- Use mildly pleasurable rewards for relatively easy tasks and more pleasurable rewards for tasks the child finds harder.
- Couple tangible extrinsic rewards with social rewards of praise, encouragement, and physical signs of pleasure like smiles, clapping, or hugs. Over time, the child will often become conditioned (or learn) to find these social rewards intrinsically rewarding. When this happens, the child will be much easier to integrate into mainstream social and educational settings where social rewards are important motivators. Remember: Although many autistic children don't naturally enjoy imitating or interacting with others, they can often learn to enjoy these activities through the use of extrinsic rewards. Nonautistic children have a natural social-reward mechanism wired

into their brain. Through training with extrinsic rewards, you're simply trying to create a new brain pathway in autistic children that will replicate this normal pathway.

Using Their Best Learning Strengths and Styles

Like other children, autistic children have both learning strengths and weaknesses.

- When assessing an autistic child's strengths and weaknesses, remember that strengths and weaknesses can exist side by side and that areas of strength can be fairly narrow. For example, a terrific ability to remember and repeat sentences (e.g., scripts from videos or TV shows) may not indicate a strong ability to understand sentences. An accurate assessment of learning pluses and minuses is crucial.

- Even though higher-level processing deficits are most characteristic of autistic learning challenges, autistic children can have deficits in low-level Information Input and Pattern Processing as well. It's essential to identify and treat these problems, as described in our previous chapters.

- All autistic children have language deficits of one form or another. Children diagnosed with high-functioning autism or PDD-NOS typically experience delayed language onset and usually show both low-level (e.g., semantics and syntax) and high-level (pragmatics) language difficulties. Children diagnosed with Asperger's syndrome typically show strengths in low-level language skills but weaknesses with higher levels of language (particularly pragmatics, but they also typically show more general weaknesses with abstract and flexible use of language of all kinds). As a result, virtually any child with an autistic disorder can benefit from the intervention of a speech-language pathologist (SLP) skilled in the diagnosis and management of autistic children.

- As we have mentioned earlier, many autistic children show difficulties with sensory and motor regulation. These children may benefit from the intervention of a skilled occupational therapist (see Chapter 9).

Simplifying Information Input and Pattern Processing

Autistic children have more difficulty processing complex inputs than simple ones. As a result, they can benefit from "information-simplification" strategies that allow information to be processed in neurologically less demanding ways. There are three primary means through which this should be accomplished:

- First, autistic children can benefit from the use of rule-based memory strategies. They have a hard time deducing the rules that govern all sorts of interactions (e.g., social, physical, moral) from observation alone. They also have a hard time applying these rules in different situations (i.e., in generalizing their use). However, they can benefit greatly from being explicitly taught these rules. There are several important principles to guide the use of rule-based learning.

  - Keep the rules simple. During the early stages of rule learning especially, focus on rules that are straightforward and easy to remember (e.g., *When another child says hi to you, say hi in return. Don't talk at the same time as your teacher unless she asks you to. Don't sing in class unless your teacher asks you to.*)
  - Teach the rules in whatever form the child finds most memorable. For Asperger's children, verbal rules usually work best. For high-functioning autism or PDD-NOS, visual rules may work better. For the latter, using pictures or symbols, role-play videos, or social-skills books that have cartoons of social interactions may all be helpful. Other forms of memory may be preferable for children with different learning strengths, including motor-kinesthetic or musical ("This is the way we brush our teeth, brush our teeth, brush our teeth . . ."). As we mentioned in our memory chapter, even children with primary language impairments can often memorize words set to music, because they are processed in a different area of the brain.
  - Make the rules as specific as possible, especially when starting out. Because autistic children have difficulty generalizing rules from one setting to another, rules should be specific enough that the

child can easily recognize when they should be applied. Begin with situations that are especially anxiety-provoking or pose special risks—either social or physical. *What would you do if you got lost at the zoo? What do you do if an adult you don't know asks you to go somewhere with him? What do you do when a dog you don't know comes up to you? What do you do if you're at school and you can't find your lunch? What do you do when a bully starts bothering you?* Troubleshoot these situations together. See if she can generate some alternate possibilities. Then help the child form specific rules to govern her actions. Try some role plays together, then go on a dry run to practice "in real life." As the child improves in her ability to think of alternative actions or to perceive different contingencies, practice developing more general rules that can be applied in a broader variety of situations. *How can you be a good conversationalist? How can you be a good friend?*

- Second, to help an autistic child learn more efficiently, try to clearly distinguish the signal you want the child to learn from the background noise that might otherwise get in his way. Several interventions can be very helpful.

  - Reduce distractions from environmental stimuli—especially those the child finds particularly distracting. Often he will fare best in quiet, predictable, small (even one-on-one) groups, but occasional exposures to more noisy or busy settings will still be important.
  - Slow down incoming information, like words, physical movements, or visual inputs. Accentuate the rhythmic qualities of speech, and use increases in tone and volume to stress important words.
  - Computer-based teaching approaches can be particularly valuable for children with autistic disorders. Potential advantages include the ability to adjust speed, color, contrast, and volume; the ability to limit extraneous distractions with the use of headphones or cubicles, the close correlation between sight and sound, and the unvarying location or the sound source; the ability to use

animated or live forms, the infinite "patience" of the electronic teacher; and the ability to finely control the incremental nature of the increase in difficulty. The downside of computer-based approaches is the loss of social interaction, but as one component of the teaching equation for children with autistic disorders, they can play an important role.

- Third, combining complex information into "linked" images that can be stored as a single memory in a single brain location can be useful to help improve memory formation. This is really very simple, so let us explain with an example.

  - Think of autistic children who have difficulty recalling multiple word meanings. Such children may be better able to remember a single pictorial word "map" (like that shown in Chapter 6, Figure 24), in which different word meanings are portrayed pictorially in one location, than multiple independent word-based files. This picture file can be memorized by exposing the child repeatedly to this map while hearing the word pronounced aloud. The dual exposure will eventually create a single strongly paired visual-verbal link, which will most likely be stored in the child's better-functioning visual memory area. As a result, when the child hears the word pronounced, he will automatically recall the picture with its multiple portrayals of word meanings. Combined memories of this type can be used to create simplified memories of all sorts and to allow children to use their strongest memory areas to support those areas in which they are weak.

Helping Children with Autistic Social Impairments

There are two key objectives in helping children with autistic social impairments: first, to improve their capacity for empathy and second, to improve the quality and frequency of their social interactions.

Helping Autistic Children to Develop Empathy

One of the most important things to understand about highly functioning autistic children is that their lack of direct emotional connection with others (i.e., empathy) does not mean that they are incapable of feeling or experiencing emotions. Unfortunately, many people believe that autistic children are emotionally barren. This is simply not true. The problem autistic children have in interacting emotionally with others arises not from defects in their deep emotional structures (e.g., amygdala, limbic system) but rather from processing problems in the higher perceptual centers that connect to those deep structures.

Remember the mirroring problems we discussed earlier? These problems make it difficult for autistic children to make the connection between the emotions displayed by others (through facial expressions, gestures, tone-of-voice cues) and their own internal emotional states. This failure prevents them in turn from imitating these outward signs to express their own internal states. In other words, it's not that their "inner world" is devoid of emotion but that there are problems with the connections linking that inner world and the "outer world" inhabited by others.

This is important to understand when we think about helping autistic children better connect with others on an emotional level. Autistic children have problems with *emotional empathy*, or the ability to immediately feel and unreflectively understand what others are feeling and experiencing, simply by observing them. It's not that they're incapable of understanding pain, frustration, fear, joy, or pleasure; it's just that they can't tell when others are feeling these things simply by observation.

One way to help autistic children improve their ability to understand and emotionally connect with others is to help them develop a sense of *cognitive* (or *reflective*) *empathy*. In contrast to *emotional* empathy, which is our ability to *unreflectively* feel with another person, *cognitive* empathy is our ability to understand *through deliberate reflection* what other people are feeling and experiencing.

Research into emotional and cognitive empathy has shown that these are two distinct neuropsychological functions that involve different brain pathways and can be distinguished on brain scans. That's why we can teach autistic children to recognize cognitively (or by reflection) that others have feelings and experiences like their own, even though they can't perceive this unreflectively.

There are also many excellent first-person accounts by people with high-functioning autism or Asperger's syndrome describing the importance of cognitive empathy. Probably the best known and most vivid is the following passage from Temple Grandin's moving account of her own experience with autism, *Thinking in Pictures*, where she describes how she came to understand cognitively the nature of emotional relationships:

> At that time I still struggled in the social arena, largely because I didn't have a concrete visual corollary [i.e., cognitive understanding] for the abstraction known as "getting along with people." An image finally presented itself to me while I was washing the bay window in the cafeteria. The bay window consisted of three glass sliding doors enclosed by storm windows. To wash the inside of the bay window, I had to crawl through the sliding door. The door jammed while I was washing the inside panes, and I was imprisoned between the two windows. In order to get out without shattering the door, I had to ease it back very carefully. It struck me that relationships operate the same way. They also shatter easily and have to be approached carefully. I then made a further association about how the careful opening of doors was related to establishing relationships in the first place. While I was trapped between the windows, it was almost impossible to communicate through the glass. Being autistic is like being trapped like this. The windows symbolized my feelings of disconnection from other people and helped me cope with the isolation. Throughout my life, door and window symbols have enabled me to make progress and connections that are unheard of for some people with autism.

Many treatment systems for children with autism focus almost exclusively on molding their behaviors rather than reshaping their thoughts and ideas. For highly functioning autistic children, building cognitive empathy through rule-based and image-based (analogical and metaphorical) instruction should be a major component of intervention. Sean, whom we described at the start of this chapter, is a perfect example of a child who needed cognitive empathy training. Although he had little direct emotional empathy, he was a highly verbal child and was well suited to learning rules for social behavior.

- The appropriate form of help will differ for different children. Verbal rules or images are often best for highly verbal children (like those with Asperger's syndrome), while visual or kinesthetic imagery works best for children (like Temple Grandin) with other thinking styles. Physical illustrations, like Temple Grandin's panes of glass or opening-door metaphor, can also be useful: Use an extended arm to simulate appropriate social distance or a lock and key to illustrate the benefits of polite phrases like "please" and "thank you" or a buzzer to signal that a child has begun to talk "off topic." It may be necessary to experiment with various illustrations to find ones that are especially meaningful for a particular child.
- Practice in cognitive empathy can be conducted using materials from social-skills publishers like LinguiSystems (see Resources), or it can simply be practiced during the normal course of the day as particular issues come up. Role-playing activities are particularly helpful.
- Watching videos of social interactions, then stopping to discuss what's been observed can also be very helpful, as can providing comments in real time to the child on your own feelings and emotions. It's important, though, to keep rules and observations simple, especially at first.
- Around the house, autistic children should be required to engage in at least some simple helping activities, and they should be provided with frequent feedback on how their activities are contributing to the successful operation of the family. Often these children will be limited in the ways they can help, but they can usually be given simple jobs like holding doors when others are taking out the trash, carrying light bags of groceries, or getting a Band-Aid or ice pack when a sibling is hurt.
- Enlist the aid of teachers, too, and maintain close communication so practice at school can be coordinated with practice at home.

Helping Autistic Children Improve
Their Social Interactions

Improving the autistic child's social understanding is only part of the solution. It's also important to improve his knowledge of what to do and how to act in different situations. In addition to the techniques we've just mentioned, the following should be helpful:

- Rule-based social learning is essential. Talking through various social situations using pictures or cartoons with word captions can be very helpful for many children. Be methodical, and provide examples for solving various social problems in a systematic way. Discuss the likely viewpoints of others involved in these situations. Role-playing various hypothetical scenarios is also helpful.
- Early on, the use of rewards may be required as well.
- Emphasize the importance of finding "win-win" solutions, and explore ways to solve social conflicts through compromise. Help these children practice putting their wants into words and explaining them to others. Help them think also about what other people might want. Provide a list of simple alternatives, like *taking turns, asking for help, changing tasks, coming back later,* or *changing partners,* that can be used to resolve many social problems in school-age children.
- Highly visual children may benefit from a wall chart or set of pocket cards that contain visual prompts for various alternatives.
- Having a responsible adult or adolescent who can "shadow" the child during real-world activities can also promote developing skills. The shadow can remind the child to use strategies to resolve problems, provide prompts to initiate social interactions with other children, help maintain focus on activities, and point out situations where the child can employ previously learned strategies or rules. Visual, verbal, or tactile prompts can be used initially, then withdrawn over time.
- Provide opportunities to learn and practice play skills. Children with distractibility or overload issues usually do better with small groups or one-on-one play.

- Different-age children may be best for different activities: older children for more intellectual interests and younger children for more physical play. Rather than thinking in terms of "best friends," it may be better to identify specific playmates for specific activities.

- For play practice, it can even be helpful to hire a fun but responsible older child or teenager to act as play coordinator for an hour or two a week. Such coordinators can provide structured interactions and model turn taking and social communication. They will also be more patient and flexible than a same-age peer yet more fun and peerlike than an adult.

Helping Children with Autistic Communication Impairments

Communication involves both comprehension and expression of both verbal and nonverbal signals. In the following four sections, we'll discuss steps to help autistic children improve their comprehension and expression of both verbal and nonverbal forms of communication.

Improving Verbal Comprehension

Verbal language comprehension involves many different functions including attention, auditory processing (or visual processing for reading), and language processing of word parts, whole words, sentences, and narratives (or broader discourse). Autistic children may show many different patterns of language deficits, even among those who receive the same diagnosis (like PDD-NOS or Asperger's syndrome). The first step in deciding how to help any child improve her communication skills is to figure out where the breakdowns in language processing are occurring.

- Auditory processing deficits are extremely common in children with autistic disorders and frequently result in problems with sound localization, hearing in the presence of background noise, acting in response to linguistic commands, and interpreting prosodic or "music of speech" cues. Interventions for these problems are discussed in detail in Chapter 5, but in general cut down on background noise and speak in a slow, clear voice with exaggerated inflection and tonal emphasis. This will improve their perception of both the verbal and nonverbal elements of speech.

- Many autistic children show difficulties at both the individual word level (with learning new words or having overly literal or concrete word understandings) and at the sentence and higher discourse level.

  - For many autistic children, individual words have very specific and concrete meanings. Often these meanings relate to some particular incident in the child's past. For example, the word *break* may mean something that happened to a particular toy at a specific time in the past. Because autistic children frequently won't volunteer when they're confused by word meanings, a bit of detective work may be needed.

  - Try not to rely too much on words to define other words. Provide physical or visual examples. For example, to broaden his or her understanding of the word *break*, the child could be allowed to handle different types of broken objects (for instance, other broken toys, a flashlight that doesn't shine, or spaghetti noodles broken for cooking).

  - Pictures (including homemade digital pictures arranged into semantic maps, as described in Chapter 6) and videos can be useful for illustrating many types of word meanings without using words. Be sure to provide multiple examples so the child can learn to distinguish the general terms represented by the items from the specific items pictured.

  - Enactments and role plays can also be used to help broaden meanings, especially for more abstract words like *fairness* or *justice* (for instance, sharing a piece of cake).

- At the whole-sentence level, autistic children often have difficulty understanding how word interactions (e.g., grammar) can affect sentence meaning. Sometimes—especially when young—they reveal their difficulties by using memorized "scripts" or echoed speech (echolalia) to express their wishes. This repetition of entire phrases often indicates an inability to break whole phrases into component words and assign meanings to each. As children age and become more verbal, these patterns diminish. However, difficulties interpreting (and expressing) tenses, pronouns, and other grammatical features may remain. At the higher language level, difficulties with narrative sequence and figurative language are extremely common.

- Problems understanding higher-order language are often best addressed using visual supports. Comprehension of figurative language or multiple word meanings can be improved through practice with workbooks that use simple drawings and straight-forward illustrations for figurative speech or idioms (e.g., "It's raining cats and dogs"). Children may need to look at several different examples of the same phrase before they can infer the general meaning and translate their understanding to new situations. (Helpful materials are listed in Resources, Chapter 6.)

  - Children with Asperger's syndrome tend to have fewer problems with individual word meanings or syntax but still have difficulty with higher-order language. The interventions just described will be appropriate for these problems as well. Children with Asperger's syndrome often have especially pronounced problems detecting the prosody of language (see Chapter 5 for descriptions and reservations).

- Children with autistic disorders often experience a leap in understanding when they learn to read. Because difficulties with auditory processing are common, they may take in information better through reading than listening.

  - Closed-captioning of TV and videos can provide excellent opportunities for accurately observing social speech and the ways words correspond with facial expressions and gestures. Many autistic children find it easier to observe (repeatedly!) word usages, actions, and gestures in video formats (especially cartoons) than in "real life."

- Caution: Many children with autistic disorders prefer fact-based information, like documentaries and nonfiction books. If not balanced by plenty of exposure to informal social language, these materials may exaggerate the child's natural tendency to sound oddly formal, like a documentary host.

Improving Nonverbal Comprehension

The nonverbal physical and contextual clues that can help a child understand what's being said, who is speaking, in what setting, in what tone of voice, with what gestures or facial expressions, and other such indicators of meaning are an important part of communication. Teaching cognitive strategies like those used to enhance empathy can help autistic children learn to reflectively process nonverbal information that most people process automatically.

- In addition, practice using the kinds of interventions described in Chapter 4 for children with face blindness (prosopagnosia) and in Chapter 5 for children with impairments in their ability to detect auditory prosody can be very helpful.
- Watching films (animated films are often a good place to start), while pausing for frequent comments on the relationship between verbal and nonverbal factors like the words used, gestures and facial expressions used, and tone of voice used, can provide clues as to the speakers' meaning. Get children to study these films like little scientists trying to study a foreign culture. Help them develop rules for what different gestures or expressions can mean and what kinds of conversations are appropriate in different kinds of places or settings or between different kinds of people.
- Because there are so many variables in different settings or situations, social context is often baffling for children with autistic disorders. Having a parent or teacher provide very specific contextual

information immediately before entering a new situation or role-playing different social situations can be helpful.

- It can also be helpful to have the child practice gestures and facial expressions in front of a mirror. Have her pretend to be a character from a favorite movie (often the script can be obtained online) and deliver some of that character's lines, while mimicking the nonverbal expressions. Give her feedback to help her "performance" become more relaxed and natural. One interesting thing about facial expressions is that some of them, like pain, disgust, surprise, and joy, are universal and innate. Even though autistic children may not make these faces intentionally, they may sometimes make them automatically. By getting them to deliberately practice these gestures, they may actually develop a better cognitive understanding of their meanings when they are used by someone else.

Improving Verbal Expression

Strategies for improving verbal expression should be tailored to the nature of the underlying language problem. Specific interventions are outlined in Chapter 6. However, several general points are important.

- Teaching about social context can improve understanding of what kinds of topics are appropriate for different settings or with different kinds of people. One helpful way to practice is to take digital photographs of various family members or colleagues at school, then make a notebook containing the pictures. Under the pictures, place information about the person's age, relationship to the child, interests, possible topics for conversation, and good opening phrases when they meet. Help the child practice conversing by pretending to be the different characters.
- Focus on different language styles that are appropriate for different settings: which words are formal, which are relaxed, and with whom to use each kind of speech. Again, videos can be helpful.
- Share your own experiences and struggles getting to know people. Let the child observe you interacting with others. When he does his

best on an interaction, praise him for his courage, then give him feedback and encouragement.

- Many children with autism have problems understanding and remembering temporal sequences—that is, remembering and expressing how things have occurred with respect to time.

  - Language problems may contribute to sequencing difficulties, especially if the child has difficulty understanding language *tenses*. To improve the understanding of tenses, practice reading or telling stories that are entirely in one tense (i.e., past, present, or future). By consistently grouping tense forms and linking them with past, present, or future events, the child can improve her sense of ordering in time.

  - Using picture sets that can be arranged to tell stories can improve a child's ability to tell stories or relate events in sequence. Story tile sets can be purchased from many educational supply stores and can be a good source of practice, but they may be too hard at first. Often it will be easier to start with a story the child already knows well. Appropriate picture sheets can be obtained by taking digital photographs of a TV screen while a favorite video is playing or by saving still frames from a DVD onto a computer drive. The child can then practice laying out the panels of the story in sequence. As the child's sequencing abilities improve, she can then practice narrating the events as she lays out the pictures.

  - Sequences of facts or to-do activities can often be better remembered by pairing items with music. Setting important lists to favorite songs can improve both memory and sequence.

Improving Nonverbal Expression

Many of the same techniques described above for improving nonverbal comprehension will be useful for improving nonverbal expression. In addition, the following interventions can help with eye contact and expressive gestures:

- Parents and teachers should be patient and flexible in their expectations regarding eye contact. While most autistic children can gradually improve their ability to make eye contact, especially with those with whom they are comfortable, their language intake and output may often become swamped if they try to make sustained eye contact while speaking or listening. In general, it's best to aim for occasional brief glances rather than sustained visual contact.

- First, tell the child why eye contact is valued by other people (i.e., that it expresses interest, communicates emotion, etc.) and why a failure to make at least occasional eye contact can be troubling to other people.
- Second, practice making direct eye contact. See how long the child can look directly into your eyes, take a break, then try again.
- Third, as eye contact improves, begin challenging the child to recite back a well-known sequence of information (like the ABCs or the number sequence) while maintaining eye contact.
- Fourth, after the child improves his ability to speak a familiar sequence while maintaining eye contact, say a sentence to him while looking into his eyes, then get him to repeat it back. With practice, his ability to avoid "overload" with eye contact can improve significantly, especially with family, teachers, and friends.

- Practice speaking while eliminating unusual body postures or limb movements. Substitute more restrained hand gestures if the child feels the need to move while speaking.

Helping Autistic Children with Attention and Self-Regulation

Helping Autistic Children Improve Attention

As we've mentioned, attention problems of all varieties are common in autistic children. The following general steps can help most autistic children:

- Provide information in the form a child can most easily process. Difficulties processing language, sound, or visual cues can worsen inattentiveness. Identify the child's strongest input and processing systems, and use those for learning. Avoid activities that require multitasking or the simultaneous use of different input and/or output systems, like hearing and moving or seeing and talking.

- Avoid overloading processing systems by providing information in small chunks and teaching strategies to divide tasks into manageable bits that can be completed without frequent shifts in attention.

- Even children with fairly severe difficulties in selective and sustained attention may learn well in frequent short snippets. Frequent reminders and redirections may be needed. In the rapid prompting method, children are frequently redirected by an aide with either verbal reminders (e.g., "Stay on task") or physical reminders (e.g., taps on the shoulder or pointing) to return focus to what they should be doing. Having an adult serve as "surrogate attention" can be a big help, especially at first.

- Engaging the autistic child's systems of motivation and reward is also crucial (see above).

- Autistic children frequently have difficulty gauging the passage of time, which can complicate pacing and transitions. Using easily visible egg (or other) timers can help in these areas.

- Difficulty generating alternative possibilities and approaches contributes greatly to cognitive inflexibility in autistic children. Generating alternative possibilities and approaches requires the work of the brain's Chief Creativity Officer, who is headquartered in the right frontal lobe and who coordinates inputs from many other brain areas. Small wonder this is hard for autistic children. To improve their mental flexibility, teach them rule-based approaches to generating alternatives. Create short lists of alternatives for frequently encountered circumstances (e.g., *What do I do if another child wants to play with something I'm playing with? What if I want to play with something she's playing with? What do I talk about when I meet a new child I've never met before? What do I do if I lose my mom at the store?*). Provide one or more answers for each question.

- Biofeedback or neurobehavioral training (as described in Chapter 7) can be helpful.
- Autistic children with attention problems can sometimes benefit from the medications used to treat ADHD. The advice of a mental health professional with expertise in both autism and attention problems will be useful.
- The first step in dealing with perseverative (repetitious) activities is discovering why the child is engaging in them. Parents usually discourage repetitive activities, because they look odd, draw undesirable attention, and stigmatize the child among his fellow schoolchildren, yet self-stimulatory behaviors like rocking, bouncing, flapping, or producing visual stimulations may be calming, alerting, or simply pleasurable for the child.

  - Some children attend better when they're standing, walking, rocking, or swinging. (Motion perception appears to integrate the processing of sight, sound, and touch.) In addition, firm touch and rhythmic activities like rocking (which stimulates position, pressure, and motion sensors) can be calming for many children. In many ways, these activities are simply more exaggerated versions of the kinds of movements like foot tapping or gum chewing that many people find soothing and alerting. If such activities do not greatly interfere (or if they help) with learning, then the child should have some freedom to engage in these behaviors. We've seen several children who showed dramatic improvements in verbal fluency when allowed to pace while talking.
  - See whether environmental factors are provoking these behaviors. Do self-stimulatory behaviors increase when lessons are not engaging or are too difficult, or when students, teachers, or other factors (e.g., noise, movement) provoke anxiety? Eliminate offending factors.
  - Often it's neither possible nor worthwhile to wholly extinguish repetitive behaviors. However, it can be necessary to channel repetitive movements into less disruptive and more socially appropriate forms. Sometimes perseverations can be redirected

with simple verbal or visual reminders. Helpful sensory fidgets include double sticks of chewing gum, executive "fidgets" like squeeze balls, bouncy seat cushions, a therapy ball for a seat, etc. These alternatives can provide "organizing" input without the social stigma. When repetitive behaviors are intrusive or unpleasant to the child and when they cross into the realm of obsessive-compulsive disorder, they require the care of a skilled mental health professional.

Helping Autistic Children Improve Emotional Self-Regulation

Children with autistic disorders often have difficulty with emotional control and self-regulation. Several factors contribute to these difficulties. First, problems with "mirroring" and imitation make it hard for them to perceive behavioral norms and to model their behavior after others. Second, autistic children often have difficulty monitoring their own feelings, internal bodily states, and emotional responses. They frequently have difficulty realizing when they're hungry, thirsty, in pain, or tired and when these sensations are contributing to emotional fluctuations or irritability. Third, autistic children often have especially intense feelings and emotions. There is actually evidence that some stimuli may more powerfully affect the brain's emotion centers in autistic than in nonautistic individuals. As a result, autistic children may experience states of neurological hyperarousal in situations of stress or sensory overload, like when they visit new places, meet new people, try new activities, face difficult processing tasks, or are forced to transition to new activities without understanding why the change is necessary, what's coming up, or what's expected of them.

- To improve a child's emotional regulation, begin by providing as much structure as possible in both scheduling and the physical environment. For children who attend school, this might mean coordinating with the teacher to provide warnings before transitions (at ten minutes, five minutes, and one minute), consistent routines for daily activities (like preparing to eat lunch or to go home), consistent seating locations in circle time, et cetera.

- Help children understand how various situations or environments contribute to their emotional meltdowns. Understanding why rage or anxiety attacks occur can be important to breaking the cycle. Look for particular sensory factors (auditory, visual, tactile, balance and motion) that may contribute to overloading.
- Help them recognize the signs that their feelings are getting out of hand, and teach them strategies for dealing with these problems (voluntary time-out, biofeedback, asking for help, etc.).
- High-functioning autistic children can also benefit from insight into the effects that bodily development (like growth spurts and hormonal surges) can have on their emotions.
- When discussing with the child how to prevent future meltdowns, focus on things each of you can do. Avoid dwelling on past failures. Obsessing on the past often precipitates additional meltdowns.
- Serious mood and emotional problems require the help of a mental health professional. Autistic children often have difficulties with anxiety and, as they age, depression. Medications or other forms of therapy may be needed.

- Reducing impulsivity can be difficult, but it is important, because impulsivity interferes greatly with learning and social relationships. Although impulsivity often improves as children age, this improvement can be hastened through efforts on the part of parents and children.

  - Both inconsistent discipline and emotional parental responses to misbehavior worsen impulsivity in children. Firm and consistent limits and coolheadedness—even when misbehavior is deliberate—are essential. Autistic children require lots of structure and fare much better with clear demands and predictable consequences.
  - Impulsivity worsens when children become more aroused. Keep an eye out for rising arousal, and help institute the calming activities described above.
  - Provide praise (and, if appropriate, rewards) when the child succeeds in patiently waiting or in self-calming if he becomes impatient.

- Encourage activities that require waiting, persistent focus, and turn taking. Games like Go Fish, Chutes and Ladders, or Candyland are good practice. Computerized versions of basic games (like Hoyle's Kids Games) where children play against computerized characters may be especially easy to play yet require waiting while the other "players" take their turns. Computerized play of this sort is often nice practice before playing unsupervised with other children.

- When impulsive episodes occur, determine whether sensory overload, bodily factors (like hunger, thirst, or growth spurts), or impaired communication played a role, and try to avoid those factors in the future.

- Remember, not all actions that appear like impulsive misbehavior really are. Autistic children may appear impulsive because of missed or misunderstood visual or auditory social cues. It's important to separate errors in understanding from errors in self-control and deliberate misbehavior.

- Homeschooling can be a good option for some children with autism. Autistic children often have a greater desire to please their parents than anyone else, and sensory distractions can often be limited. Social and academic challenges can also be increased in a more gradual and incremental fashion that will be more likely to lead to success than will forced interactions with unselected children.

9

Mixed Messages

Sensory Processing Disorder

Sensory integration is the organization of sensations for use. Our senses give us information about the physical conditions of our body and the environment around us. . . . Countless bits of sensory information enter our brain at every moment, not only from our eyes and ears but from every place in our body. . . . The brain must organize all of these sensations if a person is to move and learn and behave in a productive manner. . . . When sensations flow in a well-organized or integrated manner, the brain can use those sensations to form perceptions, behaviors, and learning. When the flow of sensations is disorganized, life can be like a rush-hour traffic jam.

—A. JEAN AYRES, *SENSORY INTEGRATION*
AND THE CHILD

Jerome was a handsome and rather shy six-year-old, who held tightly to his mother's hand the first time he walked into our clinic. Jerome didn't speak in response to our greetings, though he smiled sweetly before ducking behind his mother's leg. After a little coaxing, he quietly separated from his mother and began to explore our clinic. He passed by a number of popular "boy traps"—a group of *Star Wars* figurines, a hammock swing, and assorted gym mats—and instead picked up a book on robotics. He sat and read quietly for the next twenty minutes, while his mother told us about his recent problems. As she talked, it became harder and harder to believe that this quiet and bookish young man could be the same child she was describing: the one who'd been put on probation by his private kindergarten for repeated "behavioral problems."

Jerome, we learned, had spent most of his early life at home with his stay-at-home mom. However, several months previously, he'd begun attending a private half-day kindergarten. Because he was obviously a very bright child (he'd learned all of his numbers, colors, and the letters of the alphabet before he was two and a half, had read at three, and was currently reading at a third-grade level), his parents had assumed he would enjoy school. They could not have been more wrong. When his mother went to pick him up after his first day in class, she found him crying in a corner. The teacher gave her a tired smile. "He's an only child, isn't he?" she said knowingly. Actually, Jerome had a four-year-old sister with whom he played very well. "Well," the teacher responded, "probably just first-day jitters."

After Jerome continued to have "first-day jitters" each day for the next three weeks, this benign explanation lost much of its luster. Every day ended with the same flood of tears and some new tale of misbehavior from his teachers. Jerome seemed unable to "go along with the flow" in class. During story time, he lay down flat on the floor or stood up rather than sit cross-legged as he was told. He refused to use scissors and didn't like to draw during art time. During free play, he often stood by himself at the edge of the room or gravitated to the bookstand, where he engaged in solitary reading. During music, he was uncooperative and "rude," covering his ears whenever the other children began to sing and refusing to dance or do the motions that went with the songs. On several occasions (when things had gotten really boisterous), he began screaming and suffered a complete emotional meltdown. Often he didn't even respond when the teachers tried to speak with him. When the children formed into lines to go outside,

Jerome sometimes became hostile and physically aggressive if other children bumped him, and when they began walking, he often tripped and fell, which provoked more tears and accusations. Before the first month of school was over, Jerome's teachers informed his parents that his behavior would have to improve soon or he wouldn't be allowed back.

Jerome's parents were shocked by their son's behavior, and, to be honest, they were also deeply embarrassed. They had always worked hard to teach Jerome to be kind and considerate to others and had always believed he had taken these lessons to heart. He was usually so sweet with his sister and so good when playing with her. He was highly affectionate and tender with his family, and he was very morally sensitive. That his behavior at school could be so different from his behavior at home seemed not only inexplicable but inconceivable as well.

SENSORY PROCESSING DISORDER: WHEN INFORMATION . . . ISN'T

We see many children like Jerome in our clinic: happy and well behaved in the quiet, stable, low-stress environment at home, but confused, overwhelmed, and ultimately unruly in the complex environment at school. Like these children, Jerome had difficulty understanding what was going on around him in all the noise and commotion of the classroom. Somehow the information coming in through his senses, which was supposed to keep him informed, only confused him. Consequently he couldn't respond to his environment with appropriate feelings or actions.

Jerome was suffering from a common but frequently misunderstood condition called *sensory processing disorder*. Sensory processing disorder (also known as sensory integration disorder, or dysfunction) is a brain-based problem with information processing that is characterized by difficulty understanding and responding appropriately to sensory inputs.

Children with sensory processing disorder (which we'll hereafter refer to as SPD) typically have difficulty "feeling at home" in their environment—often even in their own skins. They find the information coming in through their senses confusing and contradictory and the task of distinguishing threats from harmless stimuli difficult and dangerously slow. As a result, they may feel as if their senses—and their very selves—are under a constant state of siege. Often they appear stressed and hypervigilant, as if at any moment expecting some new disaster, yet they may respond slowly and ineffectually when danger really does appear. They may react with terror to a relatively nonthreatening stimulus, like an inadvertent bump from a classmate, the rub of a hairbrush across the scalp, or the sound of a flute playing a happy tune, yet completely ignore the sound of an oncoming car, the sight of a dog with bared teeth and raised hackles, or the dangerous flicker of an open flame. This inability to easily process and understand sensory inputs can complicate every aspect of their interactions with the environment.

In this chapter, we'll discuss the many special problems faced by children with SPD. We'll also discuss the many ways they can be made to process sensory information more accurately, respond to it more appropriately, and feel more emotionally and behaviorally in control. Let's begin by looking at the many different behaviors that can be seen in children with SPD.

BEHAVIORS ASSOCIATED WITH SENSORY PROCESSING DISORDER

Many of the behaviors shown by children with SPD reflect (as its name suggests) difficulties processing sensory inputs. Often these difficulties arise from problems in the types of higher-order processing steps that require the smooth integration (or interactions) of different brain systems. In this respect, SPD is similar to the autistic disorders we described in the last chapter. Like many of the behaviors seen in children with autistic disorders, the behaviors seen in children with SPD often reflect the breakdown in connections between brain systems that allow these systems to work in a coordinated fashion. This similarity is further demonstrated by the fact that most autistic children also show signs of SPD. However, the majority of children with SPD are not autistic, because they do not experience breakdowns in the connections that control social affiliation and emotional empathy. Instead the behaviors they display reflect difficulties processing complex sensory information, both so they can fully understand it and so they can respond to it in an appropriate manner. (We'll have more to say about the relationship of autism and SPD in our Causes section.)

Before we look in more detail at the particular behaviors associated with SPD, we need to make an important preliminary comment: Although we'll be listing many different behaviors or symptoms and dividing them into different sensory or motor categories, these behaviors should not be thought of as each resulting from different neurological deficits. These behaviors all result from a single nervous-system process, as we'll describe below. In other words, SPD is not just a collection of isolated behaviors or deficits, but a multisystem neurological condition that results from problems connecting and coordinating different brain systems.

Now let's look in more detail at the behaviors associated with this condition.

Three Categories of Behaviors Associated with Sensory Processing Disorder

Most behaviors associated with SPD fall into one of three general categories: (1) impaired sensory discrimination, (2) impaired sensory regulation, and (3) sensory-seeking behaviors. Let's look at each.

Impaired Sensory Discrimination

Behaviors in the first category suggest that a child has difficulty identifying the nature or source of sensory stimulation — that is, *what* the source of the stimulus is or *where* it is coming from. This trait is sometimes known as *impaired sensory discrimination*. *What*-type discrimination problems can involve any sensory system, including the visual and auditory systems (see Chapters 4 and 5), touch (e.g., size, shape, or weight), movement or position, smell or taste, or internal bodily sensation (e.g., thirst, hunger, fatigue, or the need to empty bowels or bladder). *Where*-type discrimination problems include difficulties localizing sources of sensory stimulation either in three-dimensional space or on a personal body map. We'll have more to say about these difficulties in our Causes section.

Impaired Sensory Regulation

Behaviors in the second category suggest that a child has special difficulty regulating (or modulating) the amount of sensory information that enters her conscious awareness. We've spoken in previous chapters about the largely unconscious process by which sensory input is classified either as important enough to attend to or unimportant enough to ignore. Children with SPD often admit either too much or too little information to the level of conscious awareness. As you'll notice, this sounds very much like the kind of problem with selective attention we described in Chapter 7. In some ways it is, but there are also differences that distinguish these problems. First, children with SPD display these difficulties with sensory regulation in the context of a broader disorder affecting the function of the sensory and motor systems. Second, these problems don't just result in distractions that pull kids off task, but they actually produce real confusion, anxiety, and even fear, often with significant emotional and behavioral consequences. In other words, these children don't simply face a competition among various stimuli for their attention; rather they experience a real sense of threat and danger, which, as we'll see later, is connected to the action of their fight-or-flight mechanism in the autonomic (i.e., automatic) nervous system. Let's quickly take a look at the two main consequences of these difficulties with sensory regulation.

- Children who receive too much information into conscious awareness will be flooded by more information than they can reliably process. As a result, two contrasting and seemingly contradictory things may occur. First, these children may be so overwhelmed by the deluge of information that they miss important details and fail to respond appropriately to their environment. Second, they may appear overresponsive (or hypersensitive) to unimportant sensory stimuli and, as a consequence, be unable to ignore the "little distractions" most of us tune out effortlessly, like the scratching of a shirt tag or the buzzing of a fluorescent light. They may also appear overstimulated, distractible, overwhelmed, or agitated by things going on around them. To calm themselves down, they may become sensory-avoidant, "turn off" their input systems, "crawl into their shell," or engage in fight-or-flight behaviors. Jerome experienced just such problems.

- In contrast, children who receive too little information into conscious awareness will be underresponsive (or hyposensitive) to sensory stimuli. Such children may fail to respond appropriately to the environment or may appear insufficiently alert. To stay alert (which of course they must to function well in school), they may engage in self-stimulating or sensory-seeking behaviors (see below).

As we'll discuss later, children with SPD may be overresponsive to some stimuli and underresponsive to others, or their responsiveness to stimuli may vary over time. In general, it's better to think of their sensory regulation functions as poorly controlled and erratic rather than generally over- or underresponsive. Typically these children have as much difficulty regulating motor output as they do sensory input.

Sensory-Seeking Behaviors

Behaviors in the third category suggest that a child is in need of additional sensory stimulation and are known as sensory-seeking behaviors. Children with SPD frequently seek abnormally intense or frequent stimulation of various senses (primarily movement or pressure, but also touch). There appear to be two primary reasons for these behaviors.

First, children with SPD often have difficulty processing the position and pressure cues that they receive from balance and touch receptors in various parts of their bodies. As a result, they may have trouble automatically determining their body's position in space. This uncertainty about their position can leave them insecure and anxious and can result in poorly coordinated movements. By actively seeking movements that will stimulate their balance, touch, and position sensors, these children are able to obtain more precise information about their position in space, which results in greater security and stability and helps maintain posture, muscle tone, and balance.

Second, many children with SPD engage in frequent touch and movement activities with their hands. Often they will be found on exam to have a poor sense of where their fingers are in space, and touching or pressing various objects seems to help them maintain better focus, alertness, and orientation.

Specific Behaviors Associated with
Sensory Processing Disorder

The following behaviors are each associated with SPD. As you read these lists, remember that every child (even those without SPD) will show some of these behaviors at least some of the time. However, children with SPD can be distinguished from other children in that they tend to show more of these behaviors, more frequently, with greater intensity, and involving more bodily systems than do other children. Most important, for children with SPD, these behaviors do not simply irritate and annoy but cause significant functional impairment; they prevent children from doing the things they need or want to do. Let's look at these behaviors on a system-by-system basis.

Behaviors Related to Vision

Children with SPD often have difficulties with visual processing. They may show any of the behaviors discussed in Chapter 4 or:

- Display sensitivity to bright lights, strong colors, or shiny paper. (Less commonly, they may crave these stimuli.)
- Wear sunglasses or colored lenses indoors or on cloudy days.
- Complain of strobe effect from fluorescent lights.
- Have trouble seeing patterns on visually busy or crowded fields or on pages with lots of lines, like graph paper.
- Have trouble maintaining eye contact.

Behaviors Related to Hearing

Central auditory processing disorders (CAPDs) are extremely common in children with SPD. They may show any of the behaviors described in Chapter 5, and especially:

- Display hypersensitivity to sounds (e.g., cover ears to loud noises like vacuum cleaners, clothes dryers, marching bands, etc., especially when young).

- Have emotional meltdowns in noisy places, like at birthday parties, ball games, parades, or movies.
- Complain of hums or buzzes from electronic devices (lights, TVs, etc.) that others don't hear or aren't bothered by.
- Become distracted by even faint background noise.
- Speak in an unusually loud voice.
- Exhibit unusual pitch patterns (prosody) in speech.
- Fail to respond to name being called.

Behaviors Related to Touch

Children with impaired touch (or tactile) discrimination often have difficulty identifying what's touching their bodies or what they themselves are touching. They may show the following behaviors:

- Display defensiveness to touch sensations of all kinds. May react with hostility or revulsion toward friendly or affectionate touches. May avoid being hugged or held and may react strongly to being bumped or touched by others. May tolerate deep pressure but not light caresses.
- Hate grooming activities like bathing, hair combing or brushing, cutting hair or fingernails, toothbrushing.
- Feel extreme sensitivity to clothing tags, firm or irritating fabrics (like jeans or wool), socks and especially sock seams, shoes, shirts that touch the armpits or pants that squeeze the groin or thighs, underwear. May prefer to go around the house almost naked.
- Be unusually squeamish (or unusually passionate) about activities involving water or messy substances like finger paints and glue.
- Have oral touch sensitivities (lips, tongue, and mouth) that cause strong food preferences. May avoid (or seek) foods of particular textures—soft or crunchy, wet or mushy, sticky, thick, chewy—and will often avoid mixed foods.
- May engage in sensory-seeking behaviors, which may involve either pressure sensation (see below) or light touch. May constantly seek to touch different surfaces or textures, or to pick things up and feel them. May preferentially seek oral stimulation and constantly stick things in

mouth. May frequently chew on clothes, fingernails and toenails, or
even on their digits themselves. May seek out tactile experiences most
people find unpleasant, like asking to be tickled or spanked.

- Some children who are underresponsive to touch may show unusually high pain thresholds, even sustaining injuries without being
aware of them.

Behaviors Related to Taste and Smell

Children with SPD may have difficulty discriminating different smells and
tastes or have strong aversions to certain smells and tastes.

- They are often notoriously picky eaters. May prefer bland or mildly
sweet foods, like pastas, breads, and potatoes. As one mother described her son, "Sweet or wheat, he will eat."
- They may have overpowering reactions to the smells of foods, sometimes causing retching or vomiting. They may be unable to help
prepare food, clean up the dishes, or take out the trash.
- Underresponsive children may have difficulty detecting the smell of
burning objects (e.g., toast).

Behaviors Related to Balance, Body
Position, and Movement

Children with SPD often have difficulty telling where their bodies are in
space using balance (vestibular) and position (proprioceptive) systems. As a
result, they may show:

- Unexpected falls when walking or running or even standing
and turning.
- Falls from chair to floor for no apparent reason.
- Frequent bumps into things or other people.
- A tendency to avoid rapid movement or vigorous play and to stay at
the periphery of the play area.
- Anxiety in crowded situations, especially when walking.
- Anxiety walking on unstable or uneven surfaces.
- Insecurity with escalators or stairs.

- Trouble learning to ride a bike, to skip, or to jump rope.
- A tendency to cling to supports, especially in crowds or when walking, holding on to or leaning against others.
- A tendency to use vision and touch to perform movements that others do automatically.
- Problems with motion sickness and a tendency to avoid movement.
- Alternatively, seeking out heavy pressure and movement to stimulate pressure and position sensors in the large joints (e.g., jumping off heights; bouncing on beds, sofas, and trampolines; crashing into walls or onto floors; climbing under heavy objects; or asking others to lie on them).
- A tendency to seek vestibular (balance) stimulation by swinging, spinning, rocking, or rolling on the ground.
- A preference for spending time with the head in the down position (e.g., lying with lower body on bed or sofa while reading a book on the floor with upper body hanging off bed).

Behaviors Related to Internal Body Sensations

Children with SPD often have difficulty identifying and responding appropriately to internal body sensations (interoception). Often these children appear unusually "out of touch" with their bodies.

- Overresponsive children may behave like hypochondriacs, complaining often of feeling sick and worrying about every little bump or sore or bodily sensation.
- They may use the bathroom surprisingly often, because of being oversensitive to bowel or bladder stimulation.
- They may complain of feeling hot or cold when others are comfortable.
- Underresponsive children may have difficulty recognizing when they're hungry or thirsty. Children with little desire to eat may suffer growth retardation and need to be coaxed to eat every bite.
- Irregular sleep patterns are common, including difficulty falling asleep, wakening at night, trouble telling when they're tired and what to do in response. One child told us, "When I get feeling all floppy and droopy, that's when I know I should try running around more."

- Difficulty telling when they need to empty bowels or bladder may cause problems with potty training, constipation, or "accidents," often with seemingly no warning sensation beforehand.

Behaviors Related to Impaired Sensorimotor Integration

The sensory and motor (muscle-movement) systems must work closely together to create coordinated movement. Children with SPD typically have difficulty integrating these two systems. As a result, they may show poor motor coordination, or *sensorimotor dyspraxia* (literally "difficulty with action"). Children with sensorimotor dyspraxia have trouble using sensory information (including feedback from touch and position sensors) to plan, implement, monitor, and modify complex motor actions. Their movements thus appear awkward, halting, and poorly coordinated, and they may show the following behaviors:

- In infancy, they may have difficulty rolling over, controlling their head, sitting unsupported, learning to crawl on all fours (instead preferring the belly-based "commando crawl").
- Crawling often begins late (after the ninth month) and lasts only a month or less before "sofa surfing" begins. Walking is usually on time, though in some children it may be late.
- Sometimes significant *oromotor dyspraxia* (problems coordinating the mouth, tongue, swallowing and speech muscles) may cause delayed or abnormal speech, eating, and swallowing.
- In older children, problems with poor postural muscle support and poor peripheral muscle tone are common. Children may show difficulty sitting upright in a seat without a back; difficulty sitting on the floor in a normal cross-legged position (a tendency to slump or lie down, or to stand or ask for a chair); a tendency to slump down in chairs or lay the head on a desk; a preference to stand by a desk rather than sit; and arm and leg muscles that are weak and fatigue easily and may feel soft and doughy (or, less commonly, excessively rigid) to the touch (i.e., low tone).
- Problems with gross-motor control are common, including jerky, ineffectual, or poorly coordinated movements; difficulty playing games

that involve movement, running, or even walking in tight spaces or in lines with other kids; and a tendency to avoid gross motor activities altogether or become the proverbial "bull in the china shop" who's always falling or knocking into something.

- Problems with fine motor control are also common, including difficulty with handwriting; unusual grips for pens and pencils; difficulty using scissors, drawing, or coloring; difficulty dressing or grooming, especially using snaps, buttons, laces, or zippers; trouble using utensils; trouble opening doors and cabinets with knobs, pulls, and latches; and trouble with eye-muscle control for reading or near work.

Behaviors Related to Impaired Emotional Regulation

Children with SPD often have difficulties controlling and regulating their emotions. In most children, this appears to be due to the stresses caused by impaired sensory processing and integration (as described above), but in some it appears also to involve a more primary deficit in emotional regulation. The following behaviors may be seen:

- Signs of emotional intensity, including a tendency to respond to the perception of physical threats with a physical or emotional violence that seems completely out of proportion to the stimulus; severe tantrums, sometimes with seemingly little provocation but often at times of forced or unexpected transitions; the appearance of being brimful with emotion, ready to spill with the slightest tremor; the tendency when entering an overload phase to be completely lost to reason, self-control, punishments, threats, or promises (as one father told us, "When he goes into one of these binges, I could tell him I was going to throw his Xbox into Puget Sound if he didn't calm down, and it wouldn't even register"), which often results in resistance to traditional forms of discipline.
- These children often adapt poorly to changes of all kinds and especially to unexpected occurrences or transitions—even to activities they usually like—because they find the process of adjusting to new circumstances so hard.

- They may show an unusually low tolerance for frustration and appear rigid and inflexible. (Frustration may often be provoked by their own inability to perform tasks that others perform with ease, like dressing, eating, playing, or writing.)
- Emotional problems may be worsened by missed bodily cues for hunger and sleep. Often these children will experience their worst emotional problems in late morning or afternoon or in the evening before bed.

Behaviors Related to Social Functioning

Children with SPD often have difficulty with social interactions.

- Children who experience sensory confusion, especially in busy environments, often miss social cues. They may miss or misinterpret words, gestures, and expressions from adults and other children and fail to respond appropriately.
- They may also miss warning signals from animals, like bared teeth and raised hackles, and are at higher risk of being bitten.
- They may appear "odd" or simply different in the eyes of other children or adults.

  - Their difficulties controlling motor or vocal output may make them look or sound different from other children.
  - Their tendency to overload or shut down in noisy or chaotic places and to be disturbed by things that don't bother other people may make them look immature, bad, or "spacey."
  - Their difficulties perceiving "personal space" or "boundary" issues, coupled with balance insecurity, may result in a tendency to lean against, hold on to, or stand too close to other children or adults.

- Children with SPD are also frustratingly likely to have negative responses to activities or situations that appeal to most other children. Birthday parties, amusement parks, playgrounds, noisy restaurants, music class, movie theaters, and other noisy places can all cause sensory overload and meltdowns. Vigorous physical play may be avoided because of concerns about falling, sensory overload, and the potential for explosive outbursts and aggressive behaviors due to fight-or-flight reactions (see below). Perhaps most unfortunately, the kinds of things done by the teachers who work hardest to make their classrooms fun for most kids—busy, colorful places with lots of "activity stations," fun music, dancing, games—may be precisely the things that aggravate kids with SPD. As a result, these teachers may find that the harder they work to make class enjoyable and to involve these kids, the more they shut down or overload. It's hard to imagine a more potent recipe for frustration and misunderstanding on both sides.

CAUSES OF SENSORY PROCESSING DISORDER

When you read the extensive lists of behaviors presented above, two questions will probably spring to mind: Why do children with SPD display such a wide variety of problem behaviors? And what mechanisms could possibly account for this staggering array of sensory and sensorimotor problems?

The answers to these questions are suggested by the list of conditions with which SPD commonly occurs, as shown in Table 8.

One of the interesting things about this list is that most of these conditions fall into one of two basic categories:

1. Conditions that damage or disorder the brain directly, either through injury or as a result of genetic conditions that impair brain development.
2. Conditions that impair the sensory input that the brain needs to organize and develop.

Both categories of conditions have one thing in common: They disrupt the normal pattern of brain wiring that creates a functional and well-integrated nervous system. Let's see why this is so.

TABLE 8 *Conditions Associated with Sensory Processing Disorder*

- Premature birth.
- Birth injury or difficult birth (e.g., prolonged labor, prolonged induction, fetal distress).
- Premature labor, maternal bleeding, or other pregnancy-related difficulties.
- Neonatal stroke.
- Prolonged sensory deprivation (most commonly due to early prolonged hospitalization in intensive care or to institutionalization, as in overseas orphanages).
- Head trauma.
- Significant auditory or visual processing deficits (including complete blindness or deafness).
- Recurrent or prolonged seizures.
- Autism or autism spectrum disorders (see Chapter 8).
- Certain genetic conditions like fragile X syndrome or Down syndrome.
- Sensory processing disorder also appears to run in some families, particularly in association with autism-related disorders.
- Sensory processing disorder is also suspected by some experts to be more common in highly or profoundly gifted children.

Normal Brain Development: Mapping Out the World . . . Gradually

Let's review what we said in Chapter 2 about the brain's normal pattern of development. The brain isn't simply constructed according to a preset genetic or developmental plan. It's also formed (and continually re-formed) over a lengthy course of development by repeated neurological stimulation. Only after a long period of repeated interactions with the environment will a child develop the brain connections that allow her to ride a bike, catch a ball, do a math equation, or read a book about how her brain works.

As we've seen in our chapters on hearing and vision, developing a nervous system that can accurately perform all these functions depends upon a whole series of information-processing steps. The first step involves the ability to obtain accurate Information Input from the individual senses. As we've said before, "Garbage in, garbage out": If the initial input is sufficiently impaired, all the downstream processing steps will be impaired as well. Second, proper nervous system development also requires accurate Pattern Processing functions that can process, then reconcile (or integrate) the information received from each of the individual senses to create a clear, consistent, and nonconflicting picture of that world.

The importance of this integration process will be obvious to anyone who has experienced situations where the brain received conflicting messages from different senses. A common example is the condition known as vertigo, in which the eyes and the movement sensors in muscles and joints send the brain different signals about the body's movement and position in space from those being sent by the balance sensors in the inner ears. The result is chaos, confusion, imbalance, falls, and nausea. Children with SPD can experience such conflicting messages all the time. This can create significant problems for them in interacting with their world, since it's only by obtaining accurate, well-integrated, and nonconflicting signals that we can understand and respond to the world with appropriate Output for Action.

When all of these processes are working well and the nervous system is developing properly, this cycle of information among sensory Information Input, brain Pattern Processing, and motor Output for Action allows us to understand and respond to the environment quickly and accurately (see Figure 28). It allows us to identify the nature, intensity, and location of sensory stimuli; to respond to them with actions of the right type and strength; and to aim them in the right direction. It also allows us to monitor our own actions and modify them as necessary, because the senses provide the brain with a continuous flow of information it can use to make predictions and adjust its actions.

Unfortunately, in children with SPD, this information cycle does not always work well. Because their brains don't organize and integrate information in the smooth fashion we've described, they often have difficulty accurately perceiving their world and responding to it appropriately.

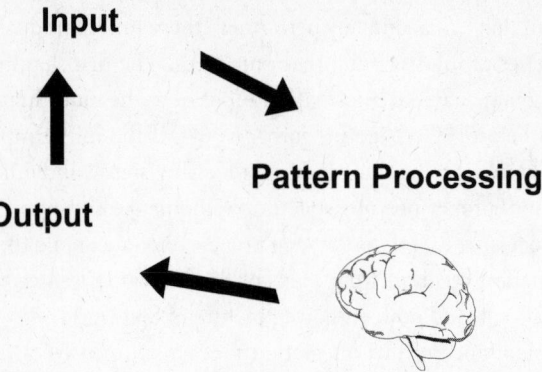

Environment

Input

Pattern Processing

Output

FIGURE 28. The Information Cycle in the Well-Integrated Nervous System

Because of the dynamic nature of brain development, these brain-based sensory processing difficulties don't remain fixed or stable over time. Instead the brain uses its capacity to develop, change, and reorganize with stimulation (that is, its plasticity) to create new and hopefully more functional connections through a continual process of rewiring. This is why children with SPD typically show gradual improvement over the course of years and why they often experience flares in symptoms (or even the development of new symptoms) during times of physical growth or physiological or emotional stress. While these rewired pathways can improve function in some areas, they can also produce inefficient connections or "crossed wiring" in others. Such inefficient and poorly integrated wiring can produce unclear, overlapping, or even contradictory signals. These imperfect connections can impair sensory and motor processing in several ways:

- They may trigger exaggerated responses or fail to respond when they should. This can result in the classic signs of sensory over- or underresponsiveness.
- They may cause mismatches between the messages received from different senses (e.g., the visual and balance mismatches in vertigo) that prevent the child from knowing where his body is in space or in relation to the things around him.

- They may also result in mismatches between sensory inputs and motor outputs, resulting in failure of coordinated or appropriately graded movement.

Understanding the Behaviors Associated with Sensory Processing Disorder

We're now in a position to better understand most of the confusing and troubling behaviors shown by children with SPD. As you remember from our Behaviors section, most of these behaviors can be grouped into three categories: those that reflect impaired sensory discrimination, those that reflect sensory over- and underresponsiveness, and those that reflect sensory seeking.

Impaired sensory discrimination often results from problems in many Information Input and Pattern Processing functions. We've discussed problems with visual and auditory processing extensively in Chapters 4 and 5, and we'll mention some of the problems resulting from balance, position, and touch sensation during our discussion of sensory seeking (below). These problems can make determining the identity, intensity, and location of various stimuli difficult, if not impossible. They can also affect the ability to plan and implement appropriate motor responses to sensory stimulation.

Sensory over- and underresponsiveness often result from the kinds of mismatches and inefficiencies in brain wiring that occur in response to brain injury or malformation. This "miswiring" can result in exaggerated, diminished, or absent responses to sensory stimulation. Children with these inefficient connections often show particular difficulties responding in a carefully nuanced or graded fashion to various stimuli, in terms of both motor output and emotional response. (We'll discuss emotional response in more detail below.)

Sensory-seeking behaviors reflect the attempts of a child with SPD to provide additional input to her body's movement, balance, and touch sensors in order to increase her level of alertness and mental focus and to help herself feel more secure of her position in space. Let's see how this works.

Recently researchers have shown that engaging in various types of physical movements can improve baseline levels of alertness and attention. Even minor body movements like finger tapping can activate various brain regions associated with learning and attention, including an important part of the brain that's associated with auditory sentence comprehension, visual search, and spatial attention. We may actually learn better if we engage in minor movements.

Your own experience probably bears this out. Many people tap their feet or fingers, swivel their chair, or chew gum when they're trying to stimulate their thinking or stay alert during meetings (or to read books on learning!). Often people speak and think more quickly when they make hand gestures, pace, or go on walks. Research supports the value of all these approaches.

Children with SPD often find that they, too, remain more alert and oriented when they move—though they may appear to experience this need in a somewhat exaggerated form. As a result, they frequently engage in sensory-seeking behaviors as a kind of "self-therapy" to promote alertness and awareness. Most often they stimulate their touch, pressure, and balance sensors. In most children, these behaviors really can improve alertness and focus—or not! If too vigorously engaged in, they can become distracting. The key is to obtain enough sensory input to organize and focus attention without allowing the sensory seeking to become the primary focus of attention.

Often the kinds of movements that are most effective in improving alertness and focus are large-scale, whole-body movements that put deep pressure on the muscles and joints. These are the areas supplied by the position and motion sensors (*proprioceptors*) that help the brain keep track of the body's position in space. The importance of proprioceptive stimulation in maintaining alertness and mental focus is well recognized by NASA: They discovered that a mechanical pressure device helped airplane pilots improve their level of alertness and spatial orientation so that they could tolerate higher speeds and g-forces.

Similarly orienting effects are exerted by movements that gently stimulate the balance (*vestibular*) sensors in the middle ear, like rocking or swinging. Large-scale balance and position stimulation not only help to increase alertness but also contribute to feelings of personal security. As we'll discuss below, a child who has difficulty monitoring the position of his body in space will frequently develop balance insecurity, which can be a big source of anxiety.

Fine-motor movements can also improve alertness and focus in children with sensory-seeking tendencies. Fine-motor sensory-seeking behaviors usually come in two varieties: finger and hand movements and oral (mouth) movements. Children who engage in extensive finger stimulation usually have impaired sensory feedback from their fingers. On exam, they show difficulty identifying which finger is being touched or moved when their eyes are closed, plus other physical signs of "sensory confusion." Children who have extensive oral sensory-seeking often get into trouble by chewing on shirtsleeves or collars, pencils, paper, nails or even fingers. We'll discuss appropriate interventions in Helping.

Emotional Responses in Children with Sensory Processing Disorder

Because sensory regulation is closely related to emotional regulation, children with SPD often have difficulty regulating and controlling certain aspects of their emotions. If you've ever unexpectedly heard a car backfire behind you or unexpectedly felt a hand on your shoulder when you were standing in a dark, lonely place, you know how closely the sensory and emotional pathways are connected. This closeness creates real difficulties for many children with SPD. In fact, the intense emotional responses they experience may be some of their most distressing problems and may result in significant anxiety and behavioral dysfunction.

Why are these symptoms so intense? The answer is simple: because children with SPD often interpret hard-to-process sensory stimuli as signs of impending danger. Remember, we don't just have senses to satisfy our curiosities, fulfill our desires, or learn our lessons in school; we have them so we can protect ourselves from danger. That's why our senses come equipped with a direct connection to the fight-or-flight defense mechanisms that help us respond to dangers in our environment. When danger comes, we need to be able to respond quickly and energetically.

Because a child's environment is usually free of threats, a child with well-functioning sensory processing systems will usually feel safe, comfortable, and free to focus attention on specific tasks. However, if that child is unable to monitor her environment effectively, she'll no longer feel confident that she's free from danger and will tend to respond in dramatic fashion to the first hint of threat.

Children (and adults) are like pilots who've been sealed into cockpits that prevent all direct connection with the outside world. Their brains have no immediate access to the sights and sounds around them, to the movements their "plane" is making or the things it might be touching. They can monitor these factors only by using their information-processing systems as "instruments" (Information Input and Pattern Processing). If those "instruments" are inconsistent or display conflicting information, they'll have no way of telling which—if any—of these systems are trustworthy and which unreliable. That's one reason why children with SPD are often so anxious and stressed out: They realize that at any moment they may experience a "crash landing." During times of sensory overload, when "instrument confusion" gets extreme, the result is not simply irritation but primal terror: the classic fight-or-flight reaction.

This fight-or-flight reaction is not something children with SPD choose to have. It's automatic, operating below the level of conscious awareness through the autonomic nervous system. This is our more "primitive" nervous system, which controls basic life-support functions and helps us respond quickly to serious threats. Significantly, this system has close ties with our emotional-response centers that control fear and panic, and it activates those response centers when it perceives a threat. It also has ties with the cerebellum, a structure at the lower back part of the brain that plays an especially important role in helping to regulate emotional arousal (and in many other functions children with SPD struggle with).

These close connections between sensory processing and emotional regulation help explain why children with SPD can respond in ways that seem so over-the-top to other people. Because they have difficulty determining both the severity of environmental threats and how intense their responses should be, both their emotional and physical responses tend to be "all or none" rather than finely graded. These automatic all-or-none responses are essentially reflexes, and when strong they can completely override conscious choice.

That's why children with SPD frequently respond to powerful environmental stimuli as if they were in mortal peril: *They truly believe that they are.* When in the grip of an "overload" reaction, they won't listen to reason, be capable of self-control, be "talked out" of terror, or be threatened into compliance. Only time and a calm, quiet environment will return them to a state of stability.

These powerful emotional and physical responses can be very frustrating to the families and teachers of children with SPD, since they often interfere with the children's abilities to socialize, learn, and enjoy themselves in different environments. These behaviors also commonly lead to their being mislabeled with ADHD, oppositional defiant disorder, bipolar affective disorder, obsessive-compulsive disorder, Asperger's syndrome, or PDD-NOS. It's important to realize that the emotional difficulties these children experience are often the direct result of their difficulties with sensory processing. As a result, treatments aimed at improving these sensory processing difficulties will usually do a better job of relieving their emotional symptoms than will treatments aimed at the diagnoses listed above (see Helping).

It's also important to understand that the emotional problems these children face are not caused simply by overwhelmingly strong fight-or-flight mechanisms. Strong fight-or-flight reactions can be good or bad, depending on the situation. Acting in an unthinking, instinctive, all-or-none fashion can be very useful when you're standing on a railroad track and a train whistle blows behind you. It's considerably less useful when you're five years old, sitting in kindergarten circle time, and you respond to the rub of your shirt tag with an intensity nature intended for protecting you from scorpions.

The problem with these all-or-none responses in children with SPD is that they are responses to the wrong things in the wrong ways. These children's sensory processing confusions make it hard for them to judge the threat level in any given stimulus. As a result, they constantly feel besieged by apparent threats and frequently respond in dramatic fashion to stimuli that pose no real threat.

Control over these behaviors is often made more difficult by the trouble many children with SPD have in monitoring their own bodily sensations or feelings. Often they may not even be fully aware of how their sensory difficulties feed into their emotional state. So they may become overwhelmed, anxious, or withdrawn, without even knowing why. Improving self-awareness—including the ability to monitor internal bodily states and reactions—is an important part of helping children with SPD.

EVALUATING CHILDREN FOR SENSORY PROCESSING DISORDER

Children suspected of SPD should receive the same thorough history, physical and neurological exam, and neuropsychological testing we have described throughout this book. Table 8 identifies some of the important historical features that should be looked for. History should also seek to elicit which of the behaviors we've described are problems for the child.

Although these behaviors are the most easily recognizable aspect of this disorder, children with SPD will *always* have physical or neurological abnormalities that can be picked up on careful examination. It is important to note that these signs will be multisystem (e.g., visual, auditory, balance, motor planning, tone, or posture) in nature, rather than confined to a single sensory or motor modality. Among the most common findings we see on exam are difficulties with finger-position sense, finger confusion, gross- and fine-motor coordination, low skeletal muscle tone (especially of the core or postural muscles in the trunk and neck), difficulties with visual motor control and visual processing, and difficulties with auditory processing. Sensory-seeking behaviors will also commonly be observed during the examination.

Making sure that your child receives appropriate care can be challenging. Ideally, the primary-care doctor should provide a referral to a skilled neurologist, occupational therapist, or other specialist familiar with SPD. However, this frequently doesn't happen. If you suspect that your child has SPD, don't settle for reassurances or a "wait and see" approach — especially if your doctor seems poorly informed about this disorder. The sooner SPD is treated, the sooner a child will get back on the road to normal development.

HELPING CHILDREN WITH SENSORY PROCESSING DISORDER

The two primary goals in helping children with SPD are to help them to function better and to feel more at home in their environment. One of their biggest barriers to reaching these goals is that they often have difficulty drawing clear "lessons" from sensory (or environmental) stimulation. The sensory mismatches we described in Causes make it hard for them to detect important signals in all the unimportant noise of a normal busy environment. As a result, they have difficulty interpreting and responding to sensory messages in a rapid, automatic, and efficient manner.

Fortunately, a well-designed set of interventions can improve their abilities to understand and respond to their environment. The same process of brain rewiring that initially caused many of their problems can be used to treat this disorder. Targeted therapy, with controlled sensory stimulation and carefully coordinated sensory and motor responses, can change the development, structure, and function of different brain pathways to improve sensory processing and behavioral responses. By simplifying sensory inputs so they're more easily recognized, children with SPD can learn to recognize these inputs more accurately, efficiently, and automatically.

In this therapeutic process, a skillful and well-trained occupational therapist can play an important role. Occupational therapists traditionally focus on improving their clients' "occupational function" and their "activities of daily living," like feeding, dressing, and so on. Since a child's primary occupation is school, an OT will be concerned with developing the basic sensory processing and sensorimotor skills needed for school success. The therapists we've found most helpful employ activities involving both isolated and multimodal sensory inputs (i.e., auditory, visual, tactile, proprioceptive, and vestibular) in combination with demands for motor output. These activities strengthen individual sensory and motor maps and help to integrate them with each other. There are, however, significant variations among therapists in their approaches to treating sensory processing difficulties. An interdisciplinary working group associated with the American Occupational Therapy Association (AOTA) is currently working to establish "best practice" recommendations based on available research.

During the course of therapy, parents should attend several sessions so they can better understand how to incorporate therapeutic activities in play at home. The benefits of therapy will be more rapid and complete when reinforcing activities are performed throughout the entire week, rather than just in a single therapy visit once a week.

In addition to occupational therapy, specific therapies may also be needed for auditory or visual disorders, speech and oro-motor speech difficulties, or social and pragmatic language difficulties. Sometimes children and families require counseling for the emotional-regulation issues that often trouble children with SPD or for the anxiety, depression, or family conflicts that arise as a consequence of this disorder. We'll discuss these in more detail below. Ideally, a medical professional familiar with SPD can help prioritize interventions if more than one therapy is needed.

There are six key steps in helping children with SPD become more comfortable and functional in their environment. We'll consider each in turn. These steps are:

1. Making the world more sensory-friendly
2. Managing sensory-seeking behaviors
3. Managing sensory-avoidant behaviors (i.e., oversensitivities)
4. Improving whole-body balance and movement
5. Improving fine-motor function
6. Improving emotional regulation

Helping Step 1: Making the World More Sensory-Friendly

The first step in helping a child with SPD become more comfortable and functional is to make her world more sensory-friendly. This is important not only in the two *external* environments where she spends most of her time—home and school—but also in the one internal environment where she spends all her time: her body.

Environmental modification is crucial in SPD, because the environment plays a key role in producing the symptoms of this disorder. The symptoms in SPD don't arise simply because of neurological wiring problems within the child. They arise because of the mismatch between the child and his environment. It's essential to work on both parties in this mismatch. As we saw with attention disorders, it's a mistake to place all responsibility for the difficulties in this disorder on the child. Jerome, whom we described at the beginning of this chapter, is a perfect example of how different environments can dramatically affect the function of a child with SPD. In this section, we'll discuss steps you can take to make the different environments inhabited by a child with SPD more sensory-friendly.

The Body

Children with SPD often show a combination of undersensitivity and over-sensitivity to various bodily signals. The following steps may be useful:

- Touch/clothing sensitivities: Children with SPD frequently show sensitivities to touch that affect their ability to wear certain types of clothes or fabrics. All children naturally vary in their sensitivity to touch stimulation from clothing, and many children who get irritated by tags or seams do not have SPD. However, children with SPD often experience clothing sensitivities so severe that they find it hard to focus on anything else. The biggest clothing offenders tend to be shirt tags, socks (especially with seams), shoes, underwear (again with seams or tags), any kind of clothing made from thick or stiff fabric (new blue jeans being a common irritant), and anything made from wool. These sensitivities tend to diminish as the child ages, with flares around growth spurts or times of emotional stress.

- When clothing sensitivities are severe, a program of tactile brushing will often help (see below).
- Schools should allow children with clothing sensitivities some flexibility in their dress, especially in the use of shoes and socks in class. The fact that most people around the world don't keep their shoes on indoors may be telling us something.
- Soft, thin, seamless cotton is often the most comfortable fabric (though children vary), and baggy sweats and tees the favorite outfit. Some parents swear by particular vendors, like Hanna Andersson (www.hannaandersson.com) for underwear or the kinds of soft clothing available from Sensory Resources (www.sensoryresources.com). Many parents also learn by

experience to cut tags, prewash, and allow their children to wear sandals year-round.

- Food preferences or aversions: Children with SPD may have very strong food preferences or aversions and be unusually picky in what they'll eat. They may have taste limitations for white, bland, or starchy foods or texture cravings for or aversions to foods that are crunchy, soggy, sticky, chewy, et cetera. These sensitivities may make a "balanced diet" extremely difficult. Gradually increasing tolerance for different tastes and textures is important but needs to be gradual. In the meantime, supplementation with a good children's multivitamin is important. When oral hypersensitivities play a role, the steps discussed next can help.

- Oral hypersensitivity: Children with oral hypersensitivity often have texture sensitivities like those mentioned above but may also resist eating in general, even to the point that they have trouble getting enough calories. These children are also notoriously defensive about toothbrushing, and tooth decay can be a big issue. These hypersensitivities can often be greatly improved by a several-week course of regular (every two hours or so) sweeping around the gums and tongue with a finger or a soft rubber troche. Bribery may be needed at first!

- Oral hyposensitivity: Children with diminished oral sensitivity have a hard time telling by feel how much is in their mouth. As a result, they may overstuff their mouth, which can cause choking. Teach this rule: "Don't take another forkful, spoonful, or bite until your mouth is empty."

- Coordination of speech and swallowing muscles: Children who have oro-motor control problems may experience fatigue while eating or difficulty chewing. As a result, they may resist eating or have problems with choking. These children may also have motor difficulties that affect their articulation of words and use of facial expressions. They generally require formal help from an OT or speech therapist. To improve strength and coordination of the lips, tongue, mouth, and throat muscles, these therapists often recommend activities such as blowing, sucking on thick drinks like milk shakes, eating crunchy or chewy foods, and chewing on bite blocks. Rarely, they may recommend a swallowing study to check for blockages or muscle problems that hinder the passage of food.

- Hunger and thirst: Children who are underresponsive to hunger and thirst need a regular routine for "refueling." Create a schedule for snacks and meals, then carefully follow it. At least some food and liquid every two hours should help prevent dramatic highs and lows. Over time, this schedule will usually become habitual, so the child no longer needs external monitoring.

- Bowels and bladder: Some children with SPD have difficulty sensing when it's time to eliminate bodily wastes. These children require regular voiding schedules. Choosing a set time after meals and/or snacks is usually helpful.

- Sleep: Children with SPD often have difficulties with sleep. Most commonly, their sleep problem results from a failure to detect their body's signals that it's time to go to bed. As a result, they keep fighting to maintain a high level of arousal and may actually become more rather than less active as they grow tired. These children may also be kept awake by environmental stimuli like noise, the touch of the blankets, the temperature of the room, et cetera. The following simple steps can help:

  - Make sure the child has enough exercise and sunlight exposure during the day, and avoid daytime naps.
  - Avoid using electronic equipment like computers, video-game consoles, or TVs while in bed.
  - Establish a regular time for bed, then stick to it (provide warnings beforehand for the child with transition problems!).
  - Have a pleasant and relaxing ritual like a warm bath or light reading before bedtime.
  - Soft background noise (like a fan or white noise generator) may help children who have difficulty falling asleep because of auditory distractibility or who are light sleepers.
  - Some children may enjoy tactile stimuli, like the feel of the fan blowing across their face (even in winter), the heavy pressure feel

of thick comforters (even in summer), U-shaped body pillows, or a large stuffed animal.

- If sleep problems cause excessive daytime drowsiness, the child should be seen by a sleep specialist. Sleep disorders are finally being recognized as a significant problem in children, with potentially dramatic effects on attention, behavior, and mood. Problems like obstructive sleep apnea (with or without enlarged tonsils) and restless leg syndrome are common and treatable, requiring the help of an appropriate sleep specialist.

The External Environment

The following steps can help create a more sensory-friendly external environment:

- Identify and eliminate the triggers in the environment that contribute to overloading. Take a break from shoes and socks, use earplugs for very noisy events, stand up from desks when needed, or lie down during circle time rather than sit cross-legged. Eliminate extra sources of motion, noise, glare, or any barriers to free movement (objects that might be bumped into or tripped over).
- Create a predictable and well-structured environment to reduce the chronic sensory and emotional stimulation experienced by a child with SPD. Remember: The goal is *predictability*, not *inflexibility*. Structured predictability means that a child knows what to expect from her environment. As a result, she can feel more relaxed and comfortable, because she does not need always to "expect the unexpected." However, this doesn't mean that she can't be allowed some degree of control over her environment. In fact, providing her with an element of control can actually improve her ability to tolerate some of the things she can't change.
- Allow the child a chance to rest and recharge when he senses he's had enough. While therapeutic activities are crucial to reducing oversensitivities (see below), sometimes oversensitive kids just need a place to hide out, calm down, and recharge their emotional batteries. Every child should have such a "safe zone" both at school and at

home where he can go when he feels like he's heading for a meltdown. For younger children, it can be a place under a table or in a
large cardboard "cave." For older kids, it can be a study carrel or a
desk in the hall, library, or resource room.

The Schedule

While regular schedules for meals, sleep/wake times, and other important
bodily activities can help children with SPD, there is a bit of a catch: Often
these children have difficulty making the transition from one place or activity to another—which is to say they often have difficulty with schedules.
Adapting to new situations is hard for them, so they tend to resist change.
When forced to switch to a new environment or activity, they often shut
down, "crawl into their shell," or overload. This difficulty with transitions is
often worsened by a poor sense of the passing of time, which makes it hard
for them to plan ahead and to understand the importance of scheduling.
Several steps can help transitions go more smoothly:

- "Advanced warnings" at five- or ten-minute intervals before transitions will give them a chance to adjust their expectations and eliminate nasty surprises.
- Allow plenty of time so transitions aren't rushed, especially if
  dressing or other preparations are required. Hurry often precipitates overload.
- Work on various tasks with a clock handy so they can develop a sense
  for time's passage and for how long various tasks take.

The Learning Environment

In addition to eliminating distractions and providing a quiet place for recharg-
ing, the learning environment can also be made more sensory-friendly using two alternative educational approaches: computer-based learning or
homeschooling.

- Several factors make computer-based learning especially sensory-
  friendly: All sensory inputs come from one unchanging direction;

volume, brightness, tone, and rate of information can all be controlled; information can be presented in a more consistent, predictable, and recognizable form; and missed information can be repeated as often as needed. In addition, computer-based learning lends itself nicely to a multisensory format: Words can be reinforced with pictures, sounds can be reinforced with pictures or text, and movement and music can be used to help memory.

- Computer-based learning can be especially helpful for children with SPD, because it typically requires less gross and fine motor control to manipulate items in a virtual (computer) world than it does in the real world. As a result, many children can perform tasks, like writing, creating art, or simulating physical motions, that are difficult for them in the real world. Mastery at such tasks can help self-esteem and become an important source of hobbies and future career interests. Computer activities can also be therapeutic: Recent research has demonstrated the benefit of video games for at least one type of visual motor integration.
- Of course, moderation is crucial. Children also need regular physical activities and practice negotiating their physical environment. Only through this means will they become more physically at ease with the real world.

- Homeschooling can be an attractive option for some children with SPD, because it provides the opportunity for more regular and controlled stimulation. Sometimes, though, schools can provide well-trained therapists and flexible teachers who are willing to help the child manage in the standard classroom.

Helping Step 2: Managing Sensory-Seeking Behaviors

Sensory-seeking activities can be divided into two general categories: those that provide whole-body or large-body-area stimulation and those that provide very local or fine motor stimulation.

Whole-Body-Movement Stimulation

There are many ways that a child can receive helpful whole-body proprioceptive stimulation. Most of these activities will involve some form of bouncing or squeezing sensation.

- Helpful bouncing activities include:

  - Jumping on a minitrampoline, pogo stick, exercise mat, or mattress.
  - Sitting on a big exercise ball or bouncy seat cushion (even when working).
  - Vigorous activities like horseback riding, gymnastics, running, or martial arts. (Private lessons in these sports are frequently preferred, both because the child is likely to be at a different skill level from age peers and because noisy group activities are more likely to cause sensory overloading.)
  - Swimming or water play is also particularly popular with these children, because it provides a combination of deep joint stimulation, pleasant tactile experiences, and freedom from concerns about falls or balance problems. As one young patient observed, "I sometimes get tired of the law of gravity, so I like to go swimming."

- Helpful squeezing or pressure-type activities include:

  - Deep muscle massage or surrounding children with mildly heavy, soft materials such as a deep beanbag, a weighted blanket or vest, or by "burrito-wrapping" (i.e., swaddling) them in a heavy blanket. Often these kids will enjoy playing "pile-on" with other kids and will have a suspicious tendency to end up at the bottom of the pile. They may spontaneously crawl under mattresses or furniture cushions and even ask others to lie on them.
  - Heavy work activities, like helping with the gardening.

- Whole-body balance/vestibular stimulation can also be provided in several ways:

- Gentle rocking on a gym ball, porch swing, glider, or rocking chair is popular.
- So are swinging activities. In addition to standard swings, indoor hammock-type swings are very popular, especially in climates where outdoor swings aren't available for much of the year.
- Spinning activities, like merry-go-rounds or sit-and-spins can help, but spinning too fast can be overstimulating. Gently spinning in a hammock chair provides the best way we've found to combine swinging and spinning.

Fine-Motor Stimulation

As we discussed above, most fine motor sensory-seeking behaviors involve either hand- and finger-related activities or oral stimulation.

- Sensory-seeking behaviors involving the fingers and hands can often be controlled and regulated through the use of sensory fidgets (like hollow rubber balls, therapy putty, executive squeeze toys, or other squishy or nonmessy substances) or through activities like folding and shredding paper.
- Children who engage in oral sensory-seeking behaviors can benefit from double sticks of gum (preferably sugarless), which can provide powerful oral proprioceptive input, or rubber chewies, which are available from sensory supply houses (see Resources).

Additional Comments on Sensory-Seeking Behaviors

A few extra points about sensory-seeking behaviors are in order:

- As you've probably noticed, many of these activities are rhythmic or regular in character. Such activities allow children to anticipate both the movements they need to make and the sensory feedback they are likely to receive, so they can prepare and plan better. Knowing what to expect helps make these activities not only alerting and focusing but also calming.
- These activities should become part of a child's regular schedule, just like meals, naps, et cetera.

- Don't be fooled by a child's "self-diagnosis" or natural choice of activities. Most children benefit from both fine- and large-scale stimulation. Although some children may naturally pursue extensive large-scale self-stimulation—even to the point of overstimulation—they may be more calmed and organized by fine-motor fidgets than by aggressive large-scale activities. They may also seek to avoid activities that would be helpful, if they find them challenging or tiring.

- Because sensory-seeking children are usually in motion, they're often diagnosed with ADHD. While some sensory-seeking children do have attention problems, many do not. If a child can maintain or improve focus while sensory seeking, that child probably does not have a primary attention problem.

- Parents, teachers, therapists, and affected children should all work together to find solutions for sensory-seeking behaviors in the classroom. Movement and pressure-seeking behaviors should be channeled into forms that are "restorative" for the children who have them and not disruptive for classroom routines or social relationships. Flexibility and understanding are essential. As a child improves in self-monitoring and regulating skills, she should receive more freedom to seek appropriate stimulation or movement when needed.

- Whenever movement or pressure-seeking behaviors become disruptive for the child or for classmates, referral for intensive sensorimotor therapy is essential.

Helping Step 3: Managing Sensory-Avoidant Behaviors

Children who are overresponsive (or oversensitive) to certain sensory stimuli may engage in sensory-avoidant behaviors—that is, behaviors designed to avoid or minimize those aggravating sensations. As we've mentioned, children may be sensory-seeking toward some sensations but sensory-avoidant toward others, so it's important to address both kinds of behaviors. Often sensory-avoidant behaviors may be even more disruptive to a child's life than sensory-seeking behaviors, because they involve distressing responses that may cripple the child's function in many environments.

Therapy for sensory-avoidant children seeks to reduce overresponsiveness to distressing sensations like touches, sights, sounds, and movements by using a daily plan of controlled sensation called a *sensory diet*. Improving sensitivities in multiple senses often does not require specific desensitization therapies for each one, because our sensory systems are so highly linked, or integrated. Addressing sensitivities in one area often improves sensitivities in many areas.

- Three forms of sensory input have generally proved most successful in reducing oversensitivities: touch, pressure (proprioception), and movement (balance/vestibular). Many successful therapists employ all three. In one common protocol (Wilbarger), a therapist firmly brushes the skin with a soft plastic surgical brush, then administers "joint pumps," or pressured contractions across the joints. Typically, a two-week course of brushing and joint pumps (administered every two hours while the child is awake) will be used initially, followed by stimulation as needed to maintain the gains. The brushing seems to "desensitize" the skin to touch sensation, while the joint stimulation seems to improve postural muscle tone and improve body-position sense. These interventions shouldn't be attempted by persons who haven't received specific training, but a description of this approach can be found in the book *Sensory Integration: Theory and Practice* (see Resources).

- Many therapists also use gentle stimulation of the balance/movement system to improve a child's sense of spatial localization and postural security. This therapy generally involves gentle swinging or rocking in a hammock, a sling, or a rocking chair, usually on the order of ten cycles a minute. Again, as with proprioceptive stimulation, this therapy appears to work by helping children improve their body-position sense.

- Each of these therapies must be performed correctly to help and if done improperly can sometimes worsen symptoms. Initially they are best performed under the guidance of a trained therapist. For the long term, though, a skilled therapist can usually train parents (and teachers) to help a child with organizing and calming activities that can be used on an ongoing basis.

- Other sensory-diet activities can be engaged in by anyone at home and may be sufficient to manage children with milder symptoms. These are essentially the kinds of whole-body and fine motor alerting and focusing activities described above. Remember: Different children may respond differently to each activity, so it's important to see what works best for each child. You may be surprised at which activities your child finds calming. We've seen boys who resembled Clark Kent more than Superman become martial-arts fanatics and girls who lived in terror of the neighbors' pet Chihuahua become daredevil horsewomen. Offer a range of activities and see what works.

- For older children, sensory diets should be paired with education about sensory symptoms and interventions (see "Emotional Self-Regulation," below).

- Sensory overresponsiveness tends to peak during preschool and early-elementary years, then diminish over time. However, therapy can greatly accelerate this improvement and prevent secondary psychological and academic harm.

- Symptoms often go in cycles, with intense flares during growth spurts or hormonal fluxes, followed by relatively milder intervals.

- In most cases, by the time a child reaches adulthood, the symptoms are much less likely to be limiting, though they may still be annoying.

Helping Step 4: Improving Whole-body Balance and Movement

The following interventions can help children with SPD improve their whole-body tone, posture, and balance, protect their bodies when they fall, and engage in complex large motor movements.

- Feedback from stretch and position receptors in the muscles is essential for maintaining muscle tone and posture. Because children with SPD can have difficulty processing such feedback, they frequently have low or weak muscle tone. This is especially true of the core postural muscles in the neck, back, and hips, which are essential for stabilizing the head and upper body. Poor postural muscle tone can make activities like handwriting, sitting upright in a chair or on the floor, or even keeping one's head off the desk while reading difficult and tiring. Formal occupational therapy is usually the best option for children with significant core-muscle weakness. However, there are some activities children can engage in at home to improve core muscle tone.

- Roll around on a scooter board, lying stomach down with the head held up.
- Lie stomach down to read or watch TV, with head and shoulders lifted off the floor, and weight supported on the elbows.
- Do reverse sit-ups, lying on the stomach while arching up the head and feet.
- Daily exercises including sit-ups and light weights (one to five pounds) can be very useful in building up the arms, shoulders, and postural muscles of the upper back.

- Improving the protective reflex that guards the head during falls is another essential intervention for children with SPD. Normally when a person trips, an automatic cascade of motor reflexes kicks into motion to counteract the lurch forward: Back and neck muscles contract, pulling the head backward, and arms extend outward to cushion the fall. Many children with SPD have problems with this protective reflex, due to problems in the visual, vestibular (inner-ear), proprioceptive, and motor-planning systems. These same factors can also cause frequent falls, resulting in a reluctance to explore new environments or a habit of clinging to adults for protection.

  - Intensive and focused therapy can build speed and strength in the muscle groups that extend the arms and pull the head back during falls, plus improve balance and coordination to prevent falls in the first place.
  - Therapy can also improve play and social behavior in children who have avoided group play due to fears of being pushed or knocked off balance by the other children.

- Training in complex (coordinated) large-muscle movements should be gradual, especially for children with balance concerns.

  - Rocking and swinging activities of gradually increasing vigor are often a good place to start, as they can help children get used to the feel of quick movements. With time, children will gain enough security to advance to running, jumping, and climbing.

- For children who enjoy running and jumping but have problems with planning, balance, coordination, or scanning, the following activities can help:

  - While standing on a balance board, play catch with a beanbag, either alone (hand-to-hand) or tossing to another person.
  - Move-and-freeze games or rule-following games like Simon Says are also good ways to practice coordinated motor control.
  - Obstacle courses requiring running, jumping, and crawling can also be fun and effective ways of building large-motor strength and coordination.

Helping Step 5: Improving Fine-Motor Function

Children with SPD often have poor fine motor coordination (or *dyspraxia*) and impaired sensory feedback from the fingers (*agnosia*). (See Chapter 11 for more details on these conditions.) They also frequently have poor hand-eye coordination and visual-spatial deficits, like those described in Chapters 4 and 11. The end result is trouble performing a wide range of fine-motor tasks including dressing, eating, building, writing, and drawing.

- Have them engage in activities that strengthen and provide deep-pressure sensation to the fingers. Helpful activities include play with heavy therapy putty, tearing folded paper, or stretching rubber bands over a pegboard. Many other therapies for preschool and early-elementary children can be found in the books *The*

Out-of-Sync Child and *The Out-of-Sync Child Has Fun* by Carol
Kranowitz.

- Arts and crafts projects like drawing and scissoring are also helpful
  and popular, as long as they're not too frustrating. Self-opening scissors are useful for children who can't operate the regular kind. During drawing activities, use short, one-inch pencils or crayons that
  must be held with a pincer grip to increase strength.

- Building tasks (like those described in Chapters 4 and 11), can also
  build fine motor strength and coordination and are generally more
  popular with older children. LEGO kits, gear sets, Lite-Brite, and
  model building can all be enjoyable and beneficial activities.

- Handwriting is often a serious problem for children with SPD.
  Handwriting is discussed in detail in Chapter 11, so we won't go
  into great depth here. Just remember: Children with SPD often require strengthening in both peripheral (hand and finger) and core
  (neck, back, and shoulder) muscle groups before they can make
  much progress in handwriting. Only after the necessary muscle supports are in place will writing interventions succeed.

Helping Step 6: Improving
Emotional Self-Regulation

Children with SPD can gain a greater measure of emotional self-regulation
and control through interventions that improve their resiliency, flexibility,
self-awareness, and self-sufficiency. The best approaches depend upon the
age of the child. In younger children, who are less self-aware, environmental modifications to minimize exposures and therapies to reduce sensitivities will be most effective. (See Steps 1 to 3, above.) However, as children
grow older, their conscious participation should be enlisted in developing
greater emotional self-regulation.

- The first step in improving self-regulation is developing a heightened
  sense of self-awareness and self-understanding. Children must be
  taught to monitor their own internal state of arousal and emotional
  well-being and to detect signs of impending overstimulation. Tell

them what you're observing about their behavior and what signs they
might use to detect the same things. For example, help them recognize how they're affected by different environments and sensory
stimuli, so they can plan and prepare more effectively for transitions and new activities. Materials from the ALERT program, like
Take Five, provide step-by-step instructions for teaching children
how to recognize their body's signals. They also provide information
on how to pursue appropriate "organizing" activities. Another good
book for nine- to twelve-year-old children is *The Goodenoughs Get
in Sync* by Carol Kranowitz. Additional materials are listed in Resources.

- The second step is to develop strategies to control emotional and behavioral responses to sensory stimulation and other frustrations. Self-
  calming activities, like the use of sensory fidgets, deep breathing,
  cognitive self-suggestion, meditation, or self-focusing activities like
  those learned through biofeedback can be extremely useful. Often
  these emotional-control strategies can be learned during a course of
  occupational therapy, in conjunction with practice at home. Sometimes, however, it may be necessary to work with a psychologist or
  counselor on a more intensive basis. It's important to find a counselor who is knowledgeable about SPD.
- While encouraging increasing self-control, it's important to provide
  the child with some control over her own environment. However,
  don't place more on her than she can handle. Provide plenty of
  warning about impending transitions and plenty of time to adjust.
  Encouragement to develop flexibility should be balanced with opportunities to make choices.
- Watch carefully for signs of overloading. When meltdowns do occur,
  give the child space and time to deal with her feelings. Remember:
  During meltdowns, the strength of her autonomic reaction will
  probably overwhelm not only her ability to cope or control herself
  but also her desire to be good, her fear of discipline, and even her
  love for you. Don't make things worse by escalating the situation. It's
  in the calm after the storm that the chance to talk about strategies
  for averting future crises will come.

10

It's as Easy as ABC . . . or as Hard

Dyslexia in Children

In 1896, in the first description of developmental reading disability in the medical literature, it was noted that a certain student could not learn to read in spite of "laborious and persistent training." However, his headmaster observed that this student "would be the smartest lad in the school if the instruction were entirely oral." The study of reading disability has frequently considered the often striking inconsistencies between high intelligence and ability coupled with surprisingly poor reading and writing skills. However, most research to date has focused mainly on the obvious problems to be corrected rather than the hidden potential to be identified and developed.

—THOMAS G. WEST, *THE ABILITIES OF THOSE WITH READING DISABILITIES*

P orter was a very bright nine-year-old boy with a measured IQ of nearly 140, who struggled with the reading, writing, and spelling demands of third grade. He had a history of mild speech delays (with first words just after eighteen months and combined words just after two years) but otherwise showed accelerated oral-language development. He'd always loved being read to and by age five was bringing his mother long chapter-books to read. But as he progressed through kindergarten and first grade, Porter showed little interest in learning to read for himself.

Initially Porter had difficulties linking sounds to individual letters. He was given intensive training in phonics, which seemed to help somewhat but he found this study very aggravating. Even when he mastered letter sounds, he showed little patience for sounding out words and instead used a guess-and-go strategy, whereby he simply guessed the identity of each word he read on the basis of the first, and occasionally last, letters or from surrounding contextual cues (like story matter or pictures). Fortunately, he was a fairly good guesser, so by the time he reached third grade, his scores on tests of silent reading comprehension usually hovered around the sixtieth percentile. Oral reading, by contrast, was pure torture, just as it was for Michael in Chapter 1. In addition to having trouble sounding out individual words, Porter also frequently skipped words and entire lines of print when reading. He also had persistent difficulty pronouncing certain sounds and, in particular, differentiating his *v* and *f* sounds.

Writing and spelling were especially big problems for Porter. His letter formation was extremely irregular and difficult to read, and he tended to ignore conventions like capitals, punctuation, and spacing in his writing. Although he was very creative and full of ideas, he had difficulty translating any of his ideas to print. When we asked him to take three minutes to provide a written description of a certain picture, he wrote: "the bay sole [i.e., stole] the cookie Jar. the Gul [girl] Push the bay [boy]. the mam [mom] fooded [flooded] the hane [home]." Unsurprisingly, despite a vocabulary in the ninety-ninth percentile, Porter tested on spelling at below the tenth percentile. In contrast, he dictated the following statement in just over one and a half minutes: "The boy is stealing cookies from the cookie jar, and the girl is saying 'shush' and asking for cookies. The mom is distracted because the sink is flooded, and she's washing a dish. The house has an open window with some gardens and a cloud and another part of the house and a tree. And on the inside there are lots of closets, and the mom is also preparing tea." As third grade continued, Porter was becoming increasingly frustrated, and was beginning to resist doing any work.

Laura was thirteen years old when she came to see us. She was a voracious reader and spent most of her free time reading—until headaches and dizziness forced her to stop. She also loved creating her own stories and wanted to write them down, but her spelling was so bad and her handwriting so messy that she often felt that it just wasn't worth the effort. One three-sentence passage she wrote for us included the mistakes "overflowes," "laughes," "oben" [for open], "supprised," and "climed." On two sentences, she began the first word with a lowercase letter, then corrected her mistake. There were several cross-outs and corrections.

Laura had easily mastered her alphabet and her letter sounds as a child, and she had initially made good progress with reading. Decoding short words in large print was no problem, but when the print got smaller and the words got longer toward the end of second grade, Laura began to struggle. She often complained of headaches and blurring and wobbling of the letters on the page. Reading glasses helped a little but didn't solve her problem. While she could read long novels for pleasure and answer oral questions about them with good comprehension, she often had difficulty on written tests of reading comprehension, because she misread or misinterpreted the questions. In fact, although she was clearly very bright and showed gifted-level performances in many areas of language and memory on oral testing, Laura had recently failed the state-mandated test for reading comprehension, because she had difficulty understanding the multiple-choice questions and answers. She was also struggling in math, due to difficulties reading story problems.

On our examination, Laura showed a strong understanding of the way sounds go together to form words and good auditory processing skills. However, she also showed difficulties with eye-movement control, visual registration, and visual memory. When we asked her to read aloud, she made multiple word and line skips, and on several long words she substituted other words that differed by only a few letters. With writing, she showed difficulties with fine-motor control and with sensory feedback from her fingers.

DYSLEXIA: IT'S MORE THAN JUST A READING DISORDER

Dyslexia is often defined as a difficulty in learning to read accurately and fluently that is unexpected in light of other cognitive abilities and the provision of adequate instruction. However, as the experiences of Porter, Laura, and Michael from Chapter 1 clearly show, dyslexia is more than just a reading disorder. Reading difficulties are just one part of this broad, neurologically based condition. Children with dyslexia often struggle not only with reading but also with handwriting, spelling, oral language, math, motor planning and coordination, organization, sequencing, orientation to time, focus and attention, right-left orientation, auditory and visual processing, and memory.

Dyslexia is a very common condition, affecting as many as ten percent (and by some measures twenty) of children in the United States. Dyslexia often runs in families, but even in families with several affected members, the signs and symptoms they display may vary both in extent and severity. This variability in symptoms is the rule with dyslexia and is believed to reflect the fact that as many as ten different genes—as well as environmental factors and other nondyslexic traits like memory and sensory processing functions—play a role in its expression. (It would really probably be more accurate to think of it as "dyslexias.") Because dyslexia varies in its origins and expression, the approaches to its treatment should be varied as well. No single one-size-fits-all approach will work for all persons with dyslexia.

Although dyslexia can vary greatly from child to child, there are also numerous similarities among dyslexic children. In this chapter, we'll describe the many ways that dyslexic children typically resemble each other and how they differ. We'll also describe an approach to evaluating and helping children with dyslexia that takes this diversity into account, so that each child can receive the kind of help that he or she needs. Let's begin by discussing the many behaviors that can be associated with dyslexia.

BEHAVIORS ASSOCIATED WITH
DYSLEXIA IN CHILDREN

Dyslexia-associated behaviors can be divided into two broad categories: those related directly to reading problems and those not directly related to reading. Let's consider each in turn.

Behaviors Associated with Reading
Problems in Dyslexia

In the sections that follow, we will divide the behaviors associated with dyslexic reading problems into four different categories, each of which corresponds roughly to one of the basic processes underlying reading. These categories are *hearing* words, *seeing* words, *saying* words, and *remembering* words (see Figure 29).

These categories are not set in stone. Sometimes they overlap—as, for example, when difficulty hearing word sounds causes difficulty saying (or pronouncing) words. However, they provide a good way of organizing our thinking about dyslexia, which will be useful throughout this chapter.

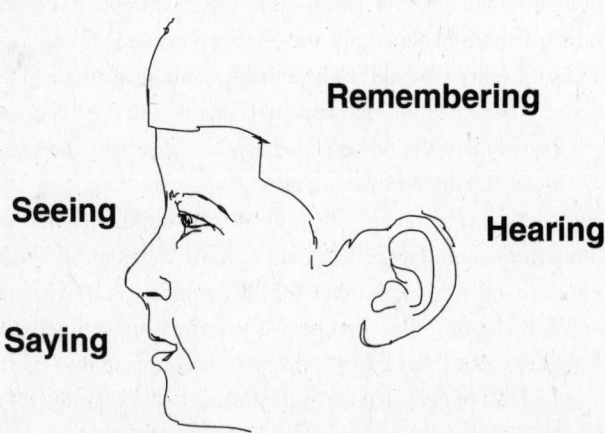

Remembering

Seeing

Hearing

Saying

FIGURE 29. The reading process involves *seeing* words, *hearing* the sounds in words, *remembering* words and their meanings, and *saying* words.

Problems Hearing Words

The following behaviors may suggest that a child is having difficulty hearing the sounds in words:

- Late onset of spoken language (failure to speak single words by eighteen months or combined words by two years) may be the earliest tip-off. Children with speech delays should be watched carefully as they enter kindergarten and first grade for other early signs of dyslexia. Many children with dyslexia don't show speech delays, and not all speech delays are caused by dyslexia, but this may be an important clue.
- Lack of interest in or understanding of rhymes, which most children will find interesting by age four or five.
- A tendency to mishear words, especially because of mistakes in subtle sounds, like *time* for *dime* or *pin* for *pen*. This mishearing is often reflected in a child's tendency to mispronounce words or to create "invented spellings" that suggest she has misheard word sounds. Children with dyslexia may also mispronounce words by inverting or missequencing word parts (see Figure 30).
- Failure to develop a clear "word attack" strategy when learning to read. Most early readers quickly learn how to break words down into smaller pieces using their component sounds, then "sound out" these smaller pieces one by one before reassembling them into the complete word. In contrast, many children with dyslexia rely on "guessing" strategies using the first and maybe the last letters. Some dyslexic children may even show an unusual tendency to substitute words with related meanings but completely different letters, such as *bird* for *hen* or *body* for *skin*. Often the reading of such children shows a combination of difficulties, as with our young patient who read the phrase "her mother gave" as "her father Dave." Dyslexic children also show difficulties learning to recognize new words. They often make the same mistakes over and over again, even on words they've encountered many times—possibly even on the same page. These difficulties with word attack often lead to slow and inaccurate reading, which is most obvious when children try to read aloud.

Mispronunciation of Word Sounds
larch instead of *large*
hod instead of *hot*

Mistakes in Sound Order
paitner instead of *painter*
bistick instead of *biscuit*

Mistakes with Rhymes
"What rhymes with *take*?"—"Rack!"

Mistakes in Spelling
"I thoot I crod clam the matin."
(I thought I could climb the mountain.)

FIGURE 30. Impaired "Hearing" Resulting in Mispronunciations, Rhyming, and Sound-Based Spelling Mistakes

Problems Seeing Words

A second set of behaviors may suggest that a child is having difficulty seeing words. These behaviors include:

- A tendency to skip over individual words or even entire lines.
- Difficulty fixing eyes in one spot.
- Difficulty with near work.
- A sensation that the words and letters on the page seem to wobble, mingle, move over each other, or even pop in and out of the page.
- Fluctuating double vision, especially when trying to focus on the middle letters in a word.
- A tendency to confuse or missequence the letters in words when reading aloud (e.g., reading *saked* for *asked* or *kwake* for *awake*). In addition, a subset of children with dyslexia will show difficulties of spatial processing that result in letter or number reversals or inversions (e.g., *b/d*, *b/q*, *b/p*, *p/q*, 6/9, 3/E, etc.).

- A tendency to omit suffixes at the ends of words (e.g., changing plural to singular forms by omitting the *s*) or to omit internal fragments of words. Sometimes these omissions can produce important changes in meaning, as when one young gentleman strained our composure by repeatedly omitting the letters *-ni-* from the word *organisms* while reading in very earnest tones an otherwise dry passage on marine biology!
- A tendency to tilt the head to the side when reading, squint, or rub the eyes.
- A tendency to use a finger or other marker to guide the eyes while reading.
- A special sensitivity to bright lights or even sensitivity to the glare from very shiny or bright white paper when reading.
- A tendency to experiment with the color settings on televisions and computer screens, preferring settings that irritate the other family members.
- Signs of visual distractibility, like difficulty focusing on words or numbers in a visually crowded background or in the middle letters of long words. When too much information is presented to these children's visual field at once, they cannot take it in, nor can they automatically narrow their field of focus to a more manageable size. Dyslexic students often find this true for visual materials of all kinds, not just printed words. One young student told us, "If my teacher would only put four math problems on a page, I could do ten pages of them, but when she puts forty on one page, I can't do any." Figure 31 illustrates schematically some of the reading difficulties seen in children with dyslexia.

Problems Saying Words

A third set of reading-related behaviors may suggest that a child is having difficulty *saying words*. These behaviors include:

- In addition to speech delays and difficulties with word pronunciation (as discussed above), children with dyslexia often have difficulty with speech articulation beyond age-appropriate norms (as we saw with Porter, and with Michael in Chapter 1).

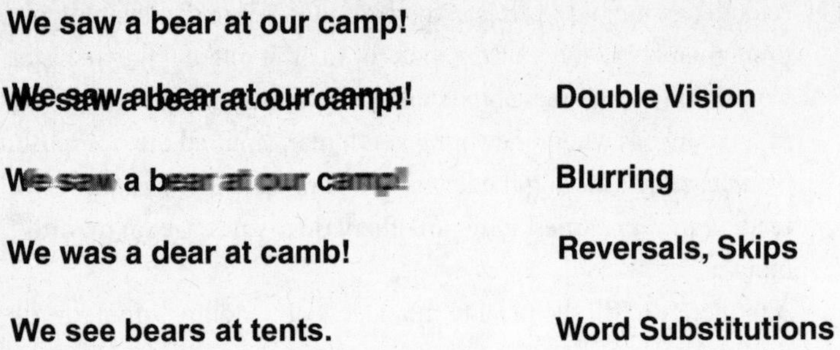

We saw a bear at our camp!

We saw a bear at our camp!   **Double Vision**

We saw a bear at our camp!   **Blurring**

We was a dear at camb!   **Reversals, Skips**

We see bears at tents.   **Word Substitutions**

FIGURE 31. Reading Difficulties Seen in Dyslexia

- Other speech difficulties, like stuttering and word-finding difficulties (see below) are also more common in children with dyslexia. As in the case of speech delays, not all children with stuttering or word-finding difficulties have dyslexia, but such children should be watched carefully for signs of dyslexia and exposed to heavy doses of reading and oral language.

Problems Remembering Words

The fourth and final set of reading-related behaviors may suggest that a child is having difficulty *remembering words or letters*. These behaviors include:

- Difficulty remembering the sounds of the letters of the alphabet.
- Difficulty learning to recognize words "by sight" or to "sight-read." This difficulty causes special problems reading the approximately 25 percent of English words that are "irregular" in the sense that they cannot be pronounced using the typical rules of phonics but must be memorized in their entirety. Examples of such words include *foreign, bowl,* and *Wednesday.*
- Difficulty rapidly retrieving words from memory. Words are both filed in and retrieved from memory on the basis of sound, so dyslexics with sound processing difficulties (see below) may have difficulty with word retrieval. Often this results in word-

finding difficulty—the common phenomenon of being "tongue-
tied."
- Difficulty with reading comprehension. Children with dyslexia often have difficulties with reading comprehension, especially when
passages have little redundancy (i.e., duplicated information)
or background context or where the sentence structures are
very complex.

Nonreading Behaviors Associated with Dyslexia

There are many other behaviors associated with dyslexia that are not directly related to reading. Some of these behaviors are language-related, like
problems with writing or spelling, while others are unrelated to language.
These behaviors include:

- Dysfunctional handwriting, or dysgraphia. This is an extremely
common problem in children with dyslexia. In fact, in dyslexic children who've been able to develop good reading skills, this will often
be the most obvious and persistent symptom. Children with dyslexia
frequently find writing slow and laborious. Their letters may be
poorly formed, and they often have trouble remembering to use
handwriting conventions such as capitals, punctuation, and spacing.
We'll discuss these handwriting difficulties further in Chapter 11 on
dysgraphia.
- Signs of working memory overload are common in children with
dyslexia. Some dyslexic children have impaired auditory working
memory, which contributes to their reading problems (see below).
Others have good working memory spans but overload on tasks like
reading and especially writing, because of the excessive working
memory demands imposed by dyslexia. These children must spend
so much mental energy on sounding out words or forming words
and letters that they often have little energy left to focus on the content and grammar of their writing, even when their speech shows
good command of language.
- Many dyslexic children show a combination of difficulties control-

ling and coordinating the movements of fingers (fine motor), limbs and trunk (gross motor), speech muscles, and eye muscles, suggesting an underlying problem with motor control. Usually dyslexic children with this combination of coordination problems have especially severe difficulties with handwriting.

- Math problems are common in children with dyslexia and may result from factors including difficulties with sequencing, number reversals, problems with visual movement control, and difficulties with the reading and language demands associated with story problems (see Chapter 12).

- Dyslexic children often develop social and emotional problems as a result of their school-related difficulties, as we saw with Michael. These problems can occur as early as first or second grade, though for some children they may not come to a head until high school or even college. Problems with diminished self-esteem, anxiety, and depression can cause physical complaints, oppositional behaviors, work resistance, aggressive outbursts, and school avoidance. These problems are especially likely to occur when the underlying dyslexia goes unrecognized and untreated and when the child is unjustly accused of lack of effort, motivation, or application. The child may feel isolated and misunderstood when he sees all his peers succeeding yet he continues to struggle. When he experiences repeated failures, he may enter a "cycle of despair" in which each new failure only increases his sense of hopelessness and confirms his growing suspicion that he is defective and worthless. J. William Adams, headmaster of Morgan Park Academy (a private primary and secondary school just south of Chicago), an expert on dyslexic education, and a person with dyslexia himself, recalled for us these feelings from his own childhood: "There's nothing worse than being told to do something you can't do, then to be asked, 'Have you really done your best?'"

- In addition, as we have mentioned above, children with dyslexia often behave in ways that suggest they are suffering from attentional disorders or ADHD. Published reports suggest that the rate of ADHD is higher in dyslexic children than in the general population. Some children with dyslexia clearly do show difficulties with sustained attention across a wide variety of activities. Others experience their greatest focusing difficulties on tasks involving reading and writing and are distractible primarily during these tasks. Many of these children have difficulties with visual distractibility and with auditory short-term memory, as mentioned above, and these problems can contribute to the appearance of ADHD. It is less clear whether this more task-specific pattern of distractibility and inattention merits the diagnosis of ADHD. It is also necessary to determine that a child is not simply showing aversion to new tasks because of a sense of hopelessness or anxiety.

- It's important to realize that many of these behaviors, while suggestive of dyslexia, are not specific for it. Dyslexia can be diagnosed only on the basis of a thorough neuropsychological evaluation. Most children with dyslexia will not show all of these behaviors, although some children may show many. Also, since nearly half of all children with a family history of dyslexia will develop dyslexia themselves, these behaviors should be regarded as especially significant in a child with such a family history. Such a child should receive early intervention, before she falls behind or experiences social and emotional problems. The longer the delay before intervention begins, the longer treatment will take due to the social, emotional, and developmental issues that accrue over time.

THE CAUSES OF READING ACQUISITION AND READING IMPAIRMENTS

In this section, we'll describe the mechanisms underlying both normal reading and dyslexia. Understanding both normal and dyslexic reading should clarify many aspects of dyslexia you've previously found confusing and help you better care for children with dyslexia. Let's begin by looking at the normal process of reading development.

Learning to Read: The Normal Process
of Reading Development

When children learn to read, they usually progress through a series of overlapping steps or phases. Understanding the nature of this reading progression will make it easier to understand where children with reading problems typically encounter difficulties.

The first step children take toward reading occurs when they begin to associate some set of letters that they see repeatedly in a particular context with a spoken word. Often this will be a product or brand name, due to the prominent visual styling of the letters. The first word our older child "read" in this fashion was *Tide* (which should give you a pretty good idea of what a messy eater he was!). At this stage, children are not actually sounding out letters. They have simply made the crucial step of associating a particular collection of *printed* letters with a particular *spoken* word. Most children develop a repertoire of a few such sight words before they begin learning to decode (or sound out) words.

Gradually children begin to make connections between individual letters and the sounds they represent. However, they're still not quite ready to sound out or decode whole words. They still identify printed words primarily by context, using their limited ability to sound out individual letters as just one among several kinds of clues. For example, they may look at the book their mom is holding and see the little word she's pointing to that begins with *d*. They know what sound the *d* makes, so they know how the word starts. But rather than continuing to decode—that is, translate letters to sounds, then blend the sounds together to form words—they look for other clues. If there's a picture of a dog on the page, they'll probably guess right.

As children develop a fuller understanding of the relationship between the different letters and the sounds they make, they gradually begin decoding words in earnest. Initially reading is slow and laborious and more an exercise in sounding out a string of words than deciphering the meaning of a text. Over time, as they become better at decoding words, speed and comprehension will improve. However, as long as a child is fully dependent upon decoding strategies, the process of reading will remain rather slow and laborious, and "irregular" words that cannot be decoded using standard phonetic rules (e.g., *benign* or *wound*—as in a cut) will still be hard to read. Many children with dyslexia remain stuck in the early decoding-dependent phases of reading, because they have difficulty mastering the associations between written letters (or combinations of letters) and their associated sounds. We'll discuss this problem in detail in the next section.

Finally, if all goes well, children will reach the stage of fully mature and rapid reading, which is often called the *orthographic* phase (from the Greek *orthos* meaning, "correct" or "see correctly," and *graphos*, meaning "writing"). This phase is characterized by the ability to recognize words or word parts "by sight" rather than by sounding them out. To enter this phase, children must begin to recognize the numerous multiletter combinations that occur together frequently. These include groups of letters that combine to make sounds that differ from a simple blend of each (like *th*, *sh*, or *ing*), prefixes and suffixes (like *pre-*, *anti-*, or *-ment*), and other commonly occurring letter combinations. Eventually they will come to recognize increasing numbers of whole words by sight, without having to decode them at all. This ability to remember these larger word and letter groups is dependent largely on a form of visual memory, as we'll discuss in more detail below. Most children develop the ability to recognize whole words by sight after repeatedly sounding out those words using decoding strategies. That's why studies have shown that interventions that improve children's decoding abilities often improve their sight-word recognition skills as well. However, some dyslexic children (like Michael) may bypass the decoding phase altogether and become entirely dependent on whole-word recognition. These children may read silently with relatively good comprehension but be utterly unable to read aloud. Other children with dyslexia seem to have special difficulty developing the ability to recognize words by sight and remain wholly dependent on the comparatively slower sound-based decoding system for reading. Truly skilled readers use a seamless blending of both sight-word reading and decoding to read most written materials; sight-word skills are used for familiar words and decoding strategies for any new or unfamiliar ones.

Pattern Processing: Reading's Sound, Sight, and Speech Systems

Now that we've considered the different phases that a child passes through when she learns to read, we're ready to look in slightly more detail at the neurological functions that are needed to pass successfully through these phases. As we'll see, there are three primary brain systems that a child can use to read: a sound-based system, a sight-based system, and a speech-based system. We'll begin by discussing the sound-based (phonological) processing system that plays a major role in the reading problems of many children with dyslexia. Then we'll discuss the often overlooked visual (orthographic) processing problems that play a role in the reading difficulties of as many as two-thirds of children with dyslexia. Finally, we'll discuss the surprising way that the speech centers of the brain can be used to help children learn to read and spell.

The Sound-Based (Phonological) Reading and Spelling System

As we mentioned in Chapter 5, one of the most important problems underlying the reading difficulties in children with dyslexia is a problem in the *phonological*, or sound processing, system of the brain (from the Greek *phone*, meaning "sound, particularly of the voice," and *logos*, meaning "word"). Experts estimate that phonological impairments are present in as many as 60 to 80 percent of children with dyslexia. As a result of this brain-based deficit in sound processing, children with dyslexia may have difficulty learning how to *decode* printed words—that is, learning how to link the printed letters on the page with the word sounds they represent.

To understand why children with dyslexia can have problems with decoding, we must first understand a crucial fact about reading. *To correctly decode words, a child must first be able to correctly align the rapidly passing sequence of sounds in a spoken word with the sequence of printed symbols on a page.* For example, to decode the word *pig*, a child must be able both to correctly hear (or process) the sounds *puh-ih-guh* and to see (or perceive) the sequence of letters *p-i-g*. Only by consistently perceiving the correspondence of the sounds in the spoken word *pig* with the letters in the printed word *pig* will she learn to decode. Anything that disrupts this mapping process—making it hard for the child to discover the correspondence between sounds and symbols—will make decoding difficult, if not impossible. As we'll see, children with dyslexia often have difficulties with *both* the sound and the visual processing aspects of the decoding process. Little wonder they struggle so greatly in learning to read. We'll discuss the visual problems associated with dyslexia in the next section. Here we'll focus on dyslexic sound-processing difficulties.

As we've said, to decode words, a child must be able to hear each of the sounds that make up those words when they're spoken. For most children, this ability comes quite naturally. Their brains have little difficulty in perceiving each one of the different, rapidly changing sounds that make up spoken words. Unfortunately, around 10 to 20 percent of children have difficulty distinguishing these sounds as they fly by in combination with other sounds in spoken words. As a result of this phonological processing deficit, these children will have difficulty hearing the differences between the sounds represented by various letters when they occur in spoken words. This may hold true for literally countless word sounds, like the sounds represented by the letters *b, d, p,* or *t,* in spoken words like *dime* and *time,* or *bin, din, pin,* and *tin;* or for sounds represented by *f* and *v; m* and *n; sh* and *ch; r, w,* and *l;* and on and on. Children who can't correctly *hear* these sounds as they fly by rapidly in spoken words have a tremendous degree of difficulty understanding how letter symbols correspond to word sounds.

For example, think of a child who has difficulties perceiving the differences between the word sounds listed above. Even if such a child can see all the letters in words clearly enough (though this is often a problem for children with dyslexia as well, as we'll discuss below), how can she hope to decipher the correspondence of letters and sounds when presented with a series of words like *pit, bit, bid, dip, pig, pick, big, dig, bet, bed, pet, peg, peck, deck, beg, bag, back,* et cetera? When spoken, these words sound nearly the same to her. There's simply no way she'll be able to learn the appropriate letter-sound associations by decoding. She'll simply have to learn to recognize all these words "by sight," while her decoding skills remain stuck in the most primitive, context-bound, "guess and go" stages.

This difficulty with sound-symbol association often shows up in the spelling problems experienced by children with phonologically based dyslexia. Look again at the sentence written by our young patient in Figure 30: "I thoot i crod clam the matin." Confusions such as *thoot* for *thought, crod* for *could, clam* for *climb,* and *matin* for *mountain* strongly suggest difficulties hearing the differences between speech sounds in words. This helps explain why the process of learning phonetic rules (or the associations of letters and sounds) is so confusing for many children with dyslexia and why the process of reading and spelling is so difficult. This relationship between sound discrimination and reading difficulty also explains why (as we shall discuss below) approaches that focus on helping children *hear* sounds more clearly can be effective in helping them learn to read.

This difficulty with phonological processing also helps to explain several other commonly seen problems in children with dyslexia. First, it helps explain why they often have difficulty with "word finding," or retrieving words from memory—the well-known phenomenon of becoming tongue-tied. Information about words (like their definitions, synonyms, antonyms, homonyms, and personal associations) is usually stored in a part of the brain known as the *auditory word memory* area. The brain files information in this area according to how it believes the word sounds and retrieves it in two ways: first, by hearing the word spoken, and second, by reading the letters that represent that word. Both of these mechanisms are critically dependent upon a child's ability to process word sounds accurately. If you don't hear a word the same way that you perceived it when you filed it, you won't look for it in the right place in the auditory memory area. Similarly, if you don't pronounce a word to yourself the same way when you read it as you did when you filed it away, you won't look for it in the right place either. Children with this phenomenon often encounter the frustrating difficulty of knowing what they want to say but being unable to find the right words.

This difficulty with phonological processing also helps to explain the process of mishearing that is commonly seen with dyslexic children. Think, for example, of what will happen when the mother of a child with these sound-discrimination and retrieval difficulties calls to him as he rushes out the door on a winter's day, "Have you got a coat?" He'll happily respond "No!" then head out wearing his jacket, satisfied that he's told his mom he doesn't have a "cold."

As we've mentioned, a child's ability to learn to read by decoding depends both on the ability to hear spoken words correctly and on the ability to see printed words correctly. In the next section, we'll discuss the important but often neglected visual problems that are a crucial part of dyslexia.

The Sight-Based (Orthographic) Reading and Spelling System

Visual abnormalities have been shown to be present in as many as 80 percent of children with dyslexia. These include abnormalities of visual contrast sensitivity, visual tracking, visual motion detection, visual fixation, visual attention, and recognition of the spatial orientation of letters and numbers. These visual difficulties correlate highly with reading ability and especially with the ability to recognize words by sight.

There is a considerable degree of controversy regarding the precise brain mechanisms underlying these visual abnormalities. However, a large and continually growing body of research suggests that they make it hard for children to consistently perceive the letters in words in their proper order (e.g., *girl* versus *gril*) and spatial orientation (e.g., *bad* versus *dad* or *dab*).

This ability to perceive letter sequences correctly is important for all aspects of reading, including word decoding and sight-word reading. At the level of decoding, you can easily see its importance when you consider the sound-symbol mapping process that underlies decoding. This mapping requires the ability to link a series of sounds (heard in their proper sequence), with a series of letters (viewed in their proper sequence). Any process that impairs the ability to correctly see a sequence of written letters will make it all but impossible to discover the relationships between spoken word sounds and letter symbols. Think, for example, of the child we described earlier who was trying to map the sounds of the word *pig* onto the visual symbols *p-i-g*. If he sees the letter sequence as *ipg, gip, gpi, igp, qig,* or *giq,* he will have an extremely hard time understanding how the sounds map onto the symbols. Unfortunately, this is precisely the kind of visual problem many children with dyslexia have, and it greatly compounds their difficulties learning to read.

These visual processing abnormalities can also cause difficulty at the level of sight-word recognition and recall. As you remember from above, skilled reading is characterized by the ability to recognize whole words (or word parts) "by sight" (i.e., without the need for decoding), using the orthographic reading system. This ability to recognize whole words on the basis of their visual appearance is made possible by a part of the brain known as the *visual word form area,* which is analogous to the auditory word memory area described above. In the visual word form area, information about words is filed away according to the visual appearance of words. As a result, when a previously learned word is seen on a page, the information stored about it (i.e., definition, associations, etc.) is rapidly retrieved from this area, bypassing the need for decoding. This visual recognition system is the primary mechanism most skilled readers use when they read, because it's much faster and more efficient than sound-based decoding. It's also crucial for remembering the pronunciations of the many words in English that can't simply be sounded out on the basis of their appearance and for remembering the spellings of those same words, which can't be deciphered on the basis of their sounds (e.g., *sponge, shoe, receipt*).

The ability to store a word properly in the visual word form area appears to be at least partially dependent upon the ability to form a stable and consistent visual tracing of a word. Because children with dyslexia often have difficulty forming such stable and consistent tracings, they may also have difficulty both storing and recalling words in their visual word form area. As a result, such children may have trouble identifying words by sight when they encounter them on the page, and thus be forced to rely on their sound-based decoding system for reading. If this sound-based decoding system works relatively well, these children may be able to read reasonably accurately, but they will usually be fairly slow readers.

It's important to stress that visual word form memory is a specialized form of visual memory that is distinct from other aspects of visual memory. For example, a dyslexic child with an extremely poor memory for visual word forms can have a phenomenal memory for visual shapes or images, because these memory areas use different pathways and are located in different parts of the brain. In fact, other aspects of visual memory can often be used to compensate for impaired visual word form memory, as we'll discuss below.

The Speech-Based (Broca's) Reading and Spelling System

There's one final word processing system that dyslexic children can use to help with reading—especially if they have difficulty with sound-based decoding. Interestingly, it's a region of the brain that's usually involved in speech output. This region is often called *Broca's area*, after the doctor who first described it. Like the auditory and visual word memory areas, Broca's area can store information about words. However, in Broca's area, this information is not organized according to word sound or appearance (as in the systems we've discussed) but according to the *motor plans* that determine which speech muscles are needed to speak the words.

This area, which works even more slowly than the auditory word memory system, is frequently the major center for individual word analysis in dyslexic children who have impairments in both their auditory and visual word form memory systems. The information stored in this area can be retrieved during reading when the visual image of the word the child sees on the page activates the vocal muscle movement patterns needed to speak the word. In this surprising way, *Broca's area essentially "reads aloud" to the child.* This is why many young readers—and dyslexic children in particular—tend to move their lips while reading, even when they are not making any sound. Several popular dyslexia-treatment strategies (described below) have been designed to employ this mechanism to help children learn to read and spell.

Conclusion: Three Main Patterns of Dyslexic Readers and Spellers

Having described the most important impairments underlying the reading and spelling problems in dyslexia, we are now in a position to understand how these problems tend to present in several common patterns.

The first pattern includes children like Michael (from Chapter 1) who show severely impaired phonological processing but somewhat less impaired visual word form memory. This group includes about one-third of children with dyslexia. Michael spoke for this whole class of children when he described his pattern of acquiring new words for reading and spelling: "[I try] to read the words in my own way, by memorizing what the words looks like." For children in this group, visual word form memory generally works well enough for them to read silently with fairly good comprehension. Often it even allows them to recognize which of the alternatives on a multiple-choice spelling test is correct (e.g., *seprate, seperate, sepperate, separate*). Typically, though, it does not work as well for spontaneous word form recall—that is, for spelling the word from memory—especially when burdened with the additional demands of letter formation and higher-order language needed for writing. Michael was characteristic in this regard as well. His visual word-recognition system worked well enough for him to score near the fortieth percentile on multiple-choice spelling-recognition tests (which was one of the reasons his school refused to recognize his disability), but his ability to spell words from memory was severely impaired. No matter how hard he tried, he was unable to commit spelling words to long-term memory simply by staring at the word and saying the letters to himself or even by writing them multiple times. The following is an example of his spontaneous writing: "On a planet farfay awaw There was a youno man by the name of uragoner who set of for the edges of his planet in surch of the plantes bengines [planet's beginnings]. His cutter [culture] had mot alwalec peen [always been] on This planet." Characteristic of children with this problem, the mistaken words do not "sound" like the words intended, indicating a breakdown in matching sound units (*phonemes*) with their appropriate letter representations (*graphemes*).

The second pattern includes children like Laura, who have relatively intact phonology but impaired visual word form memory. This group includes about 20 to 30 percent of dyslexic children. Writing samples from these children show a very different appearance. The meaning intended by the writer is usually very clear, because all the words "sound" the way they should. While children with this pattern might make similar errors of capitalization and punctuation, the spelling mistakes they tend to make would be ones they couldn't detect by sound. They often mistakenly split compound words into parts or combine words that should be separate. They double letters where a single one should be used or vice versa. They use one-letter combinations (like *ee*) where an identical-sounding but different-appearing combination (like *ea*) should be used. They also tend to have special difficulties with *homonyms*, which are words that sound alike but are spelled differently. Since these children are largely dependent on sounding-out strategies for spelling, the difference in spelling between *there* and *their* or *two*, *to*, and *too* can seem arbitrary and even cruel.

The following sample was written by another very bright eleven-year-old boy with minimal phonological impairment but significant visual symptoms. "I am a Typhoon and I am on my way to Japan and gathering spead. I mite be the Typhoon that destrois the mongls and their ships on their second invashon of Japan. . . . My stronggest power is wind wich can make trumendus waves that can capsise the stronggest mongl ship." While the spelling is still quite impaired, the meaning is much easier to decipher than in Michael's passage. Notice how these errors cannot be detected simply by sounding out the words but only by how they look.

The third pattern, which is the most common, representing about 50 to 70 percent of children with dyslexia, includes children who show more balanced problems with both visual word form memory and phonology. These children will show a pattern of reading and spelling difficulties that combine features of the two patterns described above.

Many children with dyslexia learn to read well enough—at least in certain situations—that they avoid identification. However, their dyslexia-related difficulties still cause them important problems. This pattern of difficulties is so common among the children we see in our clinic—especially among many of the most highly gifted—that we have given it its own name: *stealth dyslexia*.

Children with stealth dyslexia, like Michael (and Laura), are typically verbally skilled but on careful testing usually show signs of classic dyslexic auditory and/or visual difficulties. Because of their language strengths, they may develop into good silent readers (though often slightly later than would be expected, normally around grades two to five). Yet because of their unresolved dyslexic difficulties, they typically struggle with writing (including spelling) and oral reading. Because of their strong silent-reading abilities (and in many cases their ability to recognize correctly spelled words on multiple-choice tests), they are often not identified as having dyslexia, nor are they given the help they need to develop their skills.

All too often, children with stealth dyslexia struggle through elementary school, performing well below their potential ability, and are forced to expend incredible energy just to keep up with the average. When they meet the heavier writing demands and more complex written-language patterns in middle and high school, they all too often enter a cycle of despair that leads to eventual failure. This downward spiral is absolutely unnecessary, but unfortunately it is something we see over and over again in our practice. Children with high verbal IQs or high language-achievement tests who show a difference of more than two standard deviations between their language skills and their spelling, written language, or oral reading abilities are highly likely to have dyslexia and should be carefully evaluated and treated for it, irrespective of where their scores fall on an age- or grade-level mean. There is considerable evidence that this group of students contains some of the very brightest and most creative minds in our society, and it is an absolute tragedy that their plight should go unnoticed.

At the other end of the dyslexic spectrum are children whose difficulties with word-sound processing are so severe that they result in significant difficulties not only with reading, but also with oral language comprehension and expression. We often see such children in the early elementary grades, when they are having difficulty mastering reading and writing. Typically, like Marshall in Chapter 6, they will have a family history of dyslexia, and may even have had a parent who was diagnosed with language difficulties as a child. Technically, these children do not qualify for a diagnosis of dyslexia, because they have significant deficits in oral as well as written language comprehension; yet careful examination often suggests that their difficulties learning language arise from the same type of problems processing word-sounds that frequently contribute to the reading problems in dyslexia. It is important to properly identify these children, because when given intensive intervention for their word-sound processing difficulties (in the early elementary years especially) they will often show dramatic improvements not only in the decoding aspects of reading, but in oral language expression and comprehension as well.

Attention: The Role of Working Memory in Reading

Working memory also plays an important role in the reading process, because reading places huge demands on working memory. Children with dyslexia often show signs of working memory overload during reading and writing—times when they "just can't seem to get it all together." For many children with dyslexia, working memory overload seems to be a *result* rather than the cause of their underlying reading and writing problems. In other words, they experience working memory overload because they must work so hard to decode while reading and to form letters and words while writing. Their working memory capacity is fairly normal, but it's just not big enough to handle the extra burden imposed by the sound or visual processing problems.

For other children with reading problems, primary impairments in working memory may play a major role in producing reading problems. Often these children have primary limitations in auditory working memory that have produced problems not only with reading but also with broader language functions and often with attention. We've discussed these children already in Chapter 6.

EVALUATING READING PROBLEMS IN CHILDREN

When a child has difficulty reading or spelling, it's important to assess not only that child's reading and spelling skills but also her entire range of mental and physical strengths and weaknesses. Initially, simple problems with visual acuity and peripheral hearing should be ruled out, and then a complete evaluation should be performed. This evaluation should determine five things:

1. Why the reading and/or spelling problems are occurring.
2. Whether more severe language or attention problems or problems affecting general intellectual capacity are involved.
3. Whether other dyslexia-related difficulties (of the kinds described above) are present.
4. What an appropriate course of treatment should consist of.
5. What strengths the child has, especially in the areas of auditory and visual memory, that he can use to get around any problems that can't be eliminated.

In addition to a general evaluation of the child's motor, sensory, and memory systems, this evaluation should carefully assess the child's skills in the following reading-related areas: phonology (including the child's ability to store and retrieve information by sound), visual scanning and tracking, oral reading (including accuracy and comprehension), handwriting, and spelling. This evaluation should include not only face-to-face testing but also an inspection of the child's schoolwork. The more and better the information that can be gathered and inspected, the easier it will be to make an accurate assessment of the child's strengths and weaknesses. On occasion, it may be appropriate to perform IQ testing to rule out a more general cognitive deficit.

Remember: Assessing strengths is crucial. Even after successful intervention, many dyslexic children will still face special challenges, especially in the areas of spelling and handwriting. As we saw in Chapter 3, knowing a child's memory strengths and her preferred learning style is essential for developing an optimal learning approach for that child.

HELPING CHILDREN WITH DYSLEXIA

In this section, we'll describe the many things that can be done to help dyslexic persons of any age—even adults—learn to read and spell better. Figure 32 presents a visual guide to the treatment approaches we'll be discussing in this section. You'll probably want to refer to this figure as we go along to help keep the big picture in mind. (You may also wish to refer to the Helping sections in Chapters 3, 4, 6, and 11 for information regarding eye-movement control and spatial processing issues, working memory issues, output problems affecting speech, and writing issues, respectively.) Now let's quickly review the contents of Figure 32, before we get into our more detailed discussion.

Note at the top of Figure 32 that we've divided dyslexic children into two main categories (columns): those on the left with sound-based (phonological) reading difficulties and those on the right with visual (orthographic) reading difficulties. As we've mentioned previously, approximately 20 to 30 percent of dyslexic children will belong in the left-hand (phonological) column alone, about 50 to 70 percent will belong in both columns, and about 20 to 30 percent of children will belong primarily in the right-hand (visual) column. In general, children with phonological deficits will benefit from the therapies in the left-hand column, and children with visual problems will benefit from therapies on the right.

We can further define which children are likely to benefit from which therapies by looking at the divisions on the left of the figure. Here we've divided dyslexic children into four main categories, based on information from their neuropsychological testing about memory strengths and weaknesses.

1. The *top row* represents children with special difficulty learning by auditory pathways, who are therefore *primarily visual learners*.

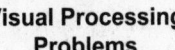

	Auditory Processing Problems	**Visual Processing Problems**
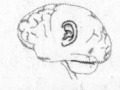 **Auditory Memory Problems**	Train Phonics Train Visualization Verbal Mediation Closed-Captioning Use Story Memory Thematic Learning Silent Speed Reading	Eye Exercises Trace Word Shape Study Word Roots Allow Finger Sweep Silent Speed Reading Multisensory Techniques (See, Hear, Touch)
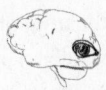 **Visual Memory Problems**	Train Phonics Verbal Mediation Motor-Sensory Memory (Air Writing) Closed-Captioning Multisensory Techniques (See, Hear, Touch)	Color and Picture Mnemonics Story Mnemonics Verbal Mediation Books on Tape
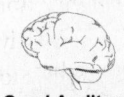 **Good Auditory & Visual Memory**	Train Phonics Teach Phonics Rules Closed-Captioning Silent Speed Reading	Eye Exercises Read Along with Books on Tape
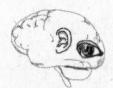 **Auditory & Visual Memory Problems**	Train Phonics Dramatize Words (Visual and Spatial Imagery) Musical Memory Multisensory Techniques (See, Hear, Touch)	Eye Exercises Use Color to Emphasize Visual Motor-Sensory Memory (Air Writing) Musical Memory Multisensory Techniques (See, Hear, Touch)

FIGURE 32. A Framework for Matching Educational Strategies with Reading Impairments

2. The *second row* represents children with special difficulty learning by visual pathways, who are therefore *primarily auditory learners*.

3. The *third row* represents children who learn well in general by either pathway and as such are *relatively balanced learners*.

4. The *fourth row* are children who experience difficulties retaining information through both auditory and visual channels. These children will require help for both their auditory and visual difficulties but will not have the benefit of relative strength in either

pathway to rely on. These children are especially dependent on *multisensory learning*.

By considering both a child's underlying auditory/phonological or visual/orthographic deficits in light of these major memory strengths and weaknesses, we can get a better idea of which interventions will prove helpful.

In the following sections, we'll describe the treatments listed in the various boxes of the figure. These treatments can be divided roughly into the three classes described in Chapter 2:

1. Remediations, or treatments that lessen (remediate) the phonological and visual impairments that cause the reading problems in dyslexia.
2. Compensations, or strategies that allow children to use areas of strength to help compensate for areas of weakness, primarily through the use of mnemonic (memory) strategies that help them learn and remember new information about words.
3. Accommodations, or special interventions that minimize the effects of any dyslexia-related impairments that can't be eliminated by these other two strategies.

When reading these sections, it's important to remember that this information is intended as a general guide to help parents, teachers, and other concerned adults understand better the kinds of treatments that are available for children with dyslexia. It should not be thought of as a complete do-it-yourself manual. Although parents have a crucial role to play in this treatment process, children with dyslexia require the help of a skilled multidisciplinary team to reach their full potential. No parent should try to "go it alone."

REMEDIATIONS FOR CHILDREN WITH DYSLEXIA

In this section, we'll discuss remediations for the two main categories of problems affecting most children with dyslexia. We'll begin by discussing remediations for the sound processing deficit, then follow with a discussion of the remediations for the visual processing deficits.

Remediations for the Sound-Based (Phonological) Problems in Dyslexia

There are two crucial steps to remediating phonological reading problems. The first is to improve the child's ability to *perceive* the way words are made up of smaller sounds. The second is to help the child *understand* how these sounds correspond to the letters that make up printed words (that is, the rules of phonics).

Many classroom-based teaching systems have been developed to help with both steps, and many schools now use a version of one of these systems. There are also programs available that can be used outside the classroom that combine both steps. Most of these programs are intended for children at the kindergarten or early-elementary level. However, most can still be used for somewhat older children with significant reading problems. A few good programs of this kind include Saxon Phonics (www.saxonpublishers. harcourtachieve.com), Hooked on Phonics (www.hookedonphonics.com), Reading Reflex (see Resources), and Sensational Strategies for Teaching Beginning Readers (www.orton-gillingham.com). The Phonics Game (www .phonicsgame.com) also provides an enjoyable game-based approach for practicing phonics.

Several computer-based programs have also been developed that focus more intensively on remediating the first of the two steps: that is, on "training" the auditory system to perceive word sounds more clearly. Two programs that work this way are called Earobics and Fast ForWord (see Chapter 4). These programs can improve sound discrimination abilities in many children, though they do not work in all, and at present there is no clear way to distinguish beforehand which children will benefit. In our experience, these programs are most helpful for children who frequently mishear and make many sound-based spelling mistakes—though again, these signs are not perfect. While these software programs do not by themselves "teach children to read," the sound discrimination improvements they produce can help children respond better to phonics training. These programs should be thought of as useful adjuncts to reading-remediation programs, but not as complete reading therapies.

Other programs combine these steps with multisensory mnemonic (memory) strategies. The most popular of these strategies are based on the Orton-Gillingham Method (www.orton-gillingham.com), which combines auditory, visual, and kinesthetic (motor-memory-based) cues to aid the faulty auditory word memory system. Strategies of this type include the Wilson method (www.wilsonlanguage.com), the Spalding method (www.spalding.org), the Herman method (www.hermanmethod.com), and the Slingerland method (www.slingerland.org). Often these methods are administered by specially trained tutors or in special schools or classes. These multisensory strategies are particularly helpful for children with combined deficits in auditory and visual processing. Some children with severe motor-planning or sensory-feedback difficulties may find that the addition of movement—and especially fine-motor movement—hinders learning more than it helps. Attention should be paid to an individual child's areas of strength and weakness. We'll describe these systems (and several other multisensory systems) in more detail in our section on mnemonic strategies.

Although these programs can help dyslexic children to lessen and circumvent the deficits in their sound-based reading systems, most children require additional help to become skilled readers. The most helpful step, not surprisingly, is to *read more*. However, not all reading is of equal value. When the experts on the National Reading Panel evaluated various reading styles to see which worked best in helping children become fast and fluent readers, they found that the procedure known as "guided repeated oral reading" showed the best results. (For a copy of their report, see www.nationalreadingpanel.org/publications/summary .htm.)

In guided repeated oral reading, an adult guide initially reads a passage aloud to a child. The passage selected should be difficult enough that the child initially makes some errors—perhaps one to two mistakes per line, but not more. Depending on the age and skill of the reader, this passage may be as little as a few sentences or as much as several paragraphs. The child then "echo-reads" the passage out loud, while the guide provides moment-by-moment feedback. This same passage should be practiced once or twice a day until mastered. Then a new passage should be selected and worked on until perfected. Practicing in this fashion can produce dramatic results—*even in adults*.

In addition to guided reading, it is important to expose a child to lots of auditory language. Reading to a child, listening to books on tape, attending plays, and watching films and documentaries with rich language content can all be very valuable. The gains in vocabulary and grammar produced by these means typically translate into improved reading comprehension and fluency.

When watching TV or videos, activate closed-captioning. Closed-captioning can provide excellent practice in letter-sound word associations as well as useful visual support for children who have frequent problems with mishearing.

Another important way to strengthen gains in the letter-sound connections is to have the child practice writing. It's important to remember, though (as we'll stress in Chapter 11), that children with dyslexia often have such severe problems with handwriting that they view writing as a form of torture. Don't overburden them to the point of frustration. Take the long view: Bit-by-bit, incremental gains are the key. Many dyslexic children with handwriting difficulties are simply on a different time frame for handwriting development than their nondyslexic peers. Also, keyboarding is essential for dyslexic writers. Having a child practice writing on a keyboard equipped with a spell-checking function (or better still with a program like Write Outloud; see below) can itself have a beneficial educational effect because of the immediate feedback it provides on spelling and, with some programs, the auditory "read-back" function that allows them to hear what they've written.

Finally, for children who are less efficient with their sounding-out system than with their visual recognition system, speed-reading can be a useful skill. While some details may be lost by speed-reading, children with this reading profile often take in more information by speed-reading a passage two or even three times than by meticulously reading word by word once. For children with visual skipping difficulties, sweeping along the passage with a finger or other marker can improve tracking. For key passages, underlining or highlighting words is helpful for some children as well. Another strategy that is especially useful for decoding long or irregular words that are especially challenging, is the "sweep-sweep-spell" method described in *The Gift of Dyslexia*. In this method, a word is swept through twice rapidly and then, if it still does not register, is sounded (or spelled) out letter by letter.

Remediations for the Visual Processing Deficits in Dyslexia

At present there is less agreement on how to treat the visual abnormalities associated with dyslexia than the phonological deficits discussed above.

However, there are a growing number of studies documenting the beneficial effects of visual remediations for certain visual problems in dyslexia.

In children with dyslexia, the remediable visual problems (not including simple non-dyslexia-related acuity and focusing problems) can be clustered into three general groups: (1) problems with visual word form memory, (2) problems with letter and symbol reversals, or (3) problems with contrast sensitivity. We'll discuss each of these issues in order.

Visual Word Memory Problems

As we discussed above, many dyslexic children have difficulty with automatic sight-word recognition due to subtle abnormalities in their visual-control systems. These children will often show abnormal symptoms or behaviors during reading, such as frequent word or line skips, a tendency to move their whole head to read instead of just their eyes, double vision, and squinting or closing or rubbing one eye. They may also complain of visual blurring or a sensation that the letters on the page are wobbling, wiggling, or popping in and out of the paper. Finally, they may show a tendency to missequence the letters in words.

Many dyslexic children with these symptoms have been found to have deficits in the visual attention and control mechanisms that are responsible for balancing visual motion and fixation. Several studies have shown that interventions designed to improve the performance of these systems can result in both significant reduction in adverse symptoms and gains in reading. In our opinion, children with difficulties of this nature should be referred to a developmental optometrist (an optometrist with specialized training who will usually have the letters FCOVD in addition to O.D. after his or her name) for evaluation and treatment. We believe that the evidence we've described provides strong justification for this approach, and in our clinic we have seen many children who've benefited greatly from such treatment.

Letter- and Symbol-Orientation Problems

While it is common for children before the age of eight (both dyslexic and nondyslexic) to reverse letters or numbers when writing or to make symmetrical letter substitutions when reading, a significant number of dyslexic children show difficulties with such reversals that persist beyond this age. These children may also show difficulties with letter formation that extend far beyond simple difficulties with reversals (see Chapter 4, Figure 12). There is evidence that in many dyslexic children, these reversals arise from the same problems controlling visual fixation and motion processing that we've just described. As a result, children with unusually extensive or persistent difficulties with reversals should be referred to a developmental optometrist for evaluation. In addition, several computer programs have been designed to help improve visual recognition, for example PTS (www.visiontherapysolutions.net/pts.html).

These interventions will be helpful for some children with extensive letter-reversal difficulties, but not all. If there is evidence that a child also has difficulty with other aspects of visual-spatial perception (e.g., object or facial recognition), we usually recommend that such a child be evaluated by a neurologist or ophthalmologist with expertise on centrally (cerebral) based visual impairments (CVIs).

Contrast Sensitivity Problems

Dyslexic children often have difficulties with poor visual contrast sensitivity. These may be experienced as glare from the paper, eyestrain, or just difficulty making out letters. Symptoms may be worse in some lights than others. Fluorescent lights frequently produce the most problems. These children may also have trouble with glare from TV or computer screens.

Several studies have shown that children with this difficulty can be helped by the use of colored filters that actually help the letters "stand out" better from their visual background. One study from Oxford University showed reading gains in children with these symptoms when they used colored overlays on the page: 23 percent of children were helped by yellow filters, 15 percent by blue, and 7 percent by red or green. While there are sources for specially designed (Irlen) filters available on the Internet (www.recordedbooks.com) and through special examiners, some of our patients have told us they have found the colored overlays available at office-supply stores to be an acceptable substitute. We have seen some children experience a big enough improvement in contrast sensitivity after three or four months of filter usage that they no longer needed to use the filters to read.

Children with contrast sensitivity problems may also experience improved vision and reduced eye fatigue by turning down brightness settings and adjusting the tints or colors on TV or computer screens. On the computer, changing the background to pale yellow or blue is often helpful, and many children prefer different font colors as well, such as burgundy or violet. Some children have also told us that they prefer to reduce the displayed colors on the Control Panel to 216.

Summing Up Visual Treatments

Many dyslexic children with visual complaints can benefit from certain simple interventions, such as increased font size, broad line spacing, reduced visual crowding, and the use of a finger or marker while reading. We would also recommend experimenting with colored overlays as described above. Some children with particularly bad horizontal eye-movement problems can also benefit from the simple trick of turning their book or music sheet on its side and tracking vertically instead of horizontally, while they're waiting for their visual therapy to help improve horizontal eye movements.

However, as we've indicated throughout this chapter, children with dyslexia are not a homogeneous group. Visual treatments are appropriate for dyslexic children who show problems with the visual aspects of reading, whether these problems present alone or in combination with phonological deficits. General principles for evaluation and treatment of children with dyslexia should include the following:

1. Any child with evidence of phonological deficits should receive the phonological remediations described above.
2. Dyslexic children with extensive visual symptoms such as headaches while reading, eyestrain, blurry vision, and letter wobbling, blurring, switching, or otherwise moving should be referred to a developmental optometrist for evaluation.
3. Dyslexic children with diffuse motor-planning and coordination problems are especially likely to have visual movement problems and should be referred early for visual evaluation.
4. Dyslexic children with visual symptoms but no demonstrable phonological deficits should be referred immediately to a developmental optometrist.

5. Significant visual perceptual problems of the kind described above also deserve early referral.
6. When a dyslexic child with phonological deficits has received a course of phonological remediation but has failed to make the expected degree of progress, an evaluation from a developmental optometrist is in order.

Compensatory Strategies for Children with Dyslexia

Many strategies have been devised to use alternative memory functions to compensate for problems in the phonological and visual word memory systems. Each of these mnemonic strategies works very well for some children and not at all for others, so their use must be tailored to an individual child's memory strengths and weaknesses, as shown in Figure 32.

Unlike the remediative strategies described above, the primary focus of these mnemonic strategies is to help children commit individual words to memory for reading and spelling, word by word. In deciding which words to learn first, it's a good idea to start with the most common words, because the twenty-five most common words account for nearly a third of all the words the child is likely to encounter when reading, and the top one hundred fully half. There are a number of excellent resources available on the Internet that contain lists of the most common words in English, such as Fry's Instant Sight-word List and the Dolch Sight-word List (www.literacyconnections .com/dolch.html).

Visual Strategies

Visual memory is one of the most powerful memory classes of all. Remember: Visual memory is not just a single entity but a diverse set of memory functions. Each of these functions deals with a different aspect of visual perception, like light and dark, shapes and edges, color, texture, movement, relations of object parts to wholes, figure-background distinctions, and the novelty or familiarity of the object. An individual may have excellent memory for one aspect of visual perception while having real difficulty with others. For example, a child with dyslexia may have a very defective visual word form memory but have a wonderful memory for colors, shapes, symbols, or pictures. By using a mnemonic strategy that takes advantage of some aspect of the child's visual memory system that is particularly strong (like colors, pictures, symbols, and even stories), we can often "trick" the brain into remembering the visual image of the word. These strategies, in other words, work by recruiting areas of nonword visual memory to remember word appearances as if they were purely visual images, rather than printed words.

One of the easiest visual strategies involves using color- and pattern-recognizing memory centers to remember word appearance. In this strategy, vivid colors, fancy fonts, or memorable patterns are used to form the different letters of a word the child is trying to remember (as, for example, the use of different colors in the letters of the words *here* and *hear* on the next page). These different visual features help draw attention to important letter patterns in "difficult" or nonphonetic segments of words and "chunk" this information into smaller and more manageable bits to make it easier to remember.

A second visual strategy is to transform the spelled word into a picture representing the word's meaning. In a study done at Oxford, "doodling" words in this fashion improved visual word memory not only for the particular words drawn but also for similarly spelled words. For example, doodling the word *bough* in the shape of a tree branch not only helped children remember the spelling of the word *bough* but also helped them remember the spelling of other *-ough* words. For this reason, it is often helpful when using this approach to learn words in "word families" that have been grouped on the basis of similar letter patterns (i.e., visual similarity). Lists of these word families are available in programs such as Target Spelling (www.nbizz.com/ampm/listings/1293.html) or at www.avko.org.

Figure 33 demonstrates how we used this "doodling approach" in two of the Visual Spelling Cards we developed as mnemonic aids for children who had difficulty spelling homonyms (www.neurolearning.com). These cards also incorporate several other mnemonic approaches. Before looking at the use of strategies, note how a "sound-dependent" reader will be unable to distinguish between the words *here* and *hear* simply by sound.

Looking at the cards, notice first our use of shading to link the two *e*'s in *here*, and to highlight the word *ear* in *hear*. Now notice how the pictures

FIGURE 33. Visual Mnemonic Strategies

link to the meanings of the words to help make the spellings more memorable. Each of these features can help children with good "picture" memories to remember these spellings as visual images. Repeated practice spelling difficult words using cards like these that bring together multiple aspects of memory can produce significant gains in a child's spelling and word-recognition abilities. (Note: Children with strong auditory memories but weaker visual memories can use cards like these to aid in the process of verbal mediation, as we'll discuss below.)

Visualization Strategies

Children can also learn to use their visual memory functions to remember information they haven't actually seen with their eyes but which they have translated into visual imagery through the process of visualization. One powerful visualization strategy involves the mental picturing of words spelled backward. Brain-imaging studies have found evidence of a reverse visual word form area on the right side of the brain that stores visual images of words backward. This area can sometimes compensate for a malfunctioning left-brain visual word form area. Some dyslexic children can successfully create reverse visual word forms in their "mind's eye" while spelling words out loud, then subsequently use these images to spell the words in their proper order.

Another mnemonic system based on visualization techniques is the commercially available Nancibell Seeing Stars Symbol Imagery Program. This program uses visualization strategies to improve word memory. Children with particularly vivid visual imaginations may find this program especially useful. Dyslexic children with auditory working-memory difficulties can use similar visualization processes to translate auditory/verbal information into pictorial information so they can retain it better (see Chapter 3).

Auditory Memory Strategies

Auditory memory areas distinct from the phonological memory system described above can also be used to improve word memory. One strategy we touched on above (and mentioned repeatedly in other chapters) is called *verbal mediation*. In this strategy, a child stores information about word spellings in verbal form, after translating the spelling into some form of word description or story. In other words, rather than trying to remember spellings simply on the basis of letter sounds or physical appearance, the child creates a description that she can use to "talk through" the structure of the word. In one variation of this strategy called *verbal elaboration*, the child memorizes short phrases describing the spelling of the word. Look, for example, back at our cards in Figure 33. A child who wanted to use verbal elaboration to describe the word *here* could say "an *h* followed by two *e*'s surrounding an *r* that points to a treasure map." This is a classic example of a *multisensory* strategy that uses multiple forms of memory to aid in remembering word forms.

Vocalization Strategies

Vocalization strategies are similar to (and at times overlapping with) auditory memory strategies, because they both involve verbal (word-based) information. However, these strategies work by "speaking" words, not by "listening" to them. In fact, they seem to work by activating the Broca's area–related speech muscle-memory centers we discussed earlier.

The simplest of these strategies is called *subvocalization*, which is basically the process of saying words to yourself to keep them in mind. This strategy works best when it combines vocal muscle-mediated memory with auditory memory, then adds the kinds of contextual/story, personal, and music-mediated memory systems we'll discuss below. These speech-related strategies can also be combined with visualization strategies for added power.

One commercially available system that has been designed to take advantage of this vocal muscle-mediated memory system is called Lindamood-Bell Phonemic Sequencing (LIPS, www.ganderpublishing.com). The LIPS method tries to improve the awareness of word sounds by teaching children to link the awareness of the positions of the vocal structures used when speaking with the speech sounds they produce. This improved phonemic awareness can then be used to help the child better understand the rules of phonics.

Peripheral Motor/Kinesthetic Strategies

Kinesthetic (or movement-based) strategies are similar to vocalization strategies in that they use motor memory to help with word memory. However, instead of speech motor memory, these strategies use the motor memory that controls the movements of the limbs and fingers.

People are often surprised that there is such a thing as motor memory. That's probably because for the most part motor memory operates subconsciously. When we're walking, for example, we may have to "tell" our legs where to go, but we don't consciously have to tell them how to take each step. Instead our legs remember what to do because they're practiced at walking. That's what motor memory is all about. When we've practiced a movement often enough, we can execute it without thinking. The plans we need to use to make the necessary movements are stored in our motor memory. That's why a good musician can converse with her audience while she plays her guitar or why most of us can talk on our cell phones while we dri—uh, forget that last example.

Motor memory can be useful for children with dyslexia because it can be used in reverse to help the conscious mind remember important information. For example, many of us have probably had the experience of forgetting a telephone number but remembering it after we started to make the movements needed to dial that number. By going through the movements, then reckoning backward, we can "remember" the number. In a similar way, strategies based on motor memory can help dyslexic children recall letter and word forms. By engaging in the simple act of "air writing" (tracing a finger or pencil over the letters on a page), a dyslexic child can often improve her memory of a word's spelling.

The memory tracings connected with large-muscle movements, like those at the shoulder, are even easier to remember than those of smaller joints, like the fingers. Large-muscle motor memory, in which letters are outlined in large, sweeping motions of the upper arm and shoulder, is often even more effective than finger muscle memory. Many children find that actually writing words with large, sweeping, shoulder-based motions on a chalkboard, a grease board, or a large roll of paper is even more effective. Another motor-based strategy some children find useful is "acting out" the shapes of the letters (e.g., in the fashion of the Village People's "Y.M.C.A." song—but without dressing up like a cowboy or a firefighter).

While kinesthetic strategies like these are helpful for many children with dyslexia, we have found them especially useful for children with visual memory impairments. These strategies also play a prominent role in many of the multisensory learning strategies mentioned above, like Orton-Gillingham, Wilson, Herman, Spalding, and Slingerland. These programs combine auditory and visual techniques with motor-memory techniques and are often helpful for children who fail to respond completely to intensive phonological remediation. One important caveat regarding motor-based memory methods is that they seem to work less well in children with significant motor-planning and coordination difficulties or those with extensive sensory-feedback and finger-position-sense difficulties. Sometimes, though, large motor movements will work well in such children, so these are still worth trying.

Musical Memory Strategies

As we mentioned in Chapter 3, words set to music are stored in a different spot in the brain from most language-based memories. In fact, it is not uncommon after strokes or accidents for people who've lost the ability to speak words still to be able to sing some of their favorite songs. Educators have long known the value of music as a memory aid, especially for long lists of noncontextual items, though this strategy has probably been drastically underutilized. Children with a musical bent should be encouraged to create their own musical mnemonics, setting spelling words to popular tunes or making up tunes of their own. For children with pitch problems, using a rap-music approach where spellings are tied to rhythms without melodies can also be useful (and may earn them the admiration of their classmates!). A few of the available phonics programs, such as Hooked on Phonics (www.hooked onphonics.com), use some musical methods in their programs.

Additional Memory Strategies

Any of the memory functions we've discussed so far can be made even more powerful by being combined with another aspect of memory. As we mentioned in Chapter 3, personal or episodic memory helps us remember information about personally relevant associations, strongly novel or surprising facts or events, or even things we find humorous. This personal memory system is strongly tied in with the parts of the brain that control feelings and emotions, so most things that cause strong feelings (whether happy, sad, funny, or disgusting) will stick in its stores. Creative spellings that contain a joke, a reference to a favorite interest or person, or that seem especially clever or interesting will all become registered in this area. This is one reason children with dyslexia can benefit greatly by using their own creativity in developing mnemonic strategies.

A related form of memory stores information that contains story or narrative elements. A well-constructed story can also activate stores in the auditory, visual, personal, musical, and kinesthetic region. The more creative a child can be in developing stories that incorporate multiple memory aspects, the more memorable and effective those stories will be. If you remember from Chapter 3, one of the most important principles in making any stored pattern particularly memorable is to link it with many associations. By tying a pattern in to a network of associated thoughts and information, you can greatly increase your chances of remembering it. If a child ties a mnemonic spelling strategy together to information about a word's meaning, to its uses in sentences, to other words with similar forms or meanings, or to stories about the way the word sounds or the way it looks, he will have a much better chance of recalling later how the word is spelled.

Accommodations for Children with Dyslexia

Despite the effectiveness of these treatments, most dyslexic children will still have residual school-related challenges. To ensure that these children are not unfairly penalized for their neurologically based disabilities, accommodations will be necessary. Schools must adjust their attitudes to these accommodations! These are not "special breaks." They are necessary interventions for neurologically challenged children. They're like a wheelchair ramp for a paraplegic child or a guide dog for a blind child or a sign-language interpreter for a deaf child. These accommodations are necessary to remove as many barriers as possible to learning and success. The goal of education is to help each child do the best she can using the neurological resources at her disposal. Requiring a child with dyslexia to meet the same spelling, writing, or oral-reading requirements as other students is unjust and, in the long run, counterproductive.

There are four major areas in which accommodations are crucial: reading, writing, classroom activities, and tests and assignments. In this section we'll consider each.

Accommodations for Reading in Dyslexia

The following reading accommodations can both decrease visual symptoms and improve the access of the dyslexic child to information through routes other than reading:

- Increasing print font size is an easy but important accommodation for children with visual symptoms such as blurring, wobbling or difficulty focusing, frequent word or line skips, headaches, squinting, or eyestrain.
- Decreasing visual crowding can also limit misreading and visual distractibility. If a child is visually distractible when reading, cover the other parts of the pages, especially pictures. You may even have to photocopy pages and cut out pictures or scan material into a word-processing document and then modify the format. If a child shows difficulty concentrating on math problems on a

crowded worksheet, try putting a single problem on an otherwise blank sheet.

- Recorded texts can be a good alternative or supplement to written texts for children with good auditory language intake. The best available source for recorded texts is Recording for the Blind and Dyslexic (www.rfbd.org). This organization maintains the largest recorded text library in the world. It has copies of most textbooks currently available.
- Help the child prelearn important new words, names, terms, or phrases before encountering them in a reading assignment or lesson. Prelearning sessions can often be valuable opportunities to help children place new information into their network of prior knowledge, so they can more easily process its meaning when they encounter it in the text.
- Discussing reading assignments, after they're completed, with a parent or teacher is crucial to making sure the child has understood key concepts, words, and facts.

Accommodations for Writing in Dyslexia

Many dyslexic children have severe handwriting problems, especially those with motor-coordination difficulties. The following writing accommodations are essential:

- Most dyslexic children should have their writing requirements reduced to at most one-third of the normally expected amount.
- Allowing dyslexic students to communicate information through means other than handwriting is also essential. As we'll discuss in more detail in Chapter 11, keyboarding, oral dictation or testing, and the use of graphic presentations can greatly improve the communication of information (compare the difference between Porter's written and dictated picture description at the beginning of the chapter). Keyboarding should be used as much as possible and should replace written work as much as possible.
- Treat both handwriting and spelling as unique disciplines with their own goals and grading. Don't take away points for mistakes on as-

signments where the goal is communication of information rather than handwriting or spelling per se.

- For more information on handwriting accommodations, see Chapter 11 on dysgraphia.

Accommodations for Classroom Activities in Dyslexia

Environmental factors can play a big role in the classroom-based difficulties experienced by dyslexic children, as can the ways in which information is presented. The following accommodations should help:

- Always seat dyslexic children where auditory and visual distractions will be minimized, preferably near the front of the room and away from windows, noisy doors, and particularly unruly or chatty classmates.
- During oral discussions, treat dyslexic children with patience and understanding, especially if they have word-finding difficulties. It's often helpful to let them know before class begins (or even the day before) what question they will be asked to discuss, then let them lead off the discussion to make sure they get a chance to participate.
- If a child with dyslexia is to be asked to read aloud in class, let him practice the reading selection overnight. If he does not feel comfortable reading before his peers, do not force him, but strongly encourage him to participate with short, prelearned passages.
- If children have problems with auditory short-term memory, chunk information into manageable bits (see Chapter 3).
- Children with auditory processing difficulties should also frequently be checked with to make sure that they understand instructions.
- Classroom notes and assignments should always be provided in writing. It is virtually impossible for most dyslexic children to take notes, and attempting to make them do so will usually significantly detract from their learning experience.
- Foreign languages are usually especially difficult for dyslexics, and they should be given a waiver if desired. (If the child strongly desires to try to learn a foreign language despite recognizing the difficulties involved, Spanish generally has the most consistent and simplest

sound-symbol associations of the modern languages and for that reason is probably the easiest to learn. American Sign Language is another good option. French, by contrast, uses many "silent letters" and should usually be avoided.)

Accommodations for Tests and Assignments in Dyslexia

Testing and timed in-class assignments often create the "perfect storm" for children with dyslexia: heightened anxiety, time pressure, sensory distractibility, challenging noncontextual materials, and need for perfect word decoding. Because children with dyslexia are always hanging halfway over the abyss of working memory overload, even the slightest extra working memory burdens can tip them over on tests or in-class assignments. The following accommodations are essential:

- Tests should be untimed and should be administered in a quiet and distraction-free environment.
- Since word-memory difficulties can complicate storage and retrieval of isolated bits of information, testing should assess a child's grasp of major concepts rather than memorization of isolated facts or details.
- Children with significant word-by-word reading difficulties should have test questions read to them, even if (like Laura or Michael) they show good comprehension on longer passages. We've seen children with advanced reading comprehension fail many tests of reading comprehension because they failed to understand the questions. The same is true for answers on multiple-choice tests.
- Scribes should be provided to write down answers for children with substantial handwriting difficulties.
- For important standardized tests (like the SAT), accommodations are often available (at least in theory), but applications for accommodations often have to be made as much as nine months in advance. Unfortunately, we've found great inconsistencies in the decisions made by the entities administering these tests regarding who will and who will not be given accommodations. It's best to apply early to leave plenty of time for appeals.

- Use forms of evaluation that depend less on timed writing whenever feasible. Recently there's been a growing recognition that standardized testing is far from the best means of assessing knowledge in children with dyslexia. Oral presentations, posters, individual and group projects, building projects, work portfolios, and so on can all provide better means of assessment.

- Finally, despite the best intentions of all involved, children with dyslexia may require more help than they can get at a regular public school. Many excellent schools now specialize in the education of children with dyslexia. We have also seen dyslexic children do well with homeschooling. Many helpful schooling resources are now available on the Internet (see Resources).

11

Handwriting and
Hand-Wringing

Dysgraphia in Children

I have terrible handwriting. I now say it is a learning
disability.

—ANDREW GREELEY, PROLIFIC NOVELIST

Benjamin was a bright and outgoing child who'd always thrived in the
hurly-burly of preschool and kindergarten. Spending several hours
each day with twenty of his closest friends was pure pleasure as far as
he was concerned! First grade seemed to offer more of the same, and he began the year with high hopes. However, before long, his parents noticed a
change. Each morning, Benjamin got ready more slowly. He began to complain of not feeling well and asking to stay home. Whenever his parents
asked how school was going, he said, "Horrible," but would give no details.

The year's first parent-teacher conference brought several rude shocks.
Though the teacher was happy to report that Ben had an excellent vocabulary, terrific memory and language skills, and was reading at a third-grade
level, she was sorry to say that both his work *and* his behavior were seriously

deficient. He regularly failed to finish his in-class work and had not yet turned in any homework. (*Homework?* His parents exchanged bewildered glances.) In addition, on several occasions, he had refused—in a very rude and forceful manner—to do assigned work. The teacher was seriously concerned that he might be showing signs of oppositional defiant disorder and that he might need medications to help manage his anger.

Benjamin's parents were mortified. After the meeting, they went home and talked to Benjamin. At first, he refused to admit there was any problem at school or that he hadn't turned in his assignments. Finally, after fifteen minutes of stonewalling, his defenses finally crumbled, and in a flood of tears he confessed to his mom and dad, "I hate school 'cause I'm stupid and I can't write!"

Sarah was a popular and highly verbal sixth-grader. Her sister, Courtney, was one year older. Sarah both looked up to her big sister and constantly compared herself to her. Courtney had always been near the top of her class, and Sarah was determined to do just as well. Through the fifth grade, she'd always been able to match Courtney's grades—though she seemed to have to work much harder than Courtney ever had.

As sixth grade wore on, Sarah found she could no longer keep pace with the high standards she'd set for herself—there just didn't seem to be enough time! Language arts and social studies were impossible—to get her work to say what she wanted it to and not look like a total mess just seemed to take *forever*. Sarah was becoming increasingly frustrated and discouraged. Sarah's parents were at a loss to explain her problems. She always seemed to work so hard and had such good focus, and (they confided to us out of Sarah's hearing) they had always considered Sarah to be the smarter of their two daughters. It just didn't make sense that she should slide from being at the top of her class to being an average or below-average student almost overnight.

DYSGRAPHIA: AN IMPORTANT BUT OFTEN OVERLOOKED PROBLEM

Benjamin and Sarah were both suffering from *dysgraphia*. Although this term sounds complex, it really just means an inability to produce clear and accurate handwriting in a functional amount of time despite sufficient teaching, motivation, and mental and physical health. Unfortunately, dysgraphia is far from uncommon: As many as one in five children (more commonly boys, but many girls as well) have serious difficulties expressing themselves through handwriting.

Dysgraphia is often extremely troubling for the children who have it. Learning to express one's thoughts through handwriting is unquestionably the toughest of all academic skills to master, because it requires the greatest simultaneous use of intellectual, physical, and working memory resources. Handwriting also plays a crucial role in almost all aspects of academic life. Dysgraphia can impair performance in subjects ranging from language to math to art. As a result, severe dysgraphia can wreak havoc upon a child's ability to succeed in school.

Academic difficulties are often only a small part of the burden imposed by dysgraphia. Children with dysgraphia are frequently not even recognized to be suffering from a specific learning challenge, so they are more likely than children with other learning impairments to be accused of laziness, lack of effort, or indifference to the quality of their work. This is especially true of children whose reading and oral-language skills are fairly intact. Dysgraphia is also an unusually public impairment. It leaves visible and permanent traces on essentially every piece of a child's schoolwork, and frequently draws criticism and teasing from classmates, teachers, and parents. For these reasons, it is especially likely to damage the spirit and self-esteem of a child who knows he is trying his best and to produce feelings of resentment, anger, and self-loathing.

Because handwriting involves so many different mental and physical functions, dysgraphia can have many causes. Each of these causes requires specific treatments. In this chapter, we'll discuss the many skills that a child needs to develop functional handwriting and the interventions that can help when problems arise.

BEHAVIORS ASSOCIATED WITH DYSGRAPHIA IN CHILDREN

There are three basic categories of behaviors associated with dysgraphia in children. First, there are the abnormal characteristics of the handwriting itself. Second, there are visible abnormalities in a child's pencil grip or posture while writing. Third, there are behaviors that result from the emotional stresses of writing. Let's consider each.

Abnormal Handwriting Appearance or Speed

Children with dysgraphia typically display many difficulties in the visible characteristics of the handwriting itself. Figure 34 shows an example of the writing of a highly gifted second-grade boy with severe dysgraphia (the same young fan of modernist painting whose drawing is displayed in Chapter 13). This writing sample displays many of the typical features of dysgraphic writing we'll describe below. Before we discuss those specific characteristics, let us point out one feature of the handwriting that may not

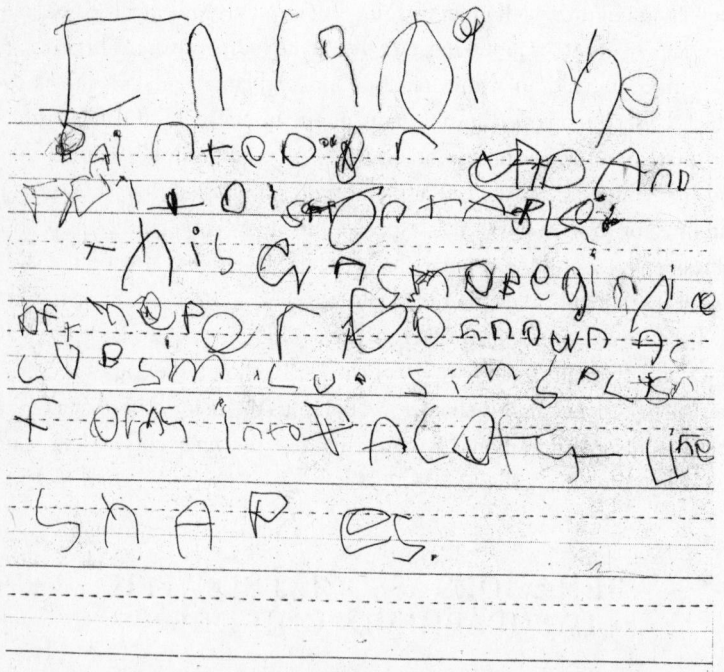

FIGURE 34. Writing Sample from a Child with Severe Dysgraphia

otherwise be obvious: Note the profound discrepancy between the highly advanced ideas discussed and the abjectly "childish" appearance of the script. The text reads, "In 1909 he [i.e., Picasso] painted 'Bread and Fruit Dish On Table.' This was the beginning of the period known as Cubism. Cubism splits forms into facets-like shapes." Small wonder dysgraphia can have such profound effects on both a child's self-image and the way others view him.

Now let's list the characteristic features of dysgraphic handwriting. (Remember: These features will vary somewhat depending on the cause of a child's dysgraphia.)

- Letters are poorly and irregularly formed. Often the same letter will appear markedly different each time it is written, even within the same word.
- The writing may appear "childish" or show signs of being especially labored, such as having unusually thick or heavy lines or even tears in the paper.
- There may be signs of difficulty managing the spatial features of the writing.

  - Spaces between words or letters are often cramped or uneven.
  - Writing wanders repeatedly above or below the lines.
  - The writer has difficulty starting at a consistent place on the left side of the paper or ending at the appropriate place on the right.
  - There is difficulty with letter orientation (backward or upside down).

- Handwriting conventions (e.g., capitalization and punctuation) may be irregularly or imperfectly observed.
- Spelling mistakes may be frequent.
- In some cases, the content of the writing may show characteristic problems, like dropped or incomplete words or sentences, missing clauses, subject/object confusion, or shifting topics in the middle of a sentence.
- In some children, handwriting legibility may vary dramatically depending upon the nature of the writing task.

- Some children may have particular difficulties writing clearly when taking notes or dictation from oral lectures.
- Others may have difficulty copying from a visual source.
- Some children may have more difficulty writing in printed letters than with cursive, while for others the opposite may be true.
- Some children may have difficulty with drawing and other fine-motor tasks as well as with writing, while others may have intact drawing and fine-motor tasks. (We will discuss the reasons for these varying conditions below.)

- Writing is dysfunctionally slow. Sometimes children with even severe dysgraphia may produce very neat and legible script, but only by being so slow and careful that handwriting is still for all practical purposes nonfunctional (like Sarah, discussed above). These children may be among the hardest workers in their class, spending two hours or more a night on homework that other children complete in twenty minutes. Occasionally these children are discovered to have handwriting impairments only when they reach junior high or even high school and are unable to take notes fast enough, complete in-class writing assignments or tests, or keep up with the expanding load of homework.
- Typically children with dysgraphia have a much easier time communicating their ideas through speech than through handwriting. Children who have difficulty communicating their ideas both by speech and handwriting are likely to have a problem with language output or word retrieval. Children with language-based difficulties will often be able to copy printed sentences rapidly and neatly, while dysgraphic children will usually struggle.

Abnormal Handgrips or Postures

The second behavioral category contains abnormal handwriting grips or postures. Figure 35 shows several common dysfunctional handgrips seen in children at our clinic.

We'll discuss the reasons for these alternate grips in more detail in Causes. For now, notice that each of these grips represents an attempt on

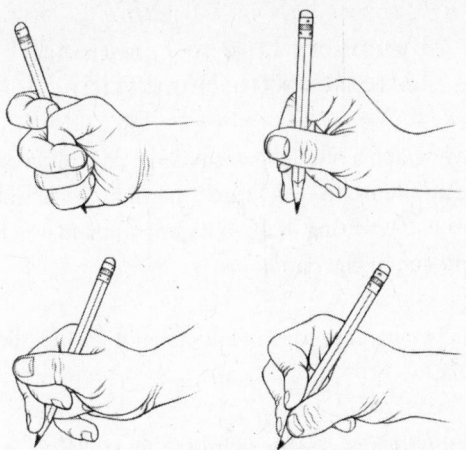

FIGURE 35. Abnormal Grips in Children with Dysgraphia

the child's part (usually unsuccessful) to gain better pencil control by increasing sensory feedback from fingers, hand, or arm.

- When a child has trouble sensing the positions or movements of her fingers, she often unthinkingly grips the pencil more tightly and may use multiple fingers, her whole hand, or even her arm to make the pencil movement required for writing. Sometimes she will hook her wrist back toward her body and write with the pencil aimed back toward her. While these strategies often work in the short run, allowing the child to form letters and words more clearly, they are laborious and usually quickly cause fatigue and cramping.
- Children with these dysfunctional grips often alternate between grips to relieve strain. They may also have tentative or uncertain grips and drop their pen or pencil while writing. Others may press too hard, breaking their pencil lead or tearing their paper.
- Children with dysgraphia also frequently assume abnormal body postures when writing. They may write with their head and eyes only inches from their pen or pencil tip or lay their head on their arm or desk because of poor postural support in the back and neck.

Behaviors Due to Emotional
Stresses with Handwriting

Children with dysgraphia often show emotional difficulties and stresses due to handwriting problems. In many cases, they may not attribute their emotional problems to the writing itself, so it's important to watch for signs that the writing is producing the symptoms.

- There are two main sources of emotional stress in children with dysgraphia:

  - The first is their own sense of frustration over their inability to master handwriting. This frustration often reflects several factors, including inability to keep up with classmates or assignments, difficulty adequately expressing their ideas in written form, and the physical and mental strains associated with writing itself.
  - The second main source of stress is the negative attention their handwriting attracts. Instead of being praised for the efforts they've expended to produce writing with which they as much as anyone are disappointed, they may be accused of laziness, inattentiveness, dawdling, low personal standards, or lack of pride in workmanship. Often it is the injustice of these charges even more than their severity that causes the greatest pain. Simple recognition from teachers and parents of how hard they are working and that they are doing their best can go a long way toward minimizing the emotional and psychological impact of this disorder and giving these kids the energy and resiliency they need to overcome it.

- Children generally begin to struggle with the emotional effects of dysgraphia at two primary points in their education.

  - The first occurs during first or second grade, when writing initially enters the curriculum. (A minor peak occurs with the introduction of cursive in third or fourth grade.)

- The second begins around the fifth to seventh grades and continues all the way through college, reflecting the progressive increase in writing demands (e.g., taking notes during lectures, copying rapidly from slides or the board, increasing frequency and length of written requirements, increases in time pressure, and the need to express increasingly complex ideas).

- When academic writing demands dramatically increase, children with dysgraphia may begin to show work resistance or avoidance.

  - They may consistently underproduce on assignments, fail to complete in-class assignments or tests, fail to turn in homework, lie about assignments, or complain of being sick and unable to go to school or do homework.
  - They may become increasingly anxious or depressed.
  - They may show an increasing frequency of tantrums or bad behaviors, with a progressively lower threshold for onset. Tantrums are especially common in children with sensory processing difficulties (see Chapter 9), who may struggle with emotional regulation.

CAUSES OF HANDWRITING PROBLEMS

To understand the different types of dysgraphia, we must first understand the different mental and physical functions normally required for handwriting. Fortunately, the process of handwriting is easier to understand than it is to carry out.

Functions Involved in Normal Handwriting

There are five major functional components involved in handwriting:

1. Generating the linguistic template for writing, which has two parts:
   a. Deciding which words to write.

    b. Sending the motor system the signals necessary to form
        those words.

2. Planning and implementing the motor output needed to carry out
   the instructions sent from the language centers.

3. Sensory feedback during the act of writing.

4. Visual feedback, which is also used to monitor the act of writing,
   and other visual functions.

5. Attention, which oversees and ties the whole process together.

That's the big picture. In the next section, we'll go through each of
the different functional components listed above in a little more detail, describing both normal functions and some of the places where breakdowns
commonly cause handwriting problems. Let's start with the first component: generating the linguistic template for writing.

Generating the Linguistic Template for Writing

To write quickly, neatly, and in a well-organized manner, a child must first
be able to generate a mental blueprint or template of the letters and symbols that need to be written. Generating this language template has two
steps: first, deciding which words to write, and second, translating these
words into signals that can inform the motor system which letters and words
to shape. Let's consider each.

Deciding Which Words to Write
(Higher-Language Functions)

Before a child *can* write, he must know *what* to write. The linguistic template
is this *what*, and the first step in generating it is to decide which words to write.

    Making this decision requires actions on each of the different lan-
guage levels we discussed in Chapter 6. At the highest level, the child must
decide what concepts and ideas he wishes to write about. On the next level,
he must decide on the overall format or structure he'll use to organize his
writing. On the next level, he must organize his thoughts into correctly
structured sentences (syntax) that contain appropriate word order and

grammar. And on the next level, he must choose appropriate individual words (semantics) to convey his ideas and concepts.

Significant difficulties at any of these language levels will prevent a child from writing easily and fluently. Language problems on these levels will not usually cause dysgraphia directly, but will contribute greatly to working memory overload, which worsens other causes of dysgraphia. When a child can't generate the language template needed to write in an automatic and fluent fashion, she must devote more of her limited working memory resources to retrieving appropriate words, recalling grammatical rules, and placing words in appropriate order. This leaves less working memory capacity to deal with aspects of handwriting we'll discuss below, like letter formation, spelling, and use of conventions like capitals and punctuation.

Once a child's language centers have decided which words to write, they must "place an order" with the motor system, telling it which letters and symbols to set down on paper. Next we'll see how this is done.

Sending the Motor System the Necessary Signals

There are two general categories of children who have difficulty translating verbal information into cues for the motor system: children with dyslexia and children who have difficulty linking particular kinds of sensory input with motor output. We'll look at each group separately.

Dyslexic Dysgraphia

To turn a mental word template into handwritten symbols on a page, a child must first break those imagined words down into smaller bits of data that can be used to tell the motor system which letters and symbols to form. If, for example, a child decides to write the word *pig*, she must be able to break this word down into its component letters, either by using visual word form memory or by sounding-out strategies. These individual letter signals can then be used to trigger her motor system to make the muscle movements needed to write them.

Most children can perform these steps without difficulty. However, children with dyslexia tend to stumble at this step. Even when they know what words they want to write, they may have difficulty turning that knowledge into signals that their motor system can recognize. As a result, their motor movements are halting, confused, and error-filled. Often this dyslexic dysgraphia is very severe. As one young patient in our clinic described this frustrating situation, "Even though my brain knows what it wants to say, it doesn't seem to tell my fingers anything." Because of their extreme difficulties in remembering how to write, dyslexic children typically experience working memory overloads at a level that makes it hard for them to remember *what* to write as well. Think back to Chapter 10 and recall the incredible disparity between Porter's lucid oral description of the picture and his very brief and error-filled written sample.

Children with dyslexia may also suffer from additional sensory, motor, and visual difficulties that worsen their dysgraphia and diminish written output, as we saw in the last chapter. Many dyslexic children also have impaired word-retrieval, and sound- and sight-based word-memory problems that complicate writing. Some struggle with spatial orientation, causing flipped or inverted letters, and difficulty managing the spatial features of writing. These children often struggle just to write the letters of the alphabet. Others have organization and sequencing problems. Some children with dyslexia have also been noted to have a condition called "mini-neglect," which leads them to ignore the left edge of the page and begin writing closer to the middle. Children with visual processing problems may have difficulty monitoring errors. Those with visual or auditory processing problems may also fail to see or hear how punctuation is used to create breaks in sentences. Finally, some dyslexic children think primarily in visual or nonverbal styles that can make the process of translating their thoughts and ideas into words difficult and slow. Small wonder, with a list like this, that most children with dyslexia find writing to be such a torture.

Not all dyslexic children suffer from sensorimotor impairments. Some (approximately one-half to two-thirds) have good fine motor skills and can copy letters and words from written samples much better than they can write them spontaneously (though they usually have to look at the sample more frequently than usual). They may also be excellent artists.

Problems Linking Sensory Input with Motor Output

In contrast to the dyslexic difficulty we've just described, which affects the ability to turn all forms of mental word imagery into motor-system signals, some children have written output difficulties only when trying to translate particular forms of sensory input (i.e., auditory or visual) into signals for their motor system.

Some children (commonly those who show auditory processing deficits or difficulties coordinating the activities of both brain hemispheres) have difficulty linking auditory-verbal input with written output. These children typically have no difficulty writing spontaneously or copying from written models. However, when they try to write down words they hear, their writing appears dysgraphic. They may have difficulty with impaired letter formation, omissions or substitutions, and impaired spellings, or their writing may simply break down altogether. Children with this problem should always be provided with lecture notes.

Less commonly, children can have difficulty linking visual input to written output. These children may have trouble taking notes from written sources or copying visual materials, like math problems, assignments, or other written instructions from a board or overhead projector. These children also require written copies of important materials.

Planning and Implementing Motor Output in Writing

When the motor system receives signals from the word memory centers telling it which letters to write, it must retrieve the appropriate "blueprints" from its store of *motor maps*. (These motor maps, or "blueprints for movement," are sometimes called *motor procedural memories*.) The motor maps triggered by these signals tell the muscles in the fingers, hands, and arms how fast to contract, how hard, and in what order.

None of us are born with the motor maps we need for writing. We must develop them through repeated trial and error. Children who have trouble forming or retrieving motor maps inevitably develop dysgraphia. Several common impairments can cause problems in this area, including impairments in sensory feedback from the fingers, visual-spatial awareness, or visual-motor integration. Each of these impairments (which we'll describe in more detail below) can prevent the motor system from successfully making the plans it needs to form letters. Children with these problems will show letter formation that is halting, tentative, and poorly executed.

Children who have difficulty storing or implementing the motor plans needed for letter writing are often said to have *graphomotor dyspraxia.* (Just remember that *graph-* means "writing," *-motor* "movement," *dys-* "problem," and *-praxia* "action," so *graphomotor dyspraxia* really just means "problems making the movements needed for writing." Easy, right? Or at least no harder than *"Caput Draconis!"* or *"Expecto patronum!"* which every seven-year-old in the world seems to have mastered!)

Like children with dyslexic dysgraphia, children with graphomotor dyspraxia have difficulty knowing what kinds of movements to make to form letters. As a result, their fingers look and feel "clumsy" when they're writing. They also have difficulty drawing and copying words. Unlike children with dyslexia, children with graphomotor dyspraxia are usually competent oral spellers.

Many children with graphomotor dyspraxia also have difficulty with other complex fine motor (hand and finger) actions, like scissoring, eating with utensils, opening wrappers, using snaps, doing up zippers, buttoning buttons, tying shoelaces, or working pencil sharpeners. They may also have difficulties with complex gross motor actions like riding a bike, throwing or catching a ball, jumping rope, skipping, or even running. However, some children with even fairly severe fine motor problems will have great gross motor skills.

Some children with graphomotor dyspraxia have an easier time with fine motor tasks that don't involve fine motor memory, like guiding a pencil through a maze, which relies primarily on visual and fine motor feedback. You should note, however, that many children with graphomotor dyspraxia also have difficulties with hand-eye coordination and/or sensory feedback from the fingers that can complicate such tasks. (We'll discuss these other problems below.)

Children with graphomotor dyspraxia often have unusual or unstable pencil grips, including many of the unusual grips shown in Figure 35. They may also frequently change grips when tired. Children with graphomotor dyspraxia often have difficulty knowing how hard to press with their pencil and may frequently break their pencil lead or even make holes in their paper.

Like most children with dyslexia, children with graphomotor dyspraxia usually find printing easier than cursive. Printed letters each have only two forms: capital and lowercase. Cursive letters, especially lowercase, can have many different forms. For example, the lowercase cursive *s* is formed differently at the beginning of a word, at the end, or following the letters *b*, *o*, *v*, or *w*. These variations in form mean that children must learn many more motor maps to write in cursive than in printed script. That's why both children with dyslexia and those with graphomotor dyspraxia often prefer printing to cursive. However, each child should be evaluated individually, because some dyspraxic children—for example, those with impaired finger-position sense (see below)—may find cursive easier.

Children with graphomotor dyspraxia often show signs of motor problems on physical examination, such as difficulty tapping their fingers quickly or imitating finger movements. They may also have poor muscle tone and strength in their hands, arms, neck, and back. Many suffer from sensory processing dysfunction or from deficits in finger-position sense, eye-muscle control, or hand-eye coordination. A small number will actually be found to have undiagnosed primary problems with their muscles or nerves, so if problems are severe, be sure to raise the issue with your child's doctor. A visit to a neurologist may be appropriate.

The Role of Sensory Feedback in Writing

For a child to write neatly, rapidly, and accurately, his brain must do more than send nerve signals out to the hands and fingers; it must also receive feedback through its various sensory inputs, so it can monitor and modify written output. Most of the feedback is provided by two systems: the visual system (which we'll discuss in the next section), and the *somatosensory system*, which includes receptors in the muscles, joints, and skin that send the brain important information about position, movement, touch, and pressure.

Position sensors (called *proprioceptors*) in the muscles and joints of the fingers play a particularly important role. When working well, they continuously inform the brain about the position and movement of each finger. However, when children have *impaired finger-position sense*—a condition known as *finger agnosia*—their fingers can't tell their brains what they are doing. Their fingers are "agnostic": They "don't know" what they're doing. Finger agnosia makes handwriting especially difficult. Often children with finger agnosia try to substitute visual for positional feedback; that's why they can often be seen with their heads bent close to the paper.

Children with finger agnosia can sometimes form neat and legible letters when they write slowly enough (like Sarah, whom we mentioned at the start of the chapter). However, their writing is far from automatic and rarely fast enough to be functional. Children with significant finger agnosia can almost never write quickly and legibly, take accurate notes in class, or write legibly about complex and demanding themes. Because they must consciously "think through" the process of letter formation (e.g., "To make a *T*, just pull your fingers down, then make a cross at the top . . ."), they often run out of working memory space to use for spelling, punctuation, and idea generation. As a result, their writing may suffer in all aspects.

Children with finger agnosia usually have difficulty drawing or imitating simple finger movements without looking at their fingers, but they may be able to navigate a pencil through a maze. Finger-tapping speed is often normal. Children with finger agnosia often show much worse handwriting when asked to write with their eyes closed, since this takes away their only functional feedback system. They sometimes find cursive easier than printing, because the fewer times their pencil leaves the paper, the easier it is to keep track of. Because sensory feedback is crucial for developing the motor maps needed to form letters, many children with finger agnosia also have graphomotor dyspraxia and may also show the signs described in that section.

The Role of the Visual System in Writing

The visual system plays several key roles in handwriting. It provides handwriting feedback, which is especially important when a child is learning to write, before the motions needed to produce letters have become automatic, and in children with finger agnosia (impaired finger-position sense). Accurate visual input is essential for accurate visual feedback. Children who have problems with visual acuity and focus or with eye-movement control in particular can have difficulty monitoring written output. This often results in problems with spacing, letter formation, and following lines.

The ability to integrate visual input with motor output also plays a crucial role in handwriting. This ability is often called *hand-eye coordination* or *visual motor integration*. Children whose visual and motor systems are poorly integrated typically have a hard time with handwriting. Their inability to link visual input with motor output makes it hard for them to modify their writing in response to visual feedback. As a result, their ability to monitor their ongoing writing depends largely on touch and pressure receptors in their fingers. Their writing frequently shows poor spacing, irregularly formed letters, and difficulty conforming to lines and margins.

Visual-spatial processing also plays an important role in word and letter formation and in the proper spatial organization of writing. Children with the most severe impairments in visual-spatial processing (usually due to brain-based impairments rather than eye-movement problems) may be completely unable to form recognizable letters. They may also have difficulty planning and organizing their use of space, such as centering their writing on the paper, observing lines and margins, and giving each letter and word its appropriate space rather than writing one letter on top of another. Also, they often have extreme difficulties with letter reversals and inversions, not simply confusing *b* with *d*, or *p* with *q*, as is common in younger children, but confusing *b*, *d*, *p*, and *q* or *m*, *n*, *w*, *v*, *u*, and even *c* (see Figure 12).

Most children with visually based dysgraphia have trouble forming letters when writing spontaneously or copying from a model. They usually show difficulty with motor tasks that require visual input or feedback, such as navigating a pencil through a maze or imitating a sequence of observed movements. Rapid finger movements and finger-position sense are usually (but not always) intact. When writing, children with visually based dysgraphia typically have fairly normal grips, except that they tend to hold their pencil or pen too tightly and may experience cramping. They may also tend to hold their face very close to the paper when writing.

The Role of Attention in Writing

Attention also plays an important role in overseeing and monitoring the writing process. In fact, each of the attention functions described in Chapter 7 is required for successful writing, and problems with any of these functions can cause difficulty with handwriting or with any step in the writing process. Such problems may result in poor idea generation and overall organization; impaired grammar and spelling; dropped words, letters or dangling clauses; sloppy formation of letters and words; inconsistent use of conventions like capital letters, spaces, and punctuation; extensive erasures and cross-outs; or crowded words at the ends of lines.

Working memory plays a particularly important role in the writing process. When a child is writing, her working memory must "keep in mind" a staggering amount of material, including overall theme or purpose; the words she's already written; what she's currently writing about; what remains to be written; conventions of grammar, spelling, and punctuation; letter formation; and spatial factors, like maintaining margins, staying close to the lines, leaving consistent spaces between words, and so on.

Often children with dysgraphia experience working memory overload even if their working memory capacity is fairly normal. There's simply not enough space to meet all the demands. This is especially true for younger children, for whom many handwriting functions have not yet become automatic. This situation is only made worse when a child has an actual impairment in working memory. Such impairments can wreak havoc at every stage of the writing process. And if a child also has dysgraphia from another source, a problem with working memory will make the dysgraphia even worse.

Many children who are diagnosed with attention problems or ADHD will also have other potential causes of dysgraphia, like impaired eye-muscle control, hand-eye coordination, or motor planning and coordination. It's important to perform a complete exam, because treatments will differ.

EVALUATING CHILDREN WITH HANDWRITING PROBLEMS

Children with dysgraphia often suffer from a combination of deficits rather than isolated problems, so treatment can vary significantly from child to child. Every child with dysgraphia needs a thorough examination covering language, memory, attention, reading, motor, and sensory functions. A detailed history should also include information on the child's birth, fine- and gross-motor development, language and reading history, academic performance, memory functions, favorite activities or hobbies, and evidence of attention problems involving activities both connected and unconnected with writing. A family history of problems with school, language, reading, vision, muscles, or nerves should also be sought.

One other important cause of dysgraphia that we sometimes see in children is medications. There are a number of potential culprits, but the most common and severe is the antiseizure medication Depakote (valproic acid). Recently this medication has been used with increasing frequency in children to treat psychiatric diagnoses, including bipolar disorder, and to control side effects related to the use of stimulants and antidepressants. Figure 36 shows the handwriting of a child who was brought to our clinic for evaluation of dysgraphia while on Depakote, and after the Depakote was discontinued. Notice the dramatic improvement. (A quick aside: *This is a good example of why you should never fall into the trap of continually adding new medications to treat the side effects of the old medications! When medicines have unacceptable side effects, try a new approach.*)

Samples of a child's written work should be examined. The child should also be asked to perform several pencil tasks, such as writing and

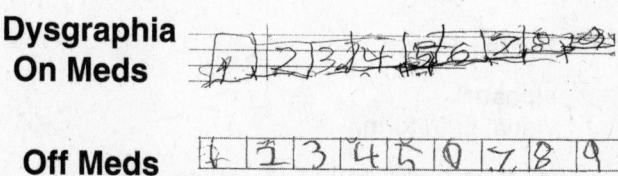

Dysgraphia On Meds

Off Meds

FIGURE 36. Medication-Induced Dysgraphia

drawing spontaneously, copying figures and a printed sentence, navigating a pencil through a maze, and (if indicated) writing from dictation. The child should also be presented with a picture and asked to describe it both orally and in writing. While the child is writing, her posture, hand grip, pencil and eye position, writing speed, and use of accessory motions such as air writing (making "practice motions" over letters) or subvocalization (whispering to herself) should be observed. The child should also be assessed for evidence of dyslexia as described in the previous chapter.

During the examination, signs of impulsivity, sensory seeking, motor hyperactivity, distractibility, or difficulty focusing should be sought. A complete neurological exam should be performed to look for evidence of tremors or unsteadiness of the fingers when the eyes are closed (*pseudochorea*, which is a sign of finger agnosia); to assess vision and hearing; to evaluate motor speed, coordination, planning and strength; and to look for right-left confusion, visual-spatial processing, and visual-motor integration.

Figure 37 presents in visual form an overview of the kinds of physical and exam findings that can be used to differentiate among the various causes of writing impairments and dysgraphia we will discuss in this section.

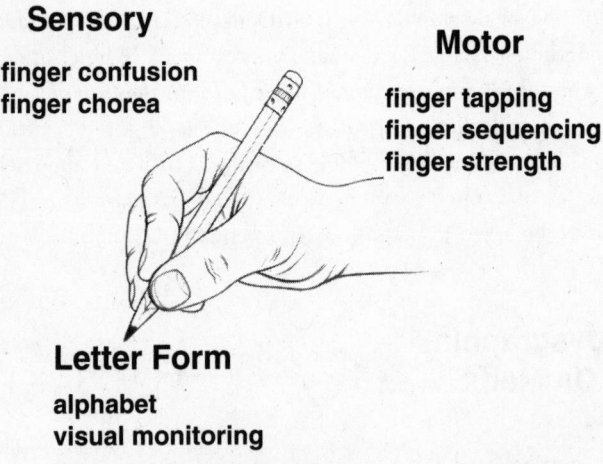

Sensory
finger confusion
finger chorea

Motor
finger tapping
finger sequencing
finger strength

Letter Form
alphabet
visual monitoring

FIGURE 37. Distinguishing Exam Features of Different Causes of Dysgraphia

HELPING CHILDREN WITH
HANDWRITING PROBLEMS

The increasing inclusion of handwriting sections on many high-stakes tests has made helping children with dysgraphia more important than ever. In this Helping section, we'll describe the steps that you can take to help a child with dysgraphia write and learn more effectively. We'll start by looking at several interventions that can help essentially all children with dysgraphia, then consider interventions that will help children with particular causes of dysgraphia.

Useful Interventions for All
Children with Dysgraphia

The most important goal in helping children with dysgraphia is to prevent their handwriting difficulties from impeding their intellectual and academic progress. Handwriting is better thought of as a means to an end, not simply as an end in itself. It should never be allowed to become a ball and chain that holds a child back from the pursuit of learning.

In this section we'll discuss interventions that can help most children with dysgraphia. First, we'll discuss steps to improve handwriting skills. Second, we'll discuss the essential role of keyboarding in helping children with dysgraphia. Finally, we'll discuss accommodations that can help children with dysgraphia achieve academic success.

Remediation: Handwriting Improvement

For children with *severe* dysgraphia, *handwriting should not be thought of as a primary means of expression*. It should be regarded as its own distinct subject and practiced for its own sake, not used as a means of communication.

- Because at least a rudimentary skill with handwriting is desirable and may be required for mandatory tests (like the SAT), handwriting practice should be undertaken by most children with dysgraphia.

(The exceptions are children with severe brain-based spatial impairments or children with such significant hand or postural weakness that they are not strong enough to write.)

- However, it's important to remember that too much practice may be counterproductive. We generally recommend initially practicing about fifteen minutes a day, then moving up to thirty minutes (split into two or three sessions) when the child begins to build stamina.
- Most children with dysgraphia benefit from multisensory hand-writing approaches. Many of the common causes of dysgraphia prevent children from remembering how to form letters in a rapid and automatic fashion. Multisensory approaches circumvent roadblocks in the letter-forming process by combining information from verbal, visual, and somatosensory sources to help children learn to form letters.
- Information from the position sensors in the muscles and joints (proprioceptors) can be used to build motor maps in the brain through a process of air writing, which can be practiced in several different ways:

  - For children with relatively intact sensory feedback in the fingers, air writing may simply involve tracing repeatedly over letters (and words) with a fingertip or pencil tip before trying to write them.
  - For children with impaired finger-position sense (agnosia), large sweeps of the shoulder often work better. Visual feedback can be added by having these children practice making very large (two to three feet high) letters on a grease board or butcher paper or with chalk on sidewalks or chalkboards.
  - Children can also use *verbal mediation* to learn proper letter formation. Verbal mediation strategies teach children to form letters by having them describe in words the various movements required to make letters. (For example, "To make a small *b*, it's full down, half up, circle down right.")
  - Finally, multisensory approaches can help children who have difficulty remembering the visual forms and spatial orientations of letters (that is, their visual appearance and the directions they

face). Children whose visual memory for objects or pictures is better than their visual memory for letters or numbers should use visual imagery to create fanciful images of letters or numbers. These images should use recognizable shapes or objects to help make proper letter shapes and orientations more memorable (see Chapter 4, Figure 19).

- Several commercially available programs can help teach multi-sensory handwriting strategies. One popular workbook-based system is called *Handwriting Without Tears* (www.hwtears.com). This popular program (developed by occupational therapist Jan Olsen and used by many schools and therapists) can be used at home with a parent or in formal sessions with a therapist, multisensory teacher, or tutor.
- Other multisensory systems can also be used, like those described in our chapter on dyslexia (e.g., Slingerland, Orton-Gillingham, Lindamood-Bell). Most often, these are used with children who have significant dyslexia or visual-spatial difficulties.
- Multisensory systems are also available to help children who have problems with math symbols and numbers, like the program Touch Math (www.touchmath.com).
- A child with severe dysgraphia should usually be evaluated by an occupational therapist with expertise in children's writing issues. An OT can be extremely helpful in deciding on an appropriate form of help and in conducting training sessions.

Keyboarding: An Essential Skill for Children with Dysgraphia

Children with dysgraphia should begin to keyboard as soon as possible, and keyboarding should become their primary means of written communication. With the help of a keyboard, letter formation is simplified from a complex sensorimotor dance to a single finger stroke. That's why keyboarding frees up so much working memory space and lets children focus on idea generation, organization, punctuation, and grammar rather than simply on moving their fingers in certain ways.

- Home can be a great place to practice keyboarding. Mavis Beacon makes several software programs that teach touch typing, as does Type to Learn, and these programs are commonly used in schools. Sometimes, though, dysgraphic children find the "timed" nature of these programs stressful and simply give up.
- Dysgraphic children often prefer the more laid-back workbook approach of Diane Hanbury King's *Keyboarding Skills* (www.eps.com). This self-paced curriculum is geared to teach ten-finger touch typing but can be modified to practice two-finger keyboarding as well.
- Learn-as-you-go methods for increasing typing skill can be even more effective than formal programs.

  - Internet-based instant messaging with friends, parents, or grandparents can be a fun and rewarding way to practice keyboarding skills.
  - Text-based computer adventure games like King's Quest (www .vintage-sierra.com/kingsquest.html) or Monkey Island (www .worldofmi.com), where written instructions are used to control the action, are also a great way to stimulate a desire to type better and to provide practice for improvement.
  - Remember: Children don't always need to become touch typists. For children with certain types of dysgraphia, two-finger hunt-and-peck typing will be the most functional. Children with visual memory or visual-spatial impairments often do best when they can keep as many keys as possible within plain view, which is easier with two than with ten-finger typing, and children with impaired finger-position sense (agnosia) often find it easier to keep track of two fingers than ten.

- In the classroom, children with dysgraphia often benefit by using a portable laptop, Alphasmart, or Dana.

  - The Alphasmart (www.alphasmart.com) is the simplest commonly used keyboard. For children in public schools, these will sometimes be available from the district. The Alphasmart is designed to be kid-friendly, with impressive "droppability," autosave features, and the ability to run for prolonged periods on an AA battery. An infrared attachment can even allow it to send files wirelessly to a printer.

- The Dana (made by the same company) has additional features that allow more complex applications, including add-on programs for more complicated word processing and math functions.

- One of the best word processing programs we've found is Write Outloud (www.donjohnston.com). This program, which can be used on PCs or Danas (and even new Alphasmarts) provides read-aloud features and offers spelling alternatives based on common misspellings. It can be valuable for children whose difficulties with attention or working memory cause them to make frequent mistakes with spelling, repeated words, or word or letter omissions. It is especially useful for children with dyslexia and will be described in more detail below in our section on dyslexic dysgraphia.

- Laptop, notebook, or tablet PCs have an even greater range of potential uses and offer far more complex visual displays. However, for younger children, they are often heavier to carry and more vulnerable to damage or theft. Desktop computers provide the greatest range of potential applications and computing power but offer the least mobility.

- Newer-generation PDAs (i.e., "personal digital assistants," like Palm or Handspring) are extremely portable and can be hooked to a portable keyboard for a very light and mobile system.

- We are often asked whether voice-recognition software is helpful for children with dysgraphia. At present, the answer is, unfortunately, no. Currently available programs rarely work well for children. Initially it is difficult to "train" the computer to recognize the child's voice, and most children lack the necessary patience. Also, these programs must be periodically retrained, as the child's voice changes and as the child begins to work on new subjects with new terminology. Even when well trained, these programs still make frequent errors, so careful proofing is required. The best programs currently available (like Dragon Naturally Speaking) are probably better suited to older teens or adults.

- Keyboards can be used to write numbers and equations as well as words, which is important when a child's dysgraphia is having a negative impact on math.

  - Some keyboard-based math programs require their own free-standing units, like Touch Pad. Others run on computers. At the elementary-school level, a program like Math Pad (www .intellitools.com) can help students perform multistepped math problems, including tasks like regrouping, without the additional work of coordinating pencil movements or recalling the correct orientation of numbers.

  - As the written load of mathematics increases through the higher grades, some students find they can work more productively and accurately using keyboard options for algebra, trigonometry, or calculus. Equation Editor, which is a part of Microsoft Word, can record such functions. An open-source program called MathCast (which is free at www.mathcast.sourceforge .net) and a commercially available program called MathSoft (www.mathsoft.com) can perform similar functions. These programs may be a bit tricky to learn at first because of the need to learn special keyboard commands; however, once these are learned, students may be able to perform math problems with little impediment from their dysgraphia. Not all students with dysgraphia will find such programs helpful, but all children whose dysgraphia appears to be hindering their math progress should be offered the chance to use one of these keyboard-based options.

Other General Handwriting Helps and Accommodations

Most children with dysgraphia require additional accommodations. This is especially true for those whose keyboarding skills are not yet good enough to enable them to keep up with required work.

- As we've said before, *for children with severe dysgraphia, the generation and expression of ideas should be separated as much as possible from the physical process of handwriting.* Until a child develops sufficient speed and automaticity, handwriting should be treated not as a major route of communication or a means of demonstrating subject mastery but as its own distinct discipline.

- While some children with severe dysgraphia will remain largely keyboard-dependent for tasks that require more than a few brief notes, many children find that handwriting difficulties begin to diminish after the onset of adolescence. Again, it's important to judge each child individually.

- Written work that cannot easily be performed on a keyboard should be reduced to at most one-third the normal level, and extra time should be allowed for any in-class assignments.

- Handwritten work should be graded on intellectual content, not on form. Points should not be deducted for mistakes in spelling, punctuation, physical organization, or general messiness (though errors should be pointed out for educational purposes). Such skills should be addressed specifically during separate training exercises.

- It's usually worthwhile for children with dysgraphia to experiment with a variety of pencils and pens (e.g., different shaft and tip thicknesses, with and without accessory grips) to see which allows the best performance. Foam grips are available from office-supply stores or pediatric- and therapy-supply catalogs. Occupational therapists can provide helpful advice about tools and grips.

- Because children with dysgraphia frequently overload their working memories when writing or keyboarding, they are often better able to detect their errors and correct their work if they proof their writing after completion. Redrafting is an essential skill for all children with dysgraphia and should be taught explicitly. Word processing helps enormously with this process.

- Improving higher-order language skills (like grammar, vocabulary, and even an understanding of paragraph and essay organization) can also make written expression easier.

- As children progress through school, note taking becomes an increasingly important skill. For children with significant dysgraphia, taking notes by hand is essentially impossible and is a distraction from learning rather than a contributor to it.

- If a child has developed good keyboarding skills, he may sometimes be able to take notes by keyboard, but this would be the exception rather than the rule.
- Allowing children to record lectures can be another alternative for those with good auditory input functions.
- Often the best solution is to provide students with notes from the teacher or from a designated student. Some teachers are concerned about the equity of providing only certain students with lecture notes. These concerns can be solved by putting notes in a place where any interested student can obtain a copy.
- When textbooks are used, students with dysgraphia should always be allowed to take a copy home. If several class alternatives are available, place students with the teacher who sticks more closely to the textbook or provides course notes.

- For tests and assignments, minimize the role of writing through:

  - Oral testing.
  - Allowing presentations or projects, like PowerPoint or graphical presentations, or audio- or videotaped reports.
  - Allowing narration to an adult scribe like a parent, classroom assistant, or teacher.
  - Multiple-choice circling or bubble-filling formats, which are preferable to written responses if written test formats are used.

- For high-stakes testing, special accommodations are essential. In most cases, a scribe should be provided, but remember: Taking a test with a scribe is very different from taking a test alone, so children should practice with a scribe in a low-pressure environment before using one on a high-stakes test. Different tests have different regulations involving the use of a scribe, and these should be reviewed before the test. It is also important to realize that some standardized tests, like the SAT, require petitioning for permission to use a scribe or keyboard up to nine months in advance so that accommodations can be made.

- Respect the dignity of children with severe dysgraphia. They are painfully aware of the defects of their handwriting and would change them if they could. Their struggles should remain a matter between themselves and their teachers. Never ask them to write on the class board or have other children check or read their handwritten work.

Interventions for Children with Specific Forms of Dysgraphia

In addition to these general interventions, more specific approaches may be required for children with particular types of dysgraphia. In this section, we'll discuss interventions that pertain specifically to children with dyslexic dysgraphia, with graphomotor dyspraxia and/or finger agnosia, and with visually related dysgraphia.

Helping Children with Dyslexic Dysgraphia

Since children with dyslexia can have writing difficulties for many reasons, interventions will be most successful when aimed at a particular child's actual mix of underlying problems. However, several interventions can help most children with dyslexic dysgraphia.

- *Keyboarding is absolutely essential for most children with dyslexia, especially when coupled with interactive word processing programs like Write Outloud.* These programs can be invaluable not only for producing more accurate, better-written documents but as a teaching tool as well.

  - Write Outloud provides immediate, out-loud feedback whenever a child types a word; alternative spelling suggestions for clearly misspelled words, based on the kinds of errors children with dyslexia are prone to make; and word pronunciations and definitions, both in print and out loud, for these alternative words.

- By providing both immediate feedback and suggestions for improvement, programs like Write Outloud can help children form tighter links between the physical process of typing letters and words and the sounds and visual appearances associated with those letter combinations. We often see significant gains in spelling and sight-word mastery in children who use such programs as their primary means of written communication. They can also show gains in their knowledge of phonics, their understanding of grammar, and their use of conventions like punctuation and spaces.

Helping Children with Graphomotor Dyspraxia and Finger Agnosia

Treatments for children with dysgraphia caused by graphomotor dyspraxia or finger agnosia (impaired finger-position sense) are quite similar (and often the same children have both), so we'll consider them together.

- Because muscle and nerve development continues through the midteen years, these children often experience a big leap in handwriting abilities as they progress through adolescence. Waiting patiently until they are ready to face the sensory and motor demands of extensive handwriting before loading them with written work is important to keep them from becoming discouraged with school in general. Until they are ready, have them continue to practice handwriting (as described above), but limit the quantity of demands.
- Be sure to address deficits in motor speed and strength. Until a sufficient level of grip strength is built up, excessive writing practice is liable to be counterproductive. Fatigue and discomfort will quickly set in, followed by frustration and despair. A long-term view is essential.
- Occupational therapy will often be helpful, but so will fine motor activities directed at improving finger strength, speed, stamina, and independence of finger movements.

- Activities that involve building or construction can be very useful. Materials should be chosen carefully to fit a child's present ability level so that the child does not become overly frustrated. Toys like Duplos, Geomags, or plastic gear sets are a good place to start for children with severe difficulties. More challenging materials like LEGOs, Bionicles, K'nex, Zoob, Quercetti Marble Runs, and Zome Tool are all good resources as the child advances in age and skill.
- Other hand activities that build fine motor strength and agility include tearing paper to make confetti or "mosaics," cutting, stapling, paper punching, and stretching rubber bands over pegboards.
- Art activities like painting, drawing, Lite-Brite, clay modeling, pottery, or play involving resistive therapy putty can also be very useful.
- Drawing or coloring using short (one-inch) pencils or crayons can also help improve strength in the small muscles of the hand.
- Musical instruments like the violin or piano can also be excellent "therapy" tasks as long as learning to play is not too frustrating for a child.

- It is also important to make sure that a child has enough strength in the postural muscles of the neck, back, and shoulders to support his hand and arm when writing, before beginning intensive handwriting therapy. Without such strength, a child will quickly fatigue while writing and, even with adequate hand and finger strength, will begin to have writing difficulties. While formal therapy is extremely useful, parents can help children gain proximal strength with activities like swimming, ball throwing, reading while lying prone with head and upper body lifted off the floor (like a reverse sit-up), and sheet or parachute toss. In this latter activity, small weights (like pillows or beanbags) are placed in the center of a sheet, and two persons standing at the opposite ends pull the sheet taut and toss the weights as high as they can.
- Several steps can also be taken to increase sensory feedback from a pen and pencil during the act of writing. Weighted pens or pencils, or a weighted glove on the writing hand, can improve a child's

sensation of hand position. (Not too heavy, though, or motor coordination will be worsened.) Softly vibrating or buzzing pens can also help improve feedback and position sense, but children differ in whether they will tolerate this sensation. A good source for these materials can be found at www.abilitations.com.

Helping Children with Visually Based Dysgraphia

Most children with visually based dysgraphia eventually develop functional handwriting—the exceptions being those who have severe brain-based visual-perceptual and visual-spatial issues. Treatment of a child's underlying visual impairments (e.g., poor acuity, defective eye-movement control, hand-eye coordination) usually goes a long way toward improving dysgraphia. Because children with visual problems often have intact sensory feedback from their fingers (proprioception), multisensory strategies that encourage them to rely more on their position sense while writing are frequently successful. In general, handwriting therapy should be pursued in the context of a broader course of visual therapy under the supervision of a developmental optometrist or well-trained occupational therapist (see Chapter 4 for details).

12

When the Numbers Won't Add Up

Math Problems in Children

Although I am not stupid, the mathematical side of my brain is like dead notes on a damaged piano.

—MARGOT ASQUITH, BRITISH SOCIALITE

As long as algebra is taught in school, there will be prayer in school.

—COKIE ROBERTS, JOURNALIST AND COMMENTATOR

Numbers were Sam's nemesis. He was in first grade before he could count to five, and well into second before he could reach twenty. In third grade, Sam had no real sense or feeling for numbers. If you asked him whether fifty-one was larger than forty-eight, he'd give you a lost expression, as if you'd asked whether green was larger than purple. Even simple calculations, like 3+4, were hard for him, because he didn't seem to understand what "add" meant. Anything dealing with numbers was mysterious to Sam.

. . .

Kailee was a bright and chatty third-grader, at the top of her class for reading and writing but near the bottom in math. She clearly understood the concepts in addition and subtraction—even multiplication and division. For example, she knew that 7×3 equaled $7+7+7$ and that 24/8 meant "How many times does 8 go into 24?" She just couldn't memorize the answers to these problems, no matter how hard she tried. Every time she faced a simple problem like $3+4$ or 5×2, she felt like she was seeing it for the first time, and out came the fingers: "One . . . two . . . three. . . ." Kailee just couldn't memorize math facts.

By sixth grade, Anna had conquered most of the visual processing problems that made her flip numbers and misread symbols when she was younger. Solving math equations was now a snap. Unfortunately, story problems were another matter. Their tight syntax and lack of redundancy give her real trouble.

Max was a puzzle to his parents: engineer dad, economist mom, both math superstars. Max looked at first as if he would carry on the tradition. He'd always loved numbers and could do single-digit addition in his head before starting kindergarten. During first grade, he mastered the times tables up to 15. If you asked him a math question—boom—he'd whip out the answer and never miss. Yet as a second-grader he was scoring 70 percent on his math papers—when you could read them at all.

Children often struggle with math, and for many different reasons. Math, like reading and writing, draws on numerous functions that are located in different parts of the brain. It requires the abilities to identify printed numbers and symbols, write them down, understand math concepts, understand math operations and procedures, read word problems, multitask in working memory, understand number quantity and the relationships between numbers, store and retrieve math facts, and perform calculations.

Children can have trouble with any of these functions. In this chapter, we'll discuss the main reasons children struggle with math, and what you can do about it.

BEHAVIORS ASSOCIATED WITH MATH PROBLEMS

Math problems are usually noticed when children fail to develop particular skills by particular ages or levels of education. Here are some important landmarks:

- By age four, children can usually count four objects. By five this number increases to fifteen.
- By eight, children should recognize and write three-digit numbers, plus and minus signs, and perform simple addition and subtraction.
- By nine, they should do simple multiplication and division.
- By twelve, they should perform all four basic functions accurately with multidigit numbers.

Specific Signs of Math Difficulties

The following are additional signs of problems that can hinder mastery of basic math functions:

- Difficulty understanding the idea of quantity (e.g., telling which number is larger than another or whether the difference between a thousand and ten is a lot more or just a bit more than the difference between thirty-five and eight).
- Handwriting that suggests spatial impairments, such as irregularly or incorrectly formed numbers or symbols, poor spacing, or unusual spacing on the page.
- A tendency to confuse or reverse numbers like 9 and 6 or 15 and 51, or to reverse symbols like < or >.
- Trouble understanding visual figures like graphs or charts.

- Trouble recognizing, remembering, copying, or naming geometric figures.
- Poor short-term memory span for numbers.
- Excessive difficulty memorizing basic (rote) math facts (like $2+3=5$, $2\times3=6$, etc.).
- Difficulty understanding math concepts like rules, procedures, and formulas (e.g., not understanding long division despite understanding simple division, not understanding how to carry numbers from one column to the next, not understanding how to "borrow" in subtraction, not understanding how decimals are handled when multiplying).
- A tendency to use inefficient strategies to avoid weaknesses—for example, treating multiplication as a series of additions (e.g., repeatedly treating $9\times6=54$ as $6+6+6+6+6+6+6+6+6$ rather than memorizing the times tables).
- Difficulty learning or acquiring new math strategies.
- Difficulty performing math procedures (like long division or multi-digit multiplication) even when well understood.
- A tendency to get lost in the middle of a problem.
- Difficulty recognizing which strategy to use to solve a problem, even when the strategy is familiar (for example, difficulty determining whether a word problem requires multiplication or division).
- Special difficulty doing word or story problems.
- "Careless errors" that are easily detected later (like performing addition on a subtraction problem or multiplication instead of division; forgetting to carry over).
- Widely fluctuating math performance.
- Problems with pacing, either doing work too quickly to be accurate or too slowly to complete.
- Poor error monitoring.
- Problems remembering previously mastered material.
- A tendency to ignore or skip questions without noticing.
- Problems with visually crowded worksheets or tests (i.e., too many problems on a page).
- Worse attention during math class or homework than with other subjects.

- Messy handwriting that makes math work difficult, especially on problems that involve multiple steps or columns of numbers.
- Worse problems with written than oral math.
- Trouble showing work, either because of handwriting problems or because "I don't know *how* I know the answer—I just know it."

THE CAUSES OF MATH CHALLENGES

Math challenges can be grouped into two large categories.

First, there are challenges that affect a child's ability to do math quickly and accurately but are not specific to math. These include problems with vision, reading, writing, language, and attention.

Second, there are more "math-specific" challenges. Children with challenges of this second type typically have either difficulty learning rote math facts or difficulty with the spatial component of math. These children are often said to have *dyscalculia*—just as children with specific reading challenges are said to have dyslexia. About 5 to 6 percent of school-age children have dyscalculia, with girls as affected as boys. There is also a strong genetic component to dyscalculia: Nearly 50 percent of the siblings of children with dyscalculia will also have it, a rate almost ten times that of the general population.

It's important to remember that the term dyscalculia should not be applied to children who are struggling with math unless we can be sure they've received adequate and appropriate math instruction. We often see children who are having trouble with math, yet who seem relatively free of any identifiable learning challenge. The true nature of their problem becomes apparent when we ask to see the materials these children are being taught with. Frequently, their parents are unable to identify the overall approach being used in school, or to provide a copy of the text the child is using, because in many cases there is none. We are instead presented with a series of seemingly random handouts with little explanatory material and no obvious sequential structure. The truth, all too often, is that these children are simply being taught in a confusing and irrational fashion.

In a recent study prepared for the U.S. Department of Education, the American Institutes for Research criticized mathematical instruction in the

United States for its failure to focus on a "centrally identified core of mathematical content" that is capable of providing true mathematical understanding. Before any child is diagnosed with a mathematical disability, it is important to assess the teaching that child has received to make sure it is capable of transmitting appropriate mathematical understanding.

Many problems can lead to math challenges. As we've seen in many other chapters, these challenges can be grouped into problems with Information Input, Pattern Processing, Output for Action, and Attention.

Math Challenges: Problems with Information Input

Although auditory problems can cause difficulty during math class, visual problems are the most important cause of input-related math difficulties. Math is a very visually demanding subject, and issues with visual acuity, convergence insufficiency, eye-movement control, visual distractibility, field impairments, visual memory impairments, or object and spatial recognition can all cause problems with math performance. Math involves complicated visual tasks like running your eyes down columns and across rows, carrying numbers between columns, reading numbers in sequence (e.g., to see that 78569342 is different from 78596342) and figures on visually crowded sheets, and discriminating between symbols like +, ×, and /, or < and >. Math also involves complex spatial and object processing tasks, including perception of number spacing and orientation, recognition of geometric figures, discrimination of parts and wholes, and the ability to read graphs and charts. Children with undiagnosed visual problems may show difficulties with any of these tasks. They may also make "careless errors," or have more difficulty doing problems on paper than they do orally.

Math Impairments: Problems with Pattern Processing

Pattern Processing deficits can harm a child's math performance. Some deficits are not specific for math and may cause problems with other functions. Others affect math specifically. Let's consider each class separately.

Pattern Processing Difficulties That Are Not Exclusively Math-Related

In this section, we'll describe the four most common Pattern Processing difficulties that can cause math challenges but not because they cause difficulties with math reasoning, per se.

Math Challenges Due to Reading Difficulties

Children with reading difficulties may experience several kinds of math challenges.

- Like Anna (whom we mentioned at the start of this chapter) and Michael (from Chapter 1), these children often have particular trouble with story problems. Story problems are often especially difficult to read because the language is typically condensed and low in redundancy. The following example is from a test for fourth-graders:

  > Sharon started the day with all her allowance in her wallet. She spent half of it taking her sister to the movies. Then she spent half of what was left on a snack. Then she gave her friend three dollars. After all this, Sharon had two dollars left. Figure out how much money Sharon started with. Show your work.

  For a nonfluent reader, the language and reading challenges of passages like this can be huge.
- Reading difficulties may also make it hard for children to understand written instructions on math tests or papers. This, too, may lead to errors.
- Some children with reading difficulties have visual and spatial processing deficits (like those described below), which can lead to "careless errors" (like misreading numbers or symbols or visually transposing numbers into different columns).
- Children with reading difficulties often also have written output problems that can affect math work, as we'll discuss below.
- Finally, children with dyslexia often have difficulties with *sequencing* that can affect math function (see below).

Math Challenges Due to Language Impairments

Like children with reading difficulties, children with language impairments often have trouble with story problems and written instructions. They can also have a hard time learning mathematical concepts, rules, and procedures. Fortunately, many of these concepts, rules, and procedures can be inferred by looking at examples when children have difficulty learning them by verbal instruction.

Math Challenges Due to Problems with Procedural, Sequential, or Rule-Based Memory

Children who have problems with procedural, sequential, or rule-based memory often have great difficulty doing math. Math requires the mastery of many rules (like how to carry numbers between columns, how to add and subtract negative numbers, how to reduce fractions, etc.) and the ability to apply these rules in many specific situations. Math also requires many multi-stepped procedures, and children who have difficulty remembering the steps for complex procedures (like long division) will have trouble getting right answers, even if they understand the concepts. Finally, math mastery requires the knowledge of sequences like the whole-number series, the even and odd number series, the prime-number series, exponential sequences (e.g., 2, 4, 8, 16, . . . or 3, 9, 27 . . .), and many others. Children who have trouble storing and recognizing these sequences often have difficulties with math.

Pattern Processing Difficulties That Produce Math-Specific Challenges

Math-specific impairments can be grouped into two primary subtypes. The first is characterized by difficulty understanding the nature of numbers or, more specifically, number quantity. The second subtype is characterized by difficulty remembering rote math facts. Let's discuss each in turn.

Math-Specific Challenges Due to Impaired
Sense of Number Quantity

Most children develop a basic sense of quantities quite early in life. By age five months, most are aware of quantities up to four and can even perform simple addition and subtraction. Unfortunately, some children (like Sam, whom we mentioned at the beginning of the chapter) fail to develop this sense of quantity. This failure has been linked to a special type of problem in visual-spatial processing.

Children with this visual-spatial processing deficit have trouble learning to count objects, because *they don't understand what numbers really mean* (i.e., that they represent quantities). They may learn to *say* the number sequence (like, from one to twenty) but will understand it only as a word sequence, not a quantity sequence.

Because the idea of quantity is so obvious to most of us, it can be hard even to understand the nature of this problem. Perhaps an example will help. Look at the following list: the presidents on Mount Rushmore, the members of the Beatles, the seasons, the points of the compass, the horsemen of the apocalypse. What do these all have in common? It's obvious, isn't it? It's their quantity, the number four. Yet this wouldn't be obvious if you lacked a concept of quantity. It would be hidden, the way the concept of color is hidden from a person born blind.

Fortunately, most children with this problem acquire a *basic* understanding of quantity and an ability to count by the midelementary years. However, they still show difficulties with quantitative reasoning and number relationships. They won't, for example, know automatically whether 5 is more than 6 or less than 4 or that the answer to the problem $78-42$ will definitely be less than 100. Often they rely on extremely basic techniques for counting, like using their fingers. But even when they do, their lack of "feeling" for quantity makes them prone to "simple" mistakes, like $10+6=4$. They also have difficulty with mathematical approximations— for example, knowing when they see the problem $972-357$ that the answer is going to be closer to 600 than to 50. They simply don't have an instinctive *feel* for number relationships. As a result, they usually have difficulty with multidigit-number calculations, which require approximations and "number sense" to solve.

Researchers investigating this type of math challenge have linked it to deficits in the parietal lobes of the brain—specifically to an area that handles spatial processing. It turns out that understanding important math concepts like quantity and number relationships, how to make approximate calculations, and how to engage in many forms of math reasoning and problem solving requires a kind of spatial reasoning that's performed in the parietal lobes. When this area works well, a child automatically develops a kind of mental "number line" or spatial sense of number quantity that can be used to perform these functions, but when this area malfunctions, a child will have difficulty with all these functions.

The relationship between parietal lobe dysfunction, spatial processing impairments, and impaired number sense was first recognized by the German neurologist Josef Gerstmann. Gerstmann noticed that this combination frequently occurred in children who also had dysgraphia (see Chapter 11), finger confusion (*agnosia*, or inability to tell which finger is moving without looking at it), difficulty naming certain objects, and difficulty distinguishing left from right—all functions known to be localized in the left parietal lobe.

One recent study has further demonstrated the relationship of parietal dysfunction and quantitative reasoning. In this study, two hundred randomly selected children were given neurological and neuropsychological (including math achievement and IQ) examinations. Remarkably, the presence of finger confusion was a better predictor of later math skills than IQ! The upshot is that very big math problems can result from very small and specialized problems in the parietal lobe in otherwise intelligent children.

Math-Specific Challenges Due to Difficulty Remembering Rote Math Facts

The second, more common, math-specific deficit is difficulty memorizing rote math facts. Rote math facts are the answers to simple math equations like 5×7, $4 + 3$, or $8 - 2$. Most of us memorize these math facts after a bit of a struggle. Some of us require extensive drilling. Still, we eventually reach the point where we know the answers to these problems without having to calculate them.

Children with rote math impairments face an entirely different level of difficulty when trying to memorize math facts: They simply cannot master their math facts through simple rote learning. Their brains don't work that way. They are impervious to drill, much to their own (and their parents' and teachers') frustration. This is the problem that Kailee faced.

To understand this problem, you should understand that mastering rote math facts doesn't mean getting faster at performing calculations. It means memorizing the results of calculations so you know them without having to do them. To master rote math facts, the brain must form a paired memory between an equation and its answer, as it does between a word and its definition. Children with rote math impairments can't create math-related memory pairs, though they usually form other types of paired memories just fine. To memorize math facts, they must use alternative strategies as described in our Helping section, below.

The distinct roles that rote memory and visual-spatial processing play in math explains why highly talented mathematicians can have extremely strong higher-order math abilities but indifferent skills in simple calculation. Problems with rote calculation should never be mistaken for fundamental difficulties with math reasoning. Too many promising mathematicians remain stuck in basic math and pre-algebra simply because of brain-based difficulties with rote math memory.

Math Impairments: Problems with Output for Action

Dysgraphia often hinders math performance, as it did for Max, whom we mentioned at the start of this chapter.

- Dysgraphia can cause working memory overload, resulting in errors and omissions. Children may focus so much on the mechanical aspects of writing that they have few working memory resources left for thinking about math.
- Children with dysgraphia sometimes struggle because they misread their own poor handwriting. If a child doing long division writes 5 but mistakes it for a 6 when he returns at the next stage, he may arrive at the wrong answer. Difficulty keeping numbers in neat columns is another common source of problems.
- Children with dysgraphia often lose points on tests and papers be-

cause their teachers cannot read their writing. Number reversals, spacing problems, and general messiness are common problems.

- Children with dysgraphia may lose points because they refuse to show their work, even for problems they know how to do. It's simply too much work.
- Dysgraphia can also cause children to fail timed tests or in-class assignments, because they can't complete their work on time.
- Finally, children with dysgraphia and finger confusion are at special risk for spatially related quantitative-reasoning problems (as discussed above). Make sure their number-quantity skills are okay before attributing their math problems to dysgraphia.

Math Impairments: Problems with Attention

Children with any of the attention problems discussed in Chapter 7 can have math difficulties.

- Math procedures must be done in order, and you can't approach them with a wandering, flickering, or halfhearted focus. That's why the Spotlight functions of selective, sustained, and stimulated attention are important.
- Math requires multitasking and constant attention to where you're at and where you're going. That's why the Juggler's working memory functions are important.
- Finally, math requires all the Creative Corporate functions. The Operations Officer has to plan and implement strategy, control pacing, and check errors, and the Creativity Officer has to suggest creative approaches.

Children with attention problems will make different kinds of errors depending on the nature of their problem, but they may include the following:

- Problems suggesting inattention to detail, like performing addition when subtraction is asked for, forgetting to carry over or borrow numbers, dropping digits during copying, or making simple computational mistakes.

- Unusually dramatic fluctuations in performance either from day to day, or even within a single paper or exam.
- A tendency to begin working on problems before determining the required strategy.
- Problems switching from one strategy to another, like difficulty switching from addition to subtraction or from the division to the subtraction steps in long division.
- Difficulty generating alternative strategies.
- Problems checking errors, with many "careless errors" left that the child easily sees later.
- A tendency to "get lost" or to inappropriately switch strategies in the middle of a problem.

Seizure disorders can mimic attention problems and often affect math more than other subjects. Math requires you to keep track of what you're doing. Children who have frequent but very brief seizures (even lasting a fraction of a second) may lack the necessary focus. Children with math difficulties should also be watched for signs of absence-type "spells" where they seem to "drift out of it" for brief bits of time with no recollection of what happened.

It's also important not to assume that a child who appears inattentive or wiggly during math has a primary attention problem. Children with math challenges often have fluctuating attention during math class, because it's hard to stay focused on things you don't understand or that make you anxious. The key is whether they show signs of attention problems in subjects other than math or whether these seem specific to math class.

EVALUATING CHILDREN WITH MATH IMPAIRMENTS

Contrary to popular belief, children usually don't hate math without a reason. If they're being well-instructed and it's still not clicking, usually they have a learning challenge that needs to be addressed. If they enter adulthood without the math skills needed to balance their checkbook, total a bill, fill out an invoice, or read a calendar or street address, they'll be at a real disadvantage. That's why math challenges should be taken seriously and seriously addressed.

Step one in evaluating a child with math challenges is to keep a log of the child's difficulties. Are they greatest with word problems? Rote math? Number inversions? Long procedures? "Careless" mistakes? Counting or computation? Does the child have problems with handwriting, memory, attention, reading, language, or spatial processing? Identifying patterns of mistakes is the key to locating the source of math challenges.

Children with severe math difficulties also need a comprehensive examination of their "neurolearning" systems. Specific math achievement tests can help sort out math difficulties as well.

HELPING CHILDREN WITH MATH CHALLENGES

Early identification and intervention are important for children with math problems. Even children with severe deficits can show good progress when given the right help, especially in the early-elementary grades. The right approach for a child with math challenges will depend on the precise nature of the challenges involved. Let's examine these challenges by category.

Helping Children with Math Challenges Due to Impaired Information Input

Many of the math problems experienced by children with Information Input impairments are the result of poor visual registration. Obviously, the best way to help such children is to improve their vision, as discussed in Chapter 4. Steps should also be taken to minimize the negative effects of any residual vision problems.

- Reduce visual crowding.

  - Limit the amount of information on pages by spacing out symbols and problems and leaving wide margins.
  - Use sufficiently large fonts.

- Teach the child to cover questions other than the one being worked on so he can maintain visual attention and focus.

- Teach the child to read through each problem several times before beginning to limit visual mistakes. Also, have the child "say" each word or symbol out loud or at least in her head to invoke auditory short-term memory and prevent confusion.
- Have the child color-code operational signs like +, −, /, ×, (,), <, >, and so on before beginning a problem using multicolored pens or highlighters.
- Have the child use large-boxed graph paper or regular lined paper turned on its side (so the lines run vertically) to help keep multidigit numbers in the appropriate columns.
- Teach the child to systematically double- (or even triple-) check his work for errors before turning it in.
- Teach the child to trace over visual figures like charts, graphs, and geometric shapes with a finger or pencil tip to improve recognition, comprehension, and memory. Verbal-mediation strategies can also help children remember, recognize, and understand visual shapes and figures, diagrams and graphs, and spatial relationships (see Chapter 4 for more details).

Helping Children with Math Challenges Due to Impaired Pattern Processing

Various steps can help children with the Pattern Processing problems we described above.

Helping Children with Math Challenges Due to Reading Difficulties

Children with reading difficulties often struggle with word problems. The biggest challenge for these children (and also for children with language or working memory issues) is to learn to translate word or story problems into mathematical equations they can solve.

Addition +	all increased more total sum combined together	Multiplication ×	multiplied by times twice product area
Subtraction −	decreased minus fewer difference less smaller than	Division ÷	divided by per ratio quotient percent
Equals =	is, are, yields, same as		

FIGURE 38. Common Operational Terms Used in Story Problems

- The key to this translation process is identifying the key words describing the operations, numbers, and units in which those numbers are expressed. (Highlighting or underlining these words can be helpful.) Word problems often employ a fairly standard repertoire of terms to denote operations (e.g., *less* or *fewer* often indicates subtraction, while *more* or *together with* often stands for addition). Learning to identify these special word clues is crucial for children with reading problems. Some of the most common words are shown in Figure 38.
- Children with reading problems should use the error-detection techniques described in the last section to limit misreading or "careless mistakes."
- For children with severe reading problems, a reader/scribe should be provided for high-stakes tests.

Helping Children with Math Challenges Due to Language Problems

Children with language problems usually require lots of explicit instruction to learn the meanings of operations, concepts, rules, and procedures.

- Often they learn best using multimodal teaching strategies, where meanings of terms and symbols are clearly demonstrated using visual and tactile examples. Manipulatives like blocks, weights, or geometric figures are useful tools.
- More than most children, those with language problems need visual examples of procedures and solved problems available while learning new skills. Focus first on the big picture of an operation or procedure, then break it down into a series of simple, self-contained steps.
- Children with certain language challenges may find that they can remember math procedures, terms, sequences, or other information better using musical mnemonics or jingles.
- Because children with language challenges often have difficulty describing the problems they encounter, it's important to keep a log of their errors to look for specific and systematic difficulties.
- Because children with language problems often have difficulty with word or story problems like those experienced by children with reading problems, they'll also benefit from specific teaching about the operational terms listed in Figure 38.

Helping Children with Math Challenges Due to Impaired Memory for Procedures and Rules

Children who have problems with procedural, sequential, or rule-based memory can benefit from several simple interventions.

- Because children who struggle with math procedures often have sequencing difficulties, they should always have a number line from zero to ten available on their desk while doing math.
- Children with procedural and rule-based memory problems often encounter working memory overload when working on complicated

problems, so they should use a calculator, number chart, or abacus when practicing specific math procedures or learning math rules. Separate calculation practice from practice learning procedures and rules.

- Children with procedural or rule-based memory problems often re-member procedures and rules more easily when they use mnemonic strategies like jingles, stories, acronyms, or rhymes made up of the first letters of the steps in a procedure, or one of the other strategies described in Chapter 3.

- Children with procedural memory problems should always be given an example of a correctly solved problem to keep before them when practicing a new procedure. They should also be encouraged to go stepwise through the example (with help) and write down (or dic-tate) a verbal description of each step, which they should memorize.

Helping Children with Math Challenges Due to Impaired Sense of Number Quantity

- Children with poor number quantity sense lack a "mental number line," so, to compensate, they should keep a visible number line on their desktop at all times.

- Because their problems understanding quantity are caused by difficulties perceiving spatial relationships, these children can of-ten develop a better sense of the relative value of numbers using nonspatial forms of "scaled perception," like touch, position, and movement.

  - A system of weights and magnets like Geomags (www.geomagsa .com) can be used to construct number "structures" that clearly dif-fer in weight as well as appearance. For example, a cluster of one bar and ball both feels and looks different from a cluster of two bars and balls, which in turn differs from a cluster of three. Helping the child to couple the variations in weight with the different numbers of rods and balls can help him understand what quantity is all about. Adding graded weights to Unifix blocks (www.didax.com/ unifix) can achieve the same effect.
  - An abacus can also help children with spatial-quantity impair-

ments, since it provides tactile, kinesthetic, and auditory feedback that can improve a child's number sense. Children who have grown up using an abacus often develop strong kinesthetic (movement) imagery that helps them perform rapid calculations.

- Note: The math manipulatives most commonly used to teach children about quantity are sticks of varying lengths. While these manipulatives are helpful for many children, they are often less useful for children with spatially based quantity problems. Length is a spatial quality, and children with spatially based quantity problems may have difficulty appreciating subtle differences in this attribute.

Helping Children with Impaired Memory for Rote Math Facts

- Children with poor memories for rote math facts rarely make much progress with conventional drilling. However, they can usually learn their math facts quickly (and permanently) using multimodal mnemonic approaches that incorporate humor, stories, picture memory, and sometimes wordplay or rhyming. We've seen many fifth- or sixth-graders who've perpetually failed to learn times tables or addition facts make tremendous progress in just a few days using such approaches.

- *Addition the Fun Way* (from www.citycreek.com) teaches addition by converting numbers into colorful animated characters, then building humorous and memorable stories around specific number relationships. (For example, for the problem $5 + 8 = 13$: "On Friday the 13th the 5 (who drives) was driving his car over the 8 (Golden Gate) bridge, and he worried that the bridge would fall down on such an unlucky day. . . .")
- The workbook available from www.multiplication.com uses a similar strategy to teach multiplication facts, as does the book *Memorize in Minutes: The Times Tables* (see Resources).

- Some children with especially good musical memories find jingles like those used in *Multiplication Rock* to be especially helpful. (Again, as with any other mnemonic strategy, it can be even more helpful for children to devise their own jingles to favorite songs.)

- While these interventions will help most children master simple math facts, many will still struggle with more complex multi-stepped or multidigit calculations. It's entirely reasonable to allow such children to use pocket-size number charts or calculators to perform complex calculations, so they can focus their attention on the conceptual and procedural aspects of math. Remember: Rote math problems in the early grades have little to do with potential aptitude for more advanced math. In fact, many eminent mathematicians had problems with (and in some cases were even held back in school because of) calculation problems in their early years. Math fact memory relies on a very different brain system than does advanced analytical or conceptual math. That's why it's important not to prevent children with a good conceptual understanding of math from moving on to higher math classes like algebra, geometry, or even calculus simply because they have difficulties with rote math facts.

Helping Children with Math Impairments: Problems with Output for Action

- As described in Chapter 11, children with significant dysgraphia should have written work decreased to about one-third of normal. A professional with expertise in this area can provide useful guidance.
- Keyboarding can also be helpful in math.

  - Software programs for number keyboarding (like Math Pad from www.intellitools.com) can eliminate the working memory drain caused by dysgraphia, freeing up resources to focus on math. However, most keyboard programs require that children learn special commands, which can be difficult. For that reason, they are likely to be preferred only by children with fairly severe dysgraphia.
  - Computer-based instruction programs like Boxermath (www

.apexlearning.com), HeyMath! (www.heymath.net), or ALEKS (www.Aleks.com) can provide an easier way to learn math, since all work is done by keyboard. However, these programs follow their own course of study and do not provide keyboarding options that are adaptable to other courses.

• Children with milder dysgraphia often find using graph paper with larger boxes helpful.
• Children with dysgraphia should receive special accommodations for testing. Tests should always be untimed, and if they are long or require extensive writing, a scribe should be provided.
• Children with dysgraphia should not be asked to show their work on large numbers of similar problems. If they can do problems well in their head (like Max), ask for only one or two examples of shown work, and let them do the rest without demonstration. (Note: Highly visual or visual-spatial thinkers often have difficulties showing work for reasons other than dysgraphia. These children are often intuitive mathematicians who do their work using nonverbal, imagery-laden processes that are not easily expressed. Frequently they find that they are not quite sure how they get their answers—they just "come to them." Such children require a careful balancing act. They should occasionally be challenged to show that they understand the principles behind their work and can generalize these principles to other kinds of problems. However, they should probably not be forced to show work on all problems, especially if it appears to be diminishing their natural love of math.

Helping Children with Math Challenges Due to Attention Problems

In addition to improving their underlying problems with attention, the following steps can help children whose attention difficulties are causing problems with math:

• Children with a poor short-term memory for numbers ("number span") often have trouble remembering numbers long enough to do math problems. Practice can increase their short-term memory for numbers.

- Begin by determining the upper limits of a child's memory for numbers (e.g., four digits), then practice retaining numbers one digit longer for about five minutes a day.
- Many children can retain numbers better in one form than another. For example, they may find (like Kendra in Chapter 3) that they can retain two digits with their auditory "tape loop" (through subvocalization) but five digits with their visual "sketch pad" or by incorporating numbers into a familiar song.

- Children with poor sustained attention or working memory challenges often find studying math in several short teaching sessions (say, two ten- to fifteen-minute sessions a day) is more productive than single sessions of thirty or sixty minutes.
- Like children with visual or reading problems, children with attention problems should learn to read through problems several times before trying to solve them. They should also highlight important operation symbols or other important features (like brackets or exponents).
- Before beginning a problem, children with attention problems should take time to generate a specific plan for approaching and solving it.

  - They should first identify the type of problem and the type of approach (or approaches) it requires. Have them practice saying or writing down this information before beginning their work.
  - Next have them describe the specific steps they will take to solve the problem.
  - Only after both steps are completed should they start actually solving the problem.

- If the child is better at identifying problems than at developing plans to solve them, then the two steps recommended for children with procedural memory problems will be helpful.

- First, make sure that the child has an example of a correctly solved problem to refer to while working on the problem.
- Second, have the child go through the sample problem and write down (or dictate, if he has dysgraphia) a verbal description of each of the steps in order. Then tackle the new problem.

- Children who frequently make errors in identifying problem types should practice identifying problems without being asked to solve them. For example, give them sheets of mixed addition, subtraction, multiplication, and division problems (or whatever combination of problems they confuse), and have them simply write down the type of problem and highlight the operation sign with the appropriate color. Score their work simply on the basis of this first step.
- Keep children with attention and working memory problems from getting overwhelmed by multistepped problems by teaching them strategies to "chunk" tasks into smaller bits that can then be tackled more easily. For example, break long division down into discrete steps, then practice solving problems one step at a time. Narrowing the child's focus will keep her from becoming overwhelmed by trying to think of too many things at once.
- Children with attention problems often have difficulty pacing their work. It can be helpful to have them work on problems using a timer. Work out an appropriate time frame for doing a problem or a set of problems, and then have them practice with the timer until an internal sense of pacing kicks in. Be generous with the times at first. Too much time pressure will overload working memory and be counterproductive.
- Children with attention problems often struggle with error detection and self-correction.

  - Many children benefit from an incentive strategy where points, stars, or other rewards are given for error-free work. Children should check their work both immediately after completing it and after a time interval, to see if they have an easier time detecting mistakes. Points can also be awarded for mistakes they find themselves.

Accommodations That Can Help All
Children with Math Challenges

The following accommodations are appropriate for any child with significant math challenges:

- Timed tests provide a poor estimate of true math knowledge and should generally be avoided in children with learning challenges.
- Children with significant math challenges should not be asked to demonstrate their work on the board unless it's a problem they've already completed and they don't have dysgraphia.
- Children with math challenges should not have other children grade their work, nor should it be posted on the board, except as a positive example.

13

The Midas Touch

How Giftedness Can Cause Learning Challenges in Children

Contrary to what most people believe, a gifted mind is not necessarily able to find its own way. Although gifted students possess exceptional capabilities, most cannot excel without assistance. They need assistance academically, but they also need assistance emotionally through understanding, acceptance, support, and encouragement.

—J. T. WEBB, E. A. MECKSTROTH, AND S. S. TOLAN, *GUIDING THE GIFTED CHILD*

An hour with Samantha left us shaking our heads in wonder. She was pint-size but strong as an ox and incredibly coordinated. She moved fast . . . talked fast . . . thought fast. She just seemed to be developing . . . *fast!* Although only five, she'd read each of the Harry Potter books several times and written detailed stories of her own. In math, she'd grown bored of simply adding, so she'd asked her mom to teach her multiplication—*for fun!* You're probably wondering, *So what were her problems?* Well, those *were* her problems. Samantha was five years old but had the mental and physical capacity of a nine-year-old and was still in kindergarten. She was a big foot in a little shoe, and she was starting to feel the pinch.

Samantha's signs of discomfort were increasing daily. She'd been thrilled to start school, but within two months she'd begun asking to stay home. By three months, she complained of headaches and pains in her stomach when it was time to catch the bus. Samantha's mother began getting reports of behavioral problems at school. Samantha had alienated some of her classmates, who saw her as bossy and aggressive. Samantha's problem was that she didn't suffer fools gladly. This was true even when the fools were doctors. During our testing, we asked her, "How many sounds are in *stop?* How many sounds are in *whistle?*" She looked at us scornfully and replied, "How many sounds are in *aborigine?* How many sounds are in *antidisestablishmentarianism?*" We began to get an inkling of her problem.

Samantha's teacher thought she might have ADHD. Her pediatrician was unsure but said a rating scale (Connors) was consistent. Samantha's mother was unconvinced. She couldn't see how Samantha could have an attention problem when she could read and write for hours at a time and was learning as fast as she could be given information. She asked us for our opinion.

GIFTEDNESS AND GIFTED CHILDREN: AN INTRODUCTION

Perhaps you find it odd that we've included a chapter on giftedness in a book on learning challenges. After all, "giftedness" sounds like such a pure, unalloyed blessing. How could a gift be a problem? Well, as any child who's received a new puppy learns, even the best gifts can have their messy aspects.

Samantha is a classic example of a child who encounters difficulties primarily as a result of her giftedness. As we'll see, giftedness can create many challenges for a child's schooling, relationships, and social and emotional development. In fact, we sometimes (only slightly facetiously) define giftedness as: "a talent for creating difficulties in ways that suggest promise." Often gifted challenges are the flip sides of the gifts themselves and the remarkable and wonderful opportunities they present. In this chapter, we'll discuss both the gifts and the gripes, the pleasures and the pains of giftedness.

There are two big problems for anyone addressing the special needs and challenges of gifted children: defining the nature of giftedness and deciding which children are gifted. Historically, most attempts to address these problems have relied on IQ tests. Shortly after World War I, researchers like Lewis Terman of Stanford University (who developed the Stanford-Binet IQ test) popularized the use of IQ testing for defining intellectual giftedness and identifying gifted children. For Terman (and most of the educational establishment that he influenced), intellectual giftedness was essentially synonymous with having a high IQ—that is, with doing well on his tests. Many school districts still admit children to gifted programs largely or even exclusively on the basis of intelligence tests.

However, almost from the beginning, it's been obvious that intelligence tests are not perfect at measuring intellectual ability nor at identifying gifted children. Intelligence tests often fail to identify some of the most highly intelligent and creative children of all. Terman's own multidecade study was illustrative. Beginning in the 1920s, Terman asked teachers to submit names of their most intelligent students. Terman then tested these students with his Stanford-Binet IQ test. He enrolled all children scoring 140 or above in his study, and excluded the rest. Over several decades of follow-up, Terman found that the above-140 students performed (for the most part) quite well in school and became successful in their careers. However, he also found that his IQ criteria excluded the only two children in the initial sample who went on to win Nobel Prizes—and many other creative and innovative people as well.

Through the years, IQ tests have frequently been criticized for being better at identifying children who are likely to do well in school than at identifying those with outstanding creative potential. Even with regard to their ability to predict academic success, IQ tests are less than perfect. In fact, current intelligence tests can predict just 40 to 50 percent of a child's school achievement.

IQ tests have also been criticized for suggesting that there is only a single uniform kind of intelligence. Educational experts like Howard Gardner have argued convincingly that there is no single "general intelligence," but rather "multiple intelligences" that correspond to different kinds of giftedness.

Broadening the concept of giftedness is unquestionably appropriate. In our clinical practice, we see many "neuropsychological aptitudes" that can serve as a basis for creativity, innovation, and success both in school and in life. We also see (as we've described throughout this book) many neuropsychological or neurolearning strengths that can be used to develop learning strategies. What characterizes gifted children is both the number and magnitude of their learning strengths (particularly in Pattern Processing and Attention) and, frequently, their insight into how they can use these strengths.

In this chapter, we'll discuss the characteristics that distinguish intellectually gifted children and how these characteristics can lead to the benefits and the challenges commonly seen in gifted children.

BEHAVIORS ASSOCIATED WITH GIFTED CHALLENGES

The following behaviors are often seen in gifted children. For ease of consideration, we'll split these behaviors into two categories: those relating to learning and the learning environment and those relating to emotional and social/interpersonal factors.

Behaviors Related to Learning Styles and Preferences

Gifted children may exhibit the following behaviors:

- Often unusually motivated to learn.
- May focus on particular interests to an extent that seems obsessive or perseverant or may become so wrapped up in interests that they withdraw into them.
- May show unusually long attention spans and prefer to work on single topics for extended periods of time.

- May demand unusual depth in teaching and learn best with lots of time for reflection.
- May be novelty-dependent and require constant exposure to new topics and new information. As opposed to children with attention problems, these children learn well with sufficient stimulation. Indeed, part of their problem is that they learn so rapidly and efficiently they may become bored or impatient waiting for others.
- May have unusually good and efficient memories.
- Often show a tendency to become bored with excessive repetition.
- Are frequently good incidental learners who acquire broad vocabularies and knowledge bases from many sources without explicit instruction.
- May be highly, even fiercely, independent in their thinking and learning styles and have strong opinions about how they learn best.
- May become impatient with classroom routines and lesson plans if they don't match their own preferences regarding depth, breadth, or pace.
- May take knowledge and learning extremely personally.
- Tend to "love" favorite topics and feel strongly about their work.
- May show excessive perfectionism, never feel satisfied with work, experience frequent disappointments, and avoid activities they cannot perform to their satisfaction, which may lead to school refusal or underachievement.
- May be overly sensitive to criticism.
- May show intellectual independence and confidence in opinions unusual for their age.
- May tend to argue or debate, question authority, and refuse to take anyone's word.
- May question the value of lesson plans, whole subjects, or school in general, and ask for justifications for doing work.
- May show very vivid imaginations and powerful creative abilities.

Behaviors Related to
Emotional/Social/Interpersonal Factors

Gifted children also often:

- Are highly sensitive to environmental, internal, and emotional stimuli and may become overwhelmed by intense or prolonged sensory input.
- Are emotionally intense.
- Are introverted and may prefer quiet or solitary pursuits.
- Show unusual sensitivity to moral concerns like justice, fairness, and the welfare of others, even to the point of preoccupation. When they are young, this may result in unusual consideration for others or an incessant "scorekeeping" mentality and a tendency to get upset when things seem unfair.
- Feel personally responsible when bad things happen, even things that are entirely out of their control, like natural disasters, wars, or famines.
- Have difficulty finding friends with shared interests.
- Prefer the company of older children or adults, or occasionally younger children whom they can mentor.
- Have an unusual knowledge base or vocabulary, and advanced interests may make them appear as a know-it-all or show-off without their intending to.

CAUSES OF GIFTEDNESS AND
GIFTED CHALLENGES

Studies indicate that gifted children are remarkably "whole-brained" thinkers who use many parts of their brains for creative and demanding tasks. Often they show especially strong abilities in Pattern Processing and Attention. In this section, we'll discuss these special abilities and how they contribute to the behavioral and learning challenges that often affect these children.

Pattern Processing in Gifted Children

Gifted children frequently excel in their abilities to store, recognize, and manipulate patterns of many types, including sensory, abstract, and emotional. In this section, we'll divide these enhanced abilities into four categories: enhanced sensitivity to patterns, enhanced working memory for patterns, enhanced speed and efficiency of pattern retrieval, and enhanced pattern reflection. Let's consider each in turn.

Enhanced Sensitivity to Sensory Patterns

Gifted children are often unusually sensitive to sensory stimulation. They may notice things others miss and remember sights, sounds, and smells for years afterward, as if they happened only yesterday. One of the most important—and in some ways most surprising—sources of this sensitivity is related to "problems" with one of the Spotlight functions we discussed in Chapter 7: selective attention. Gifted children often show the kind of "wobbly" Spotlight control that characterizes children with impaired selective attention: They seem to notice everything and may actually seem distractible. However, these children typically don't suffer from this distractibility and may actually benefit from it. That's because they have two additional strengths that keep the downside of their sensitivity in check and milk the upside for all it's worth:

1. While their selective attention may be wobbly, gifted children often have a special strength in sustained attention, which gives them task persistence. Although they may get pulled off task by enticing stimuli, they'll usually go right back when their curiosity is satisfied. This ability to persist despite distractions is one of the key features that separates highly observant and sensitive children from those with significant selective attention problems.
2. As we'll discuss in more detail in the next section, gifted children usually have an enhanced working memory capacity that lets them process more patterns at a single time than other children are able to.

Still, this extra sensitivity does not come without a cost. In addition to the demands it places on attention and working memory, it also places tremendous demands on physical and mental energy stores. Metabolically, the brain acts like any other organ: The more it works, the more energy it consumes. It can even become "fatigued" through overuse—and gifted children are big-time brain users. Studies using functional magnetic resonance imaging (fMRI) have shown that highly creative and talented individuals often activate unusually broad areas of cortex when engaged in difficult tasks. One study looked at the brain of a math prodigy while he tackled complex math problems. Not only did he use the same brain parts most people use to do math (as we discussed in Chapter 12), but he also used additional areas responsible for *personal memory and emotion!* He literally *loved his numbers!*

Such intense intellectual activity can result in fatigue and irritability. In younger children (and especially thinner children, who seem to burn through their easily available glucose stores more rapidly), it can even cause violent mood swings, typically late in the morning and in mid-afternoon. It can also result in meltdowns with sensory or information overload. Such a pattern of extreme sensitivity to intellectual and physical stimulation (with exhaustion and overload) during childhood can be seen with surprising frequency in the biographies of eminent women and men.

This special sensitivity to sensory stimulation (and accompanying intellectual and emotional stimulation) may be one reason gifted children tend more commonly than peers to be introverts and to enjoy time alone. Research using the Myers-Briggs Personality Inventory has shown that while 77 percent of the U.S. population (and 53 percent of teachers) are *extroverts* who tend to gain energy from being with other people, fully 67 percent of gifted children are *introverts* who gain energy from being alone. A gifted child who asks for periods of solitude may be responding to internal signals telling her it's time to recharge. Extroverted parents and teachers need to be careful not to label such a child as socially backward, lacking in self-confidence, or excessively self-preoccupied. Introverted parents and teachers should likewise avoid labeling extroverted children as overly dependent on the opinions and approval of others, involved with too many people and ideas at once, or even afflicted with ADHD. A carefully balanced view is required. Introverted children should sometimes be encouraged to mix more in society, but occasional interactions with plenty of downtime afterward are preferable to extended immersions with no available escape.

Enhanced Working Memory: Span, Encoding, and Reflection

Gifted children can often keep large amounts of information "in mind" at once and quickly and efficiently file large numbers of new patterns into long-term storage. These, as you probably recognize by now, are the products of a strong working memory.

Gifted children may show strong working memory function in several domains (i.e., auditory-verbal, visual, motor-kinesthetic) or only one, but in areas of special ability, gifted children will typically show a large working memory capacity. This extra capacity (or span) means they can keep large and complex patterns "in mind" for extended periods. This gives them a special edge in both encoding and reflection. Let's look at encoding now and discuss reflection later.

Gifted children are typically gifted encoders. As we discussed in Chapters 2 and 3, encoding is the process of modifying information patterns so they can be properly filed in (and later retrieved from) long-term memory. The success of the encoding process is largely dependent upon the use of encoding strategies. Gifted children are often unusually sophisticated in their ability to develop and use encoding strategies. For example, most gifted children are good at using rehearsal strategies with their "tape loop" or "sketch pad" functions to keep patterns in mind. Many are also especially good at using verbal mediation or visualization to recode patterns into more easily processed forms. Gifted children tend as well to be especially good at using personal memory to encode patterns. Because they "love" their ideas, they often invest them with deep feeling and personal meaning.

Gifted children with this combination of enhanced sensitivity and enhanced encoding have a special talent for acquiring new information. We call their brains "cognitive flypaper," because they seem to catch—and keep—everything they touch. There are three important consequences to having such a sticky brain:

1. Often these children enter school equipped with lots of knowledge that they've picked up incidentally. They may enter a grade already knowing everything they're expected to know at the end of the year or even several years in advance.

2. Because they typically need less time and require fewer repetitions to master new material, they may grow bored or even resistant if forced to do too much repetition or review.

3. Because they can file patterns so easily in their memory stores, if they're not careful to organize them well (during the encoding process), they may have difficulty retrieving them when needed. We'll discuss this problem below.

Enhanced Speed of Pattern Retrieval (Recognition and Recall)

Many (but not all) gifted children show a special ability to rapidly retrieve patterns. This is what gives them their "sharpness" or "quickness" of mind.

Rapid pattern retrieval is also a reflection of expertise: The better you know something, the more quickly and automatically you can retrieve it. Gifted children often become experts in favorite areas. Such expertise can be very useful to them, because the ease and speed with which they retrieve well-known patterns leaves them more room in working memory to creatively reflect on and modify patterns. Think, for example, of music, where a child must practice until the mechanics of playing have become automatic before she can play with full musical expression.

Of course, simply developing expertise or automaticity does not make a child creative, either in music or in any other sphere. In fact, there is even a risk that when thinking becomes too easy and automatic, it may blunt a child's creative development. As we'll discuss in the next section, creativity is the ability to perceive new associations between patterns, not the ability to recognize and retrieve patterns quickly. Unless rapidly processing "expert" children are pushed to develop their creative skills, they may actually be at risk of stunted creative development. If they too easily solve problems and answer questions using automatic or "overlearned" pathways, they may never engage in the kind of far-flung mental struggle that helps children discover new and creative connections. Unless they are intentionally presented with roadblocks, they may get little experience in looking for alternate routes, and their mental associations may remain excessively direct and conventional. If the use of their creative faculties is not encouraged, these children, who are perfectly suited for the standardized multiple-choice test, may achieve great success in the K–12 years only to face frustration and underachievement in college and the working world, where the questions are neither obvious nor direct and where appropriate answers are more dependent on creative synthesis than on simple recall from memory.

Rapid retrievers are also at risk for boredom and misbehavior if they regularly finish in-class work with a great deal of time to spare. They may also dominate classroom discussions or small groups, become impatient with the relative slowness of peers (as we saw with Samantha), and look like a show-off or know-it-all, even without intending to. In our Helping section, we'll discuss ways to help rapid processors avoid these negative consequences.

Before moving on, we should stress what you probably already suspect: that rapid retrieval is far from universal among gifted children. In fact, there is considerable evidence that many of the most profoundly gifted children often appear mentally "slow"—even to the point of suggesting mental deficiency. For example, Isaac Newton, one of the greatest scientific minds of all time, as a child was so slow in responding to questions that household servants laughed at him and called him a fool and his mother doubted he could ever care for himself as an adult.

Enhanced Reflection: Detecting Associations Between Patterns

Gifted children—especially the most highly gifted—typically show a special aptitude for reflecting on patterns and discovering new connections and associations between them. As we discussed in Chapter 3, reflection is the process of manipulating and modifying patterns so that we can better understand and remember them, discover new associations and analogies between them, organize these associations into networks, and imagine or create new patterns using the old ones.

Because gifted children have powerful working memories, they're well equipped to engage in these processes. That's why they're so often highly creative, good reasoners, and powerful problem solvers. In fact, there are strong reasons to believe that this kind of *reflective pattern manipulation* is crucial for all creative and higher-order intellectual work. This kind of reflection helps us discover relationships between concepts and ideas and see how old problems (to which we know the solutions) can be used to solve new ones through the use of analogy. Think, for example, of a child who's asked to identify five energy sources (other than gasoline) that could be used for powering cars. He'll solve this problem quite easily if he can think (through reflection) of categories analogous to "known energy sources for cars," like "energy sources in general," "combustible materials," or "metabolic fuels." If so, he'll probably think of solar energy, electricity, gravitational energy, magnetic energy, atomic energy, hydrodynamic energy, and energy from other fuels, like sugars, alcohols, fats, et cetera. However, he'll have a much harder time if his mind makes no associations outside the category "known energy sources for cars."

As with other gifted strengths, there are potential downsides to this highly reflective and associational thinking style. Sometimes these children may see so many associations between patterns that they literally get lost wandering among their associational networks whenever they're asked a question. Such highly associational thinkers can really get bogged down. (This was probably a big part of young Isaac Newton's problem.)

Fortunately, all this mental meandering has its upside: Although it makes thinking slow, it can make it extremely powerful as well. Children with this highly associational (and often slow) processing style are the proverbial absentminded professors. They may appear either spacey or profound and are often lost in their own thoughts. They are intellectual ruminants who digest their thoughts like cows digest grass, using four "mental stomachs" rather than the typical one. Often their unusual processing style causes them to be misunderstood and their tremendous intellectual and creative potential to be underestimated.

Highly reflective and associational children can appear "different" in ways other than speed. Because their thinking proceeds through so many analogies and associations, these children may reach conclusions without being fully aware of how they got there. As a result, they may have difficulty "showing their work" or "supporting their conclusions," even when they know the correct answer. Often they have very high standards for *what counts as knowledge* and will not be satisfied with teaching that fails to meet their criteria. They dislike learning naked facts and are always looking for the meanings behind the facts. Frequently they prefer learning formats that allow them to test the uses of information—to play with it and apply it in different ways. For instance, rather than simply being told about the theory of gravity, they may want to see how they could experimentally deduce it and see what practical uses they could put it to, like erecting water towers or reservoirs on hills, or building dams, or constructing locks for ships to pass through. This comes from their desire to seek connections and associations between ideas.

These differences in learning style can create challenges for highly reflective and associational thinkers when they are trying to learn in the typical educational setting. They are often interested in (and even obsessed with) questions that other people don't see or find important. They also have a gift for making simple tasks complicated, because they tend to see eight sides to everything. They often approach multiple-choice tests like lawyers vetting a contract—and with similarly confusing results! Ask them to explain how they could miss such a simple question on a topic they've mastered, and they'll give you so many multiple word meanings, conditionals, and hypotheticals that it makes the plot of *The Da Vinci Code* seem straightforward!

Small wonder these children often get so overwhelmed by their mad rush of ideas that they fail to work productively. Unless they learn to manage the tremendous richness of their thinking, they risk being deluged by the very limitlessness of their ideas and suffering from a case of terminal "analysis paralysis."

These children are also at risk of becoming habitual contrarians, adopting unusual and oppositional ideas just because they can imagine them. They may also become so impressed by their own ideas—especially their most complicated ones—that they can be sidetracked by irrelevancies, trivia, or even obvious errors. As a friend once said of Winston Churchill (a highly associational thinker if ever there was one), "Winston was often right, but when he was wrong . . . well . . . my God."

Attention in Gifted Children

Gifted thinkers who function well typically show a synergy or "partnership" in their attentional functions that enables them to be focused yet flexible in their thinking. As we discussed in Chapter 7, we call this partnership Creative Corporate Intelligence, because it represents the balance between creativity and discipline that is found in most successful businesses.

Ideally, gifted thinkers will combine the skills of both their Chief Operations Officer and their Chief Creativity Officer to create a truly Creative Corporate Intelligence, characterized by creativity and disciplined management. Although different thinkers give different amounts of power to each "executive," input from each is essential for truly creative thinking, no matter what one is trying to create.

Take two creative thinkers who in many ways would seem opposites: the creative painter and the creative mathematician. You might expect that the painter would show a big imbalance of "creativity-to-operations" or "talent-to-suits" skills. Yet creating a work of art requires extensive oversight by the Operations Officer. The Creativity Officer produces the general conception and explores different artistic possibilities, but the Operations Officer must coordinate the use of canvas, plan the steps for laying down the paint, and continually monitor progress to see how the product is matching the conception.

Likewise, the gifted mathematician needs both creative and operational input. Despite the analytical appearance of many math functions (like deriving cube roots), mathematicians use many creative and intuitive approaches to solve them, like proposing alternative solutions, employing personal reasoning, and using analogies and approximations to arrive at answers by creative leaps rather than step-by-step.

Sometimes gifted children experience difficulties because their Creativity and Operations Officers fail to work well together as a team. Imbalances in these executives may result in undisciplined flightiness or uncreative and obsessive expertise. In our Helping section, we'll describe ways to address these imbalances.

Special Problems Confronting
Gifted Children

Gifted children can also face challenges from specific learning problems or encounter social, emotional, and psychological difficulties. Many people mistakenly assume that gifted children are gifted in all capacities. This is far from true. Gifted children can suffer from any of the learning challenges we've described in this book and from the same social, emotional, and psychological problems that confront other growing children. In addition, when they experience these problems, they often experience additional challenges as a result of their giftedness. In this section, we'll discuss this entire range of challenges.

"Twice-Exceptional" Children (2e)

Children who are *both* gifted and learning-disabled are often called *twice-exceptional* (or *2e*), because their abilities lie outside the norms at both ends of the bell curve. These 2e children are immensely diverse. In fact, they embody every imaginable combination of strengths and weaknesses. The difficulties a 2e child faces largely depend upon her own combination of strengths and weaknesses; still, the broad divergence between strengths and weaknesses that all 2e children face produces several characteristic challenges.

Paradoxically, the greatest challenges many 2e children face arise because their strengths *hide* or *mask* their weaknesses, obscuring their need for help. As we saw with Michael in Chapter 1, many schools provide remediative services only to children whose performance falls more than two standard deviations or one grade level below age norms. Yet this way of identifying special needs is entirely unsuited to gifted children, because their strengths often allow them to compensate sufficiently to keep their scores above levels where they would qualify for special help. *So where's the problem?* you might ask. *If they're able to meet norms on standardized tests, isn't that good enough?* No, it's not, and for four main reasons:

1. Failure to treat a 2e child's weaknesses will keep her from learning to her full potential. Weaknesses should be identified using individual

norms, not age or grade norms. Any child with a splay of two or more standard deviations (SD) between his strongest and weakest skills needs special help. A child who's three SD above age norms in oral language but one SD below in written expression needs help as much as a child with average oral language who's two SD behind in written expression. Failure to address a gifted child's weaknesses inevitably holds back progress in areas of strength.

2. Often 2e children must make superhuman efforts in their areas of weakness just to meet age norms. We see gifted children with dysgraphia in second or third grade who must spend several hours a night to do homework that takes other children thirty minutes. In the long run, this kind of effort is not sustainable, either physically or emotionally.

3. Most of the time, the 2e child's "failure" to fall far enough behind to qualify for help is only temporary. As the school workload grows, the child falls further and further behind and eventually fails, with devastating consequences for learning, self-esteem, mood, and behavior.

4. Although the 2e child's disability may stay hidden from others, it is always apparent to the child—often overwhelmingly so. In our own practice, we often see 2e children as young as first grade who are so despondent over their school problems that they've literally lost all joy in life. They begin to see themselves as defective or as mistakes that need to be blotted out, like the gifted second-grader we saw who told her mother that she wanted Santa Claus to "bring her death" for Christmas. As these children progress through school, they often blame themselves for the gap between their abilities and their actual performance. They may also shift blame to others. They may become anxious, self-loathing, bitter, rebellious, and depressed. Sometimes they just give up and begin underachieving even in areas of strength. These things should never be allowed to happen.

Fortunately, with early remediation, compensation, and accommodations, they needn't be. These 2e children should be helped to expand their strengths as well as overcome their weaknesses. They should also be given a hopeful vision for their future, because there is indeed strong reason for hope. Many of the world's most successful and creative people, both now and in the past, have been twice-exceptional as children. In fact, this pattern is so common that many people (ourselves included) believe that childhood disability often fosters adult creativity and success. Children who've been forced to find creative approaches for doing things most people do without effort often develop a "habit for creativity"—but only if they don't lose sight of their gifts and fall into a cycle of underachievement and despair. That's why, as we mentioned in Chapter 2, it's absolutely crucial to help children who are struggling in school maintain a positive vision of themselves and their future. This is especially true for 2e children, who are often troubled by the tremendous disparity they perceive between their abilities and their performance.

Social and Emotional Problems in Gifted Children

Gifted children are subject to the same social and emotional problems that affect other children, but their giftedness sometimes complicates these problems. They're also subject to certain special social and emotional problems simply because of their giftedness.

Developmental Asynchrony in Gifted Children

Many gifted children experience social and emotional problems because their minds, emotions, and bodies are all maturing at widely different rates. This pattern of growth is sometimes called *developmental asynchrony*. For example, a six-year-old child may do math like a ten-year-old, read like a twelve-year-old, and know dinosaurs like a college paleontology major but still respond to his brother's "borrowing" his plastic brachiosaurus like a typical six-year-old.

Often gifted children will have critical and analytical skills that exceed their judgment and restraint. Younger gifted children may have difficulty containing their outrage when their sense of fairness is violated. Older gifted children (and adults) may have difficulty controlling verbal retorts. The quick and cutting remark is a special skill (of dubious value) that often accompanies verbal giftedness and, if not controlled, may imperil relationships with peers and adults. We often refer to this problem as the "Emma dilemma," after Jane Austen's precocious heroine whose cleverness frequently outpaced her wisdom.

Gifted children also develop in very different ways than do most other children. Typically they will have different and often more "mature" interests than peers, which may lead to charges of being "stuck up," odd, or different and result in feelings of alienation or social rejection. This was the case for the children whose drawings are represented in Figures 39a and b: a seven-year-old who preferred spending art class drawing like Magritte, Bosch, and Picasso rather than sketching trucks and soldiers like the rest of his peers (Figure 39a) and a ten-year-old who got so tired of writing his name in regular script that he began signing his name in Mayan glyphs (Figure 39b). Imagine how hard it is for young enthusiasts like these to find others who share their vision. Unfortunately, it's all too easy to find others who'll ridicule them for it. Many studies have documented the pressures put on gifted children to "dumb down" their performance for the sake of conformity. Often gifted children choose instead to spend time with older children or even adults. While this may provide friends to share particular interests, it usually fails to provide a "best friend" because of differences in experience, emotional maturity, and stage-of-life issues.

"Difficult" Gifted Character Traits

Gifted children may also experience social and emotional problems because of character or temperament traits commonly seen in gifted children.

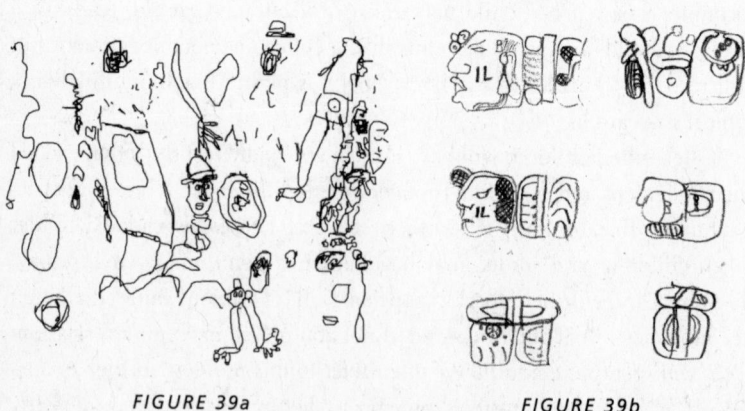

FIGURE 39a   FIGURE 39b

Gifted children are often highly perfectionistic—that is, they're dissatisfied with anything that's less than perfect, which is . . . everything! Perfectionistic children are often harshly critical of their own performances and forever unsatisfied with their work. These children require careful handling. The drive to improve oneself and one's performance is crucial for achievement and innovation and should not be extinguished. Only when it's coupled with a refusal to enjoy anything less than perfection does it become destructive. Striking the right balance requires careful guidance and encouragement. Perfectionistic children may also encounter problems when they try to foist their own high standards onto others. These exacting standards often make them particularly demanding, critical, and persistent, and they may develop reputations as "control freaks," "hairsplitters," and "sticklers for detail."

Gifted children often also display unusual personal sensitivity and emotional intensity. Highly observant and emotionally intense children are particularly vulnerable to slights from others, just as they are to the failure to meet their own expectations. They are especially likely to encounter difficulties when involved in poor interpersonal matches with parents, teachers, and other authority figures.

Despite being sensitive to the opinions of others, many gifted children may also have a strong sense of self-direction and individual dignity, which makes them fiercely independent in their approaches to learning and to life. When their vision conflicts with that of their elders, they can stubbornly resist all attempts at correction, counsel, or compromise. Attempts to "break them" like skittish horses seldom work and may leave them embittered and rebellious. These children need correction, guidance, and firmness, but within limits they should be given options as well, so they can learn to exercise their judgment within a range of acceptable choices. We'll discuss ways of dealing with these traits in our Helping section.

Specific Psychological Diagnoses in Gifted Children

Gifted children can experience the same kinds of mood, anxiety, and behavioral disorders as other children. We don't have room to discuss these all here, but for those interested in reading more about the psychological or emotional problems in gifted children, we would strongly recommend

Misdiagnosis and Dual Diagnosis of Gifted Children and Adults (see Resources). We would, however, like to mention several disorders that are more commonly diagnosed in gifted children.

Existential Depression in Gifted Children

Existential depression arises when persons become preoccupied with, then overwhelmed by, the "big questions" of existence (e.g., the meaning of life, the reality of death, the existence of injustice, the nature of evil, etc.). Because gifted children are often especially concerned with issues of fairness and tend to adopt idealized standards because of perfectionistic tendencies, they may become distressed by the disparity between the perfect world of their conceptions and the real world around them. This distress may be worsened by their emotional intensity, sensitivity, and sense of alienation from peers, and by learning challenges in 2e children.

Anorexia Nervosa in Gifted Children

Anorexia nervosa is a disorder primarily affecting adolescent girls and young women, characterized by an obsessive interest in weight loss and resulting in self-starvation. Parents with gifted girls should be especially alert for signs of excessive preoccupation with weight and dieting, distorted body image, or obsessive exercise routines.

ADHD and Gifted Children

Gifted children are frequently diagnosed—and misdiagnosed—with ADHD, because they often display behaviors used to diagnose ADHD. However, as we discussed in Chapter 7, these behaviors may—and in the case of gifted children commonly do—result from causes other than attention deficits. Gifted children may appear inattentive in class if activities aren't challenging enough or, if they are already familiar, seem irrelevant or are too quickly finished. These children may appear impulsive because they're intense, independent, willing to question rules, because they may speak their minds without fully assessing consequences (the "Emma dilemma") or may blurt out answers in class. They may also appear hyperactive if they become bored and restless, overstimulated, or even highly enthusiastic. In addition, they are sometimes mislabeled as "hyperfocusers" when they concentrate so intently that they "block out" the rest of the world.

We often observe two patterns of behaviors that lead gifted children to be mislabeled with ADHD. The first is a combination of inattentiveness in class and hyperfocusing on personal interests. This is a common pattern among highly gifted children *and adults* and can be a sign of great creativity.

Focused intensity may cause problems in a second-grade class, but it is a challenging strength, not a deficit. In fact, this focused state of consciousness is what the psychologist Mihaly Csikszentmihalyi has called *flow*. Csikszentmihalyi has defined flow as a state persons enter into when they are involved in a personally rewarding activity that has "stretched [their] capacity and involved an element of novelty and discovery." Flow is not a pathological state. It is the state of "higher awareness" that creative individuals enter when they are captivated by some question or project. This flow state results from the same kind of whole-brain activity we described earlier in our passionate mathematician. It is the kind of mental state that our educational systems should help children reach, not one we should stigmatize.

A second behavioral profile that leads gifted children to be suspected of ADHD consists of environmental sensitivity (or distractibility), a love of novelty (or new information), and a Creativity Officer that tends to dominate his Operational partner. These children are easily distracted by things in their environment (or, perhaps more accurately, are highly observant), require constant access to new materials, and are full of ideas, observations, and possibilities.

To distinguish a gifted child's ADHD-like behaviors from a true attention deficit, it's important to ask several questions: Is she falling behind on her learning curve? Is he actually having difficulty learning because he's inattentive, or impulsive, or hyperactive, or is he behaving in these ways because he's bored, or too far ahead, or requires less time to master the material, or fails to see why he should learn what's being taught? Does she appear inattentive because she needs to devote only part of her attentional resources to follow what's going on in class? Can he learn and focus well when information is presented in a way he finds interesting and informative?

While some gifted students clearly have significant attention problems, we see far too many gifted children who can focus well on materials they find interesting and informative and are in no way educationally behind, yet are placed on medications for "ADHD" because they aren't sufficiently engaged by the routine of the classroom. This is not right. When gifted children have trouble paying attention in class, it's essential to make sure they're adequately challenged and that they aren't having difficulties with vision, hearing, language, and memory that prevent their attending and focusing. Only then should primary disorders of attention be considered.

Autistic Diagnoses and Gifted Children

As we discussed in Chapter 8, there has recently been an explosion in the numbers of children diagnosed with autistic disorders like Asperger's syndrome, PDD-NOS, or high-functioning autism. In our experience, gifted children are especially likely to be mislabeled with these diagnoses, because many behaviors commonly seen in gifted children resemble behaviors used to diagnose autistic disorders. Many gifted children show intense and sometimes specialized interests and strong preferences for particular activities; are socially awkward and often isolated because of temperamental introversion, personal sensitivity, and developmental asynchrony; and speak using words and facts not typical for children their age.

Gifted children with other learning challenges (i.e., 2e children) are especially likely to be diagnosed with autistic disorders. Visual difficulties may impair their ability to pick up on facial expressions and body language or to understand "interpersonal space" boundaries. Auditory difficulties may make it hard for them to hear speech in the presence of background noise or pick up on tone-of-voice cues. Sensory sensitivities may cause them to overload or melt down in noisy or crowded public places.

As we said in Chapter 8, autistic diagnoses are best reserved for children with severe impairments in their ability to understand the emotions or motivations of others, to display appropriate empathy and sympathy, to understand what emotions are appropriate to various situations, to generalize knowledge outside the context in which it was learned, to share their intense interests with others in a reciprocal and mutual fashion, and to comprehend abstractions or tolerate imposed transitions and changes in routine. Too often we see gifted children mislabeled with these diagnoses—especially Asperger's syndrome—because they are socially awkward, verbally precocious, and display intense interests, even though they are affectionate, empathetic, manifest emotional reciprocity with their families and others who share their interests, are flexible and imaginative in their use of humor and abstract or metaphorical language, and show strong capacities for fluid creativity and analogical reasoning.

Before any gifted child is labeled autistic, she should have a complete neurological and neuropsychological evaluation to screen for deficits in auditory and visual processing, sensory integration, language processing, and other psychological diagnoses. Interventions should be aimed specifically at identified deficits.

EVALUATING GIFTED CHILDREN WITH SCHOOL-RELATED PROBLEMS

When a gifted child struggles in school, it's important to determine what roles both giftedness and other learning challenges are playing. A general history and examination should be performed as we've described, but additional steps may also be needed.

Gifted abilities are sometimes easier to identify by examining past work than through formal testing. A child who shows signs of truly creative work is likely to be gifted, even if formal assessment criteria fail to confirm this. Every effort should be made to provide the child opportunities to develop in their areas of strength.

It's also important not to overlook gifted abilities in children with learning challenges. Many, many children with reading and spelling difficulties, poor verbal fluency, specific math impairment, or other focal disabilities also have high intellectual potential. It's important to identify their strengths as well as their weaknesses and to foster growth in their areas of strength.

Regarding standardized testing, several comments may be helpful. Achievement tests often do a better job of revealing focal areas of giftedness (for example, in math) than do standard IQ tests. In addition, some highly gifted children do poorly on tests that reward rapid responses. Children who seem creative and insightful, but not particularly fast, will be more accurately assessed using untimed tests.

HELPING GIFTED CHILDREN WITH SCHOOL-RELATED PROBLEMS

Gifted children, like Ferraris and racehorses, are high-maintenance machines. They require lots of food and fuel, plenty of training and tinkering, and occasionally someone to clean up their messes. Below, you'll find our "gifted-child maintenance manual."

Help for Gifted Pattern Processing Issues

In this section, we'll look at ways to help gifted children facing challenges with the four Pattern Processing issues we discussed in our Causes section.

Helping Gifted Children with Enhanced Sensitivity to Sensory Patterns

Highly sensitive gifted children face two primary challenges: sensory overload (with resulting intellectual, physical, and emotional consequences) and distractibility.

Helping Gifted Children with Sensory Overload

The first key to managing sensory overload is to *stop it before it starts.*

- Watch carefully for signs of overload or hints that the child needs time to rest or to be alone. Remember: Gifted children are often introverts who need quiet to recharge their batteries. A preference for solitary activities is not necessarily a sign of pathology. Gifted children often need time to work through ideas, and they may prefer to do this alone. They'll usually let you know when they want more time with friends.
- Watch for environmental triggers that provoke overload, and manage exposures carefully—especially for younger children. Environments with lots of noise and movement, physical jostling and bumping, or visual stimulation are typical culprits.

- Frequently refuel the child's high-consumption engine. High-protein or complex-carbohydrate snacks (e.g., cheese and crackers, jerky, nuts) every two hours can prevent burnout and emotional instability, especially during intense activities—whether physical, mental, or emotional.

Helping Sensitive Gifted Children
Deal with Sensory Distractibility

Don't sweat distractibility unless it's preventing a child from learning. "Noticing everything" may actually foster intelligence and creativity. The mere fact that a child's eyes are out the window one second, focused on her neighbor the next, then scanning her fingernail after that is not necessarily a problem if she's still able to absorb what she needs to. Remember also that *focus and persistence are skills that can be taught and practiced, not chemicals or brain parts that children either have or lack.*

- If distractibility harms learning, the first step is to minimize environmental distracters by modifying the environment.
- The next step is to make sure there are no treatable sensory problems (e.g., vision, hearing) worsening the distractibility.
- Call the child's attention to the distractibility problem, and work with him to improve focus. Provide reminders and, if need be, rewards. Don't jump immediately to medicines unless his problem is truly disabling, and then only until he can learn good focus skills. Children whose focus is easily redirected will eventually learn to direct their own attention without reminders.
- Monitor your own focus. Remember: Alertness and awareness can be great gifts. See how they can be used to further the child's learning.
- Don't forget about variations in learning styles. Gifted children vary dramatically in their approaches to learning. Some are like hummingbirds and prefer frequent small sips of information. Others are like snakes, who take large, infrequent meals, then spend a long time digesting.
- Highly sensitive children are apt to need lots of encouragement and support. Be sure to provide them.

Helping Gifted Children with Enhanced Working Memory Functions

Gifted children often require less time than other children do to master new material. This carries several implications:

- Don't use the time saved to simply rush through the standard curriculum or add more facts. Broaden the curriculum to provide more associations or connections for new information, like historical or thematic context, analogies to other events or facts, and links that embed new information within the network of things they already know through a process of comparing and contrasting. Break down artificial barriers between fields of knowledge. Help them see how ideas are connected. Bring more science into history, more physics or engineering or chemistry into math, and more history into language arts.
- Because these children are "cognitive flypaper," they typically come to class with more incidentally acquired knowledge. Take advantage of their extra "whats" and "whens" to spend more time looking at whys, hows, and what-ifs. In other words, help them draw out the implications of the facts they already know. This is classic Socratic teaching. Not only is it fun and a good way to teach specific information, but it can also teach gifted children how to learn and to teach themselves.
- Because gifted children are often strong incidental learners, remember to use spare moments or the passing events of the day as potential learning experiences. The world is the gifted child's classroom.

Helping Gifted Children with Enhanced Speed of Pattern Retrieval

Gifted children with enhanced pattern retrieval speed require several kinds of special maintenance.

- Put up "roadblocks" that keep them from relying on automatic associations and force them to develop new pathways.

- If a child masters multiplication tables before her classmates do, don't simply rush her to more complex multiplication problems or long division (though acceleration is *part* of the solution). Broaden her exposure to problems that don't rely on rote memory or calculation but require more complicated forms of pattern recognition and reasoning, like interesting number series, story problems, or brainteasers that require spatial or abstract reasoning.
- Similar principles apply in all subjects. If a child quickly masters simple factual knowledge in history and social sciences, challenge him with questions that require inference, analysis of principles, adopting different points of view, and comparing and contrasting different historical events.

- In addition, encourage gifted children to occasionally try processing styles and learning approaches other than their preferred form. For example, a verbally proficient child who easily masters facts about the American Revolution could be asked to design a flag to rally colonists in support of the war. Have him pick colors and images and explain why they would be likely to inspire. Likewise, the artistically or dramatically gifted child could be challenged to create a supply chain to supply bullets and shoes to the Continental Army after the British had blockaded the ports. In other words, pull children into activities where they can't simply rely on "automatic" modes of reasoning to solve problems.

Helping Gifted Children with Enhanced Capacity for Reflection

Highly associational and reflective children need lots of time to process their thoughts and think deeply, not just quickly. If too much information is presented at once (especially if it is presented in a superficial or poorly connected fashion), they will have difficulty learning to their full potential. They may zero in on gaps in their knowledge and focus more on what they don't know than on what they do.

Giving them more time to see how information is connected, helping them to draw out its implications, and providing them with access to resources so they can "fill in the holes" in their knowledge is crucial for these children.

- Highly associational children learn best when information is embedded in a network of detailed connections. They are big-picture thinkers who learn better when they can see how new information fits in with what they already know. Often they prefer to start with broad overviews that describe main themes and overall structures, then gradually "move in" to higher "magnifications" where themes and events are examined in detail.

- Typically they feel more comfortable when they know in advance where they are headed in a particular unit, assignment, or lecture.

- Often they'll want to know why they are studying particular topics and what the information is good for. They are, in other words, interested in the philosophy as well as the substance of their education. Parents and teachers should be able to provide them with convincing answers.

- Highly associational children often need special help to organize their oral and written output. The richness of their ideas may make these ideas difficult to express, either in speech or in writing. Their difficulties with language output may make them seem disorganized and scattered and may obscure their creativity and insight. This is especially true for gifted children with strongly nonverbal (e.g., visual or visual-spatial) reasoning styles. These children typically benefit from organizational strategies like those we've described in our Helping sections in Chapter 6 on language and Chapter 11 on dysgraphia.

Help for Gifted Attention Issues

Many gifted children benefit from steps that help to improve the cooperation between the Chief Creativity and Chief Operations officers. Optimal "gifted attention" involves a balance between these officers that permits both fluid creativity and careful oversight.

- Children who excessively favor their Operations Officer need practice looking for multiple approaches and solutions to problems. They tend to begin detailed planning as soon as the first possible approach pops into their heads, rather than generating a range of approaches from which to choose. These children can benefit from assignments that have fewer problems but ask for multiple different solutions, as opposed to large numbers of problems each requiring only a single solution.

- In contrast, children who tend to excessively favor their Creativity Officer need practice developing detailed operational plans to specific approaches, rather than simply generating multiple possible approaches. They will often need help making and sticking with decisions about which possibilities they'll pursue and which they'll ignore. Often they love their ideas so much that it can feel like a form of punishment to have to abandon any. Sometimes a little bargaining is appropriate. Trade them the opportunity to do several detailed outlines on different topics rather than one fully formed report. Have them practice thinking through the steps of complex procedures, listing overall objectives, materials, starting points, finishing points, et cetera.

- Remember to accommodate variations in working and planning styles. Children may have widely different work patterns yet still maintain functional relationships between their Creativity and Operations officers. Some may prefer to spend more time planning and generating ideas before starting a project, while others may prefer to begin with a few tentative experiments to see if they can determine experimentally which is the right way to head. Either style can work just fine. Just make sure that children of the first type don't become so terrified of failure that they never begin or that children of the second type don't become so overeager to begin that they get themselves into trouble or fritter away their time.

- Also, some children may work best by sticking with a project for extended periods, while others prefer shorter work sessions with time for rest and reflection between. Either style (styles that seem to be innate rather than learned) may be appropriate.

- For more ideas on helping children balance creativity and organization, see Chapter 7.

Interventions That Can Help
All Gifted Children

Gifted children should be taught in detail how their brains think and learn. Most gifted children are naturally interested in "thinking about thinking" (or *metacognition*), and by enlisting their intelligence, creativity, and cooperation in this process they can become skilled thinking and learning strategists.

Understanding the Nature of Thinking

Teaching children the information we've presented in this book about Information Input, Pattern Processing, Output for Action, and Attention can help them better understand and manage their own thinking and learning. They can learn what kinds of thinking and learning styles work best for them and how to develop learning and problem-solving strategies that accentuate their strengths and avoid their weaknesses. This instruction will be fairly basic in younger children, but over time it can grow more complex.

- Gifted children should be taught the importance of linking new information with as many associations as possible. Specific mnemonic (memory) strategies (like those discussed in Chapter 3 and elsewhere) can help children use associations to improve retrieval, creativity, and problem solving.
- Gifted children should also be taught the important role of analogy (i.e., detecting likeness or resemblance) in creativity in problem solving. Gifted children should constantly ask themselves, *What is this like, or what does it remind me of? Or if I break it into smaller parts, what are the parts like? Or is the whole already part of something larger?* This will make finding analogies and building associations automatic and habitual for them.
- Teaching children about different learning and thinking styles can also help them realize that no single individual or thinking style

functions optimally in every situation. That's why we can all benefit from learning to work with others who possess different abilities and talents. For example, a highly creative person can often accomplish more when paired with a highly organized partner. Verbal and visual thinkers can help each other. A great thinker who is pessimistic or timid can benefit from an energetic and upbeat partner. By learning what they're good at—and what they lack— gifted kids can learn to form partnerships with those whose skills complement their own.

Understanding the Nature of Knowledge

Gifted children can also benefit from learning about the nature of knowledge. Knowledge is often presented as if it were acquired primarily by taking classes or reading books. Expertise is likewise presented as mastery of an existing body of information. Both presentations are misleading.

- While gifted children need to master the existing knowledge base, they must also learn how knowledge is acquired and develops as a human endeavor. They need, in other words, to learn that all the information they read about in books was discovered or created by particular persons, at particular times, and in particular places. They also need to learn that they, too, can participate in the process of advancing the stores of human knowledge.
- One critical fact that gifted children must learn is that knowledge is not advanced by focusing solely on what is already known, but also on what is not. Schools sometimes imply the opposite: that expertise means mastering the available knowledge base better than other people. While expertise does require mastering a body of knowledge, it's also true that the greatest experts are those with the clearest sense of what remains unknown or still to be discovered.
- Children should learn the difference between *academic expertise*, which consists of mastering a knowledge base, and *creative expertise*, which combines academic mastery with the ability to see what remains unknown—the holes and gaps that need filling and the questions that need answering. In all the creative fields that gifted children are ideally suited for, expertise consists of being able to see the

problems that haven't been solved, the needs that haven't been met, and the avenues that haven't been explored. This is true in science, art, business, or any other truly creative field. We must do a better job teaching our students how to look for the holes in existing knowledge or available techniques. Spending too much time teaching facts and not enough pointing out what's still unknown conveys the impression that everything worth knowing has already been discovered.

- To help your gifted children avoid this mistake, teach them to develop the habit of compiling lists of "nonknowledge": that is, things we still have more to learn about (like how the brain works or what mediates gravitational force) or technologies that could be made to work better (like home video technology or cars that run on entirely clean and renewable energy sources). Have them start with problems they experience, questions they can't answer, things they wish were real but aren't, or things they wish they could do but can't; then have them imagine ways these things might be otherwise. This is the heart of creativity.

- Although it might seem that training children to habitually "look for problems" would make them pessimistic or faultfinding, actually the opposite is true. The goal of this process is to teach children to see problems as opportunities and to realize how many opportunities they actually have to contribute to the world something really new and valuable. We see too many young Alexander the Greats, who complain that there are no more worlds to conquer and that all the great discoveries have been made. This procedure is the perfect antidote to the paralysis this oversight can cause.

- Gifted children should also be taught that most advances in knowledge result from attempts to solve *practical problems*. This is true in science, mathematics, technology, languages, political theory, history, and even art. Teaching subjects like science and math not simply as abstract bodies of knowledge but as collections of solutions to practical problems can make them far more interesting and personally meaningful to gifted children.

- Linking particular facts to stories about their discovery or development can both make them more memorable and illustrate their uses and benefits. By describing the needs or circumstances that led to particular discoveries or inventions, we can show our students both how particular information has proven useful in the past and how it might be useful in the present. These real-world examples can prove especially beneficial with gifted children who often ask, "Why should I learn this?" or "What's this stuff good for?"

- In addition, showing children how people have solved problems in the past gives them an invaluable store of analogies for future problem solving. Each academic discipline is essentially a long history of searching for solutions to problems. Bringing this process to the fore can greatly help children develop their own problem-solving abilities.

- Finally, it is vital to teach gifted children to assess the quality and reliability of information. In the pre-Internet age, when most students got their information for school projects or personal study through a library, source materials were often relatively few in number, but what was available had been screened by a librarian to make sure it was acceptable. Today most students have access to a virtually unlimited supply of electronic information, but they lack an "Internet librarian" to recommend or screen resources. Teaching students the critical skills they need to assess this information is crucial. (Specific materials that can be used to help children develop their critical thinking skills are listed in Resources.)

Special Help for Twice-Exceptional Students

As important as it is to help 2e students overcome their weaknesses, it's even more important to maintain the primary focus of their education on their strengths.

- Often it's difficult to convince 2e children to accept accommodations, especially as they grow older. Many aren't comfortable having needs that differ from their classmates' or with being singled out for "preferential" treatment. For example, a dysgraphic child may resent a laptop; a child with background-noise difficulties may resist a headset or desktop speaker. These children should be encouraged to see both the importance of maximizing their abilities to learn and the valuable role they can play in educating others about learning differences, twice-exceptionality, and the value of accepting one's individuality. When 2e children realize they can teach valuable lessons, they may be more willing to accept special accommodations.

- One of our favorite things to do with 2e children is to share stories from the lives of famous 2e people throughout history. Finding such examples is remarkably easy (e.g., Winston Churchill, Albert Einstein, Helen Keller, Thomas Edison, Isaac Newton, Barbara McClintoch, Ansel Adams, Agatha Christie etc.).

Help for Gifted Children with Social and Emotional Problems

Many of the social and emotional problems gifted children face can be lessened by helping them find friends and peers, by providing an educational setting where they fit in both socially and intellectually, and by eliminating problems that arise from the "difficult" character traits. In the sections that follow, we'll discuss each.

Helping Gifted Children Find Friends and Peers

One of the chief challenges facing gifted children is avoiding a sense of personal isolation and alienation. Establishing relationships with appropriate peers or mentors is the key.

- The combination of highly asynchronous development, strong personal interests, independent judgment, and (usually) introversion often makes finding an ideal best friend or "band of brothers/sisters" hard for the gifted child. In many cases, it's both easier and more satisfying to help the child build "specialized" relationships with others (whether children or older mentors) who share particular interests.

- The opportunities for finding same-age friends with whom they can form more typical "best friend" attachments will usually be greater in special gifted programs, like magnet schools or districtwide gifted programs. There are various national organizations, Internet lists, and local gifted groups that can help bring gifted children together (see Resources).

Helping Gifted Children Find the Right School Placement

- For children who are capable of higher-level work across all academic subjects, grade acceleration or "skipping" (sometimes even by several grades) is an excellent but often underused option. Many school districts tend to frown on grade acceleration, usually out of a concern that it may harm a child's social development. Yet the clear preponderance of research on grade acceleration, as reviewed in the 2004 Templeton National Report on Acceleration, entitled *A Nation Deceived*, shows such concerns to be unfounded. *A Nation Deceived* lays out a thorough (and in our belief convincing) case that grade acceleration can be beneficial for many highly gifted children. (This report can be downloaded from the Internet for free at www.nationdeceived.org.)

- Gifted children who vary markedly in their abilities in different academic subjects may require acceleration in only one or a few subjects. Multigrade classrooms (where students work independently and at their own pace) are often a good option for such children.

- Gifted children often flourish in magnet schools or private schools for gifted children, yet even these schools typically have difficulty meeting the needs of the most highly gifted and 2e children. Home-schooling can be a good option for these children, as we'll discuss below.

Help for Challenges Due to "Difficult" Gifted Character Traits

In this section, we'll discuss ways to help gifted children who face challenges due to three types or clusters of character traits: introversion; perfectionism, personal sensitivity, and emotional intensity; and independence.

Help for Challenges Due to Introversion

The first step in dealing with introversion-related challenges is to become familiar with the nature and extent of normal temperamental differences. For this purpose, we highly recommend Mary Sheedy Kurcinka's excellent book *Raising Your Spirited Child* and Dr. William Carey's *Temperament and the Child*. There are also helpful articles on introversion by the psychologist and giftedness specialist Linda Silverman at the Gifted Development Center's Web site, www.gifteddevelopment.com.

While it is neither desirable nor even possible to turn an introverted child into an extroverted one, most introverted gifted children can grow up to be socially and interpersonally adept adults who display few or no outward signs of "shyness" (although they usually prefer to spend free time in quiet or solitary ways). It is important to foster the growth of the introverted child's social and communication skills so that the child can learn to interact and communicate effectively with others.

- Provide occasional opportunities for social interactions, especially with those who share similar interests, but do not deprive the child of necessary time for rest and reflection.
- For children whose introversion makes speaking in class difficult, providing practice in public speaking and the formal exchange of ideas is essential. Junior Toastmasters, debate or forensics clubs, or even drama societies are all useful formats to help children get over their fear of speaking in public. Local information about such groups, which are often affiliated with 4-H clubs, churches or synagogues, or local schools, can be found on the Internet.

Perfectionism, Personal Sensitivity, and Emotional Intensity

Excessive perfectionism, personal sensitivity, and emotional intensity often (though not always) present as a cluster in certain gifted children. As we mentioned above, helping these children requires carefully balancing their desire for perfection with their need to become more accepting of their own and others' shortcomings.

- Often gifted children experience perfectionism problems when they possess advanced critical judgment but only age-appropriate performance skills. They may be all too aware of how their performances fall short of their conceptions, and unforgiving of their defects. It is important not to try to convince these children that their critical judgments are wrong and that their performances are actually wonderful. They will spot your lie and become even angrier. Instead discuss their frustrations realistically. Tell them what you struggled with at their age and how you worked to develop your skills. Read them biographies of famous people who struggled to succeed (as nearly all have), and help them develop a realistic assessment of how much hard work is required to build skill in any area. One excellent book that provides more information on this topic is Dr. Martin Seligman's *The Optimistic Child*.

- It's also important that these children see the adults in their lives struggle to master tasks they find difficult. Too often, our children see us engaged only in tasks we like and do well, so they never see us flounder, fail, or struggle to make progress. Yet they must constantly perform a whole range of tasks that they can perform only at beginner levels—including activities they have little natural talent for. Well, it's time to even up the score. If your child struggles with perfectionism and you're a klutz, then dust off that tennis racket. If second languages have always been tough for you, why don't you try to learn Spanish along with her? Lousy bowler? Bad at math? Do your drawings look like you sketched them on the back of a galloping horse? Then you— and your child—are in luck. These are all excellent opportunities for you to model perseverance, self-acceptance, good sportsmanship, and optimism. Remember: Your inability is your child's opportunity!

- It's also important to discuss perfectionism, intensity, and emotional sensitivity openly with these children. An excellent book that can be used to facilitate discussions is *Perfectionism: What's Bad About Being Too Good* by Miriam Adderholt and Jan Goldberg.

The Fiercely Independent Learner

Dealing with fiercely independent and self-directed gifted children also involves a careful balancing act in which it's all too easy to go to one extreme or the other. On the one side, we've seen unfortunate numbers of adults (including some "experts") who promote an almost idolatrous reverence for the supposed capacity of even very young gifted children to make wise choices with very little adult guidance, even on very important matters. This is nonsense, and in some cases very harmful nonsense. Gifted children are still children—irrespective of their intelligence—and there are many matters about which they have insufficient experience to choose wisely. At the other extreme, we've seen parents who believe that the proper approach to strongly independent children is to try to break their will.

- A healthy approach should avoid both extremes. Highly independent gifted children should be gradually given increasing responsibility to manage their own freedom—as they show they are ready for it—while also being taught to respect necessary limits. Where limits are absolutely necessary, adults must perform the tricky job of providing consistent and clearly explained guidelines, while providing freedom in areas where mistakes will yield tolerable consequences. Adults should also provide reasons for the limits they set, to avoid appearing arbitrary and to demonstrate that they have the child's best interests at heart. On important issues, though, it's crucial for adults to uphold the limits they set. These children must learn to control their emotions and delay gratification.

Counseling for Gifted Children

Gifted children who are significantly anxious or depressed require the help of an experienced mental-health professional. Because the child's giftedness may play a key role in these problems, it is important to find a mental-health professional with experience dealing with gifted children. A list of such practitioners is available on the Web site of the organization SENG (Supporting Emotional Needs of the Gifted, www.sengifted.org).

A Special Kind of Help:
Homeschooling for Gifted Children

Many gifted children have special educational needs and "unusual" learning styles that make it hard to find a school that's just right for them. This is doubly true of 2e children. As a result, many parents of gifted children have turned to homeschooling. Homeschooling is attractive for several reasons:

- Homeschooling provides a completely customizable education. This is particularly helpful for children whose abilities vary widely from subject to subject. Such children can accelerate in areas of strength while also receiving remediation in areas of disability. This individualized education is also useful for children who are working at a markedly different level than same-age peers and would have to be skipped several grade levels at school to find a class at an appropriate instructional level.
- Homeschooling can also be tailored to fit the special needs of gifted children with unusual pattern processing and attention styles. The "python" who learns best from intense and prolonged "digestion" of a single topic and the "hummingbird" who prefers frequent little "sips" from many different subjects can both be accommodated. Children who learn best through personal experience are often particularly well served by homeschooling.
- A homeschool curriculum can also be tailored to focus more intensively on higher-order thinking, problem solving, special interest-based activities, and interdisciplinary study than can most standard class curricula.

In the United States, homeschooling is an increasingly popular option for teaching gifted students. One study by gifted-education specialist Kathi

Kearney of gifted children with IQs in the 148 to 200-plus range showed that 43 percent had homeschooled at some point during their K-12 years, and 22 percent were currently homeschooling. In their excellent book on gifted challenges, *Genius Denied*, Jan and Bob Davidson (founders of the Davidson Institute for Talent Development, which provides educational support for some of the nation's most highly gifted young people) reported that approximately 50 percent of their young scholarship recipients have been homeschooled.

Many parents who are attracted by the potential advantages of homeschooling hesitate to try it for several reasons.

- First, they are concerned that homeschooling might harm their child's academic progress, primarily because of their own lack of training as teachers. This issue was recently reviewed by Dr. Brian Ray in the *Journal of College Admission*. He concluded, based on an examination of the nine available studies that have addressed this question, that "parents' teacher-certification has little relationship with their children's academic achievement" while homeschooling. In the same paper, Ray also cited "dozens" of available studies of educational outcome of homeschooled children. These studies show consistently that homeschooled children, as a group, outperform children in mainstream institutional schools on standardized tests. On tests like the SAT and the ACT, homeschoolers as a group average from the sixty-fifth to the eightieth percentile, versus the public-school average of the fiftieth percentile. For parents who still feel uncertain of their ability to be their child's primary teacher, other homeschooling options are available, including online instruction, teaching consortiums, and home tutoring (see Resources).
- Second, many parents are concerned that homeschooling may hinder their child's social development (socialization). Research again belies this concern. Socialization is not the process of turning a child into a copy of same-age peers but of helping a child develop into a happy, well-functioning, and emotionally mature adult. Recently researchers surveyed over seven thousand U.S. adults who'd been homeschooled as children. They found that when analyzed using various psychological constructs designed to measure emotional

and social health, these adults appeared to be at least as well off as adults who received conventional schooling. In fact, when looking at measures of civic involvement, they participated in some form of on-going community-service activity at almost twice the rate of the general population (71 percent versus 37 percent) and voted at more than twice the rate of same-age peers (76 percent versus 29 percent).

• Third, many parents are concerned that homeschooling may hurt their child's ability to get into a desirable college. Such a concern may have been justified in the past, but at present there is little cause for worry. Homeschoolers are very competitive in gaining admission to colleges—even elite universities. A recent survey of college admissions officers showed that over half of the college admissions officers they surveyed expected homeschooled students to be at least as successful in college as traditional high-school graduates, and an additional 22 percent expected homeschooled students to be more successful. *Time* magazine cited data from Stanford University's 2000 admission cycle showing that its acceptance rate for homeschoolers (26 percent) was nearly double its general acceptance rate. In the review cited earlier, Dr. Brian Ray quoted an admissions officer at Stanford University as saying that homeschoolers' applications showed an "unusually high occurrence of a key ingredient, which they term, 'intellectual vitality.'" The article also quoted an admissions officer at Dartmouth University as stating that "homeschoolers have a distinct advantage [in performing well once they get to college] because of the individualized instruction they have received." Ray also quoted Joyce Reed, an associate dean at Brown, who called homeschoolers "the epitome of Brown students," because "they've learned to be self-directed, they take risks, they face challenges with total fervor, and they don't back off."

Homeschooling is not for everyone: Families must have a parent or other adult who can be at home much of the time and who feels emotionally, physically, and mentally up for the job. But for those for whom it might be possible, homeschooling should be seriously considered whenever a child has difficulties in a classroom setting.

Resources
and References

In this section, we include books, research literature, and Web resources available for those interested in further study or finding helpful products. This is not intended as a full resource reference for information presented in this book. The books and Web resources are for the most part written at a level that can be approached by anyone reading this book. The research literature is intended for the professional or highly motivated parent who is interested in understanding the latest scientific and medical findings.

General Web Resources for *Learning and Learning Challenges*

www.mislabeledchild.com (Additional resources and important updates for the information presented in this book.)

www.neurolearning.com (Our home Web site, which contains helpful information, articles, educational products, links to other sites, information about our clinic and upcoming speaking engagements, and an index for the articles on our blog.)

www.eideneurolearningblog.blogspot.com (A daily review of recent research and information related to education, learning, and the brain.)

www.allkindsofminds.com (Web site for children's education and the learning challenges pioneer Mel Levine's All Kinds of Minds, with lots of wonderful links and information.)

www.cec.org (Council for Exceptional Children.)

www.devdelay.org (A nonprofit site listing many Internet links helpful to parents and professionals working with developmentally delayed children.)

www.ldonline.com (Wonderful online library of resources containing many articles about learning disabilities and helpful educational strategies.)

www.schwablearning.com (Terrific resource for online articles about learning, learning differences, and strategies to help the kids who have them, from the innovative businessman—and dyslexic—Charles Schwab. Every year, Schwab Learning also provides updates about federal tax law and tax benefits for parents of children with learning disabilities.)

www.edutopia.org (Site for the George Lucas Foundation's educational magazine. Articles cover promising practices in alternative learning and general news of interest to the educational community.)

www.wrightslaw.com (Very helpful reference site about issues relevant to special-education law. The site is updated regularly.)

Chapter 1. The Mislabeled Child

Books

Diagnostic and Statistical Manual of Mental Disorders, 4th edition, Text Revision (DSM-IV-TR). 2000. Arlington, VA: American Psychiatric Publishing, Inc. The source from which labels are most commonly drawn to describe the learning challenges of children.

Web Sites and References

www.cass.city.ac.uk/media/stories/story_9_1148_44300.html (Dyslexic entrepreneurs.)

Chapter 2. How to Get the Most from This Book

Books

Carter, Rita. 1998. *Mapping the Mind*. Berkeley, CA: University of California Press. A beautifully constructed and fairly recent review of the relationship between brain structure and function.

Hawkins, Jeff, and Sandra Blakeslee. 2004. *On Intelligence*. New York, NY: Times Books. A fascinating look at information processing in the brain and the nature of intelligence by a prominent high-tech entrepreneur with an expert understanding of neuroscience.

Stafford, Tom, and Matt Webb. 2005. *Mind Hacks: Tips & Tools for Using Your Brain*. Sebastopol, CA: O'Reilly Media. A fascinating journey into the phenomenology of brain function that explains many of the surprising features of perception. This is why we love the brain!

Chapter 3. Gone in Sixty Seconds

Books

Bell, Nanci. 1991. *Visualizing and Verbalizing*. San Luis Obispo, CA: Gander Educational Publishing. This is the "text" for the Lindamood-Bell's Visualizing and Verbalizing method for using visualization to keep auditory information "in mind."

Levine, Mel. 2002. *A Mind at a Time*. New York, NY: Simon & Schuster. Dr. Levine, one of America's foremost learning experts, shares helpful information about the varying experiences of children with different learning and memory problems.

Vitale, Barbara Meister. 1982. *Unicorns Are Real*. Torrance, CA: Jalmar Press. Unable to read until the age of twelve, Barbara Vitale went on to earn a master's degree in early childhood education. This book has many practical strategies to help children with visual, auditory, and combined difficulties in memory.

West, Thomas G. 1997. *In the Mind's Eye*. Amherst, NY: Prometheus Books. A fascinating account of the importance of nonverbal reasoning as displayed in the lives of some of history's most important thinkers and scientists.

Williams, Linda VerLee. 1983. *Teaching for the Two-Sided Mind*. New York, NY: Simon & Schuster. This very readable book was far ahead of its time: It provides practical tips for using direct experience, multisensory learning, visual thinking, fantasy, and metaphor in teaching.

Research Literature

Goldin-Meadow, S., and S. M. Wagner. 2005. How our hands help us learn. *TRENDS in Cognitive Sciences* 9:234–41.

Klingberg, T., E. Fernell, P. J. Olesen, M. Johnson, P. Gustafsson, K. Dahlstrom, C. Gillberg, H. Forssberg, and H. Westerberg. 2005. Computerized training of working memory in children with ADHD—a randomized, controlled trial. *Journal of the American Academy of Child Adolescent Psychiatry*, 44:177–86.

Meister, I. G., T. Krings, H. Foltys, B. Boroojerdi, M. Muller, R. Topper, and A. Thron. 2004. Playing piano in the mind—an fMRI study on music imagery and performance in pianists. *Cognitive Brain Research* 19:219–28.

Montgomery, J. W. 2003. Working memory comprehension in children with specific language impairment: what we know so far. *Journal of Communication Disorders* 36:221–31.

Rowe, K., K. Rowe, and J. Pollard. 2004. Literacy, behaviour and auditory processing: building "fences" at the top of the "cliff" in preference to "ambulance services" at the bottom. *ACER: Improving Learning, Research Conference*. www.acer.edu.au/research/programs/documents/Rowe-ACERResearchConf_2004Paper.pdf

Wright, I., and J. Limond. 2004. A developmental framework for memory rehabilitation in children. *Pediatric Rehabilitation* 7:85–96.

Web Sites and Resources

www.ldonline.org/article.php?max=20&special_grouping=&id=1087&loc=89   (Regina Richards article describing helpful memory strategies.)

www.mindtools.com (Although directed to business managers who want to optimize their learning and memory, this site will also be helpful to many students who want to learn more about how to improve skills like time management, remembering, and organization.)

www.readingrockets.org (PBS site with articles about good books for younger readers, along with reading and teaching helps.)

journals.sped.org/EC/Archive_Articles/VOL.36NO.2NovDec2003_TEC_Kleinheksel36-2.pdf (Helpful article from Kleinheksel and Summy about how to improve learning and social behavior with memory strategies.)

www.betterendings.org/Homeschool/Fun/mnemonic.htm (Site with good mnemonic strategies.)

www.ldonline.org.ld/ld_indepth/teachers/mnemonic_strategies.html (A great article on mnemonic strategies.)

Chapter 4. Overlooking the Obvious

Books

Hull, John M. 1990. *Touching the Rock*. New York, NY: Pantheon Press. This is a moving diary of a university lecturer going blind. Hull shares many insights that will be valuable for parents of children with significant visual challenges—even though their deficits may be partial. Hull talks sensitively about interpersonal interactions, the sense of time, the compensations of touch and hearing, emotions, and spiritual issues.

Lane, Kenneth A. 1993. *Developing Your Child for Success*. Lewisville, TX: Learning Potentials Publishers. Workbook for many at-home vision exercises that cover eye movements for reading, hand-eye coordination, right-left orientation problems, reversals, and helping the eyes work together. This book would be most helpful for a child who has been diagnosed by an eye professional.

Vermeij, Geerat. 1998. *Privileged Hands: A Scientific Life*. New York, NY: W. H. Freeman. This is an inspirational biography of a scientist who lost all vision as a toddler. His whole family pulled together, learning Braille and also learning how to translate the visual world into words. He became a university professor and won a MacArthur "genius" grant.

Willey, Liane Holliday. 1999. *Pretending to Be Normal*. London, UK: Jessica Kingsley Publishers. Liane is writing about her personal experiences with Asperger's syndrome, but she relates challenges that come with visual memory and visual perceptual difficulties. This would be a helpful book for parents learning to understand what day-to-day challenges their child faces with getting around, trying to interpret emotions from faces, and more.

Research Literature

Bravo, M. J., and H. Farid. 2004. Search for a category target in clutter. *Perception* 33:643–52.

Dutton, G. N. 2003. Cognitive vision, its disorders and differential diagnosis in adults and children: knowing where and what things are. *Eye* 17:289–304.

Laeng, B., and D. S. Teodorescu. 2002. Eye scanpaths during visual imagery reenact those of perception of the same visual scene. *Cognitive Science* 26:207–31.

Oppenheimer, J. 1972. All about me. *Journal of Learning Disabilities* 5:407–22.

Porro, G., E. M. Dekker, O. Van Nieuwenhuizen, D. Wittebol-Post, M. B. H. Schilder, A. J. F. Schenk-Rootlieb, and W. F. Treffers. 1998. Visual behaviors of neurologically impaired children with cerebral visual impairment: an ethological study. *British Journal of Ophthalmology* 82:1231–35.

Riesenhuber, M. 2004. An action video game modifies visual processing. *TRENDS in Neurosciences* 27:72–74.

Rosenberg, T., T. Flage, E. Hansen, R. Riise, S. L. Rudanko, G. Viggosson, and K. Tornqvist. 1996. Incidence of registered visual impairment in the Nordic child population. *British Journal of Ophthalmology* 80:49–53.

Scheiman, M. M., R. W. Hertle, R. W. Beck, A. R. Edwards, E. Birch, S. A. Cotter, E. R. Crouch, Jr., O. A. Cruz, B. V. Davitt, S. Donahue, J. M. Holmes, D. W. Lyon, M. X. Repka, N. A. Sala, D. I. Silbert, D. W. Suh, and S. M. Tamkins. 2005. Randomized trial of treatment of amblyopia in children aged 7 to 17 years. *Archives of Ophthalmology* 123:437–47.

Scheiman, M., L. Mitchell, S. Cotter, J. Cooper, M. Kulp, M. Rouse, E. Borsting, R. London, and J. Wensveen. 2005. A randomized clinical trial of treatments for convergence insufficiency in children. *Archives of Ophthalmology* 123:14–24.

Sigmundsson, H., P. C. Hanson, and J. B. Talcott. 2003. Do "clumsy" children have visual deficits? *Behavioural Brain Research* 139:123–29.

von Karolyi, C., E. Winner, W. Gray, and G. F. Sherman. 2003. Dyslexia linked to talent: global visual-spatial ability. *Brain and Language* 85:427–31.

Web Sites and Resources

www.covd.org (College of Optometrists in Vision Development.)

www.oep.org (Optometric Extension Program Foundation, has lots of good visual materials.)

www.pavevision.org (Parents Active for Vision Education.)

www.prosopagnosia.com (Great site by a person with prosopagnosia.)

www.findarticles.com/p/articles/mi_m1175/is_n5_v31/ai_21050185/print (Helpful article originally published by *Psychology Today* and written by Deborah Blum entitled "Face It! Facial Expressions Are Crucial to Emotional Health.")

Games to Promote Visual Attention

Side Tracking: Old computer games, like Pong, PacMan, Super Mario Brothers. The screen should be large, and children should follow targets without moving head. Free games are available on the Internet at sites like www.play.vg. Sing-along songs with a bouncing ball for lyrics are also good for younger children.

Visual Attention: The best games for enhancing central visual attention require focusing on the center area rather than at the periphery, and a large screen (TV or PC rather than handheld). Good games include Lucas Arts' Droidworks, Disney's Tarzan, Tony Hawk Snowboarding. Also useful is 3-D Pong (www.addictinggames.com/3dpong.html).

Visual Planning: LEGOs, K'nex, Zoobs, Tinker Toys, Marble Runs, Roller Coasters, Mazes, Tetris (if a child struggles with Tetris, she may fare better with the plastic or wooden version of Tetris or a software program like Tetris Worlds, which projects the falling shape to help children select the correctly fitting pieces), LEGO Architecture (www.Edventures.com), Rush Hour.

Chapter 5. What? Huh? Auditory Problems in Children

Books

Bellis, Teri James. 2002. *When the Brain Can't Hear.* New York, NY: Pocket Books. This is a wonderful book for parents, teachers, and other professionals on auditory processing disorders. Writing with sensitivity and expertise, Dr. Bellis describes interventions for auditory processing disorders at all ages.

———. 2003. *Assessment and Management of Central Auditory Processing Disorders.* New York, NY: Delmar Learning. This is a more technical book for auditory and other clinical professionals who require more details about individual tests and general management of CAPD.

Biderman, Beverly. 1998. *Wired for Sound.* Toronto, Canada: Trifolium Books. This is a wonderful personal account of one woman's experience with hearing loss and cochlear implantation. Beverly Biderman is sensitive and insightful, and she relates many experiences of auditory processing impairment that will be helpful for parents trying to understand their children's experiences.

Kaplan, Harriet, Scott J. Bally, and Carol Garretson. 1991. *Speechreading.* Washington, D.C.: Gallaudet University Press. This book was designed for deaf or extremely hard-of-hearing individuals, but selected sections are helpful for parents of children with milder hearing issues. Topics covered include details about environmental factors that affect hearing, anticipating vocabulary, developing "self-help" vocabulary to clarify hearing, et cetera.

Research Literature

Dean, A., and M. Davison. 2002. Pediatric hearing loss. *Clinician Reviews:* www.findarticles.com/p/articles/mi_m0BUY/is_11_12/ai_94871263.

Mengler, E. D., J. H. Hogben, P. Michie, and D. V. M. Bishop. 2005. Poor frequency discrimination is related to oral language disorder in children: a psychoacoustic study. *Dyslexia* 11:155–73.

Moore, D. R., J. F. Rosenberg, and J. S. Coleman. 2005. Discrimination training of phonemic contrasts enhances phonological processing in mainstream school education. *Brain and Language* 94:72–85.

Mraz, N. R., and R. L. Folmer. Overprotection-hyperacusis-phonophobia and tinnitus retraining therapy: a case study. www.healthyhearing.com/healthyhearing/newroot/articles

Niskar, A. S., S. M. Kieszak, A. E. Holmes, E. Esteban, C. Rubin, and D. J. Brody. 2001. Estimated prevalence of noise-induced hearing threshold shifts among children 6 to 19 years of age: the Third National Health and Nutrition Examination Survey, 1988–1994, United States. *Pediatrics* 108:40–43.

Working Group of the American Speech-Language-Hearing Association on Auditory Processing Disorders. 2005. (Central) Auditory Processing Disorders. 2005. 1–20. www.asha.org/members/deskref-journals/deskref/default

Web Sites and Resources

www.asha.org (Home page for American Speech-Language-Hearing Association. Good articles and resources are available.)

www.eslgold.com (Free English teaching and learning site with materials for practice with speaking, listening, reading, writing, grammar, vocabulary, and idioms.)

www.esl-lab.com (Randall's cyberlistening lab. Great auditory practice.)

www.lifelineamp.com/research_13facts.cfm (Useful facts about hearing problems in children.)

www.tsbvi.edu/Outreach/seehear/spring00/centralauditory.htm (CAPD overview.)

Chapter 6. The Communication Gap

Books

Christopher, Doris. 1999. *Come to the Table: A Celebration of Family Life*. New York, NY: Warner Books. Fun and helpful suggestions for enlivening family conversation.

Garner, Alan. 1997. *Conversationally Speaking*. Los Angeles, CA: Lowell House. Excellent simple resource to teach children the basics of drawing others out in conversation.

Hoffman, Gary. 1986. *Writeful*. Huntington Beach, CA: Verve Press. Although this was written for older students, selected ideas and lessons will be useful for children who have strong visual or personal memory-based learning styles. Topics include capturing complex subjects, simplifying complex subjects, explaining with dialogue.

Kellaher, Karen. 1999. *101 Picture Prompts to Spark Super Writing (Grades 3–5)*. New York, NY: Scholastic Press. Many young students have an easier time writing from pictures than from stories.

Lattyak, James, and Susan Dedrick. 2002. *Multiple Word Meanings*. Austin, TX: Pro-Ed. A helpful collection of picture worksheets demonstrating and encouraging practice with multiple word meanings.

Margulies, Nancy, and Nusa Maal. 2001. *Mapping Inner Space: Learning and Teaching Visual Mapping*. Chicago, IL: Zephyr Press. Great ideas for visually mapping ideas.

Noden, Harry R. 1999. *Image Grammar*. Portsmouth, NH: Heinemann. This is a wonderful book to teach the art of writing to older students and some gifted younger visual learners. It provides practical illustrations for descriptive writing and is a cinematographer's guide to writing.

Silverman, Linda Krieger. 2002. *Upside-Down Brilliance: The Visual-Spatial Learner*. Denver, CO: DeLeon Publishing. A wonderful reference full of good advice for parents of children who think and learn best through nonverbal channels.

Simonson, Les. 1996. *Writing in Narrative*. Crossville, TN: Elijah Press. These inexpensive books are out of print but are still available with some distributors. They are very simple, but helpful for some reluctant writers. Describes a seven-sentence organization for writing that includes graphic prompts for when, who, where, starting event, problem, problem solution, and conclusion.

Sowell, Thomas. 2001. *The Einstein Syndrome*. New York, NY: Basic Books. Excellent resource for gifted late-talking children.

Terban, Melvin. 1998. *Scholastic Dictionary of Idioms*. New York, NY: Scholastic Reference Press. Great source for idioms, which also reinforces wordplay and multiple word meanings.

Winner, Michelle Garcia. 2000. *Inside Out: What Makes a Person with Social Cognitive Deficits Tick?* Published by Michelle Garcia Winner (mwinner@worldnet.att.net). A wonderful social-skills book, intended for children with autistic spectrum disorders but useful for any child who has difficulties with social interactions.

Research Literature

Booth, J. R., B. MacWhinney, and Y. Harasaki. 2000. Developmental differences in visual and auditory processing of complex sentences. *Child Development* 71:981–1003.

Botting, N., and G. Conti-Ramsden. 1999. Pragmatic language impairment without autism. *Autism* 3:371–96.

Demonet, J.-F., G. Thierry, and D. Cardebat. 2005. Renewal of the neurophysiology of language: functional neuroimaging. *Physiological Reviews* 85:49–95.

Web Sites and Resources

www.linguisystems.com (Web site for LinguiSystems, publisher of some excellent materials for a variety of the problems discussed in this chapter. Two of our favorites are the social-language books *Room 14* and *Room 28*.)

http://members.tripod.com/Caroline_Bowen/devel2.htm (Helpful developmental milestones.)

www.writing-edu.com (Dvds and videos to help students organize their writing and uses a key-word approach to help students learn how to use paraphrase and "dress" up their writing.)

www.longleaf.net/ggrow/WriteVisual/WriteVisual.html (Helpful writing approaches for nonverbal thinkers.)

www.writeathome.net. (Online writing tutorials.)

Chapter 7. Getting It All Together

Books

Adams, James L. 1986. *Conceptual Blockbusting: A Guide to Better Ideas*. Reading, MA: Addison-Wesley Publishing. Fascinating and useful book on innovation by a design professor at Stanford.

Amabile, Teresa M. 1989. *Growing Up Creative*. Buffalo, NY: Creative Education Foundation Press. This is a good introductory book for parents who want to think about how to encourage intrinsic motivation and creativity in their children.

———. 1996. *Creativity in Context*. Boulder, CO: Westview Press. A more detailed book on creativity suitable for parents or professionals.

Black, Howard and Sandra. 1992. *Organizing Thinking Book II*. Pacific Grove, CA: Critical Thinking Books & Software. This is a book with common formats for graphic organizers. Subject areas include language arts, writing, social studies, math, science, and personal problem solving.

Brooks, Robert, and Sam Goldstein. 2001. *Raising Resilient Children*. Lincolnwood, IL: Contemporary Books. This is a wonderful and practical guide to help parents foster optimism and resiliency in their children.

Carey, William B. 1998. *Understanding Your Child's Temperament*. New York, NY: Simon & Schuster. This classic work by Dr. Carey may be a bit hard to find, but it's worth it. This book has helpful information for every parent.

Dornbush, Marilyn P., and Sheryl K. Pruitt. 2000. *Teaching the Tiger*. Duarte, CA: Hope Press. This manual lists common school accommodations for children with attention disorders, Tourette's syndrome, and obsessive-compulsive disorder. It may be helpful for parents or for other professionals trying to decide on appropriate accommodations.

Freed, Jeffrey, and L. Parson. 1998. *Right-Brained Children in a Left-Brained World*. New York, NY: Simon & Schuster. This is a short and very readable book with practical advice for parents regarding education and specific help in areas such as organization, spelling, reading, math, writing, and study in general.

Greene, Ross W. 2001. *The Explosive Child*. New York, NY: Quill. Because children with sensory processing disorder are particularly prone to emotional volatility, this book can be a godsend. It is a no-nonsense approach to helping children and families gain better emotional control.

Jones, Morgan D. 1998. *The Thinker's Toolkit: 14 Powerful Techniques for Problem Solving*. New York, NY: Three Rivers Press. Another fascinating book on creative thinking, this time by a former CIA analyst.

Kilpatrick, William, Gregory Wolfe, and Suzanne M. Wolfe. 1994. *Books That Build Character*. New York, NY: Touchstone Press. A very nice book by a professor of education at Boston College and a husband-and-wife set of publishers and writers, which both advises how to use literature to discuss issues of character with children and provides a nice reading list as well that covers volumes for children of all ages and stages of reading.

Kolberg, Judith, and Kathleen Nadeau. 2002. *ADD-Friendly Ways to Organize Your Life*. New York, NY: Brunner-Routledge. This book has practical strategies for paper, task, and time organization.

Moser, Adolph, and David Melton. 1994. *Don't Rant & Rave on Wednesday*. Kansas City, MO: Landmark Editions. This is a helpful little book for young children trying to grapple with strong feelings and rage. It has funny comic-book illustrations and carries the reassuring message that we all struggle with angry feelings from time to time and need to work at controlling our feelings.

Nadeau, Kathleen G., and Ellen B. Dixon. 1997. *Learning to Slow Down and Pay Attention*. Washington, D.C.: Magination Press. This is a younger (elementary) kids' guide that may be helpful for children having behavioral and attention problems at school. It is generally upbeat, has many cartoons, provides practical ideas for organizing, anger management, problem solving, and relaxation.

Quinn, Patricia O., and Judith M. Stern. 2001. *Putting On the Brakes*. Washington, D.C.: Magination Press. This is a short "older kid's" guide to ADHD. It covers topics such as what ADHD is all about, medication, and becoming more organized.

Research Literature

Aronen, E. T., V. Vuontela, M.-R. Steenari, J. Salmi, and S. Carlson. 2005. Working memory, psychiatric symptoms, and academic performance at school. *Neurobiology of Learning and Memory* 83:33–42.

Bolanos, C. A., M. Barrot, O. Berton, D. Wallace-Black, and E. J. Nestler. 2003. Methylphenidate treatment during pre- and periadolescence alters behavioral responses to emotional stimuli at adulthood. *Biological Psychiatry* 54:1317–29.

Carey, W. B. 2002. Is ADHD a valid disorder? In *Attention Deficit Hyperactivity Disorder: State of the Science*, eds., P. S. Jensen and J. R. Cooper. Kingston, NJ: Civic Research Institute.

——. 2000. What the Multimodal Treatment Study of children with attention deficit/ hyperactivity disorder did and did not say about the use of methylphenidate for attention deficits. *Pediatrics* 105:863–4.

Carlezon, W. A., Jr., S. D. Mague, and S. L. Andersen. 2003. Enduring behavioral effects of early exposure to methylphenidate in rats. *Biological Psychiatry* 54:1330–37.

Chang, L., L. M. Smith, C. LoPresti, M. L. Yonekura, J. Kuo, I. Walot, and T. Ernst. Smaller subcortical volumes and cognitive deficits in children with prenatal methamphetamine exposure. *Psychiatry Research* 132:95–106.

Cools, R., and T. W. Robbins. 2004. Chemistry of the adaptive mind. *Philosophical Transactions of the Royal Society of London* 362:2871–88.

Elliott, V. S. 2004. Think beyond drug therapy for treating ADHD: Study says medicate and modify. *AMNews* April 19, 2004. www.ama-assn.org/amednews/2004/04/19/hll20419.htm.

Evenden, J. L. 1999. Varieties of impulsivity. *Psychopharmacology* 146:348–61.

Farrar, R., M. Call, and W. C. Maples. 2001. A comparison of the visual symptoms between ADD/ADHD and normal children. *Optometry* 72:441–51.

Fuchs, T., N. Birbaumer, W. Lutzenberger, J. H. Gruzelier, and J. Kaiser. 2003. Neurofeedback treatment for attention-deficit/hyperactivity disorder in children: a comparison with methylphenidate. *Applied Psychophysiology and Biofeedback* 28:1–12.

Golan, N., E. Shahar, S. Ravid, and G. Pillar. 2004. Sleep disorders and daytime sleepiness in children with attention deficit/hyperactivity disorder. *Sleep* 27:261–66.

Heinrich, H., H. Gevensleben, F. J. Friesleder, G. H. Moll, and A. Rothenberger. 2004. Training of slow cortical potentials in attention-deficit/hyperactivity disorder. *Biological psychiatry* 55:772–75.

Iyo, M., H. Namba, M. Yanagisawa, S. Hirai, M. Yui, and S. Fukui. 1997. Abnormal cerebral perfusion in chronic methamphetamine abusers. *Progress in Neuro-Psychopharmacology Biological Psychiatry* 5:789–96.

Kessler, R. C., L. A. Adler, R. Barkley, J. Biederman, C. K. Conner, S. V. Faraone, L. L. Greenhill, S. Jaeger, K. Secnik, T. Spencer, T. B. Ustun, and A. M. Zaslavsky. 2005. Patterns and predictors of attention-deficit/hyperactivity disorder persistence into adulthood: results from the National Comorbidity Survey replication. *Biological Psychiatry* 57:1442–51.

Mague, S. D., S. L. Andersen, and W. A. Carlezon Jr. 2005. Early developmental exposure to methylphenidate reduces cocaine-induced potentiation of brain stimulation reward in rats. *Biological Psychiatry* 57:120–25.

MTA Cooperative Group. 1999. A 14-month randomized clinical trial of treatment strategies for attention-deficit/hyperactivity disorder. *Archives of General Psychiatry* 56:1073–86.

——. 2004. National Institute of Mental Health Multimodal Treatment Study of ADHD follow-up: changes in effectiveness and growth after the end of treatment. *Pediatrics* 113:762–69.

Nasrallah, H. A., J. Loney, S. C. Olson, M. McCalley-Whitters, J. Kramer, and C. G. Jacoby. 1986. Cortical atrophy in young adults with a history of hyperactivity in childhood. *Psychiatry Research* 17:241–46.

National Institutes of Health Consensus Development Conference Statement. 2001. Diagnosis and treatment of attention-deficit/hyperactivity disorder (ADHD). *Journal of the American Academy of Child and Adolescent Psychiatry* 39:182–93.

Nelson, W. M., and J. J. Behler. 1989. Cognitive impulsivity training: the effects of peer teaching. *Journal Behavioral Therapy and Experiments Psychiatry* 20:303–9.

Schachter, H. M., B. Pham, J. King, S. Langford, and D. Moher. 2001. Long-term effectiveness of Ritalin questioned. *Canadian Medical Association Journal* 165:1475–88.

Shoda, Y., W. Mischel, and P. K. Peake. 1990. Predicting adolescent cognitive and self-regulatory competencies from preschool delay of gratification. *Psychology* 26:978–86. As recounted in Goleman, D. 1995. *Emotional Intelligence.* New York: Bantam.

Williams, R. J., L. A. Goodale, M. A. Shay-Fiddler, S. P. Gloster, and S. Y. Chang. 2004. Methylphenidate and dextroamphetamine abuse in substance-abusing adolescents. *American Journal on Addictions* 13:381–89.

Woods, S. P., J. D. Rippeth, E. Conover, A. Gongvatana, R. Gonzalez, C. L. Carey, M. Cherner, R. K. Heaton, and I. Grant. 2005. *Neuropsychology* 19:35–43.

Web Sites and Resources

www.calendarscope.com (Inexpensive computer-based visual organizer for schedules, planning, and reminding.)

http://addconsults.com/store (Online store with a wide range of resources to aid in improving organization.)

www.additudemag.com (Magazine for children and adults with ADHD.)

www.timetimer.com (Visual timer—clock or computer software—that helps people follow the passage of time.)

www.mindtools.com (The Mindtools site has many useful resources and articles about time and task management, creativity, problem solving, and decision making.)

www.eadhd.com (Online store with various electronic organizer or reminder gadgets for kids and adults.)

www.addresources.org (There are many excellent free online articles and resources at this Web site. Especially check out the articles by Rob Tudisco, a lawyer "who, through study and insight, has learned many ways to manage his ADHD.")

www.adders.org/links7.htm (Resource for ADHD "coaches.")

www.artofproblemsolving.com (Higher-level mathematics.)

www.fpsp.org (Future Problem-Solving program: Resources and materials to help students and complex issues and devise creative solutions.)

www.206.152.229.6/Problems/strategies.html (Problem Solving in Math Counts: Site provides examples of different math problem-solving strategies.)

www.vanderbilt.edu/cft/resources/teaching_resources/activities/problem_solving.htm# experts (Tips and techniques from Vanderbilt University about teaching problem-solving.)

Chapter 8. Making the Right Connections

Books

Frith, Uta, ed. 1991. *Autism and Asperger Syndrome.* Cambridge, UK: Cambridge University Press. Excellent professional-level text with especially good information on Asperger's syndrome.

Grandin, Temple. 1995. *Thinking in Pictures.* New York, NY: Vintage Books. Temple Grandin's remarkable autobiography has many insightful observations about her experiences with autism.

Klass, Perri, and Eileen Costello. 2003. *Quirky Kids.* New York, NY: Ballantine Books. An extremely helpful and warmly human book by two practicing pediatricians on the special rewards and challenges of raising children who display autistic-type behaviors.

Shure, Myrna B. 1994. *Raising a Thinking Child.* New York, NY: Pocket Books. This is a very practical book that offers a structured program to improve a child's ability to independently problem-solve.

Siegel, Bryna. 2003. *Helping Children with Autism Learn.* New York, NY: Oxford University Press. Although this book is long and fairly technical, there's much good information here. Dr. Siegel writes from a behavioral perspective on autism.

———. 1996. *The World of the Autistic Child.* New York, NY: Oxford University Press. In this book, Dr. Siegel provides a rich overview of what it means to have autism and gives treatment resources.

Winner, Michelle Garcia. 2002. *Inside Out: What Makes the Person with Social-Cognitive Deficits Tick?* San Jose, CA: Michelle Winner. This is a workbook that Michelle Winner uses with her social-skills groups. It includes topics such as listening, inferential thinking, perspective taking, getting the big picture, and humor. It can be used with older children and adolescents.

Research Literature

Courchesne, E., and K. Pierce. 2005. Why the frontal cortex in autism might be talking only to itself: local over-connectivity but long-distance disconnection. *Current Opinion in Neurobiology* 15:225–30.

Decety, J., and P. L. Jackson. 2004. The functional architecture of human empathy. *Behavioral and Cognitive Neuroscience Reviews* 3:71–100.

Doherty-Sneddon, G., B. V. Bonner, S. Longbotham, and C. Doyle. 2002. Development of gaze aversion as disengagement from visual information. *Developmental Psychology* 38:438–45.

Donnelly, J., and J.-P. Bovee. 2003. Reflections on play: recollections from a mother and her son with Asperger syndrome. *Autism* 7:471–76.

Fogassi, L., P. F. Ferrari, B. Gesierich, S. Ross, F. Chersi, and G. Rizzolatti. 2005. Parietal lobe: from action organization to intention understanding. *Science* 308:662–67.

Gallese, V., L. Fadiga, L. Fogassi, and G. Rizzolatti. 1996. Action recognition in the premotor cortex. *Brain* 119:593–609.

Grelotti, D. J., I. Gauthier, and R. T. Schultz. 2001. Social interest and the development of cortical face specialization: what autism teaches us about face processing. *Developmental Psychobiology* 40:213–25.

Just, M. A., S. D. Newman, T. A. Keller, A. McEleney, and P. A. Carpenter. 2004. Imagery in sentence comprehension: an fMRI study. *Neuroimage* 21:112–24.

———, V. L. Cherkassky, T. A. Keller, and N. J. Minshew. 2004. Cortical activation and synchronization during sentence comprehension in high-functioning autism: evidence of underconnectivity. *Brain* 127:1811–21.

Justus, T. 2004. The cerebellum and English grammatical morphology: evidence from production, comprehension, and grammaticality judgments. *Journal of Cognitive Neuroscience* 16:1115–30.

Kemper, T. L., and M. Bauman. 1998. Neuropathology of infantile autism. *Journal of Neuropathology and Experimental Neurology* 57:645–52.

Koshino, H., P. A. Carpenter, N. J. Minshew, V. L. Cherkassky, T. A. Keller, and M. A. Just. 2005. Functional connectivity in an fMRI working memory task in high-functioning autism. *NeuroImage* 24:810–21.

Miller, G. 2005. Reflecting on another's mind. *Science* 308: 945–47.

Shamay-Tsoory, S. G., R. Tomer, D. Goldsher, B. D. Berger, and J. Aharon-Peretz. 2004. Impairment in cognitive and affective empathy in patients with brain lesions: anatomical and cognitive correlates. *Journal of Clinical and Experimental Neuropsychology* 26:1113–27.

Vargas, D. L., C. Nascimbene, C. Krishnan, A. W. Zimmerman, and C. A. Pardo. Neuroglial activation and neuroinflammation in the brain of patients with autism. *Annals of Neurology* 57:67–81.

Web Sites and Resources

www.rdiconnect.com (Relationship Development Intervention, an excellent program for helping children with autism and other social difficulties develop their abilities to interact with others.)

www.info.med.yale.edu/chldstdy/autism/aspergers.html (Yale Developmental Disabilities Clinic site on Asperger's has helpful articles about assessment, behaviors, interventions, and training.)

www.autismeducation.net (This parent-initiated site has resources of education, advocacy, and many excellent links to online articles.)

www.autism-resources.com (This site has an extensive collection of links—including many sites, organizations, and mailing lists.)

www.ddhealthinfo.org (Free online resource guide about autism spectrum disorders from the California Department of Developmental Services.)

www.childnett.tv (This site requires free registration, but it's worth it. Contains many wonderful videos and resources.)

www.nichd.nih.gov/autism (The National Institute of Child Health and Human Development [NICHD's] site for autism research has several free online publications.)

www.teacch.com (The University of North Carolina's site for TEACCH: Treatment and Education of Autistic and related Communication Handicapped Children.)

www.autism.org/music.html (Web Site for musical approaches to teaching autistic children.)

www.floortime.org/whatisfloortime.htm (Web Site for Floortime therapy: An approach to helping children with autism and related disorders through one-on-one interactions that use a child's interests to encourage development.)

Chapter 9. Mixed Messages

Books

Ayres, A. Jean. 2005. *Sensory Integration and the Child: Understanding Hidden Sensory Challenges*. Los Angeles, CA: Western Psychological Services. A recently updated version of the classic and groundbreaking book on sensory processing disorder by the pioneering therapist who first described it.

Biel, Lindsey, and Nancy Peske. 2005. *Raising a Sensory Smart Child*. New York, NY: Penguin Books. A wonderful resource with an abundance of practical tips for parents.

Bundy, Anita C., Shelly L. Lane, and Elizabeth Murray, eds. 2002 (2nd ed.). *Sensory Integration: Theory and Practice*. Philadelphia, PA: F. A. Davis.

Kranowitz, Carol Stock. 2005 (updated ed). *The Out-of-Sync Child*. New York, NY: Perigee Books. Carol Kranowitz's brilliant book that helped catapult sensory disorders into public awareness.

———. 2003. *The Out-of-Sync Child Has Fun*. New York, NY. Perigee Books. Fun activities and exercises to relieve symptoms and improve skills in children with SPD.

———. 2004. *The Goodenoughs Get in Sync*. Las Vegas, NV: Sensory Resources Press. Fun book for the under-ten crowd explaining the nature of SPD and what to do about it.

Miller, Lucy Jane. 2006. *Sensational Kids*. New York, NY: Putnam. A book on SPD by one of the leading authorities in the field.

Smith, Karen A., and Karen R. Gouze. 2004. *The Sensory Sensitive Child*. New York, NY: HarperCollins. This very practical book provides helpful advice about how parents can help their children with sensory processing dysfunction.

Williams, Mary Sue, and Sherry Shellenberger. 2001. *Take Five! Staying Alert at Home and School*. Albuquerque, NM: TherapyWorks. This workbook from the ALERT program provides practical information about how to set up an at-home or at-school "sensory diet."

———. 1996. *How Does Your Engine Run: A Leader's Guide to the ALERT Program for Self-Regulation*. Albuquerque, NM: TherapyWorks. A companion to the previous book, with excellent information on helping children with self-regulation skills.

Research Literature

Ahn, R. R., L. J. Miller, S. Milberger, and D. N. McIntosh. 2004. Prevalence of parents' perceptions of sensory processing disorders among kindergarten children. *American Journal of Occupational Therapy* 58:287–93.

Allin, M., H. Matsumoto, A. M. Santhouse, C. Nosarti, M. AlAsady, A. L. Stewart, L. Rifkin, and R. M. Murray. 2005. Cognitive and motor function and the size of the cerebellum in adolescents born very pre-term. *Brain* 124:60–66.

Chaminade, T., A. N. Meltzoff, and J. Decety. 2005. An fMRI study of imitation: action representation and body schema. *Neuropsychologia* 43:115–27.

Clapp, Sally, and A. M. Wing. 1999. Light touch contribution to balance in normal bipedal stance. *Experimental Brain Research* 125:521–24.

Cooke, D. F., and M. Graziano. 2004. Sensorimotor integration in the precentral gyrus: polysensory neurons and defensive motions. *Journal of Neurophysiology* 91: 1648–60.

Edelson, S. M., M. G. Edelson, D. C. Kerr, and T. Grandin. 1999. Behavioral and physiological effects of deep pressure on children with autism: a pilot study evaluating the efficacy of Grandin's Hug Machine. *American Journal of Occupational Therapy* 53:145–52.

Eide, F. F. 2003. Sensory integration: current concepts and practical implications. *Sensory Integration Special Interest Section Quarterly* 13:1–3.

Erez, O., C. R. Gordon, J. Sever, A. Sadeh, and M. Mintz. 2004. Balance dysfunction in childhood anxiety: findings and theoretical approach. *Journal of Anxiety Disorders* 18:341–56.

Miller, L. J., J. Robinson, and D. Moulton. 2004. Sensory Modulation Dysfunction: identification in early childhood. In Delcarmen-Wiggins, Rebecca, and Carter, Alice, eds. *Handbook of Infant, Toddler, and Preschool Mental Health Assessment*. Oxford, UK: Oxford University Press.

Perna, G., A. Dario, D. Caldirola, B. Stefania, A. Cesarani, and L. Bellodi. 2001. Panic disorder: the role of the balance system. *Journal of Psychiatric Research* 35:279–86.

Pfeiffer, B., and M. Kinnealey. 2003. Treatment of sensory defensiveness in adults. *Occupational Therapy International* 10:175–84.

Rupert, A. H. 2000. Tactile situation awareness system: proprioceptive prostheses for sensory deficiencies. *Aviation, Space, and Environmental Medicine* 71:A92–99.

van Nes, I. J., A. C. Geurts, H. T. Hendricks, and J. Duysens. 2004. Short-term effects of whole-body vibration on postural control in unilateral chronic stroke patients: preliminary evidence. *American Journal of Physical Medicine Rehabilitation* 83:867–73.

Web Sites and Resources

www.SIfocus.com (Web site for *SIfocus* magazine, an international magazine "dedicated to improving sensory integration.")

www.henryot.com (Diane Henry's site has informative articles about the "sensory diet" and environmental accommodations.)

www.spdnetwork.org (Dr. Lucy Miller's site for sensory processing disorders. Includes an SPD resource directory for sensory professionals.)

Online Therapy-Supply Stores

www.theraproducts.com

www.integrationscatalog.com

www.southpawenterprises.com

www.sensoryresources.com

www.abilitations.com

Chapter 10. It's as Easy as ABC . . . or as Hard

Books

Bell, Nanci. 2001. *Seeing Stars*. San Luis Obispo, CA: Gander Educational Publishing. A good visualization program to increase word memory.

Davis, Ronald D. 1994. *The Gift of Dyslexia*. New York, NY: Perigee. This is the Davis dyslexia system in a nutshell. Some of its multisensory techniques are particularly helpful for some persons with dyslexia. The Davis system focuses on the visual and spatial aspects of dyslexia rather than on phonology. Some of the explanations given for the techniques used are a bit questionable, but the advice given is generally very good and practically based.

Fry, Edward Bernard, Jacqueline E. Kress, and Dona Lee Fountoukidis. 2000. *The Reading Teacher's Book of Lists*. San Francisco, CA: Jossey-Bass. This is a terrific comprehensive list-based reading resource. Topics include common and irregular phonograms, syllabication rules, easily confused words, spelling demons, word families, special vocabulary (math, science), proofreading checklists, and good ideas of improving reading comprehension and study skills.

McGuiness, Carmen, and Geoffrey McGuiness. 1999. *Reading Reflex*. New York, NY: Free Press. An excellent resource for phonics training in children.

Orton, Samuel Torrey. 1989. *Reading, Writing, and Speech Problems in Children and Selected Papers*. Austin, TX: Pro-Ed. A remarkable collection of papers by Orton, one of the pioneers in the field of reading disorders and the father of a child with dyslexia. His phenomenal powers of observation are a useful reminder in an age of scanners and checklists of the tremendous value of simply looking at and listening to our patients. Although he died in 1948, Orton's writings are still a treasure trove of valuable information for those interested in reading, writing, and speech.

Shaywitz, Sally. 2003. *Overcoming Dyslexia*. New York, NY: Alfred A. Knopf. Dr. Shaywitz's book provides a comprehensive discussion and many helpful recommendations for children with phonological dyslexia.

Research Literature

Agnew, J. A., C. Dorn, and G. F. Eden. 2004. Effect of training on auditory processing and reading skills. *Brain and Language* 88:21–25.

Badian, N. A. 2005. Does a visual-orthographic deficit contribute to reading disability? *Annals of Dyslexia* 55:28–52.

Brunsden, R. K., T. J. Hannan, M. Coltheart, and L. Nickels. 2002. Treatment of lexical processing in mixed dyslexia: a case study. *Neuropsychological Rehabilitation* 12: 385–418.

Fisher, S. E., and J. C. DeFries. Developmental dyslexia: genetic dissection of a complex cognitive trait. *Nature Reviews: Neuroscience* 3:767–80.

Gottfried, J. A., F. Sancar, and A. Chatterjee. 2003. Acquired mirror writing and reading: evidence for reflected graphemic representations. *Neuropsychologia* 41:96–107.

Habib, M. 2000. The Neurological basis of developmental dyslexia. *Brain* 123:2373–99.

McCandliss, B. D., L. Cohen, and S. Dehaene. 2003. The visual word form area: expertise for reading in the fusiform gyrus. *Trends in Cognitive Science* 7:293–99.

Ramus, F. 2004. Neurobiology of dyslexia: a reinterpretation of the data. *Trends in Neuroscience* 27:720–26.

Schulte-Korne, G., J. Bartling, W. Deimel, and H. Remschmidt. 2004. Motion-onset VEPs in dyslexia: evidence for visual perceptual defect. *NeuroReport* 15:1075–78.

Solan, H. A., S. Larson, J. Shelley-Tremblay, A. Ficarra, and M. Silverman. 2001. Role of visual attention in cognitive control of oculomotor readiness in students with reading disabilities. *Journal of Learning Disabilities* 34:107–18.

———, J. Shelley-Tremblay, A. Ficarra, M. Silverman, and S. Larson. 2003. Effect of attention therapy on reading comprehension. *Journal of Learning Disabilities* 36:556–63.

Stein, J. 2003. Visual motion sensitivity and reading. *Neuropsychologia* 41:1785–93.

———, and J. Talcott. 1999. Impaired neuronal timing in developmental dyslexia—the magnocellular hypothesis. *Dyslexia* 5:59–77.

Temple, E., G. K. Deutsch, R. A. Poldrack, S. L. Miller, P. Tallal, M. Merzenich, and J. Gabrielli. 2003. Neuronal deficits in children with dyslexia ameliorated by behavioral remediation: evidence from functional MRI. *Proceedings of the National Academy of Sciences* 100:2860–65.

Temple, E., R. A. Poldrack, A. Protopapas, S. Nagarajan, T. Salz, P. Tallal, M. Merzenich, and J. Gabrielli. 2000. Disruption of the neural response to rapid acoustic stimuli in dyslexia: evidence from functional MRI. *Proceedings of the National Academy of Sciences* 97:13907–12.

Turkeltaub, P. E., L. Gareau, D. L. Flowers, T. A. Zeffiro, and G. F. Eden. 2003. Development of neural mechanisms for reading. *Nature Neuroscience* 6:767–73.

West, Thomas G. 1999. The abilities of those who have reading disabilities. In Duane, Drake D., ed. *Reading and Attention Disorders—Neurobiological Correlates*.

Whitney, C., and P. L. Cornelisson. 2005. Letter-position encoding and dyslexia. *Journal of Research in Reading* 28:274–301.

Witton, C., J. B. Talcott, P. C. Hansen, A. J. Richardson, T. D. Griffiths, A. Rees, J. F. Stein, and G. Green. 1998. Sensitivity to dynamic auditory and visual stimuli predicts non-word reading ability in both dyslexic and normal readers. *Current Biology* 8:791–97.

Web Sites and Resources

www.dyslexia-parent.com/mag39.html (Very helpful parents' site for information.)

www.uiowa.edu/~acadtech/phonetics (This phonetics site is a wonderful resource for phonics and language pronunciation. Using animations and video, you can see how different sounds and blends are generated. This is a free site from the University of Iowa.)

www.ldonline.org (Fantastic storehouse of articles and information on dyslexia and other learning challenges.)

www.interdys.org (The Web site of the International Dyslexia Association.)

www.dyslexia-inst.org.uk (A great site in the UK with more information on visual aspects of dyslexia.)

www.bda-dyslexia.org.uk (Site of the British Dyslexia Association.)

www.starfall.com (Good phonics practice on the Web for children in K–2 grade levels.)

www.kidsdomain.com/games/read1html (Game-based phonics practice on the Web.)

Chapter 11. Handwriting and Hand-Wringing

See also Chapters 4, 6, and 10.

Books

Levine, Mel. 2003. *The Myth of Laziness*. New York, NY: Simon & Schuster. A great discussion of dysgraphia and of helping children with written-output failure.

Research Literature

Deuel, R. 2002. Dysgraphia. *Continuum* 8:37–69.

Moretti, R., P. Torre, R. M. Antonello, F. Fabbro, G. Cazzato, and A. Bava. 2003. Writing errors by normal subjects. *Perceptual and Motor Skills* 97:215–29.

Web Sites and Resources

www.hwtears.com (The best handwriting-teaching approach for most children.)

www.donjohnston.com (Source for WriteOutloud.)

www.alphasmart.com (Information on Alphasmart and Dana keyboards.)

www.abilitations.com (Excellent source of different pens and handwriting adapters.)

Chapter 12. When the Numbers Won't Add Up

Books

Butterworth, Brian, and Dorian Yeo, eds. 2004. *Dyscalculia Guidance: Helping Pupils with Specific Learning Difficulties in Maths*. London, UK: Routledge. A great discussion of teaching ideas in math for younger children, many with a multisensory approach.

Ma, Liping. 1999. *Knowing and Teaching Elementary School Mathematics*. Mahwah, NJ: Lawrence Erlbaum Associates. A fascinating comparison of mathematics teaching in the United States and China. Dr. Ma reveals the weakness of procedural math teaching without conceptual understanding.

Miles, T. R., and E. Miles, eds. 1992. *Dyslexia and Mathematics*. London, UK: Routledge. A fairly technical discussion of dyslexia and mathematics.
Walker, Alan. 2000. *Memorize in Minutes: The Times Tables*. Prosser, Washington, D.C.:
Krimsten Publishing. This book uses cartoons and short stories to help children
memorize their multiplication/division math facts quickly.

Research Literature

Dehaene, S., N. Molko, L. Cohen, and A. J. Wilson. 2004. Arithmetic and the brain. *Cur-
rent Opinion in Neurobiology* 14:218–24.
Geary, D. C., M. K. Hoard, and C. O. Hamson. 1999. Numerical and arithmetical cogni-
tion: patterns of functions and deficits in children at risk for a mathematical disability.
Journal of Experimental Child Psychology 74:213–39.
Luna, B. 2004. Algebra and the adolescent brain. *TRENDS in Cognitive Science*
8:437–39.
Molko, N., A. Cachia, D. Riviere, J. F. Mangin, M. Bruandet, D. LeBihan, L. Cohen, and
S. Dehaene. 2003. Functional and structural alterations of the intraparietal sulcus in
a developmental dyscalculia of genetic origin. *Neuron* 40:847–58.
Pinel, P., S. Dehaene, D. Riviere, and D. LeBihan. 2001. Modulation of parietal activa-
tion by semantic distance in a number comparison task. *Neuroimage* 14:1013–26.
Qin, Y., C. S. Carter, E. M. Silk, V. A. Stenger, K. Fissell, A. Goode, and J. R. Anderson.
2004. The change of the brain activation patterns as children learn algebra equation
solving. *Proceedings of the National Academy of Sciences* 101:5686–91.
Shalev, R. 2002. Dyscalculia. *Continuum* 8:60–73.

Web Sites and Resources

www.borenson.com (Hands On Equations: This is a simple, inexpensive, yet useful ma-
nipulative program to help children "get the idea" behind math calculations and
equations, and word problems. The program does not use word problems per se, but
when used in parallel with assigned word problems, it can help children understand
the meanings behind the equations.)
www.singaporemath.com (Singapore Math is helpful particularly for elementary-school
students struggling with basic math concepts, because math symbols are presented
with visual examples.)

Chapter 13. The Midas Touch

Books

Adderholt, Miriam, and Jan Goldberg. 1999. *Perfectionism: What's Bad About Being Too
Good*. Minneapolis, MN: Free Spirit Publishing. Great advice for helping perfectionistic children and their families deal with the disappointments that come from being
less than perfect.
Adler, Mortimer. 1984. *The Paideia Program*. New York, NY: Touchstone Press. Great resource for the classical approach to education.
Bloom, Benjamin. 1985. *Developing Talent in Young People*. New York, NY: Ballantine
Books. This classic work interviewed the talented concert pianists, sculptors, Olympic
swimmers, world-class tennis players, mathematicians, and academic neurologists
and found out what motivated them when they were young, what their learning and
family environments were like, and what ideas their parents had about parenting
when they were growing up.

Csikszentmihalyi, Mihaly. 1991. *Flow: The Psychology of Optimal Experience*. New York, NY: Harper Perennial. Why it's so important to provide children an opportunity to develop in their areas of interest.

Davidson, Jan, and Bob Davidson. 2004. *Genius Denied: How to Stop Wasting Our Brightest Young Minds*. New York, NY: Simon & Schuster. An excellent discussion of the current neglect of gifted education and what can be done to improve it by the founders of the Davidson Institute for Talent Development.

Gardner, Howard. 1983. *Frames of Mind: The Theory of Multiple Intelligences*. New York, NY: Basic Books. Psychologist describes his well-known theory of multiple intelligences.

Hollingworth, Leta S. 1997. *Children Above 180 IQ*. North Stratford, NH: Ayer Company Publishers. This classic book by Leta Hollingworth has detailed interviews with parents and teachers of profoundly gifted children, plus the children themselves. Many parents of profoundly gifted children enjoy reading the vignettes of these extraordinary children. There are many unique challenges to parenting these kids, and they are uncommon enough that it's helpful to reread this book every now and then.

Kerr, Barbara A. and Sanford J. Cohn. 2001. *Smart Boys*. Scottsdale, AZ: Great Potential Press. This is a wonderful book that discusses some of the most common social and emotional issues of gifted boys. Topics and chapters include underachievement, "Redeemable Rebels," and "Nerds."

Kinger, Jonni. 1992. *The First Honest Book About Lies*. Minneapolis, MN: Free Spirit Publishing. When young children have school difficulties, they may have problems reconciling their feelings about absolute good and bad, and how they feel about others and themselves. This book discusses lies but also introduces children to a more complex understanding of morality and truth, by discussing topics such as optical illusions (when your senses can deceive you), being true to yourself (lies you can tell yourself), and social lies (lying versus being polite).

Kurcinka, Mary Sheedy. 1998. *Raising Your Spirited Child*. New York, NY: Harper Perennial. Help for dealing with the highly spirited and independent child.

Rivero, Lisa. 2002. *Creative Homeschooling for Gifted Children*. Scottsdale, AZ: Great Potential Press. A classic reference for homeschooling parents of gifted children.

Ruf, Deborah. 2005. *Losing Our Minds: Gifted Children Left Behind*. Scottsdale, AZ: Great Potential Press. An excellent discussion of some of the special risks and challenges confronting highly gifted children.

Rupp, Rebecca. 1998. *The Complete Home Learning Source Book*. Three Rivers Press: New York, NY. A great big book full of all kinds of helpful homeschool resources.

Seligman, Martin E. P. 1995. *The Optimistic Child*. New York, NY: Houghton Mifflin. This is a wonderful book to counter catastrophism and pessimism in your child. Writing simply and straightforwardly, Dr. Seligman provides step-by-step instructions on how to teach a child optimism and mastery.

Silverman, Linda Kreger. 2002. *Upside-Down Brilliance*. Denver, CO: DeLeon Publishing. In this very readable book, Dr. Silverman provides practical tips about how to foster a gifted child's particular learning style and gifts.

Webb, James T., Elizabeth A. Meckstroth, and Stephanie S. Tolan. 1994. *Guiding the Gifted Child*. Scottsdale, AZ: Gifted Psychology Press. This book is a reality check for many gifted parents. Insightful, encouraging, and wise.

Webb, James T., Edward R. Amend, Nadia E. Webb, Jean Goerss, Paul Beljan, and F. Richard Olenchak. 2005. *Misdiagnosis and Dual Diagnoses of Gifted Children and Adults: ADD Bipolar, OCD, Asperger's Depression, and Other Disorders*. Scottsdale, AZ: Great Potential Press. Misdiagnoses are common for gifted children. This book helps parents to understand key issues surrounding the misdiagnosis and dual diagnosis of gifted children.

Wise, Jessie, and Susan Wise Bauer. 1999. *The Well-Trained Mind: A Guide to Classical Education at Home.* New York, NY: Norton. A great source for classical homeschool education.

Research Literature

Jones, P., and G. Gloeckner. 2004a. A study of admission officers' perceptions of and attitudes toward homeschool students. *Journal of College Admission* 184:12–21.

———. 2004b. First-Year college performance: a study of home school graduates and traditional school graduates. *Journal of College Admission* 183:17–20.

Kearney, K. 1991. What do highly gifted children and their families really need? Paper presented at the 38th annual conference of the *National Association for Gifted Children*, 1991.

Kumari, V., D. H. ffytche, S. Williams, and J. A. Gray. 2004. Personality predicts brain responses to cognitive demands. *Journal of Neuroscience* 24:10636–41.

Pesenti, M., L. Zago, F. Crivello, E. Mellet, D. Samson, B. Duroux, X. Seron, B. Mazoyer, and N. Tzourio-Mazoyer. 2001. Mental calculation in a prodigy is sustained by right prefrontal and medial temporal areas. *Nature Neuroscience* 4: 103–7.

Ray, B. D. 2004a. Homeschoolers on to college: what research shows us. *Journal of College Admission* 184:5–11.

———. 2004b. Home educated and now adults: their community and civic involvement, views about homeschooling, and other traits. Salem, OR: National Home Education Research Institute (www.nheri.org).

Solso, R. L. 2001. Brain activities in a skilled versus a novice artist: an fMRI study. *Leonardo* 34:31–34.

Winters, R. 2000. From Home to Harvard: Homeschooled kids have carved a college of their own and admission to elite, traditional campuses. *Time*, September 11, 2000. (While not a research paper, this interesting article was cited in this chapter.)

Web Sites and Resources

www.gifteddevelopment.com/Articles/On%20Introversion.html (Great information on introversion in gifted kids.)

www.giftedservices.com.au (More great information in introversion from Lesley Sword.)

www.sengifted.org (Web site of SENG, an organization dedicated to serving the Social and Emotional Needs of the Gifted.)

www.nagc.org (Web site of the National Association of Gifted Children.)

www.2eNewsletter.com (Fabulous resource for the 2e community, full of informative and helpful articles.)

www.apexlearning.com (Resources for a wide selection of online courses, including AP.)

www.hoagiesgifted.org (Carolyn K's supersite of links for all aspects of gifted learning and education.)

www.uniquelygifted.org (Meredith Warshaw's wonderful site, with links and other resources helpful to 2e or gifted-LD children.)

www.gifteddevelopment.com (Dr. Linda Silverman's site, with many helpful articles about giftedness, and social-emotional issues.)

www.tagfam.org (Wonderful online forums for discussing giftedness and school issues, giftedness and homeschooling.)

www-epgy.stanford.edu (Stanford's Education Program for Gifted Youth has online classes for gifted students, with topics that include writing, mathematics, physics, and more.)

www.gt-cybersource.org/ (Davidson Institute for Talent Development's great site, with original articles and links to others on many aspects of giftedness; curriculum and program reviews are also very helpful.)

www.ctd.northwestern.edu (Resource for many online gifted courses, including AP.)

www.giftedbooks.com (Site for Great Potential Press, wonderful resource for gifted books.)

www.neiu.edu/~ourgift (A labor of love from Sally L., free online conferences with gifted experts.)

www.nheri.org (Web site for Dr. Brian Ray's National Home Education Research Institute.)

Critical-Thinking Resources

www.datanation.com/fallacies (Stephen's Guide to the Logical Fallacies.)

www.idebate.org/debatabase/alphaindex.asp (Debatabase: resource for debate and critical thinking.)

www.austhink.org/critical (Tim van Gelder's Critical Thinking on the Web.)

www.criticalthinking.com (Critical Thinking Press.)

www.paideia.org/links/default.htm#hi (Paideia Active Learning.)

www.essentialschools.org/cs/resources/view/ces_res/137#figure1(Essential Questions.)

Permissions

Index

Brock Eide, M.D., M.A., and Fernette Eide, M.D.,
are leading researchers and clinicians on learning disabilities.
They run the Eide Neurolearning Clinic in Edmonds,
Washington, and lecture throughout the United States and
Canada to parents, educators, therapists, and doctors.